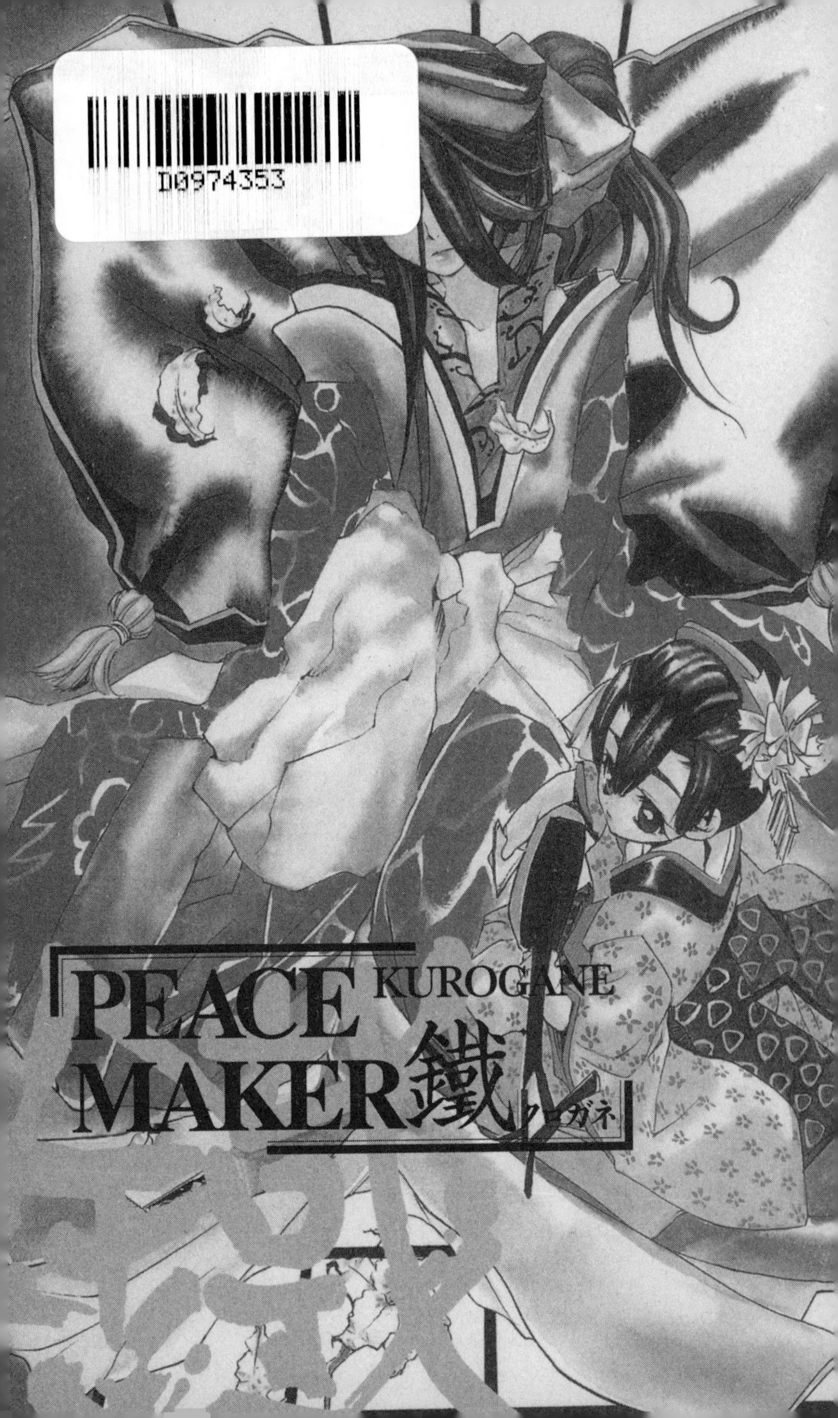
PEACE MAKER
KUROGANE
鐵
ガネ

Peace Maker Kurogane 2
Created by NANAE CHRONO

Translation - Ryan Flake
English Adaptation - Christine Boylan
Retouch and Lettering - Star Print Brokers
Production Artist - Rui Kyo
Graphic Designer - Al-Insan Lashley

Editor - Lillian Diaz-Przybyl
Print Production Manager - Lucas Rivera
Managing Editor - Vy Nguyen
Senior Designer - Louis Csontos
Associate Publisher - Marco F. Pavia
President and C.O.O. - John Parker
C.E.O. and Chief Creative Officer - Stu Levy

A  Manga

TOKYOPOP and 🐢 are trademarks or registered trademarks of TOKYOPOP Inc.

TOKYOPOP Inc.
5900 Wilshire Blvd. Suite 2000
Los Angeles, CA 90036

E-mail: info@TOKYOPOP.com
Come visit us online at www.TOKYOPOP.com

ISBN: 978-1-4278-1417-3

First TOKYOPOP printing: June 2009
10 9 8 7 6 5 4 3 2 1
Printed in the USA

PEACE MAKER 鐵
KUROGANE

Volume 2
by Nanae Chrono

HAMBURG // LONDON // LOS ANGELES // TOKYO

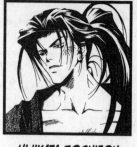

HIJIKATA TOSHIZOU

VICE COMMANDER

BECAUSE OF HIS COLD DEMEANOR AND BRUTALITY, HE IS KNOWN AS THE "DEMON VICE COMMANDER."

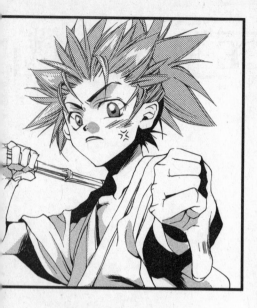

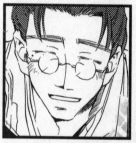

YAMANAMI KEISUKE

VICE COMMANDER

THIS BUDDHA-LIKE VICE COMMANDER COULDN'T BE LESS LIKE HIJIKATA. HE'S OFTEN SEEN CARRYING HIS ABACUS.

ICHIMURA TETSUNOSUKE

HIJIKATA'S PAGE

TETSU HAS JOINED THE SHINSENGUMI TO LEARN TO BECOME STRONG. 'S TO GET REVENGE ON HIS PARENTS' MURDERERS, CHOUSHUU REBELS. UGH HE JOINED THE SHINSENGUMI WITH ASPIRATIONS OF BECOMING A SMAN, HE'S BEEN ASSIGNED THE THANKLESS DUTY OF HIJIKATA'S PAGE.

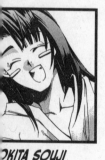

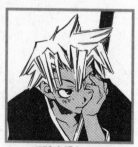

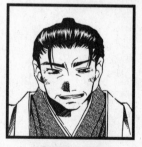

KONDOU ISAMI

DIRECTOR

A FOUNDING MEMBER OF THE SHINSENGUMI AND ALSO A MASTER AT THE SHIEIKAN DOJO IN EDO, THE MAIN DOJO OF THE TENNEN RISHIN STYLE.

KITAMURA SUZU

A BOY WITH SILVER HAIR. HE HAS NO FAMILY AND LIVED WITH HIS MASTER, YOSHIDA TOSHIMARO, UNTIL YOSHIDA WAS SLAIN DURING THE IKEDAYA INCIDENT. NOW SUZU IS...?

OKITA SOUJI

N OF THE FIRST SQUAD

EST SWORDSMAN IN THE ENGUMI. HE'S GENERALLY ND FRIENDLY, BUT WIELDING DE CAN TRANSFORM HIM A HEARTLESS KILLER.

MAIN CHARACTERS

NAGAKURA SHINPACHI

CAPTAIN OF THE SECOND SQUAD

SMALL BUT STRONG. A SWORDSMAN LIKE OKITA. HE FIGHTS IN THE SHINTO-MUNEN SCHOOL STYLE.

TOUDOU HEISUKE

CAPTAIN OF THE EIGHTH SQUAD

ONE OF THE THREE STOOGES OF THE SHINSENGUMI. HE LIKES CUTE THINGS, INCLUDING TETSU.

HARADA SANOSUKE

CAPTAIN OF THE TENTH SQUAD

A GIANT AMONG MEN, HE'S A MASTER OF THE SPEAR IN THE HOZOIN SCHOOL. HE'S GOOD FRIENDS WITH SHINPACHI.

ICHIMURA TATSUNOSUKE

TETSU'S OLDER BROTHER AND GUARDIAN. HE'S ALWAYS WORRYING ABOUT TETSU. TATSU WANTS NOTHING TO DO WITH SWORDFIGHTING, AND IS A BOOKKEEPER FOR THE SHINSENGUMI.

YAMAZAKI SUSUMU

SHINSENGUMI NINJA

A SPY FOR THE SHINSENGUMI, HE REPORTS TO HIJIKATA. TACITURN AND COLD, HE HOLDS MANY SECRETS.

SAYA

TETSU SAVED HER FROM SOME RUFFIANS AND NOW THE TWO ARE FRIENDS. SHE CANNOT SPEAK, BUT COMMUNICATES THROUGH HAND GESTURES AND WRITING.

☐ SHINSENGUMI MEMBERS

☐ PERSONS OUTSIDE THE SHINSENGUMI

THE STORY OF PEACE MAKER

IN THE FIRST YEAR OF GENJI, 1864, JAPAN IS IN GREAT TURMOIL. MILITANT AND XENOPHOBIC FORCES, WHICH HAD LONG OPPOSED THE TOKUGAWA SHOGUNATE, ADVOCATED EXPELLING WESTERN INFLUENCE AND RESTORING THE EMPEROR IN KYOTO TO POWER. TO PROTECT THE SHOGUNATE'S INTEREST IN KYOTO, A LEGENDARY PEACEKEEPING FORCE WAS FORMED FROM HUNDRED-SOME RONIN. THEY WERE THE SHINSENGUMI. THIS IS THE STORY OF ICHIMURA TETSUNOSUKE, WHO SOUGHT TO JOIN THEM.

CONTENTS

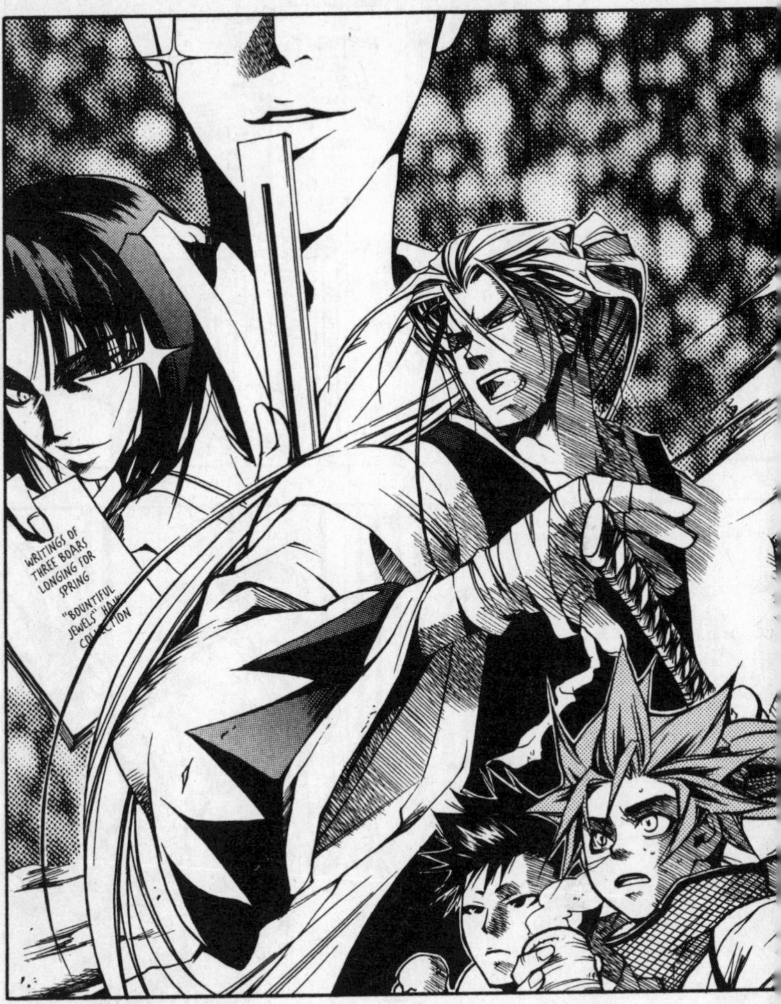
WRITINGS OF THREE BOARS LONGING FOR SPRING
"BOUNTIFUL JEWELS"

Act 6
Troubles

第六話 難

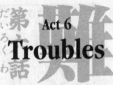

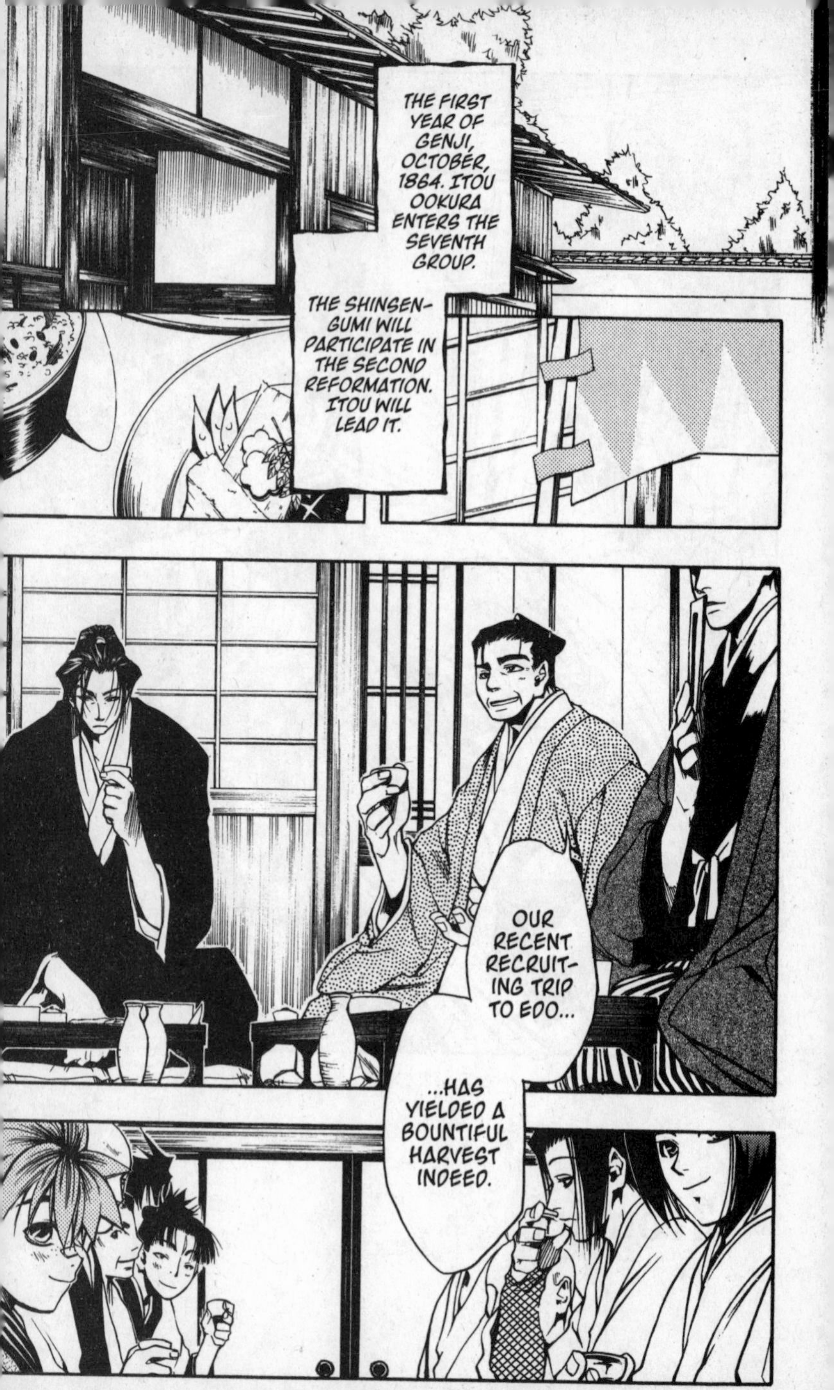
THE FIRST YEAR OF GENJI, OCTOBER, 1864. ITOU OOKURA ENTERS THE SEVENTH GROUP.
THE SHINSEN-GUMI WILL PARTICIPATE IN THE SECOND REFORMATION. ITOU WILL LEAD IT.
OUR RECENT RECRUIT-ING TRIP TO EDO...
...HAS YIELDED A BOUNTIFUL HARVEST INDEED.

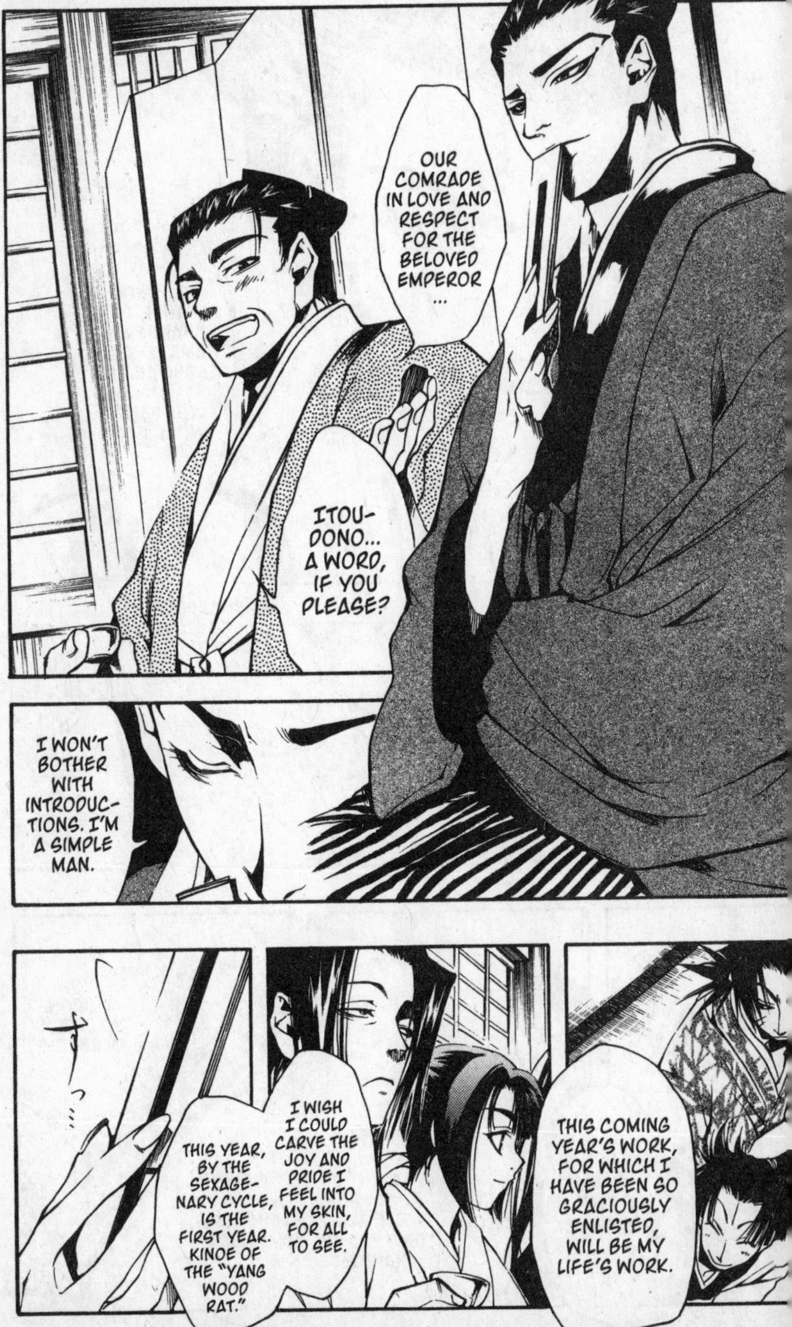
OUR COMRADE IN LOVE AND RESPECT FOR THE BELOVED EMPEROR ...
ITOU-DONO... A WORD, IF YOU PLEASE?
I WON'T BOTHER WITH INTRODUC-TIONS. I'M A SIMPLE MAN.
THIS COMING YEAR'S WORK, FOR WHICH I HAVE BEEN SO GRACIOUSLY ENLISTED, WILL BE MY LIFE'S WORK.
I WISH I COULD CARVE THE JOY AND PRIDE I FEEL INTO MY SKIN, FOR ALL TO SEE.
THIS YEAR, BY THE SEXAGE-NARY CYCLE, IS THE FIRST YEAR. KINOE OF THE "YANG WOOD RAT."

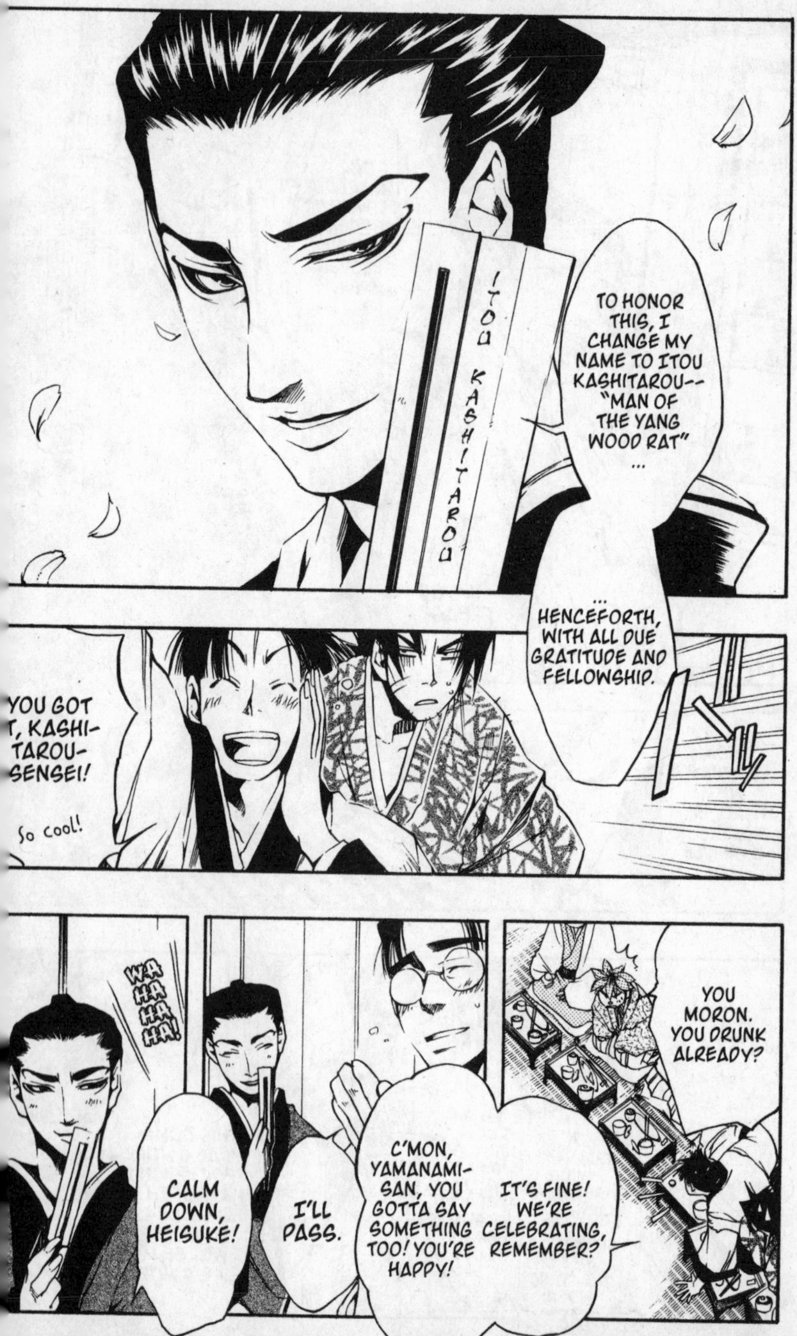
ITOU KASHITAROU
TO HONOR THIS, I CHANGE MY NAME TO ITOU KASHITAROU-- "MAN OF THE YANG WOOD RAT" ...
... HENCEFORTH, WITH ALL DUE GRATITUDE AND FELLOWSHIP.
YOU GOT T, KASHI-TAROU-SENSEI!
So cool!
YOU MORON. YOU DRUNK ALREADY?
IT'S FINE! WE'RE CELEBRATING, REMEMBER?
C'MON, YAMANAMI-SAN, YOU GOTTA SAY SOMETHING TOO! YOU'RE HAPPY!
I'LL PASS.
WA HA HA HA HA!
CALM DOWN, HEISUKE!

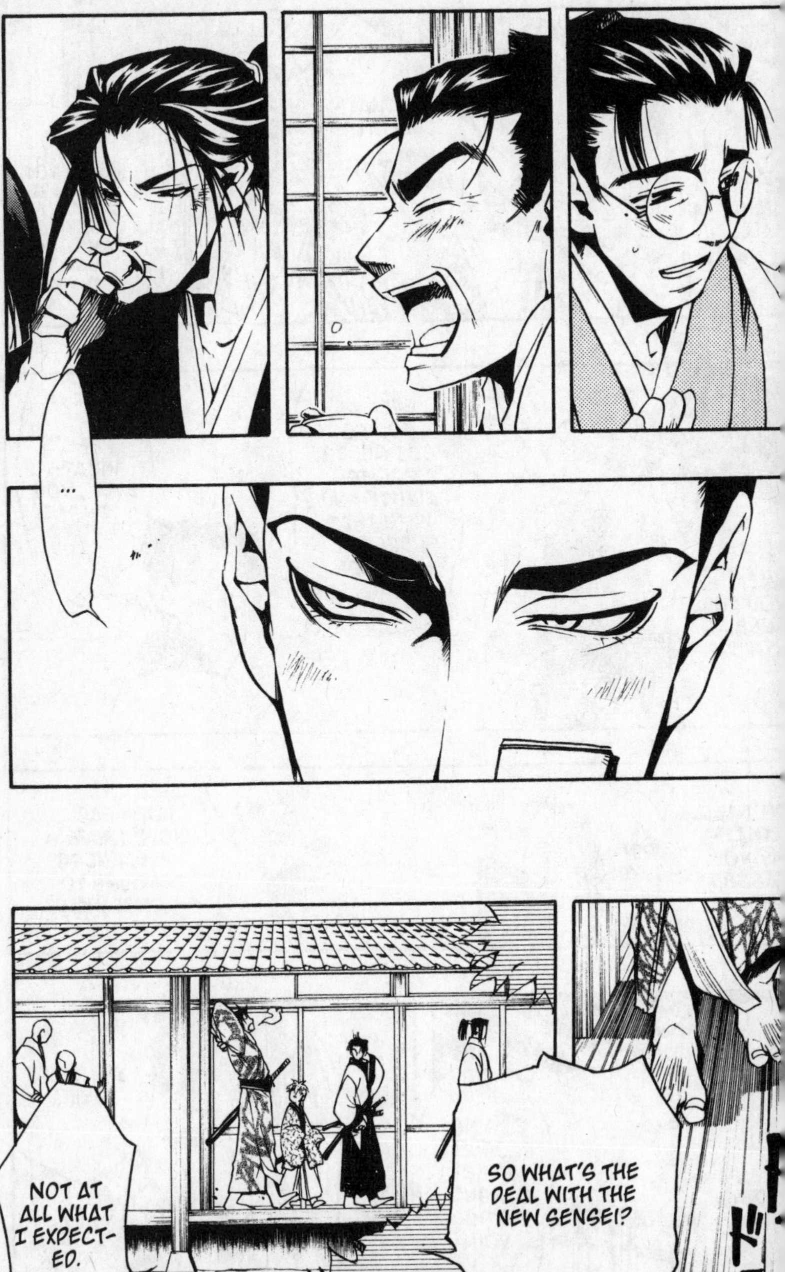
...
SO WHAT'S THE DEAL WITH THE NEW SENSEI?
ドド
NOT AT ALL WHAT I EXPECTED.

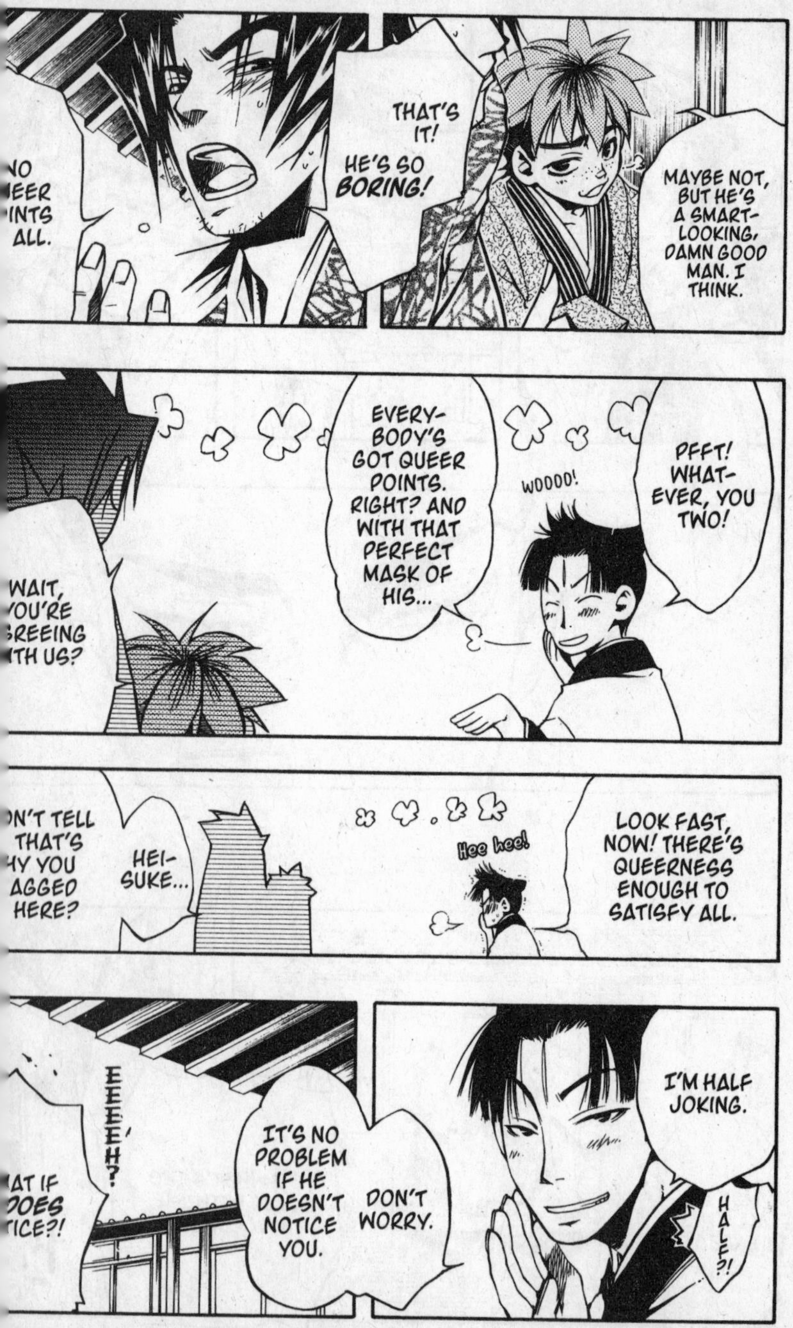
MAYBE NOT, BUT HE'S A SMART-LOOKING, DAMN GOOD MAN. I THINK.
THAT'S IT! HE'S SO BORING!
NO EER INTS ALL.
PFFT! WHAT-EVER, YOU TWO!
WOOOO!
EVERY-BODY'S GOT QUEER POINTS. RIGHT? AND WITH THAT PERFECT MASK OF HIS...
WAIT, YOU'RE GREEING ITH US?
LOOK FAST, NOW! THERE'S QUEERNESS ENOUGH TO SATISFY ALL.
Hee hee!
HEI-SUKE...
N'T TELL THAT'S HY YOU AGGED HERE?
I'M HALF JOKING.
HALF?!
DON'T WORRY.
IT'S NO PROBLEM IF HE DOESN'T NOTICE YOU.
EEEEEH?
AT IF OES TICE?!

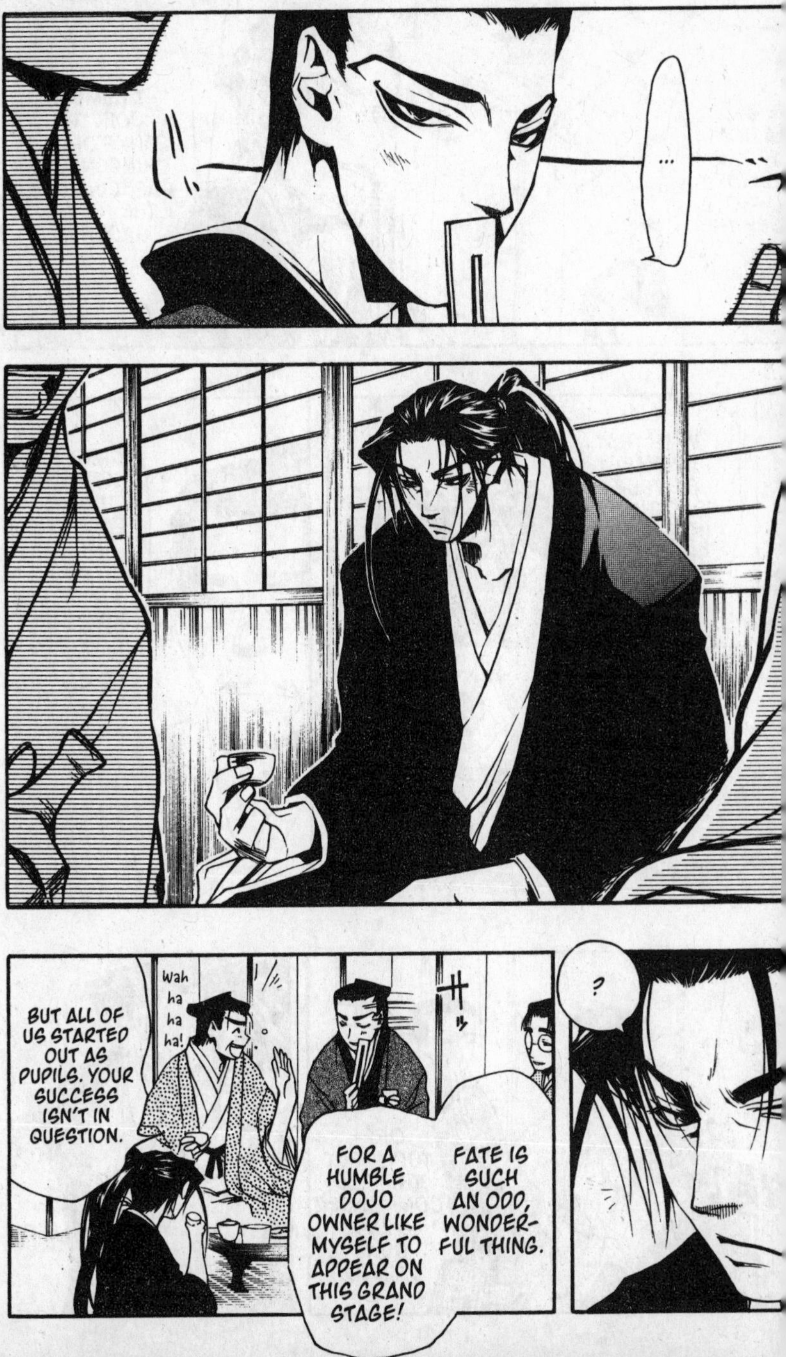
...
?
FATE IS SUCH AN ODD, WONDERFUL THING.
FOR A HUMBLE DOJO OWNER LIKE MYSELF TO APPEAR ON THIS GRAND STAGE!
Wah ha ha ha!
BUT ALL OF US STARTED OUT AS PUPILS. YOUR SUCCESS ISN'T IN QUESTION.

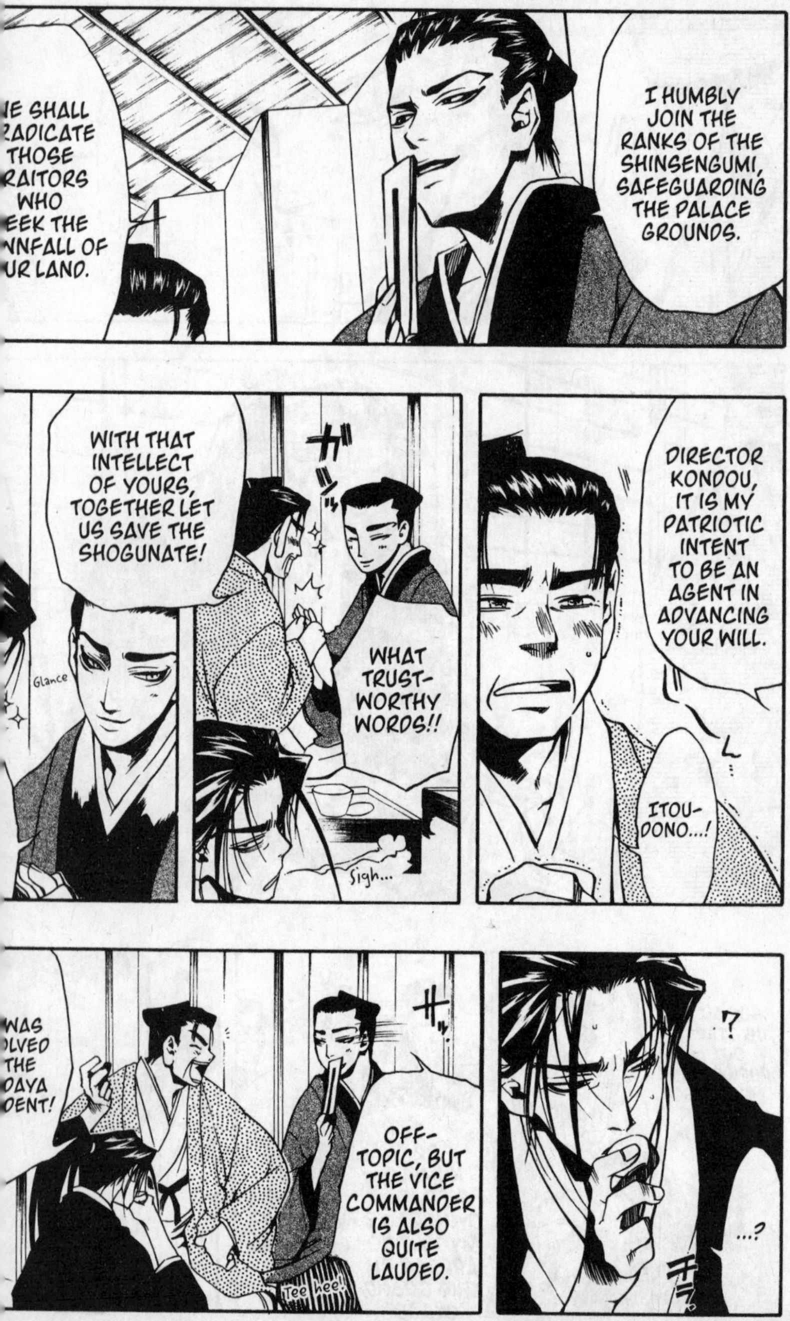
I HUMBLY JOIN THE RANKS OF THE SHINSENGUMI, SAFEGUARDING THE PALACE GROUNDS.
E SHALL RADICATE THOSE RAITORS WHO EEK THE NNFALL OF UR LAND.
DIRECTOR KONDOU, IT IS MY PATRIOTIC INTENT TO BE AN AGENT IN ADVANCING YOUR WILL.
ITOU-DONO...!
WITH THAT INTELLECT OF YOURS, TOGETHER LET US SAVE THE SHOGUNATE!
WHAT TRUST-WORTHY WORDS!!
Glance
Sigh...
?
...?
OFF-TOPIC, BUT THE VICE COMMANDER IS ALSO QUITE LAUDED.
WAS LVED THE DAYA DENT!
Tee hee!

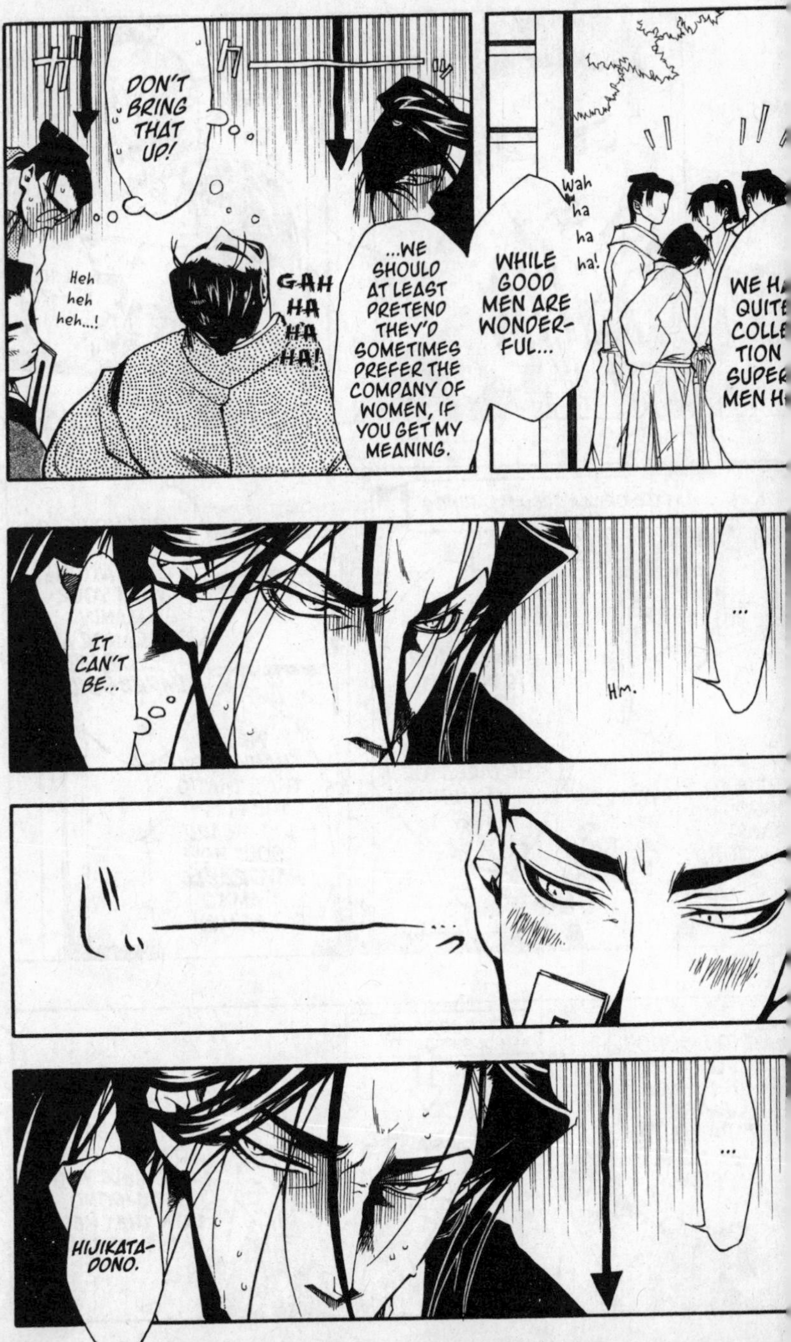
WE HA QUITE COLLE TION SUPER MEN H
Wah ha ha ha!
WHILE GOOD MEN ARE WONDER-FUL...
...WE SHOULD AT LEAST PRETEND THEY'D SOMETIMES PREFER THE COMPANY OF WOMEN, IF YOU GET MY MEANING.
GAH HA HA HA!
DON'T BRING THAT UP!
Heh heh heh...!
...
Hm.
IT CAN'T BE...
...
HIJIKATA-DONO.

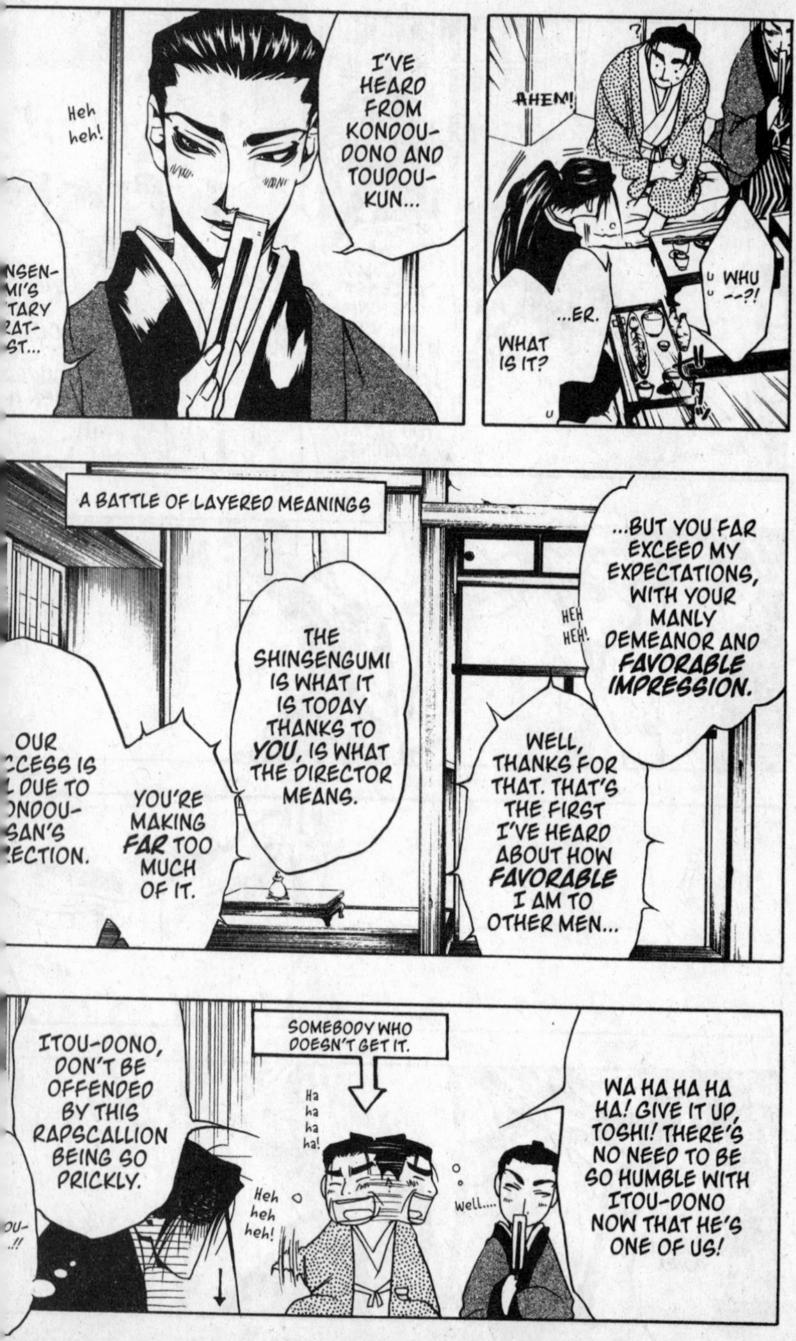

AHEM!
WHU --?!
...ER.
WHAT IS IT?
I'VE HEARD FROM KONDOU-DONO AND TOUDOU-KUN...
Heh heh!
NSEN-MI'S TARY RAT-ST...
...BUT YOU FAR EXCEED MY EXPECTATIONS, WITH YOUR MANLY DEMEANOR AND FAVORABLE IMPRESSION.
HEH HEH!
WELL, THANKS FOR THAT. THAT'S THE FIRST I'VE HEARD ABOUT HOW FAVORABLE I AM TO OTHER MEN...
A BATTLE OF LAYERED MEANINGS
THE SHINSENGUMI IS WHAT IT IS TODAY THANKS TO YOU, IS WHAT THE DIRECTOR MEANS.
YOU'RE MAKING FAR TOO MUCH OF IT.
OUR CCESS IS L DUE TO ONDOU-SAN'S ECTION.
WA HA HA HA HA! GIVE IT UP, TOSHI! THERE'S NO NEED TO BE SO HUMBLE WITH ITOU-DONO NOW THAT HE'S ONE OF US!
Well....
SOMEBODY WHO DOESN'T GET IT.
Ha ha ha ha!
Heh heh heh!
ITOU-DONO, DON'T BE OFFENDED BY THIS RAPSCALLION BEING SO PRICKLY.
OU-!!

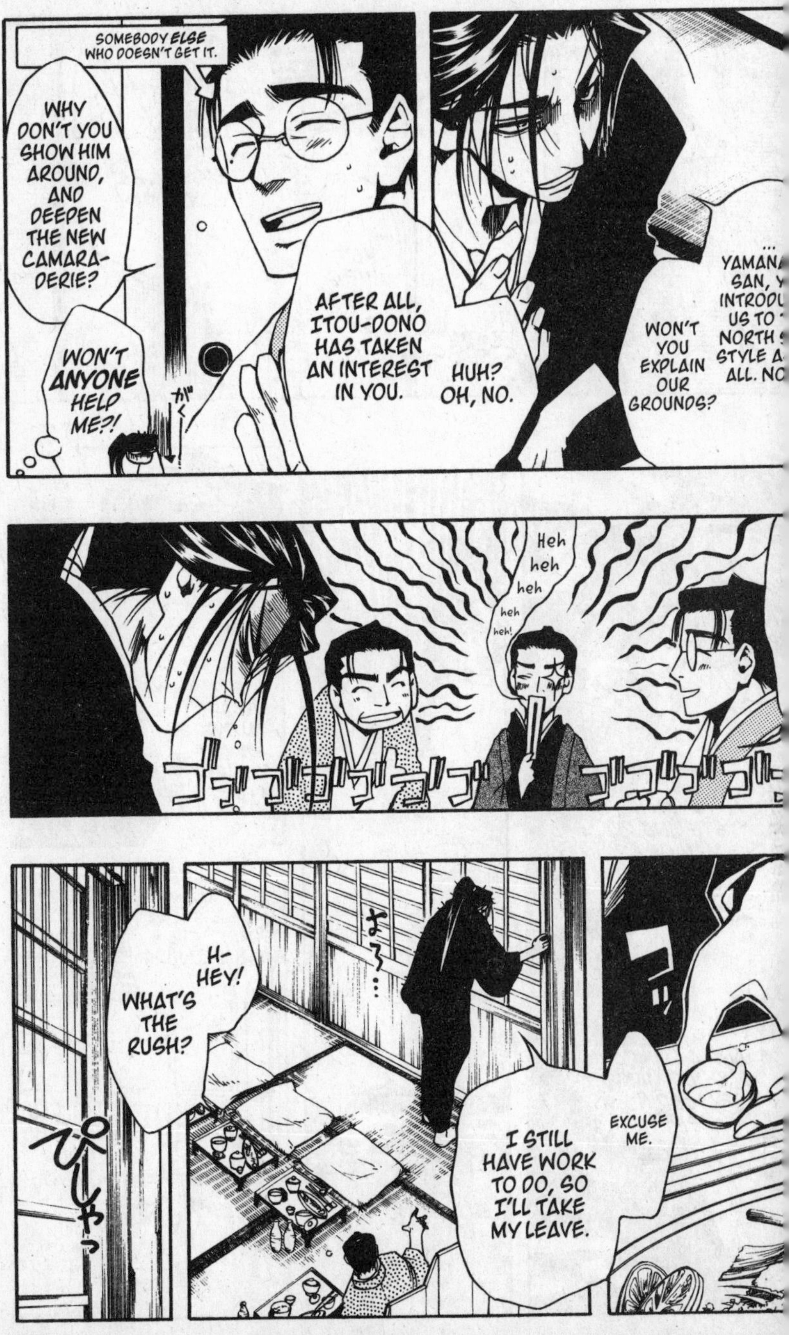
... YAMANA SAN, Y INTRODU US TO NORTH STYLE A ALL. NO
WON'T YOU EXPLAIN OUR GROUNDS?
SOMEBODY ELSE WHO DOESN'T GET IT.
HUH? OH, NO.
AFTER ALL, ITOU-DONO HAS TAKEN AN INTEREST IN YOU.
WHY DON'T YOU SHOW HIM AROUND, AND DEEPEN THE NEW CAMARADERIE?
WON'T ANYONE HELP ME?!
Heh heh heh heh heh!
EXCUSE ME.
I STILL HAVE WORK TO DO, SO I'LL TAKE MY LEAVE.
H-HEY! WHAT'S THE RUSH?

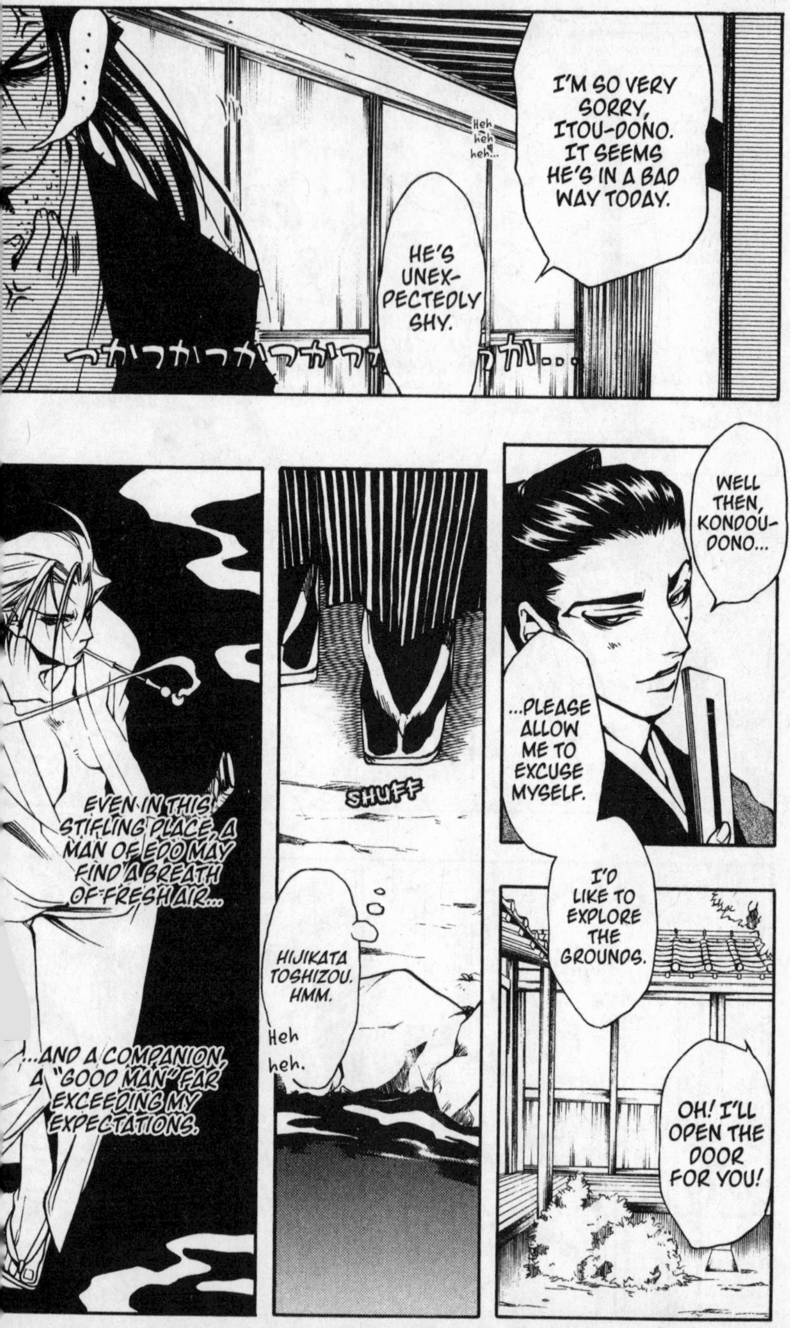
I'M SO VERY SORRY, ITOU-DONO. IT SEEMS HE'S IN A BAD WAY TODAY.
Heh heh heh...
HE'S UNEX-PECTEDLY SHY.
WELL THEN, KONDOU-DONO...
...PLEASE ALLOW ME TO EXCUSE MYSELF.
I'D LIKE TO EXPLORE THE GROUNDS.
OH! I'LL OPEN THE DOOR FOR YOU!
SHUFF
HIJIKATA TOSHIZOU. HMM.
Heh heh.
EVEN IN THIS STIFLING PLACE, A MAN OF EDO MAY FIND A BREATH OF FRESH AIR...
...AND A COMPANION, A "GOOD MAN" FAR EXCEEDING MY EXPECTATIONS.

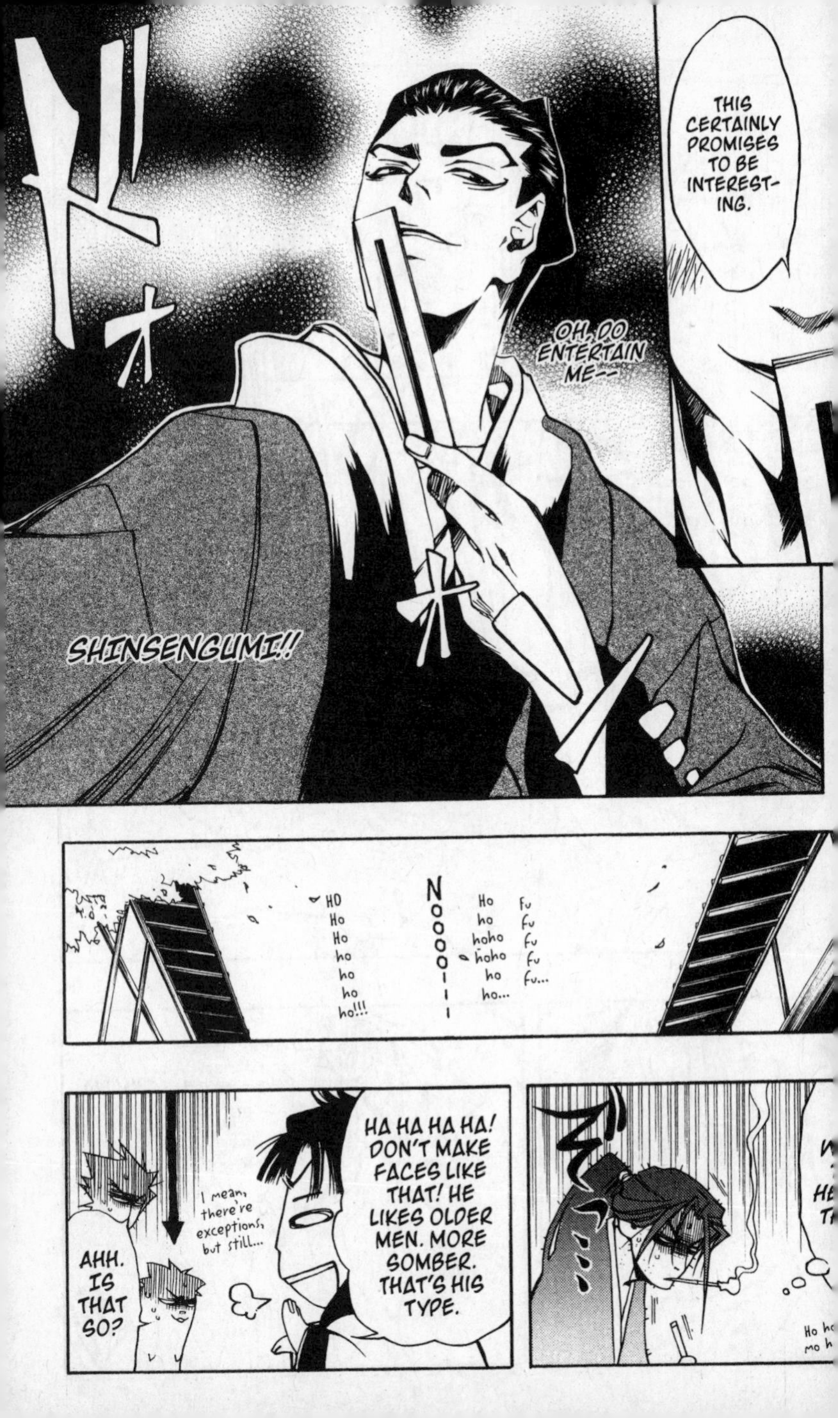
THIS CERTAINLY PROMISES TO BE INTERESTING.
OH, DO ENTERTAIN ME--
SHINSENGUMI!!
HO Ho Ho ho ho ho ho!!!
Noooo!!!
Ho ho hoho hoho ho ho...
fu fu fu fu fu...
HA HA HA HA! DON'T MAKE FACES LIKE THAT! HE LIKES OLDER MEN. MORE SOMBER. THAT'S HIS TYPE.
I mean, there're exceptions, but still...
AHH. IS THAT SO?

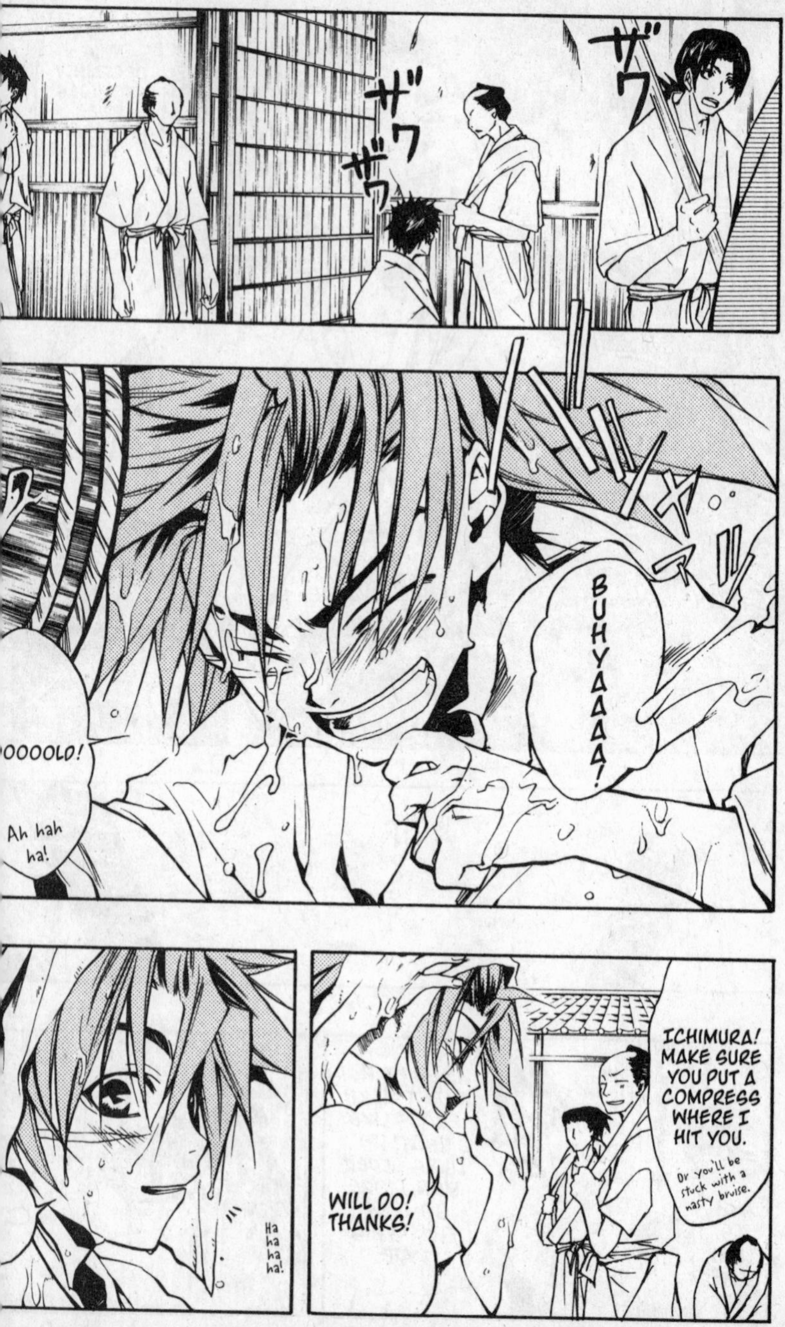
ザワ
ザワ
ザワ
BUHYAAAAAA!
OOOOLD!
Ah hah ha!
ICHIMURA! MAKE SURE YOU PUT A COMPRESS WHERE I HIT YOU.
Or you'll be stuck with a nasty bruise.
WILL DO! THANKS!
Ha ha ha ha ha!

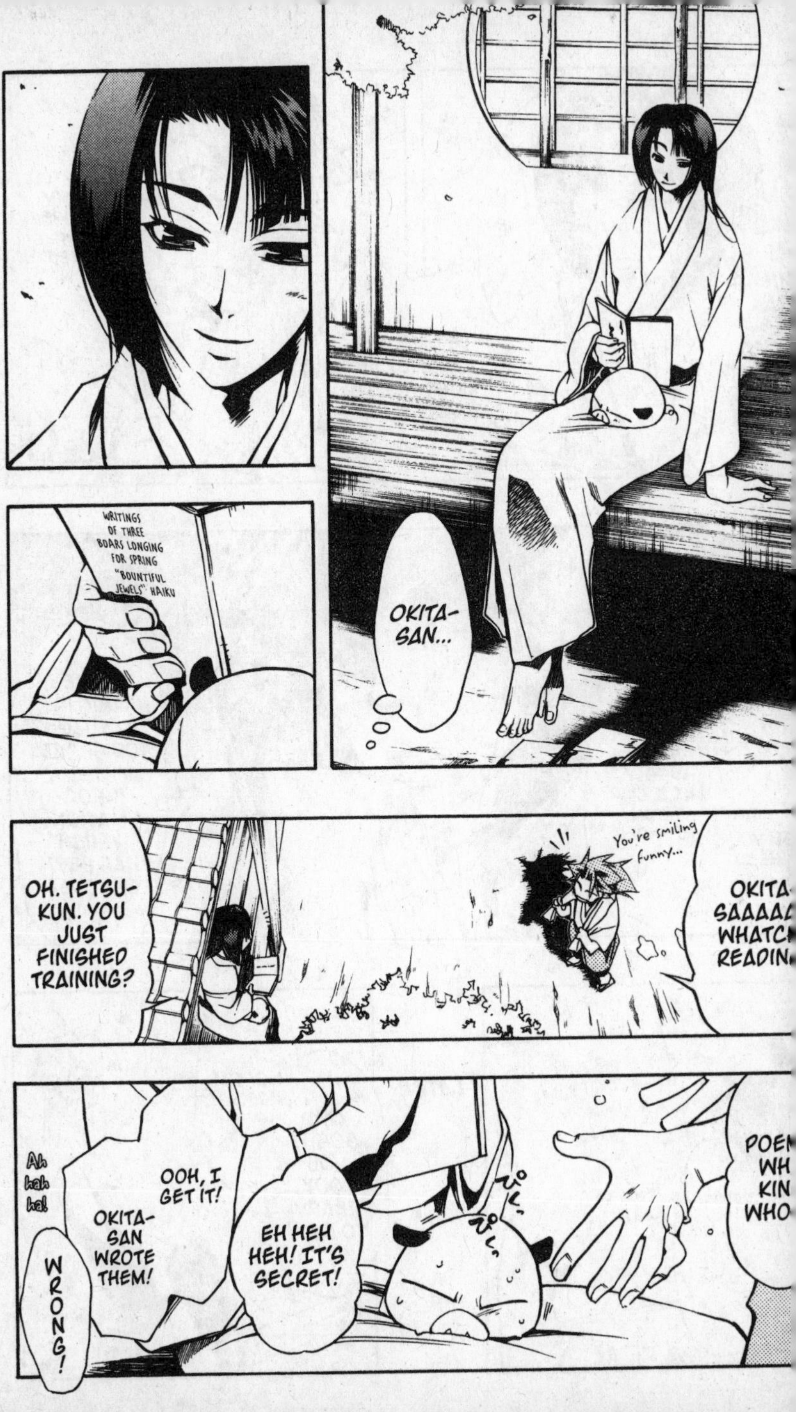
OKITA-SAN...
WRITINGS OF THREE BOARS LONGING FOR SPRING "BOUNTIFUL JEWELS" HAIKU
OKITA-SAAAAA WHATCH READIN
You're smiling funny...
OH. TETSU-KUN. YOU JUST FINISHED TRAINING?
POE WH KIN WHO
EH HEH HEH! IT'S SECRET!
OOH, I GET IT! OKITA-SAN WROTE THEM!
WRONG!
Ah hah ha!

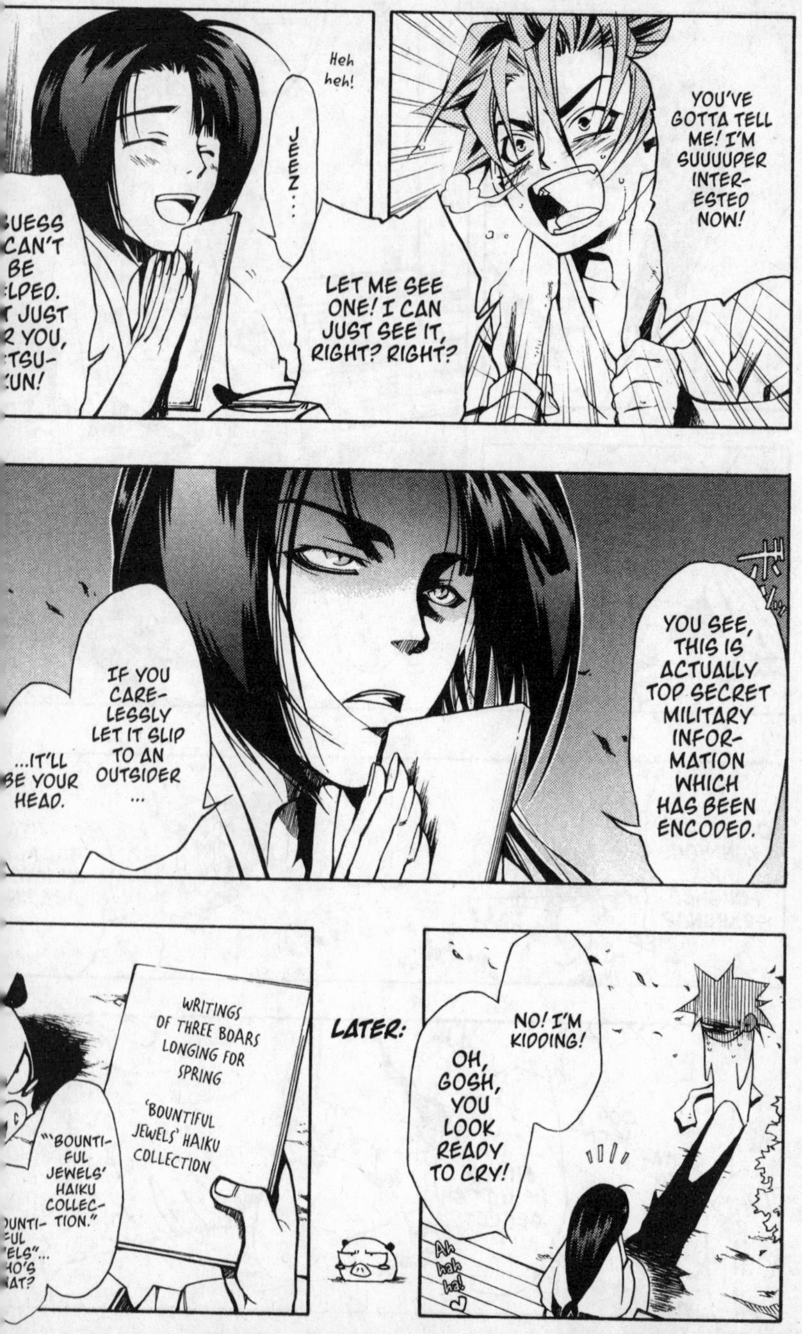
YOU'VE GOTTA TELL ME! I'M SUUUUPER INTER-ESTED NOW!
LET ME SEE ONE! I CAN JUST SEE IT, RIGHT? RIGHT?
Heh heh!
JEEZ...
UESS CAN'T BE LPED. T JUST R YOU, TSU-UN!
YOU SEE, THIS IS ACTUALLY TOP SECRET MILITARY INFOR-MATION WHICH HAS BEEN ENCODED.
IF YOU CARE-LESSLY LET IT SLIP TO AN OUTSIDER...
...IT'LL BE YOUR HEAD.
NO! I'M KIDDING!
OH, GOSH, YOU LOOK READY TO CRY!
Ah hah ha!
LATER:
WRITINGS OF THREE BOARS LONGING FOR SPRING
'BOUNTIFUL JEWELS' HAIKU COLLECTION
"'BOUNTI-FUL JEWELS' HAIKU COLLEC-TION."
OUNTI-FUL EWELS"... HO'S AT?

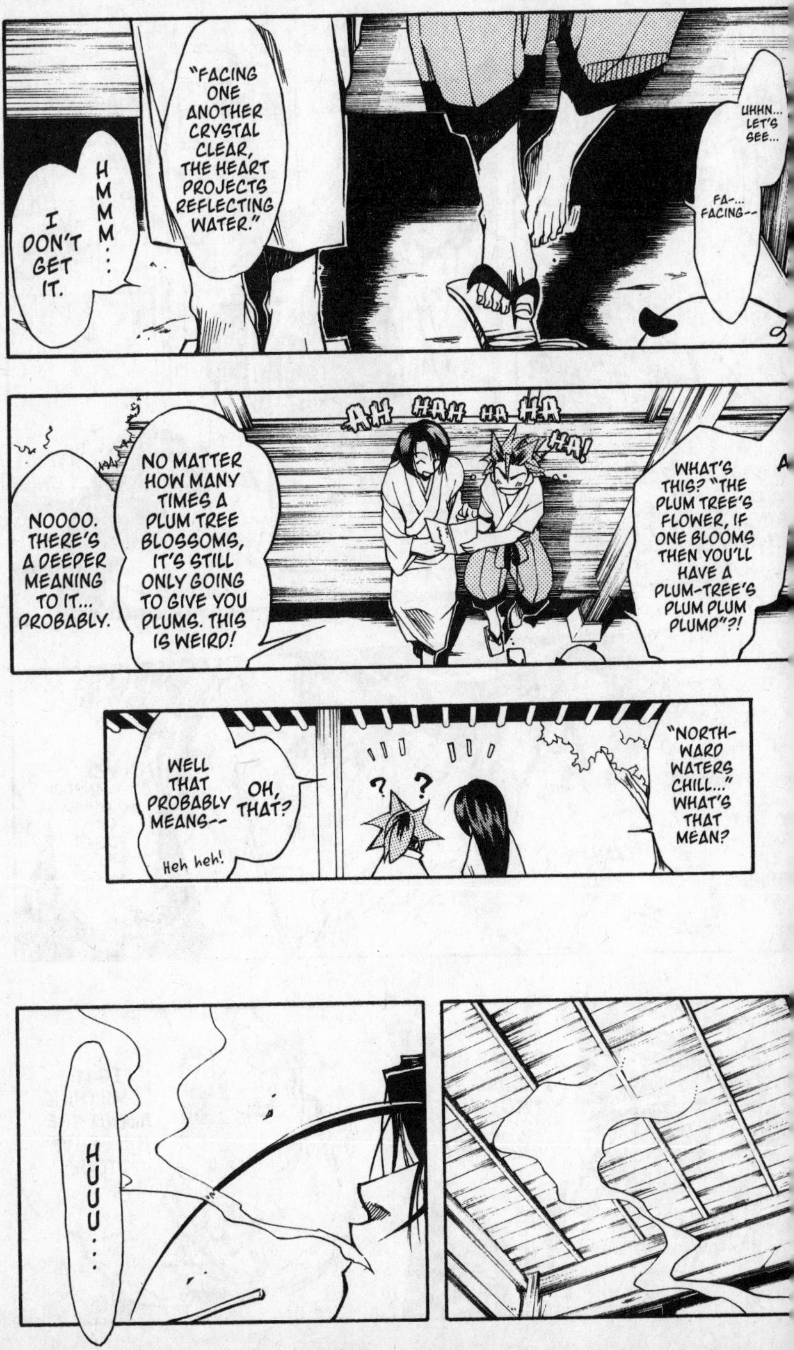
UHHN... LET'S SEE...
FA-... FACING--
"FACING ONE ANOTHER CRYSTAL CLEAR, THE HEART PROJECTS REFLECTING WATER."
HMMM...
I DON'T GET IT.
AH HAH HA HA HA!
WHAT'S THIS? "THE PLUM TREE'S FLOWER, IF ONE BLOOMS THEN YOU'LL HAVE A PLUM-TREE'S PLUM PLUM PLUMP"?!
NO MATTER HOW MANY TIMES A PLUM TREE BLOSSOMS, IT'S STILL ONLY GOING TO GIVE YOU PLUMS. THIS IS WEIRD!
NOOOO. THERE'S A DEEPER MEANING TO IT... PROBABLY.
"NORTHWARD WATERS CHILL..." WHAT'S THAT MEAN?
OH, THAT?
WELL THAT PROBABLY MEANS--
Heh heh!
HUUU...

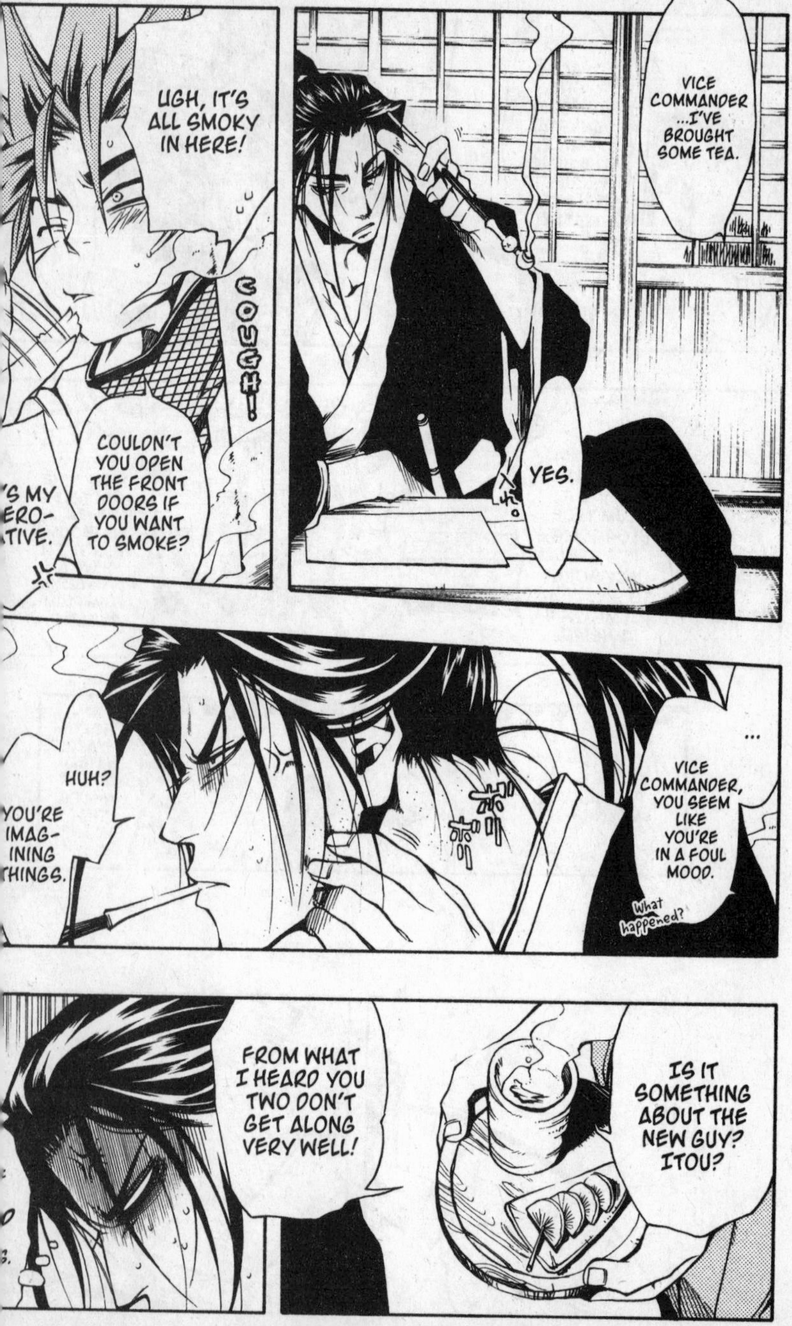
VICE COMMANDER ...I'VE BROUGHT SOME TEA.
YES.
UGH, IT'S ALL SMOKY IN HERE!
COUGH!
COULDN'T YOU OPEN THE FRONT DOORS IF YOU WANT TO SMOKE?
...
VICE COMMANDER, YOU SEEM LIKE YOU'RE IN A FOUL MOOD.
What happened?
HUH?
YOU'RE IMAGINING THINGS.
IS IT SOMETHING ABOUT THE NEW GUY? ITOU?
FROM WHAT I HEARD YOU TWO DON'T GET ALONG VERY WELL!

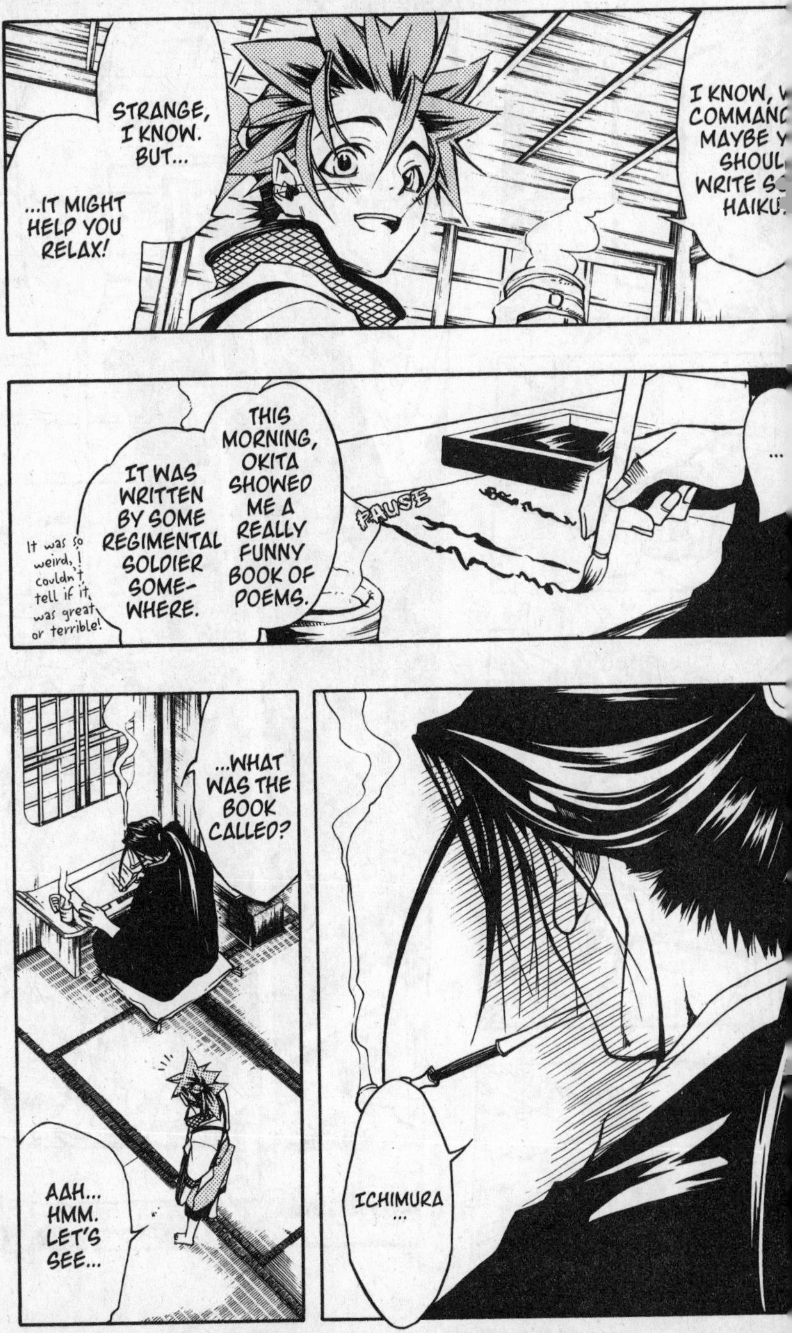
I KNOW, COMMAND MAYBE Y SHOUL WRITE S HAIKU
STRANGE, I KNOW. BUT...
...IT MIGHT HELP YOU RELAX!
...
PAUSE
THIS MORNING, OKITA SHOWED ME A REALLY FUNNY BOOK OF POEMS.
IT WAS WRITTEN BY SOME REGIMENTAL SOLDIER SOME-WHERE.
It was so weird, I couldn't tell if it was great or terrible!
ICHIMURA ...
...WHAT WAS THE BOOK CALLED?
AAH... HMM. LET'S SEE...

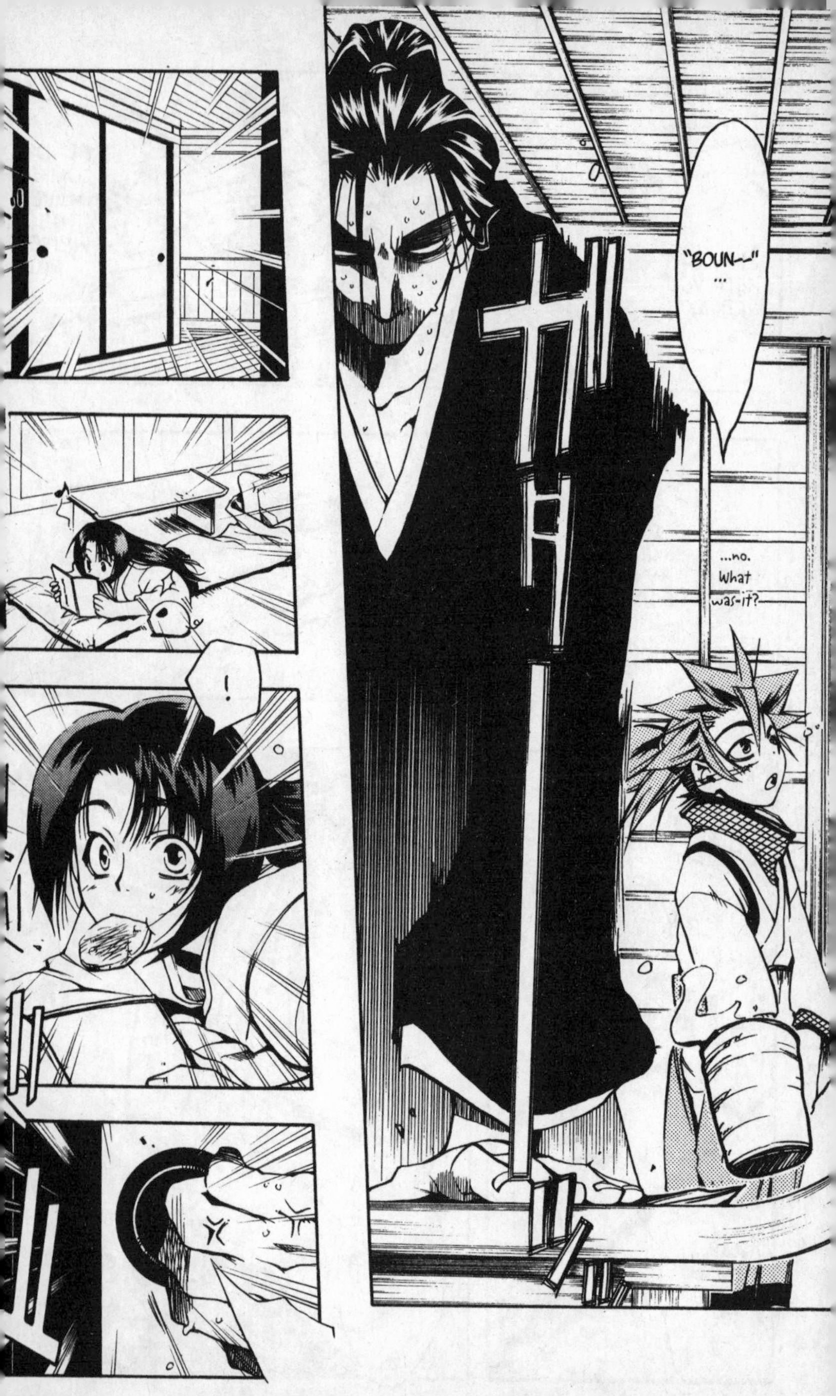
"BOUN--" ...
...no. What was-it?
!

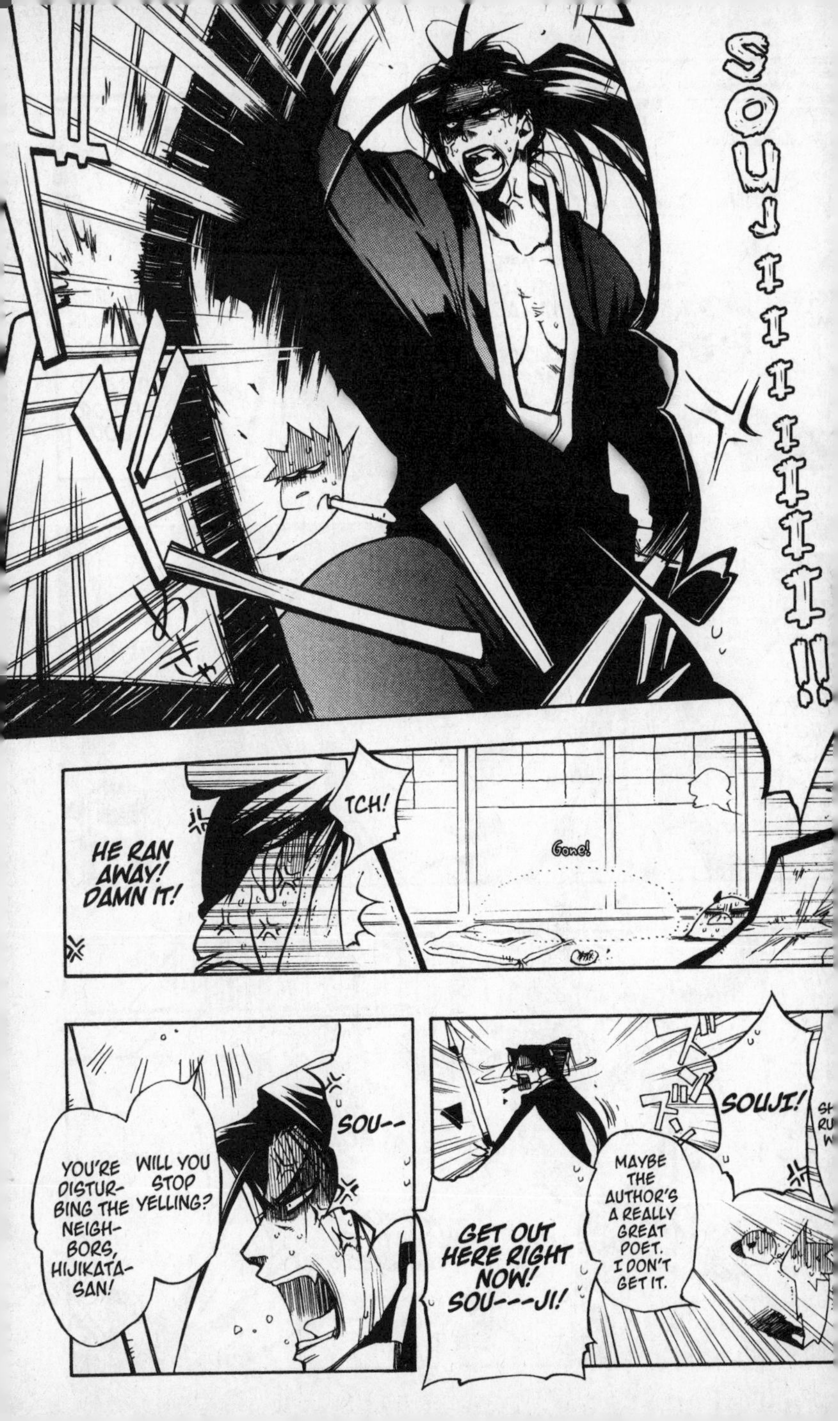
SOUJIIIIIII!!
Gone!
TCH!
HE RAN AWAY! DAMN IT!
SOUJI!
MAYBE THE AUTHOR'S A REALLY GREAT POET. I DON'T GET IT.
GET OUT HERE RIGHT NOW! SOU---JI!
SOU--
WILL YOU STOP YELLING?
YOU'RE DISTURBING THE NEIGHBORS, HIJIKATA-SAN!

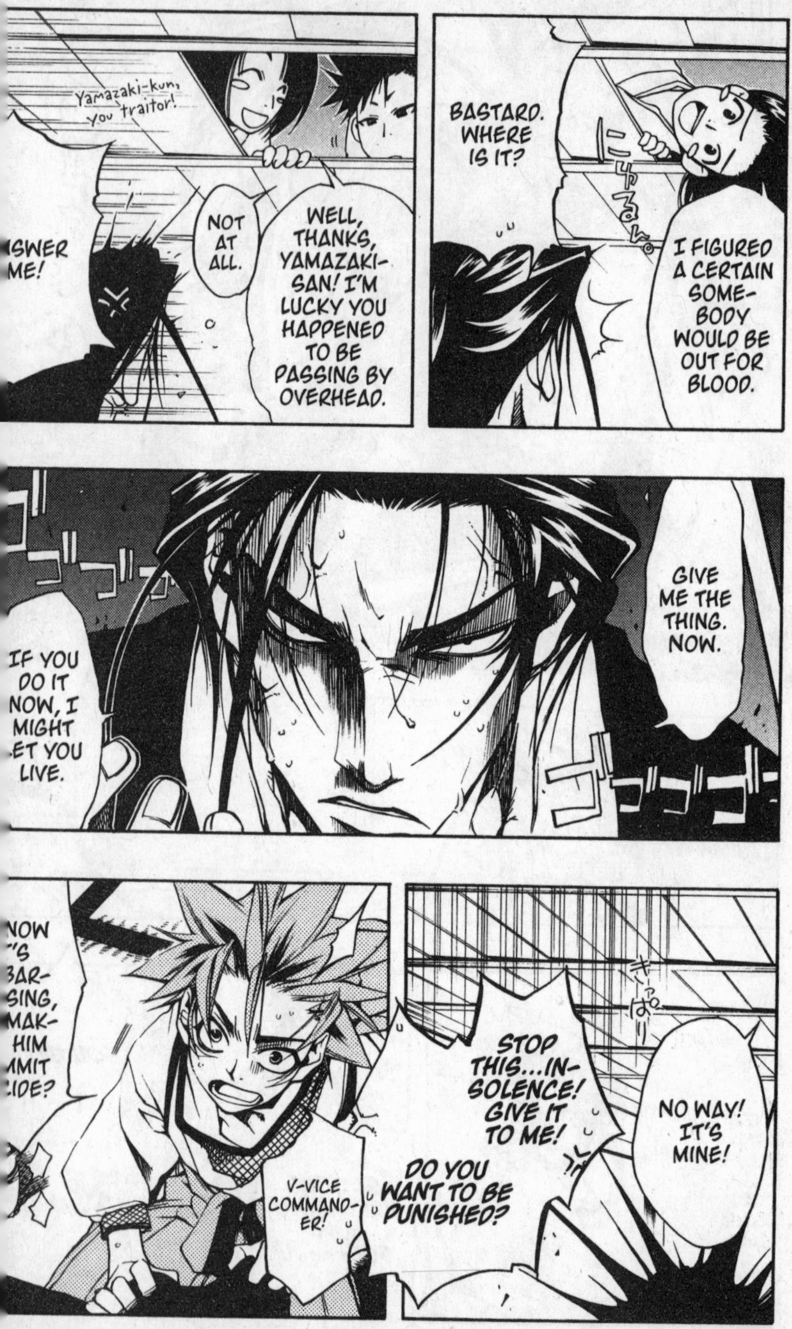

BASTARD. WHERE IS IT?
にゅるん
I FIGURED A CERTAIN SOMEBODY WOULD BE OUT FOR BLOOD.
Yamazaki-kun, you traitor!
WELL, THANKS, YAMAZAKI-SAN! I'M LUCKY YOU HAPPENED TO BE PASSING BY OVERHEAD.
NOT AT ALL.
NSWER ME!
GIVE ME THE THING. NOW.
IF YOU DO IT NOW, I MIGHT .ET YOU LIVE.
NO WAY! IT'S MINE!
STOP THIS...IN-SOLENCE! GIVE IT TO ME!
DO YOU WANT TO BE PUNISHED?
V-VICE COMMAND-ER!
NOW 'S BAR-SING, MAK- HIM MMIT CIDE?

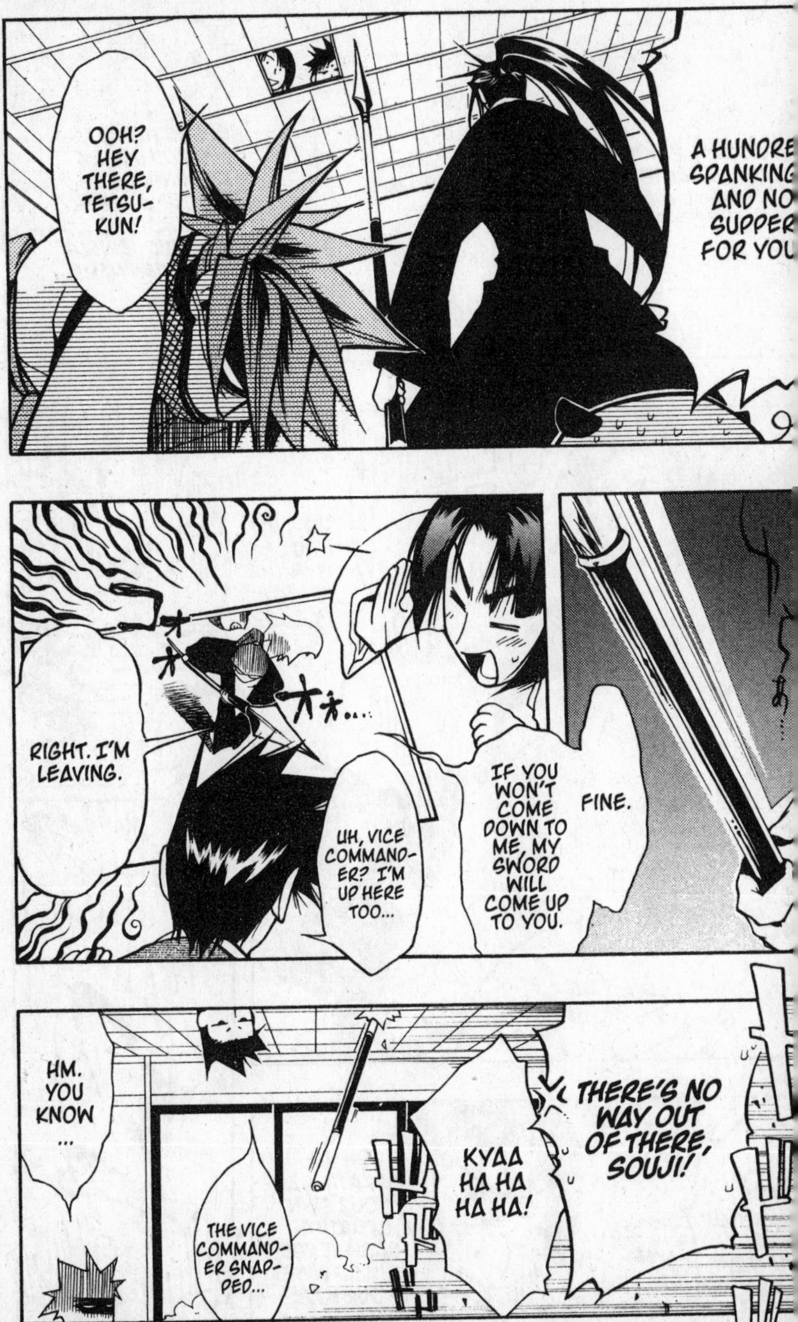
A HUNDRE SPANKING AND NO SUPPER FOR YOU
OOH? HEY THERE, TETSU-KUN!
FINE.
IF YOU WON'T COME DOWN TO ME, MY SWORD WILL COME UP TO YOU.
UH, VICE COMMANDER? I'M UP HERE TOO...
RIGHT. I'M LEAVING.
THERE'S NO WAY OUT OF THERE, SOUJI!
KYAA HA HA HA HA!
THE VICE COMMANDER SNAPPED...
HM. YOU KNOW ...

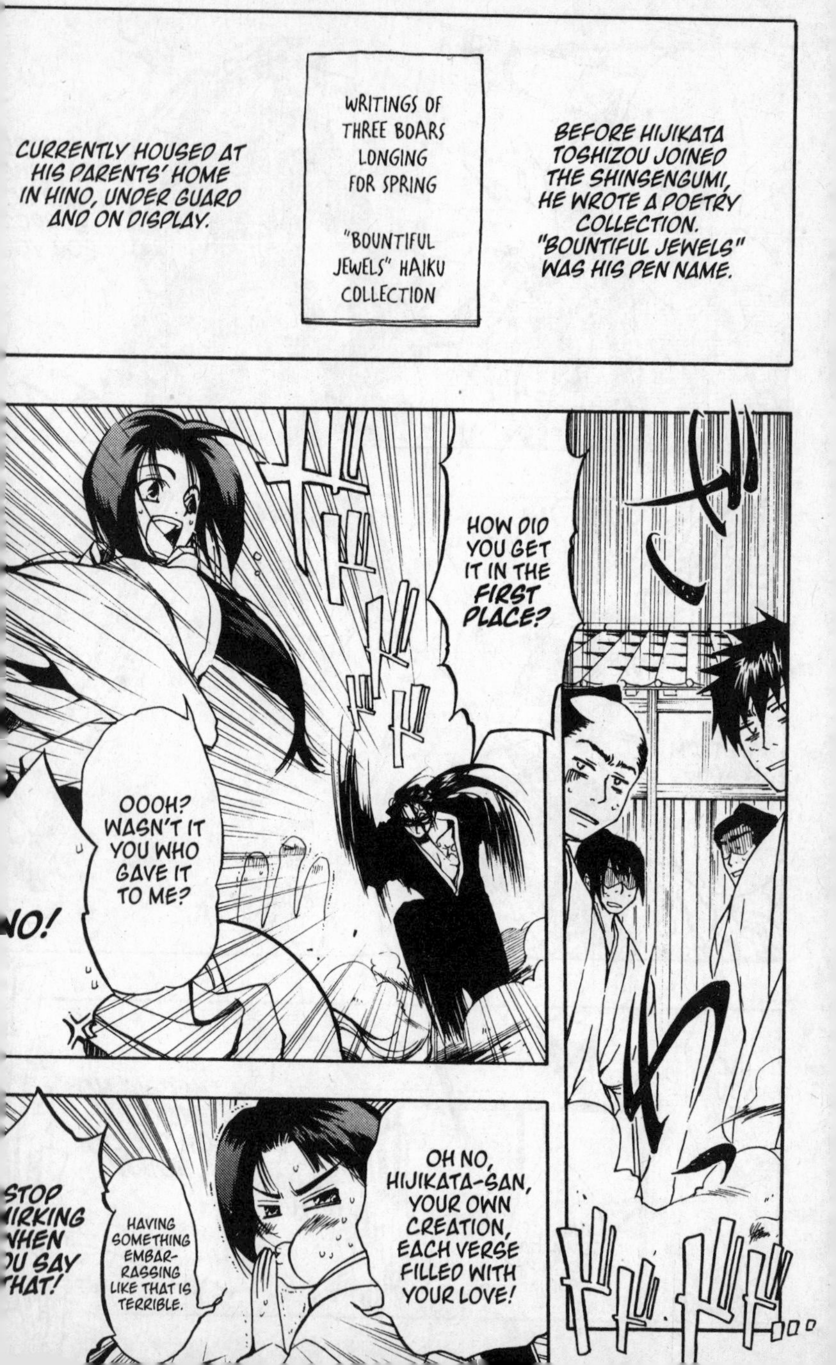
BEFORE HIJIKATA TOSHIZOU JOINED THE SHINSENGUMI, HE WROTE A POETRY COLLECTION. "BOUNTIFUL JEWELS" WAS HIS PEN NAME.
WRITINGS OF THREE BOARS LONGING FOR SPRING
"BOUNTIFUL JEWELS" HAIKU COLLECTION
CURRENTLY HOUSED AT HIS PARENTS' HOME IN HINO, UNDER GUARD AND ON DISPLAY.
HOW DID YOU GET IT IN THE FIRST PLACE?
OOOH? WASN'T IT YOU WHO GAVE IT TO ME?
NO!
OH NO, HIJIKATA-SAN, YOUR OWN CREATION, EACH VERSE FILLED WITH YOUR LOVE!
HAVING SOMETHING EMBARRASSING LIKE THAT IS TERRIBLE.

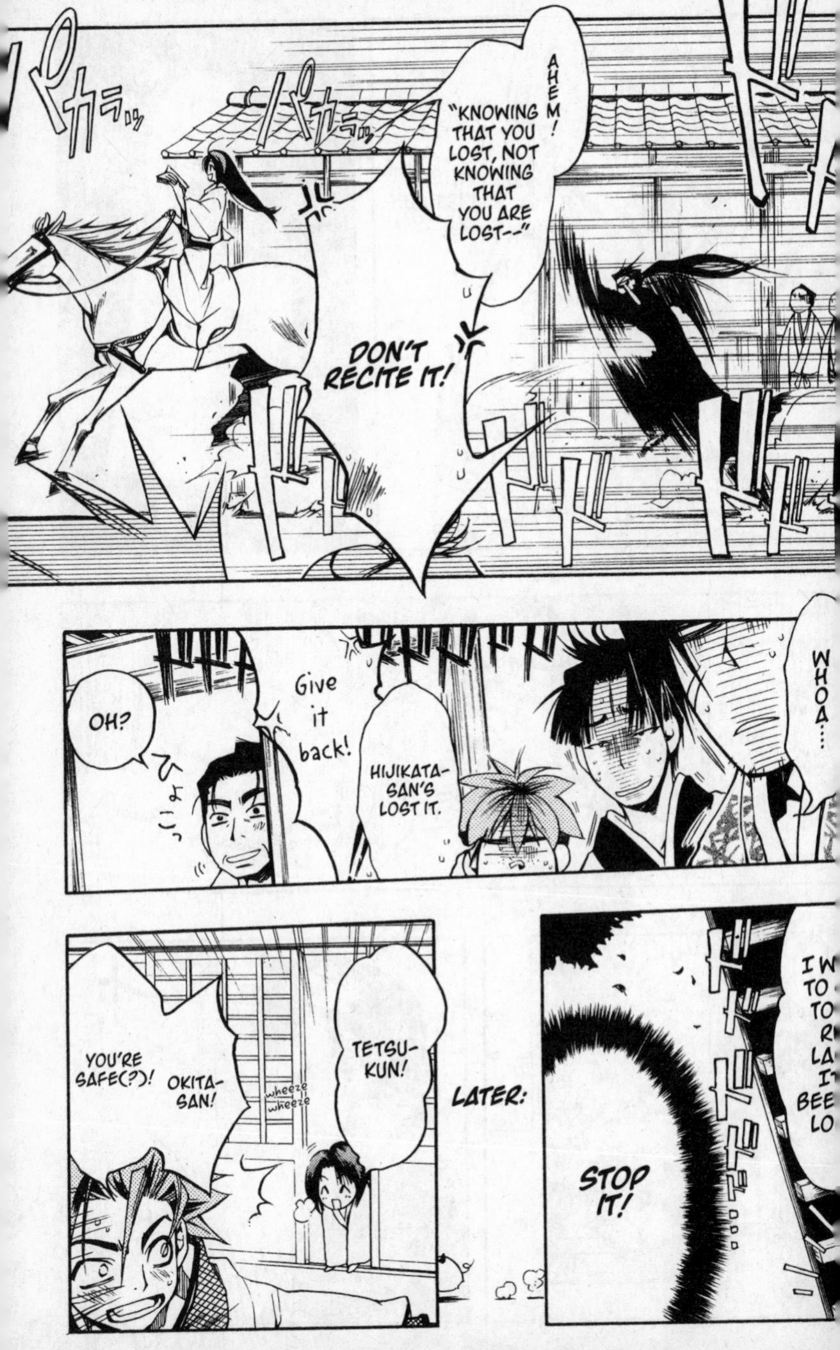
AHEM! "KNOWING THAT YOU LOST, NOT KNOWING THAT YOU ARE LOST--"
DON'T RECITE IT!
WHOA...
HIJIKATA-SAN'S LOST IT.
Give it back!
OH?
STOP IT!
LATER:
TETSU-KUN!
wheeze wheeze
OKITA-SAN!
YOU'RE SAFE(?)!

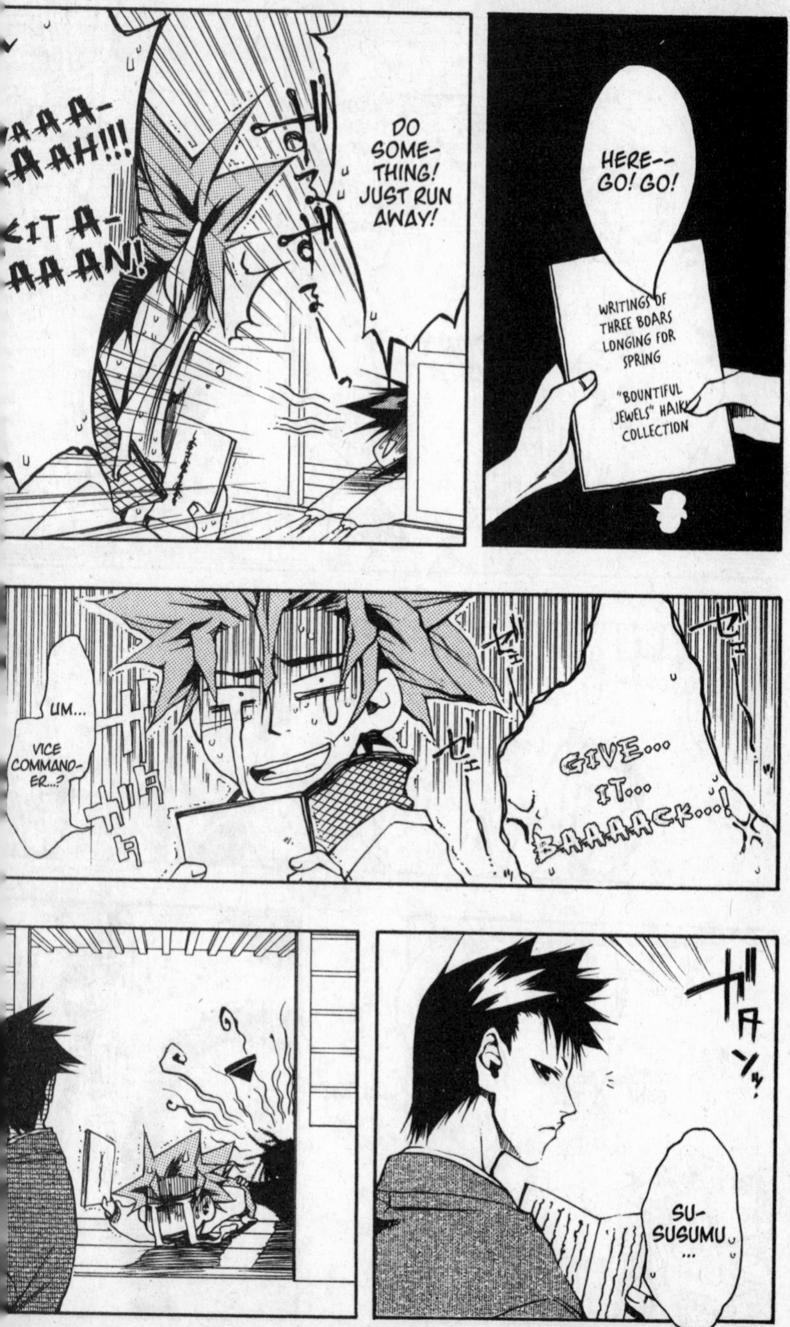
HERE-- GO! GO!
WRITINGS OF THREE BOARS LONGING FOR SPRING
"BOUNTIFUL JEWELS" HAIKU COLLECTION
DO SOMETHING! JUST RUN AWAY!
AAA-AAH!!!
EIT A-AAAN!
GIVE... IT... BAAAAACK...!
UM... VICE COMMANDER...?
SU-SUSUMU...

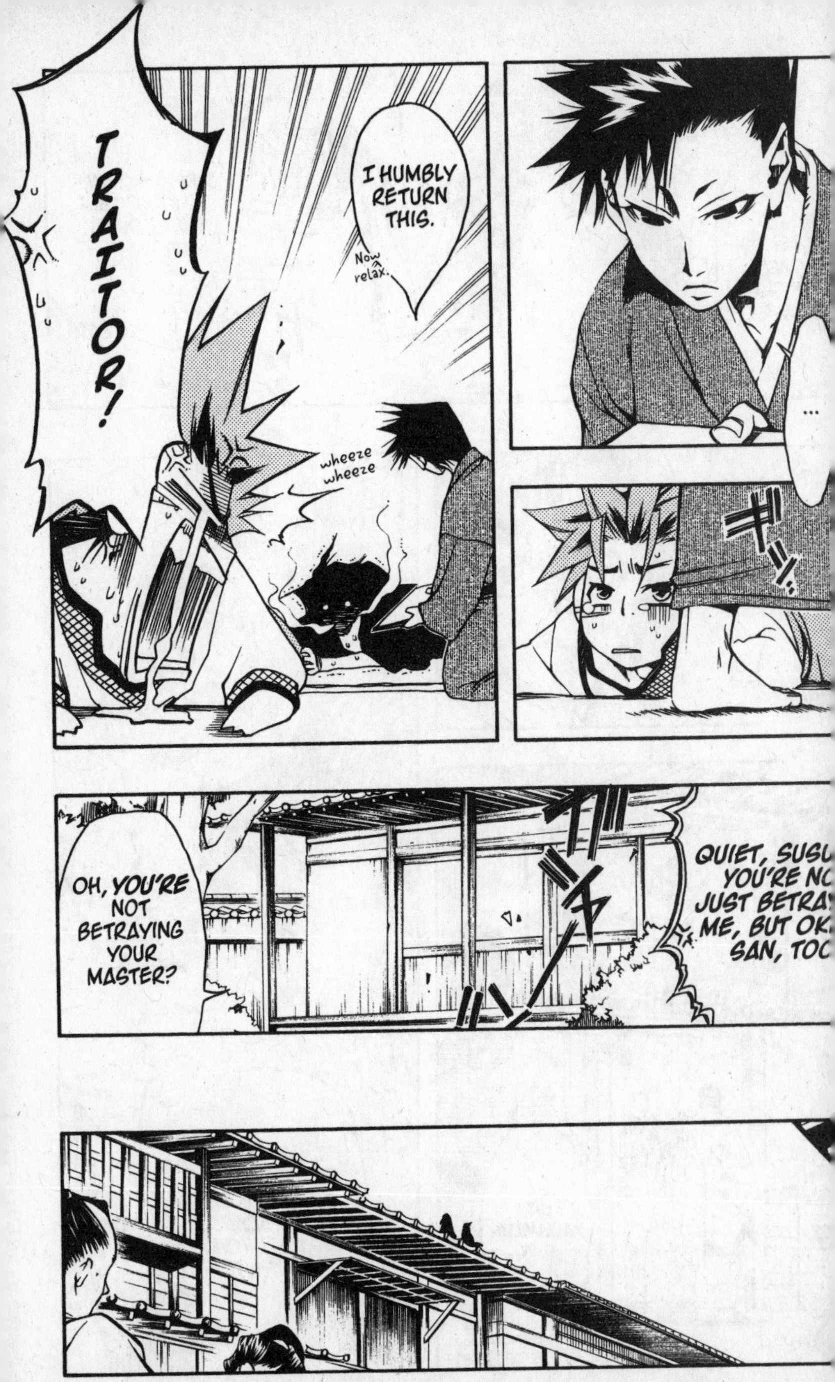
...
I HUMBLY RETURN THIS.
Now relax.
wheeze wheeze
TRAITOR!
QUIET, SUSU YOU'RE NO JUST BETRAY ME, BUT OK SAN, TOO
OH, YOU'RE NOT BETRAYING YOUR MASTER?

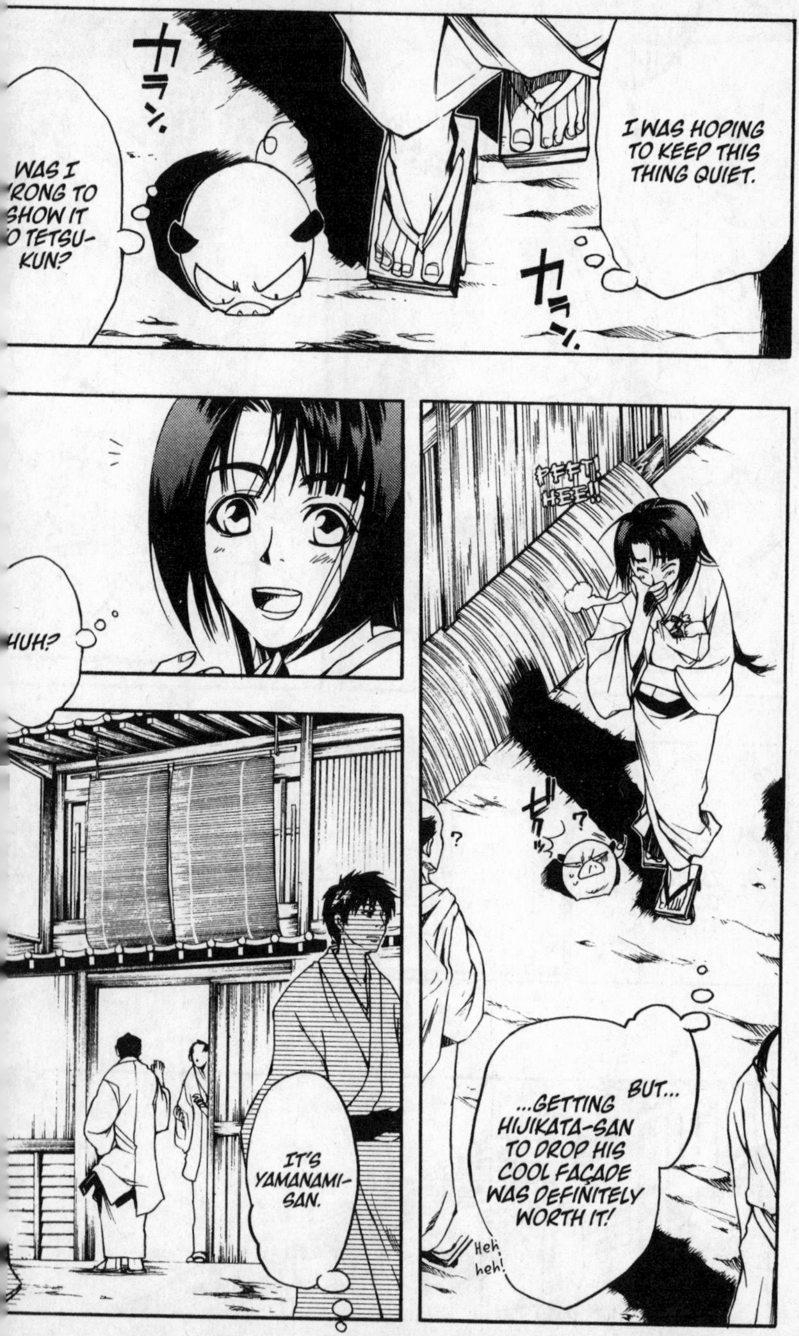
I WAS HOPING TO KEEP THIS THING QUIET.
カラン
カラン
WAS I RONG TO SHOW IT O TETSU-KUN?
PFFT! HEE!!
BUT...
...GETTING HIJIKATA-SAN TO DROP HIS COOL FAÇADE WAS DEFINITELY WORTH IT!
Heh heh!
HUH?
IT'S YAMANAMI-SAN.

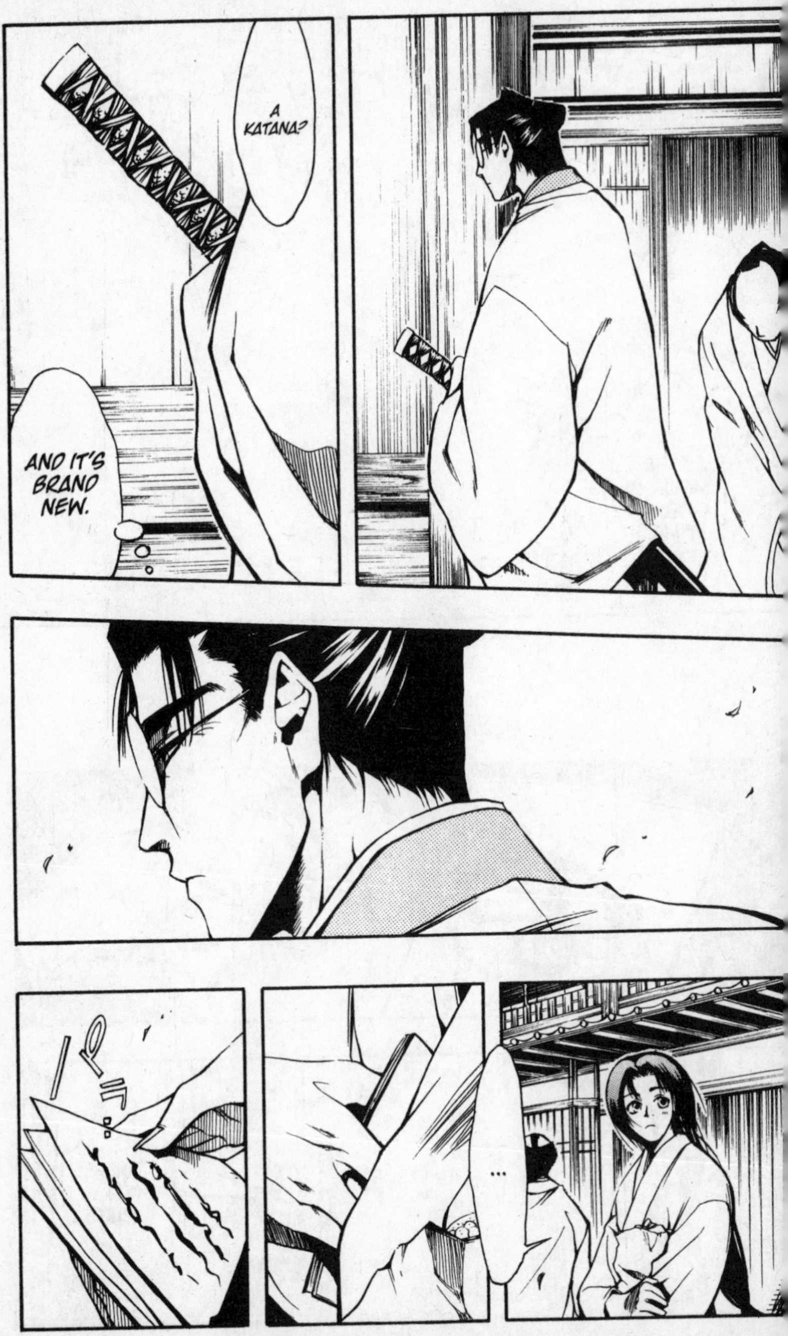
A KATANA?
AND IT'S BRAND NEW.
...

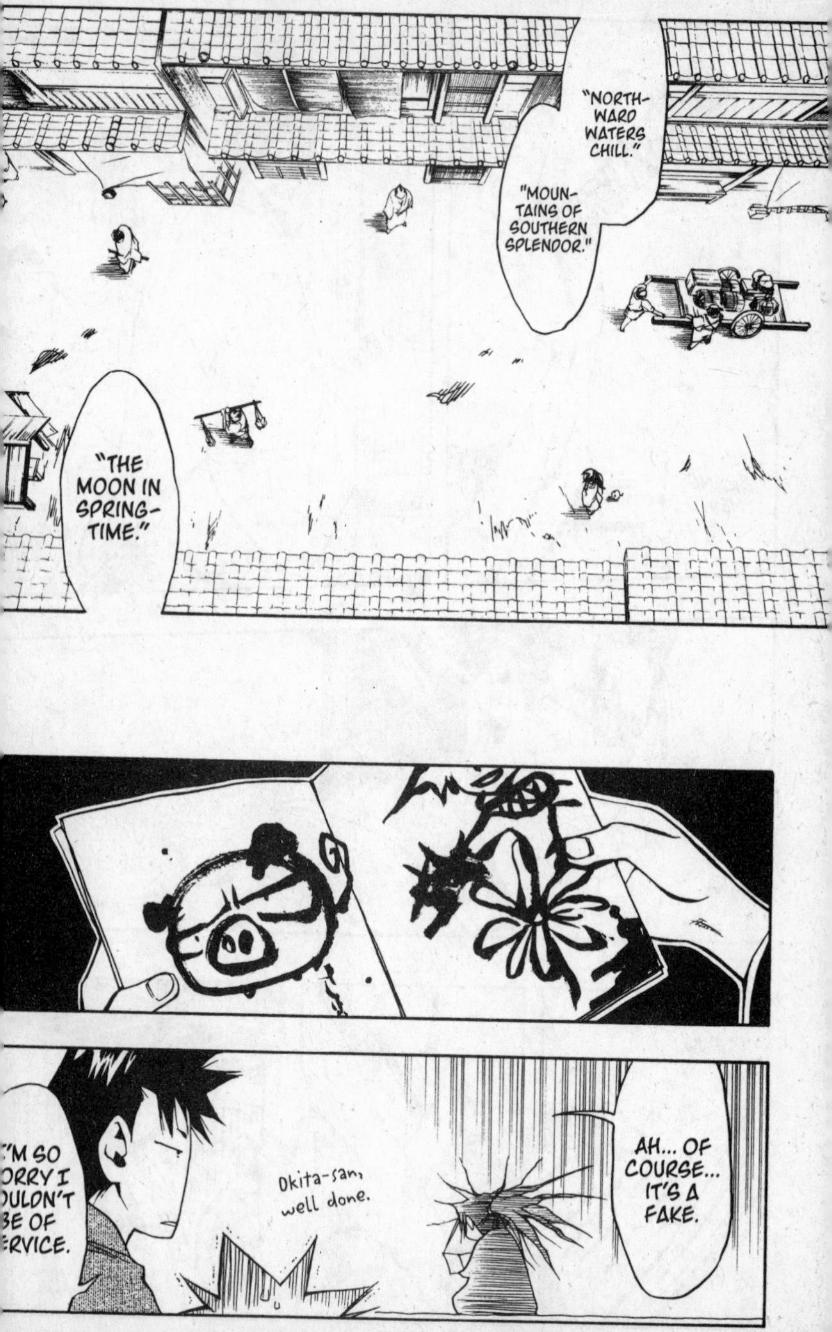
"NORTH-WARD WATERS CHILL."
"MOUN-TAINS OF SOUTHERN SPLENDOR."
"THE MOON IN SPRING-TIME."
AH... OF COURSE... IT'S A FAKE.
Okita-san, well done.
'M SO ORRY I OULDN'T BE OF ERVICE.

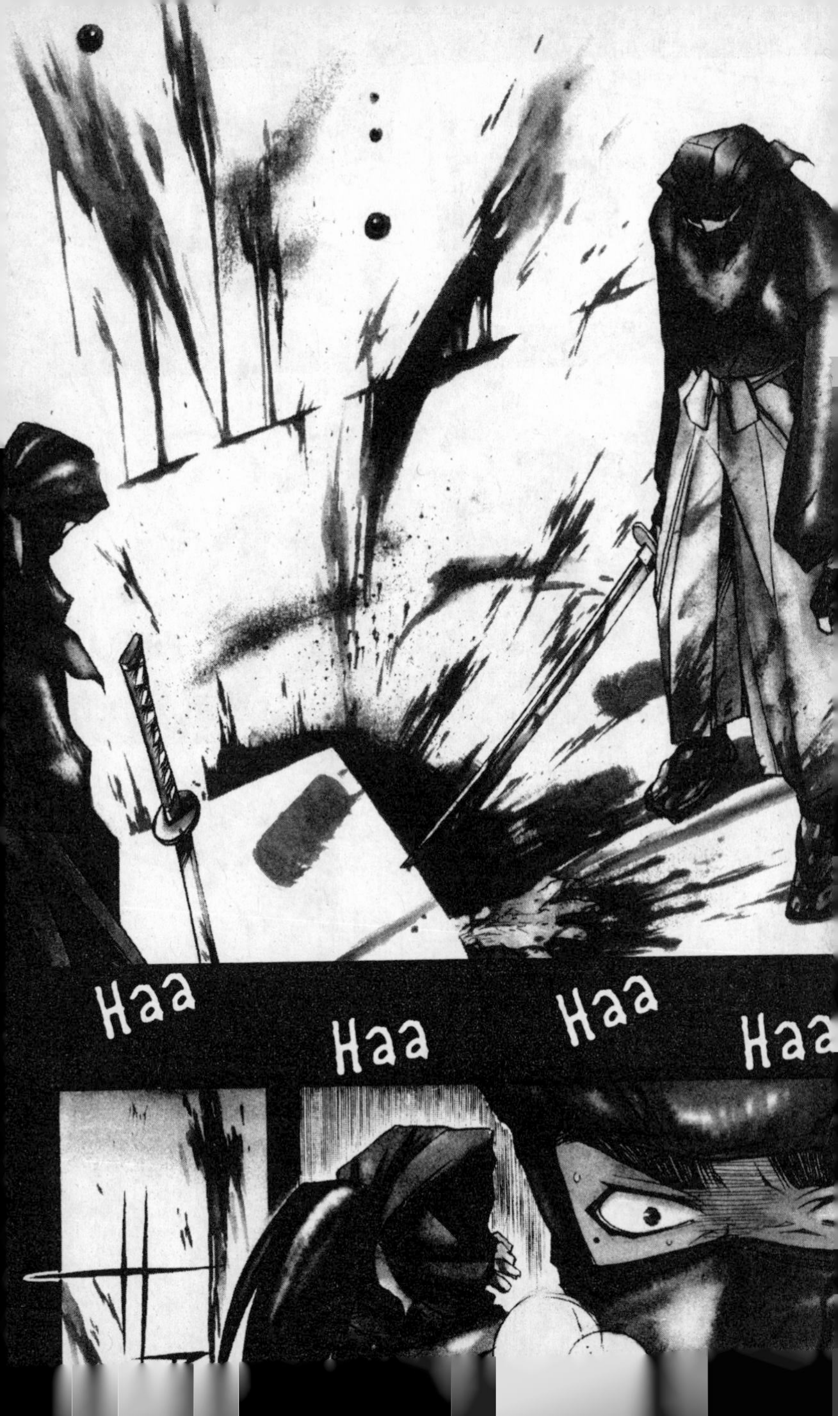
Haa
Haa
Haa
Haa

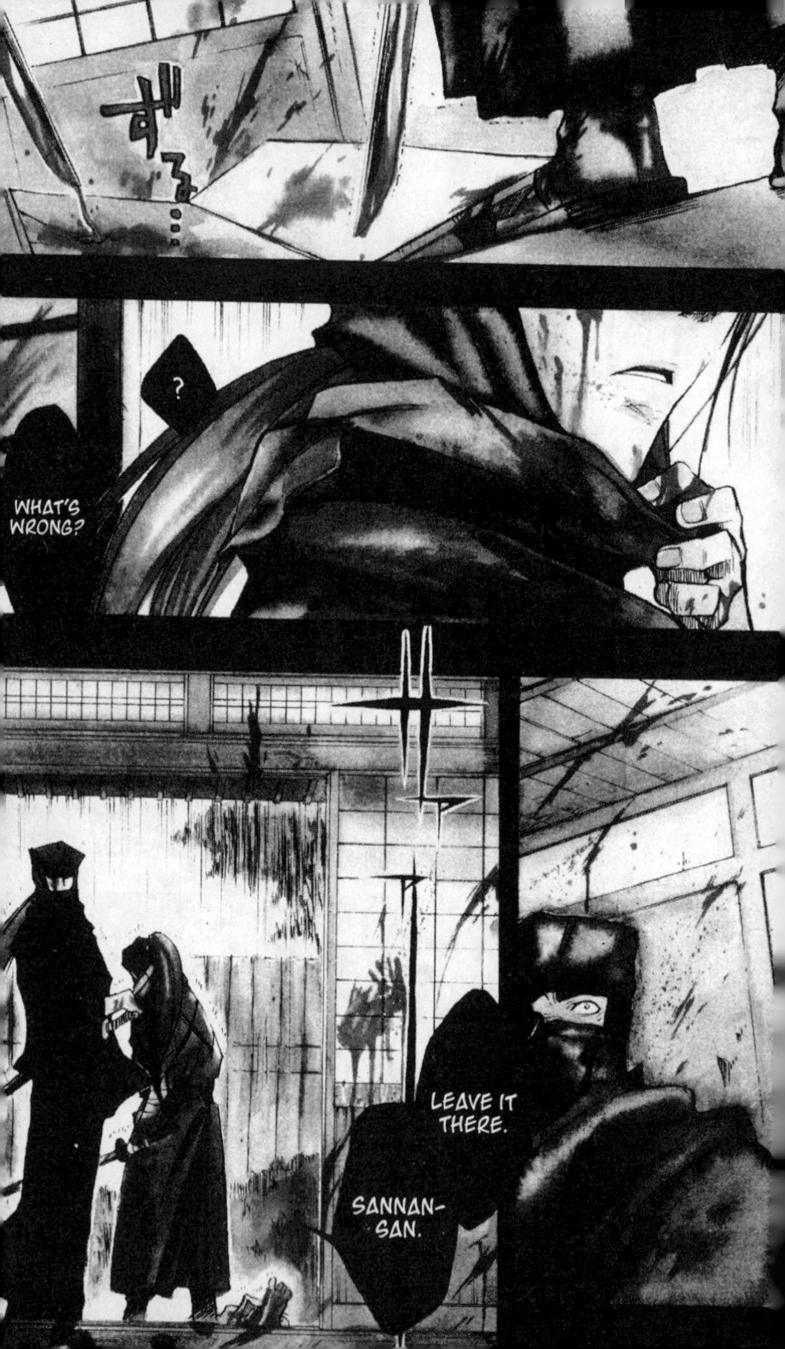
ずる…
?
WHAT'S WRONG?
LEAVE IT THERE.
SANNAN-SAN.

第七話
だいななわ
Act 7
Rain
雨
あめ

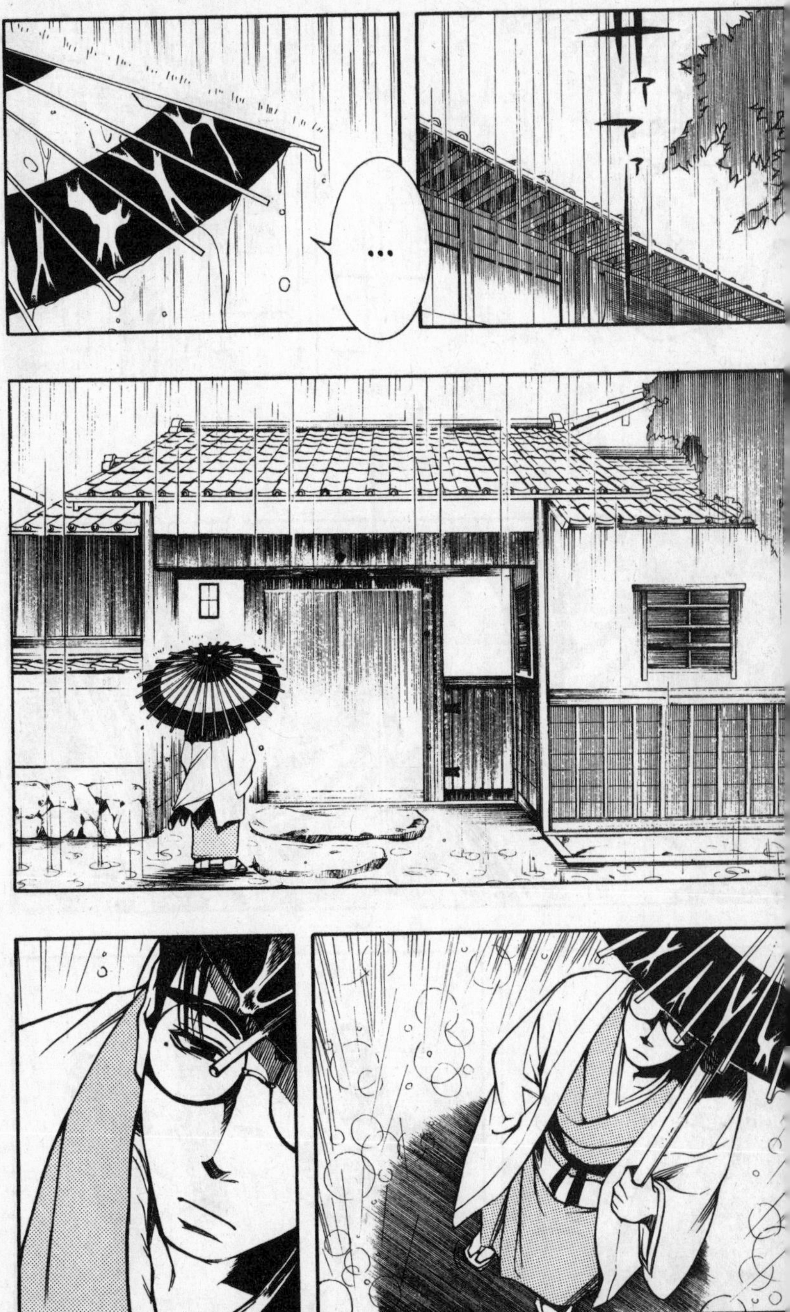
サァアァ
...

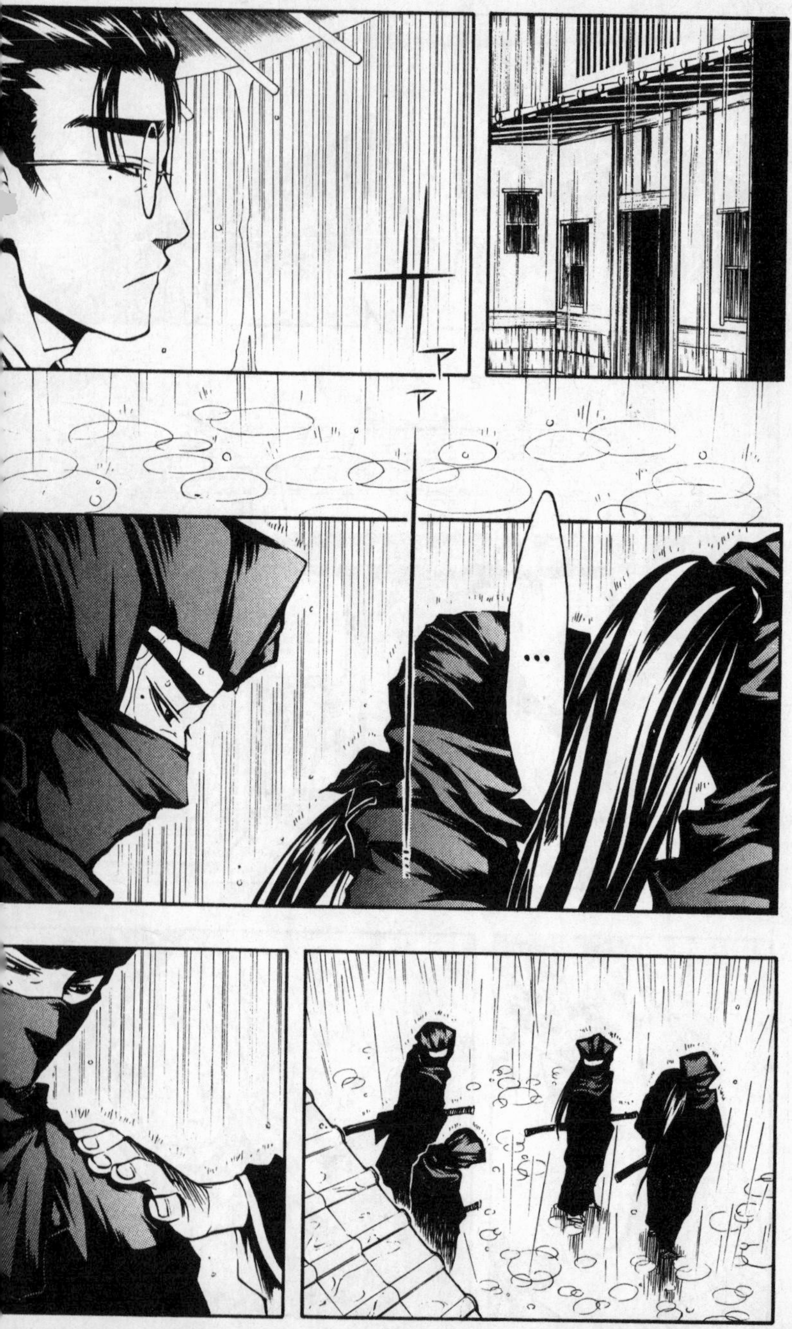
...

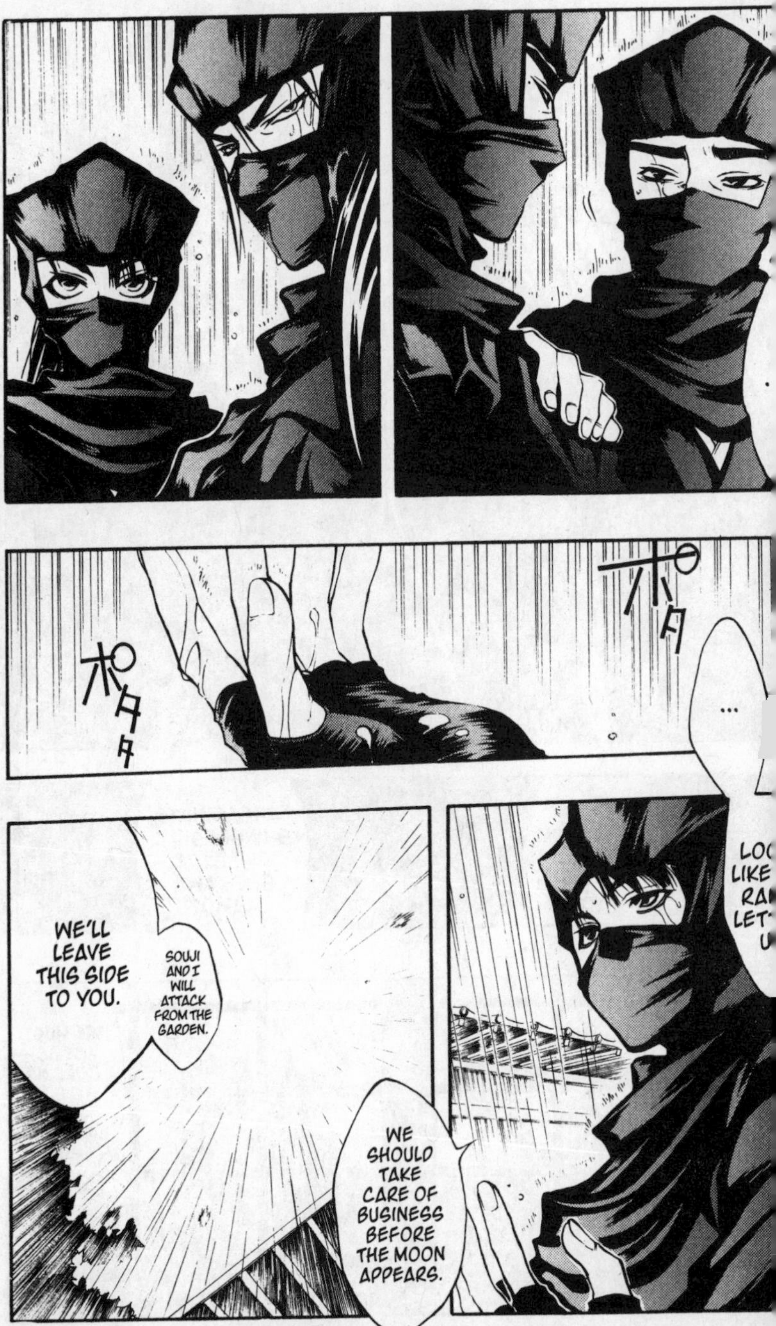
ポタ
...
ポタタ
WE SHOULD TAKE CARE OF BUSINESS BEFORE THE MOON APPEARS.
WE'LL LEAVE THIS SIDE TO YOU.
SOUJI AND I WILL ATTACK FROM THE GARDEN.

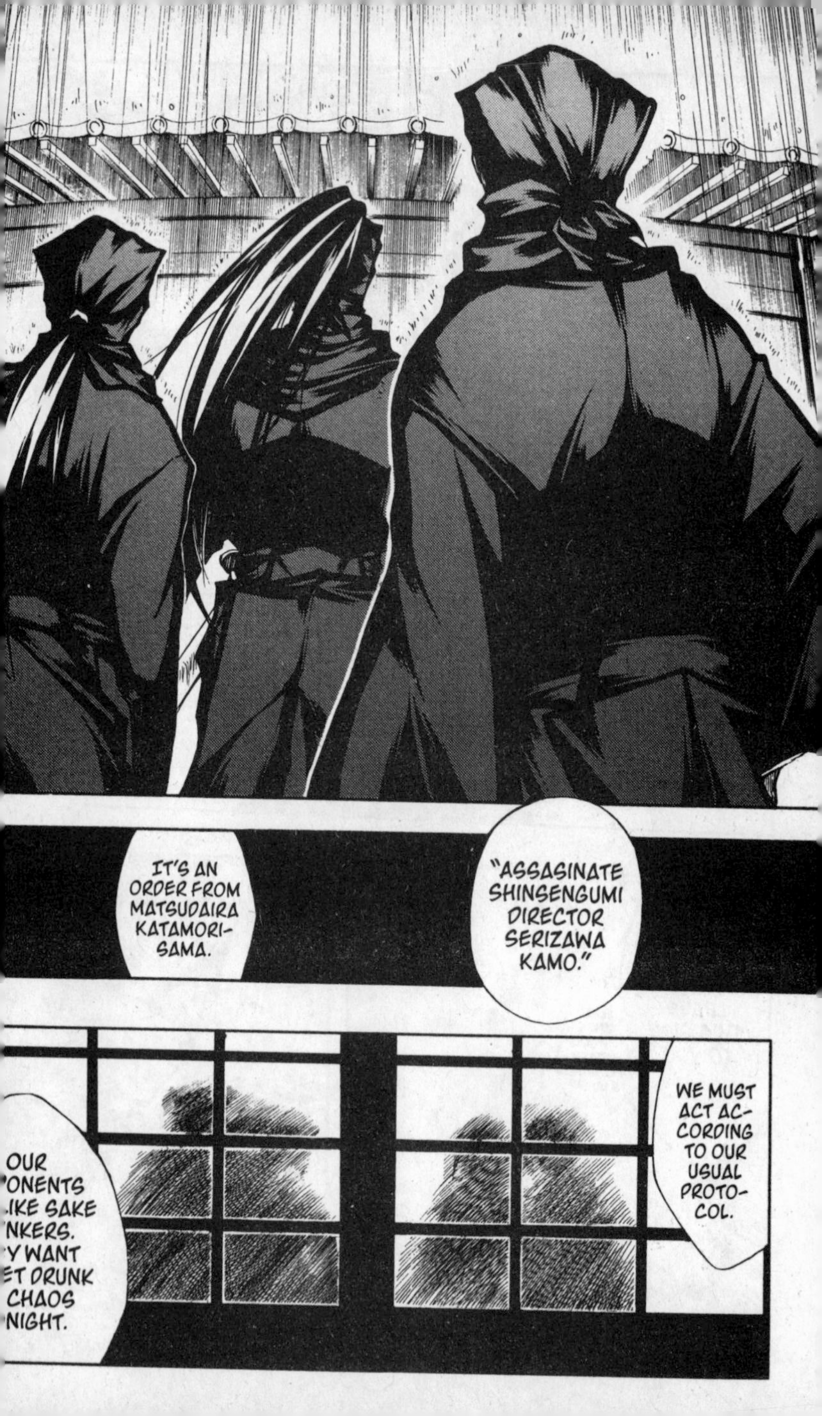
"ASSASINATE SHINSENGUMI DIRECTOR SERIZAWA KAMO."
IT'S AN ORDER FROM MATSUDAIRA KATAMORI-SAMA.
WE MUST ACT ACCORDING TO OUR USUAL PROTOCOL.
OUR ONENTS IKE SAKE NKERS. Y WANT T DRUNK CHAOS NIGHT.

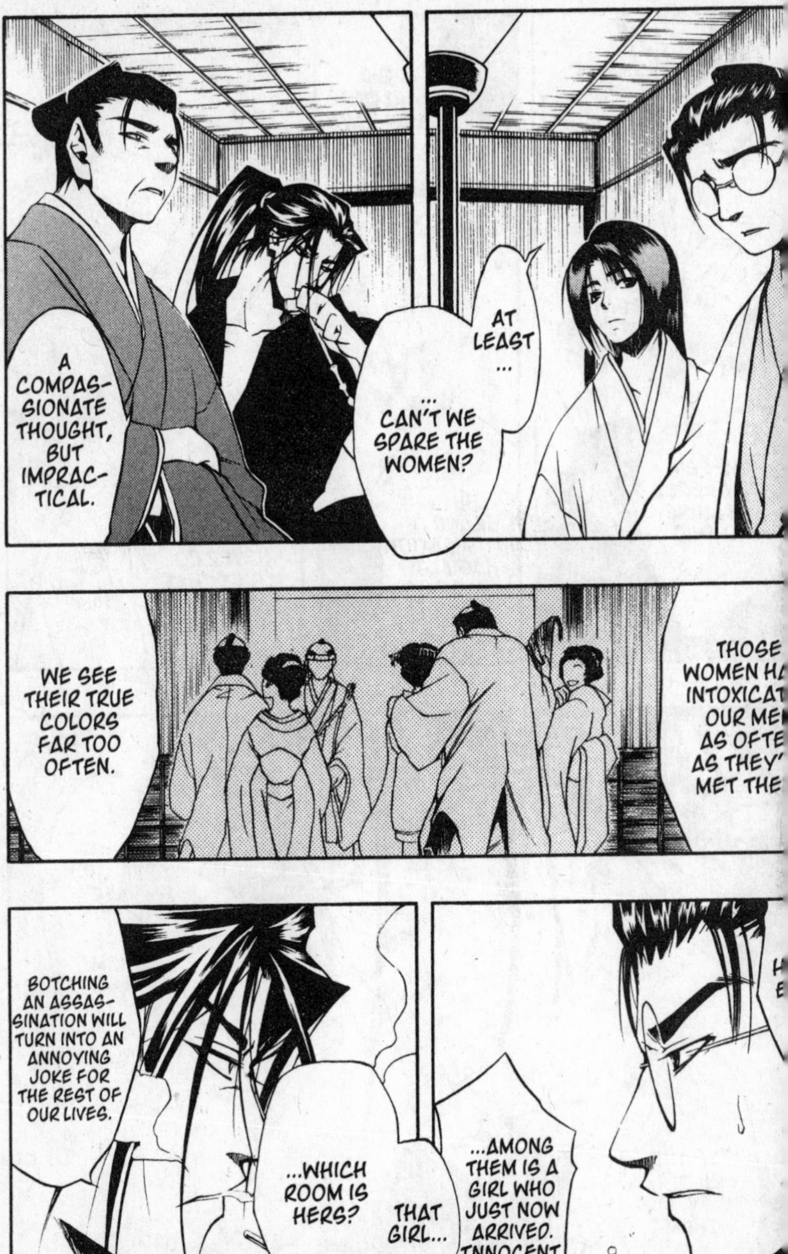
AT LEAST ...
... CAN'T WE SPARE THE WOMEN?
A COMPAS- SIONATE THOUGHT, BUT IMPRAC- TICAL.
THOSE WOMEN HA INTOXICAT OUR ME AS OFTE AS THEY' MET THE
WE SEE THEIR TRUE COLORS FAR TOO OFTEN.
...AMONG THEM IS A GIRL WHO JUST NOW ARRIVED. INNOCENT.
THAT GIRL...
...WHICH ROOM IS HERS?
BOTCHING AN ASSAS- SINATION WILL TURN INTO AN ANNOYING JOKE FOR THE REST OF OUR LIVES.

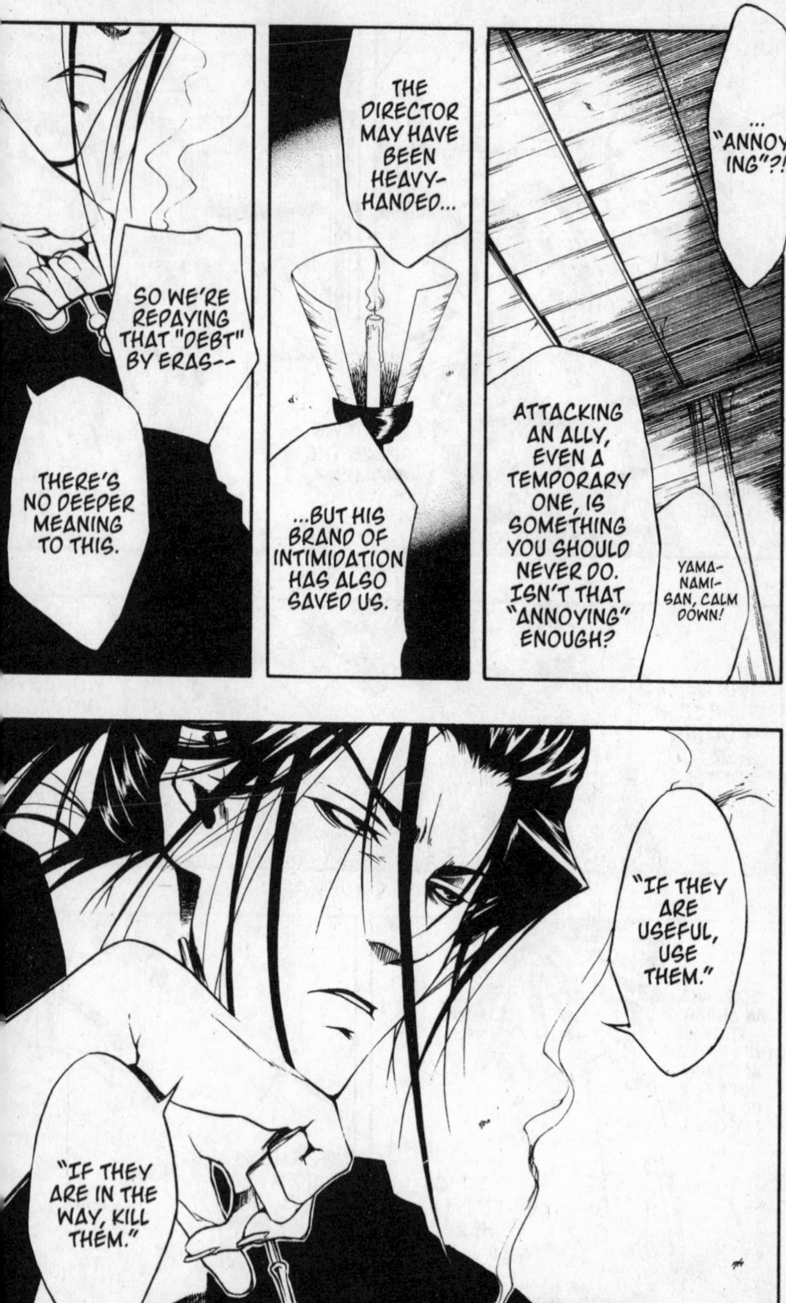
...
"ANNOYING"?!
ATTACKING AN ALLY, EVEN A TEMPORARY ONE, IS SOMETHING YOU SHOULD NEVER DO. ISN'T THAT "ANNOYING" ENOUGH?
YAMANAMI-SAN, CALM DOWN!
THE DIRECTOR MAY HAVE BEEN HEAVY-HANDED...
...BUT HIS BRAND OF INTIMIDATION HAS ALSO SAVED US.
SO WE'RE REPAYING THAT "DEBT" BY ERAS--
THERE'S NO DEEPER MEANING TO THIS.
"IF THEY ARE USEFUL, USE THEM."
"IF THEY ARE IN THE WAY, KILL THEM."

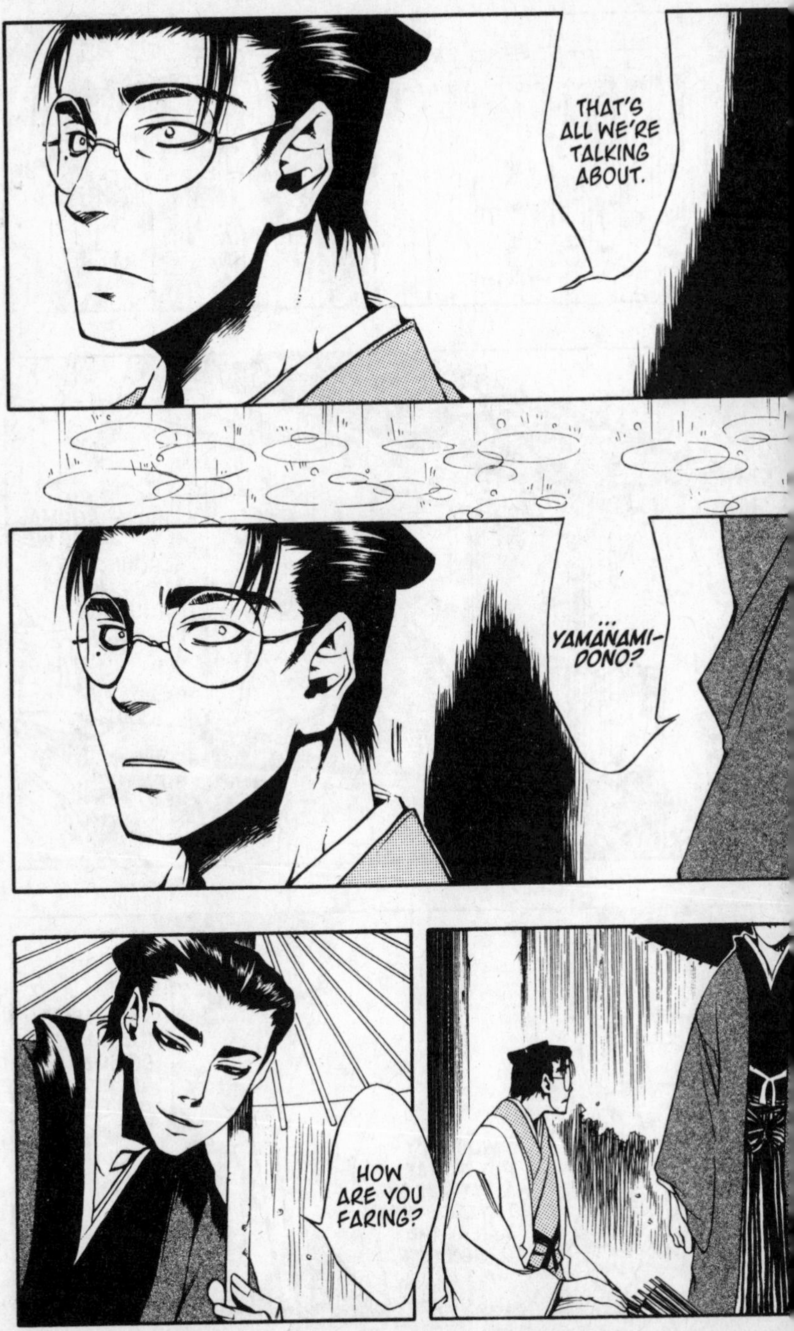
THAT'S ALL WE'RE TALKING ABOUT.
... YAMANAMI-DONO?
HOW ARE YOU FARING?

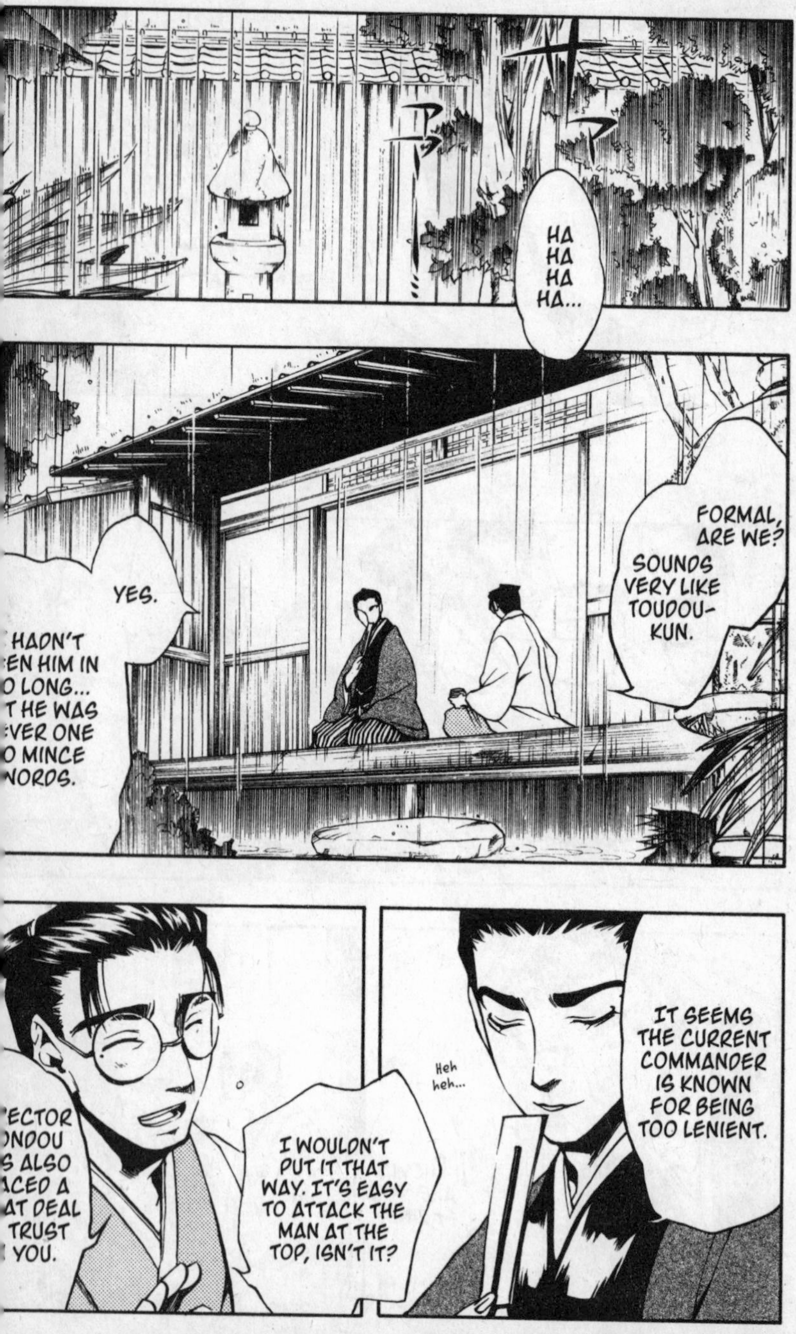
HA HA HA HA...
FORMAL, ARE WE?
SOUNDS VERY LIKE TOUDOU-KUN.
YES.
HADN'T EEN HIM IN O LONG... T HE WAS EVER ONE O MINCE WORDS.
IT SEEMS THE CURRENT COMMANDER IS KNOWN FOR BEING TOO LENIENT.
Heh heh...
I WOULDN'T PUT IT THAT WAY. IT'S EASY TO ATTACK THE MAN AT THE TOP, ISN'T IT?
ECTOR ONDOU S ALSO ACED A AT DEAL TRUST YOU.

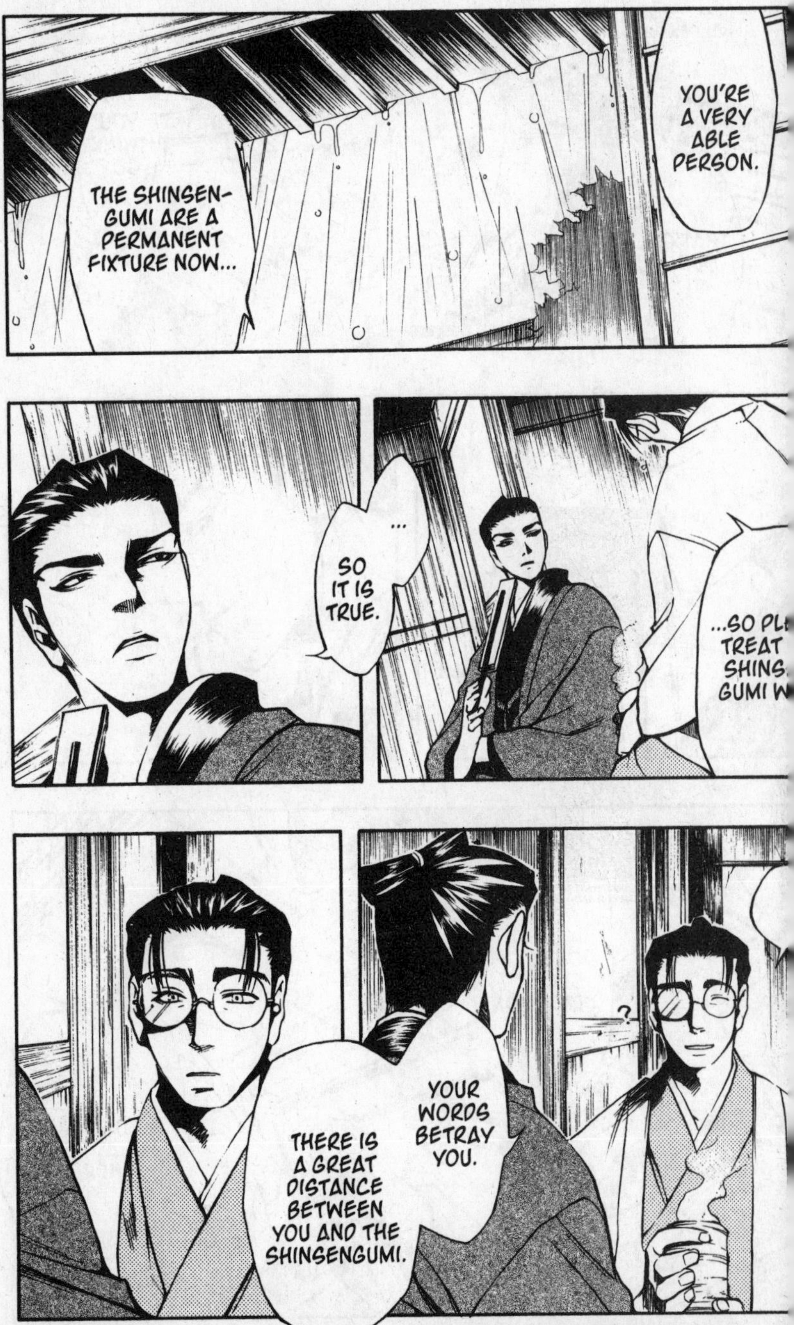
YOU'RE A VERY ABLE PERSON.
THE SHINSEN-GUMI ARE A PERMANENT FIXTURE NOW...
...SO PL TREAT SHINS GUMI W
...
SO IT IS TRUE.
?
YOUR WORDS BETRAY YOU.
THERE IS A GREAT DISTANCE BETWEEN YOU AND THE SHINSENGUMI.

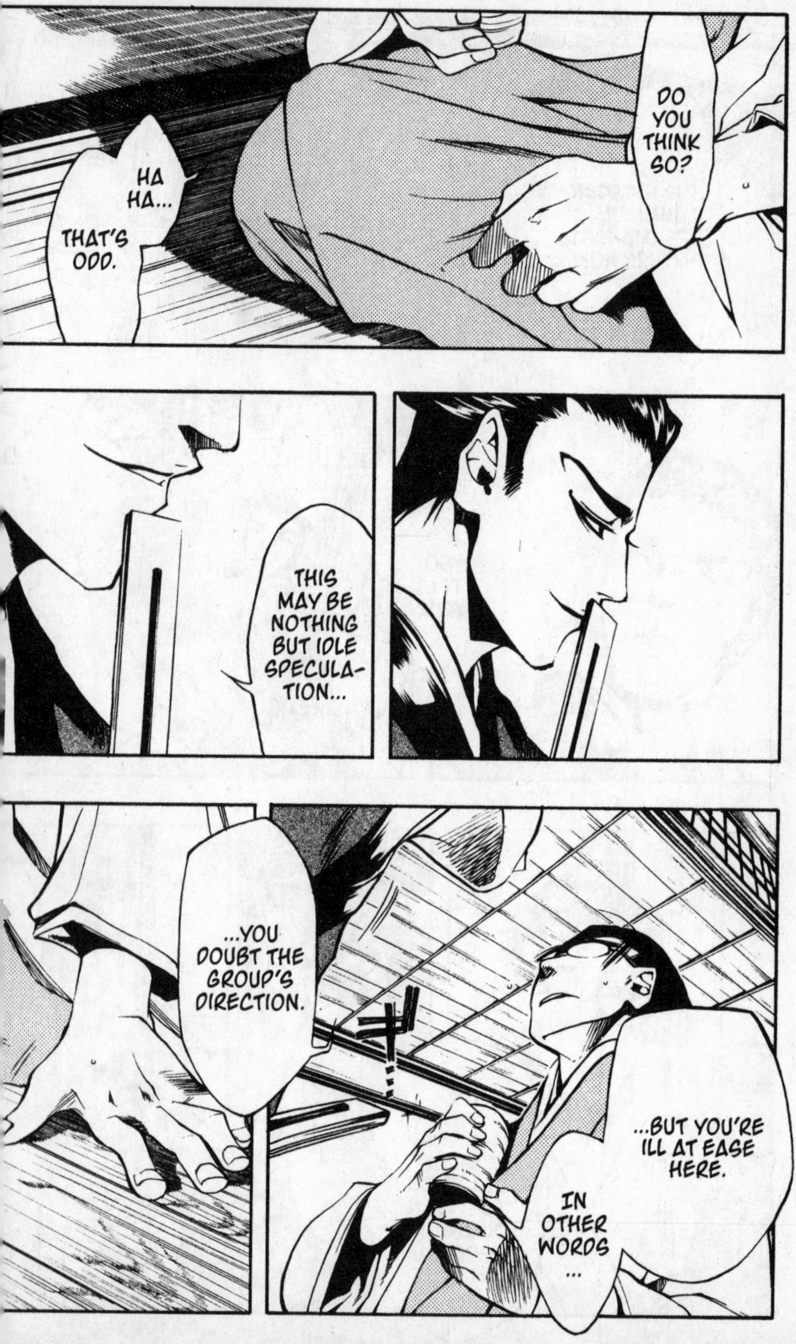
DO YOU THINK SO?
HA HA... THAT'S ODD.
THIS MAY BE NOTHING BUT IDLE SPECULA-TION...
...BUT YOU'RE ILL AT EASE HERE.
IN OTHER WORDS ...
...YOU DOUBT THE GROUP'S DIRECTION.

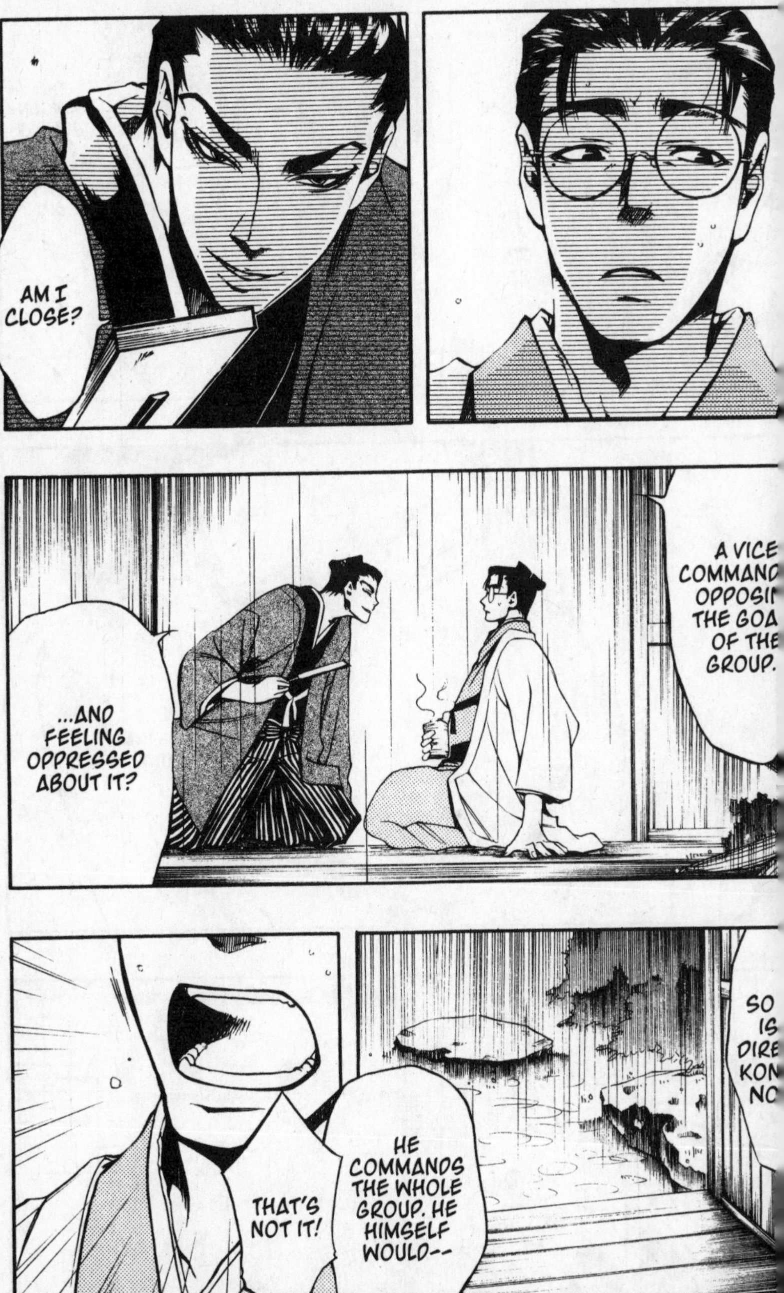
AM I CLOSE?
A VICE COMMAND OPPOSI THE GOA OF THE GROUP.
...AND FEELING OPPRESSED ABOUT IT?
SO IS DIRE KON NC
HE COMMANDS THE WHOLE GROUP. HE HIMSELF WOULD--
THAT'S NOT IT!

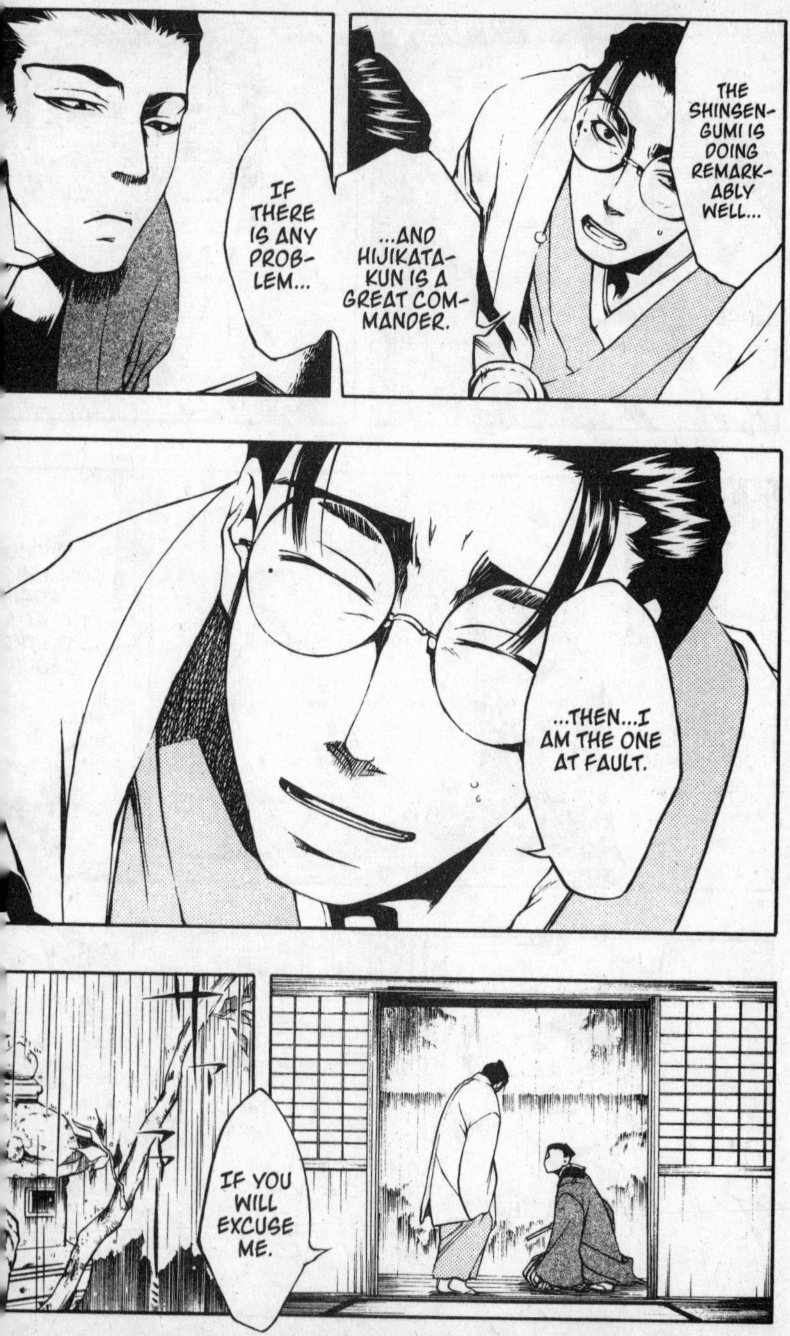
THE SHINSEN-GUMI IS DOING REMARKABLY WELL...
...AND HIJIKATA-KUN IS A GREAT COMMANDER.
IF THERE IS ANY PROBLEM...
...THEN...I AM THE ONE AT FAULT.
IF YOU WILL EXCUSE ME.

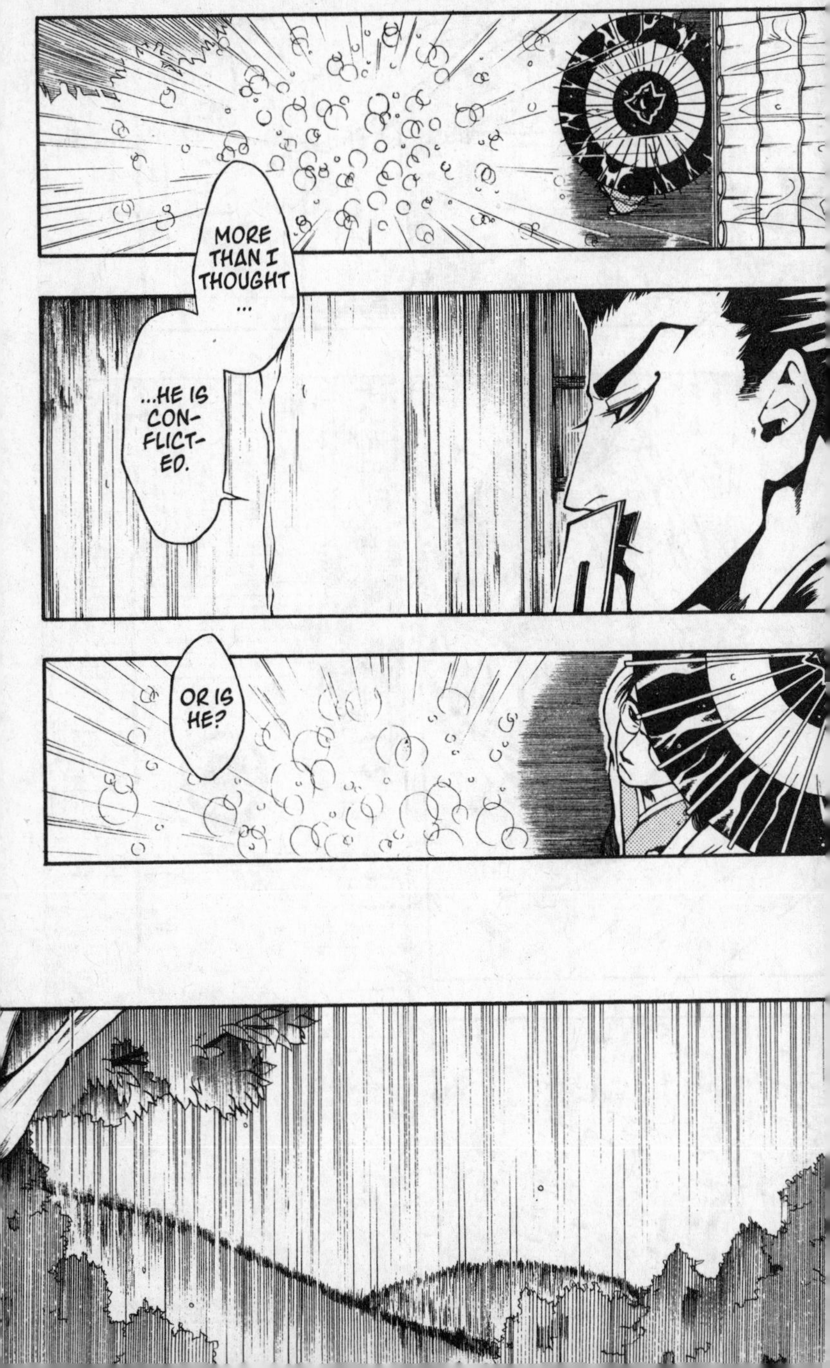
MORE THAN I THOUGHT ...
...HE IS CON-FLICT-ED.
OR IS HE?

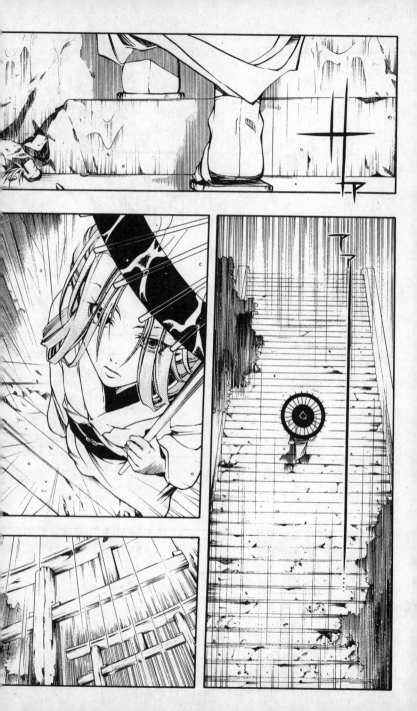

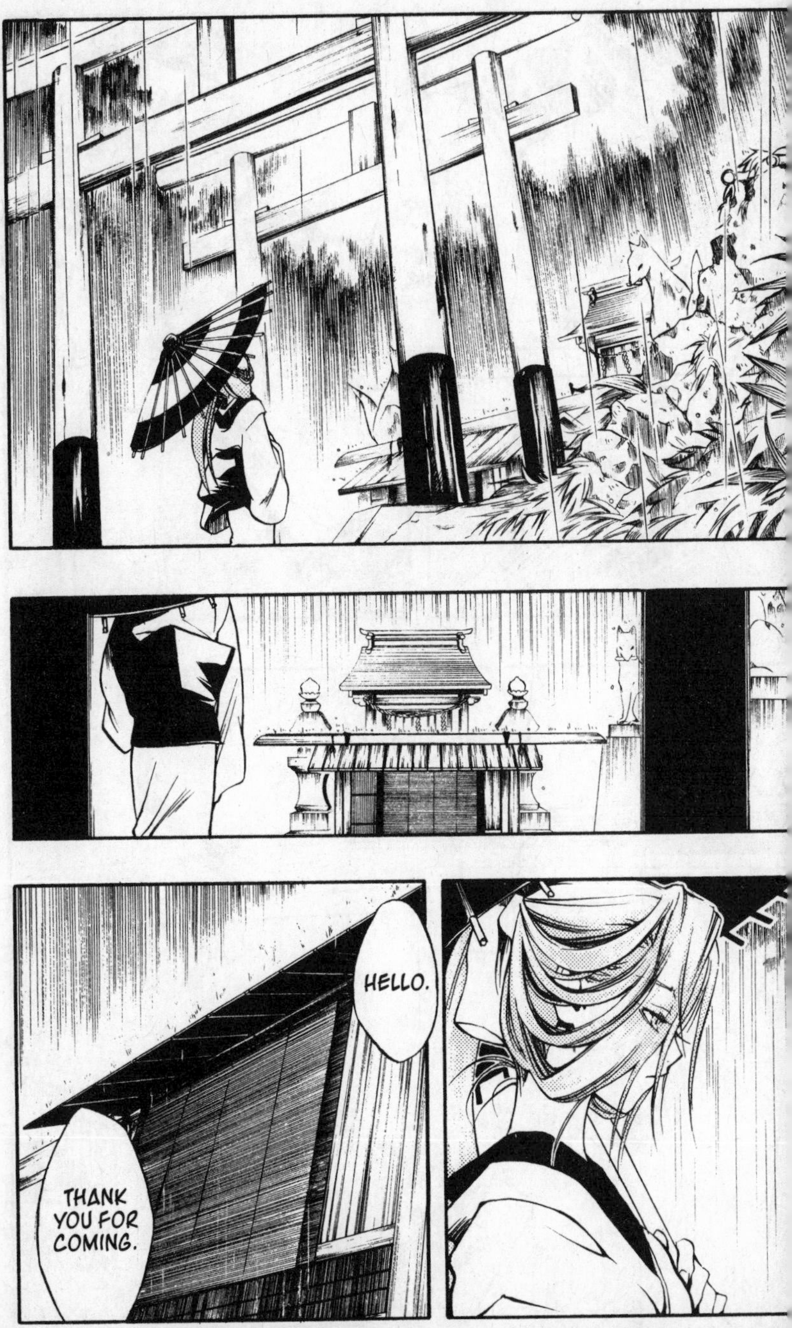
HELLO.
THANK YOU FOR COMING.

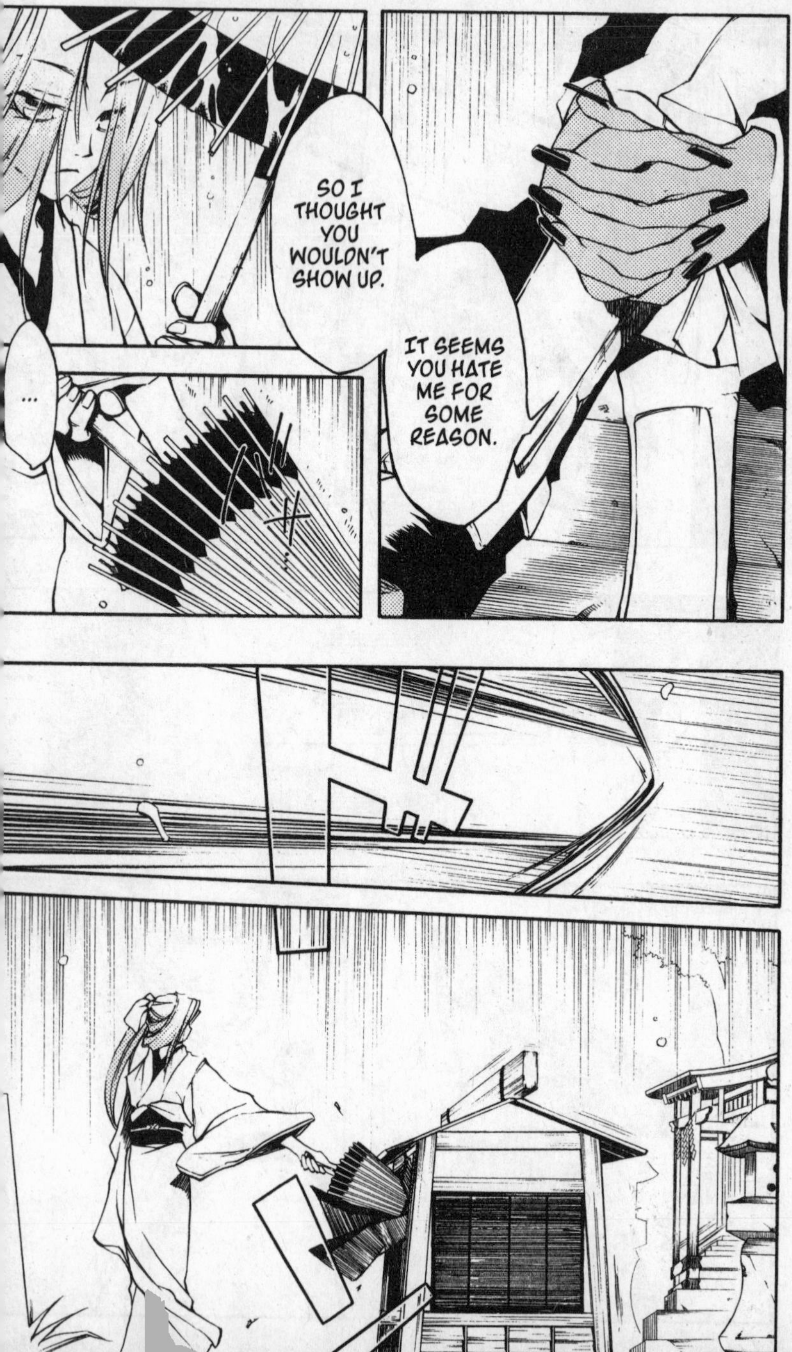
SO I THOUGHT YOU WOULDN'T SHOW UP.
IT SEEMS YOU HATE ME FOR SOME REASON.
...

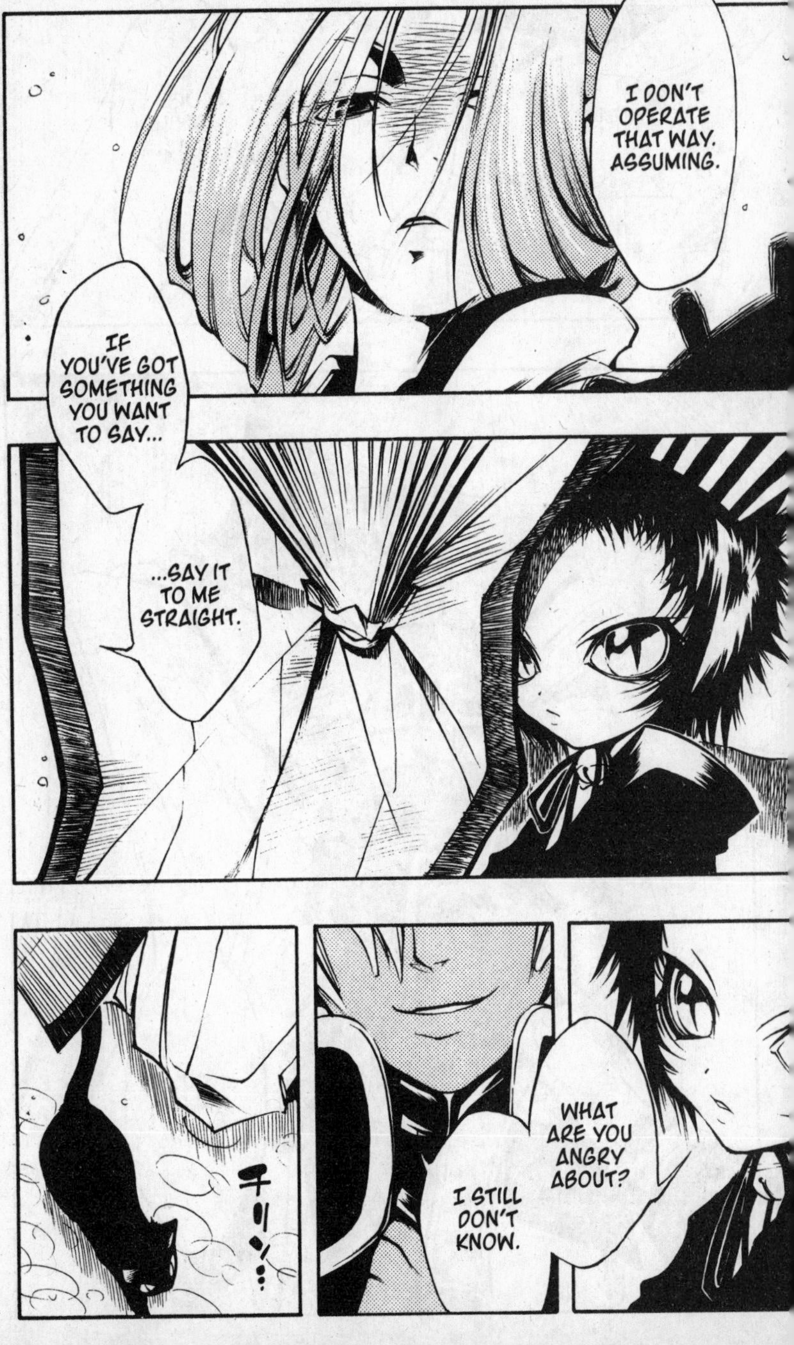
I DON'T OPERATE THAT WAY. ASSUMING.
IF YOU'VE GOT SOMETHING YOU WANT TO SAY...
...SAY IT TO ME STRAIGHT.
WHAT ARE YOU ANGRY ABOUT?
I STILL DON'T KNOW.
チリン…

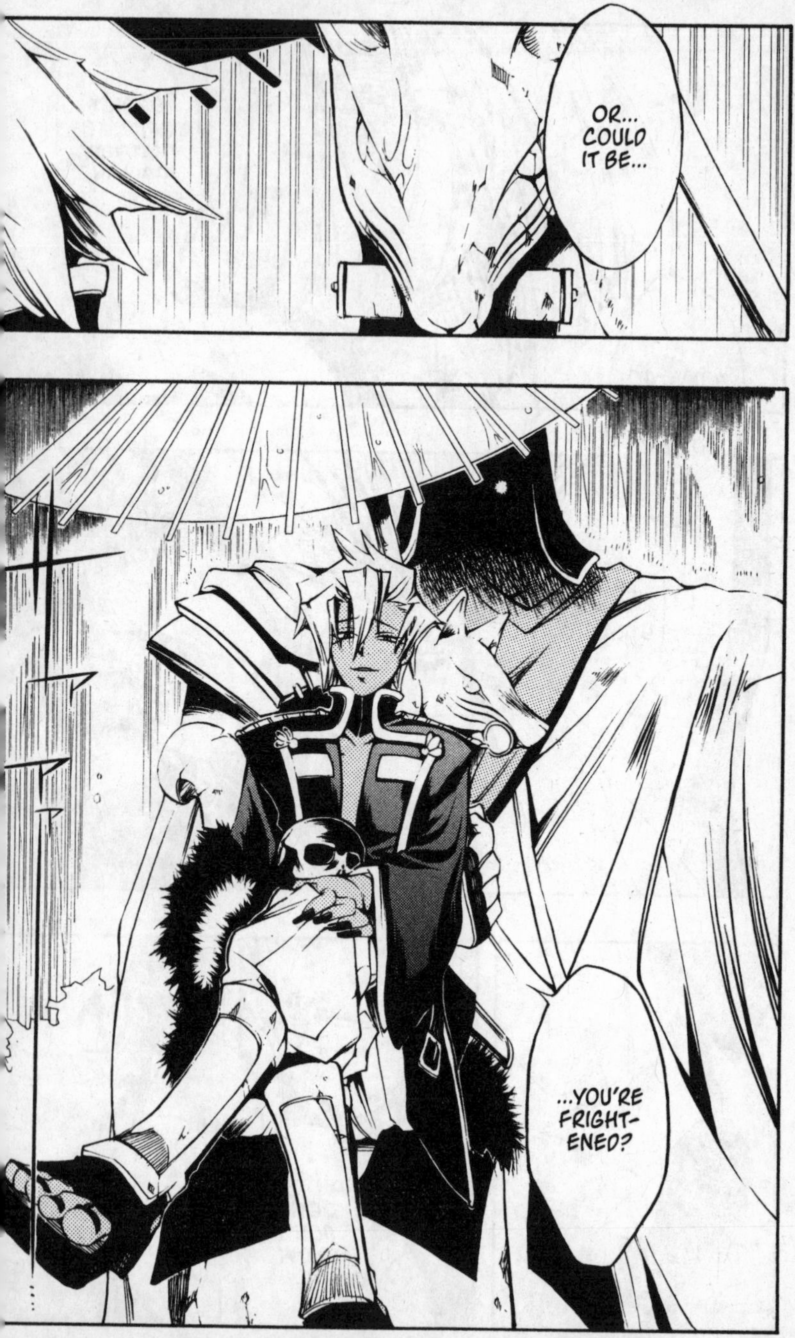
OR... COULD IT BE...
...YOU'RE FRIGHT-ENED?

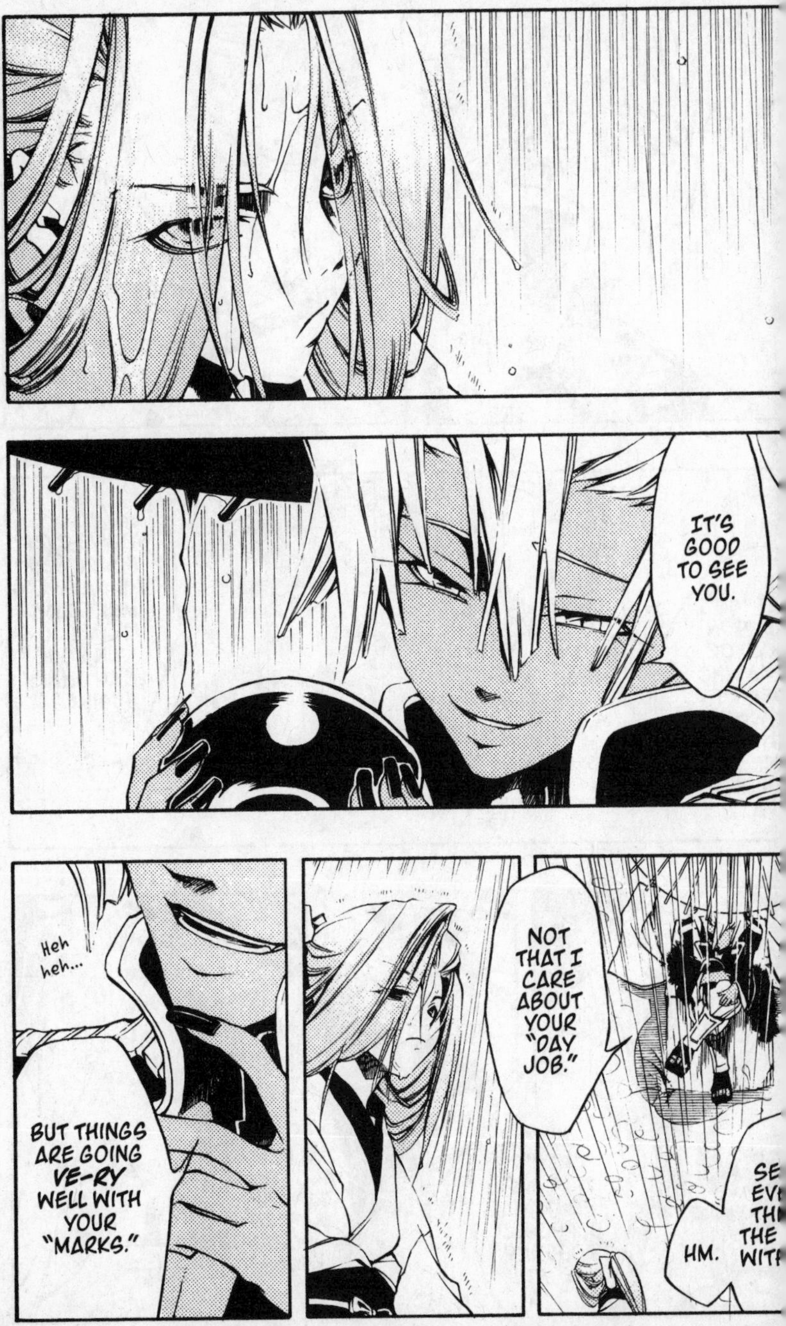
IT'S GOOD TO SEE YOU.
NOT THAT I CARE ABOUT YOUR "DAY JOB."
HM.
Heh heh...
BUT THINGS ARE GOING VE-RY WELL WITH YOUR "MARKS."

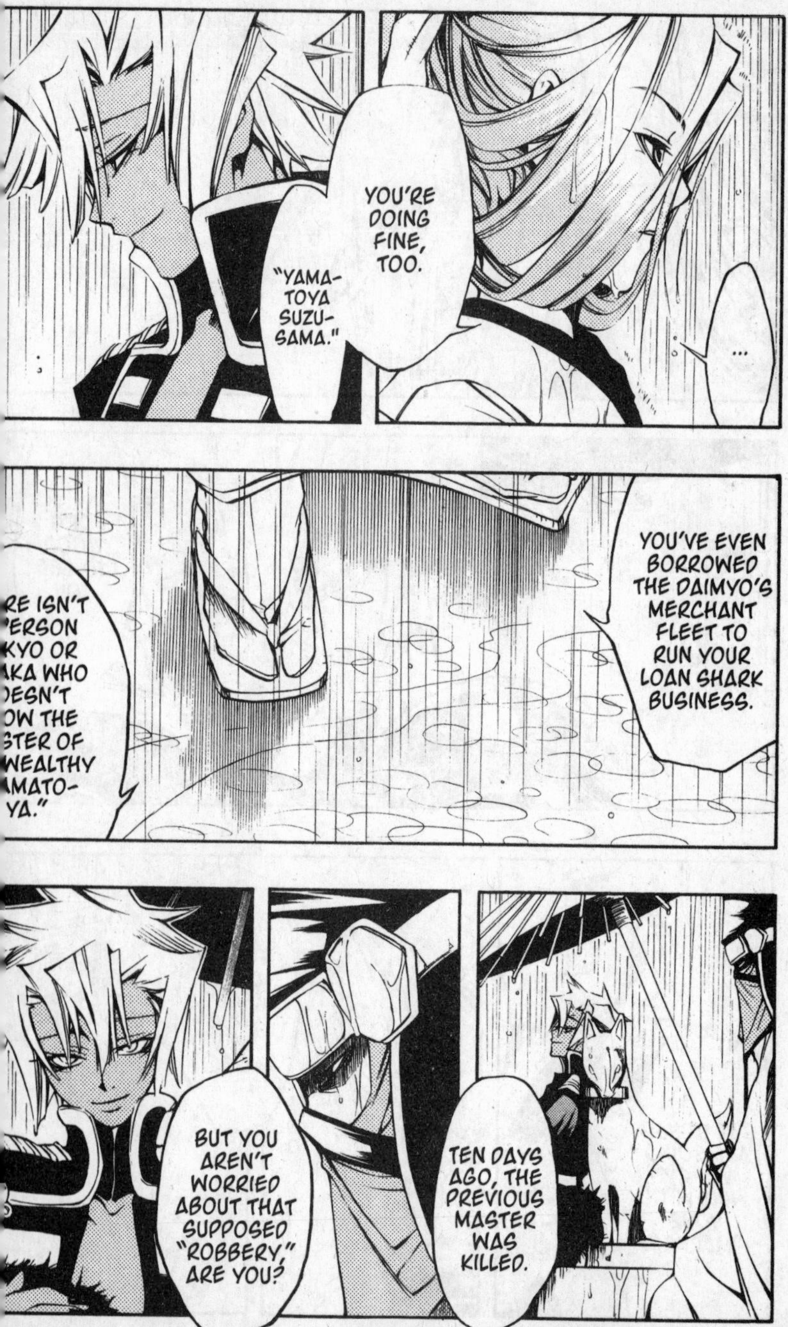
...
YOU'RE DOING FINE, TOO. "YAMATOYA SUZUSAMA."
YOU'VE EVEN BORROWED THE DAIMYO'S MERCHANT FLEET TO RUN YOUR LOAN SHARK BUSINESS.
RE ISN'T PERSON KYO OR AKA WHO DESN'T OW THE STER OF WEALTHY AMATO-YA."
TEN DAYS AGO, THE PREVIOUS MASTER WAS KILLED.
BUT YOU AREN'T WORRIED ABOUT THAT SUPPOSED "ROBBERY," ARE YOU?

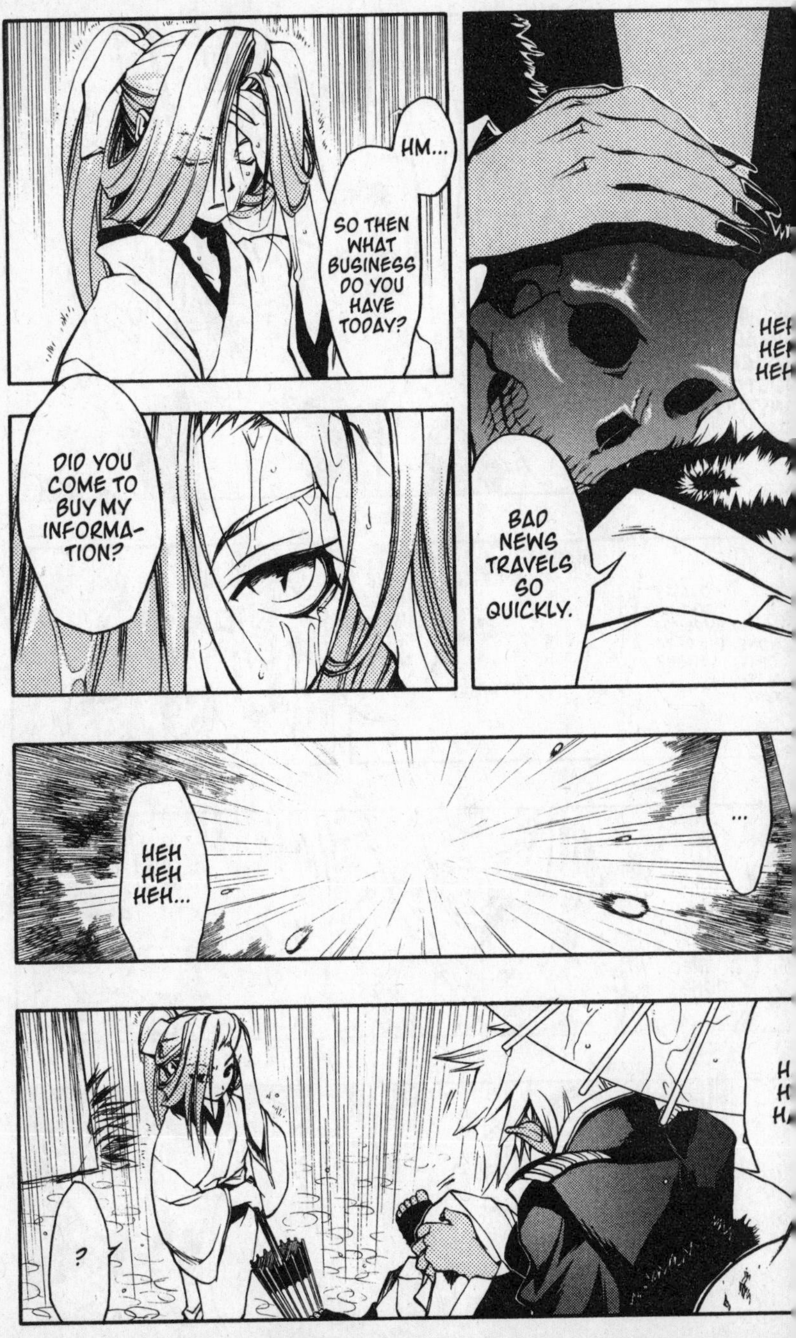
HE HE HEH
BAD NEWS TRAVELS SO QUICKLY.
HM...
SO THEN WHAT BUSINESS DO YOU HAVE TODAY?
DID YOU COME TO BUY MY INFORMATION?
...
HEH HEH HEH...
?

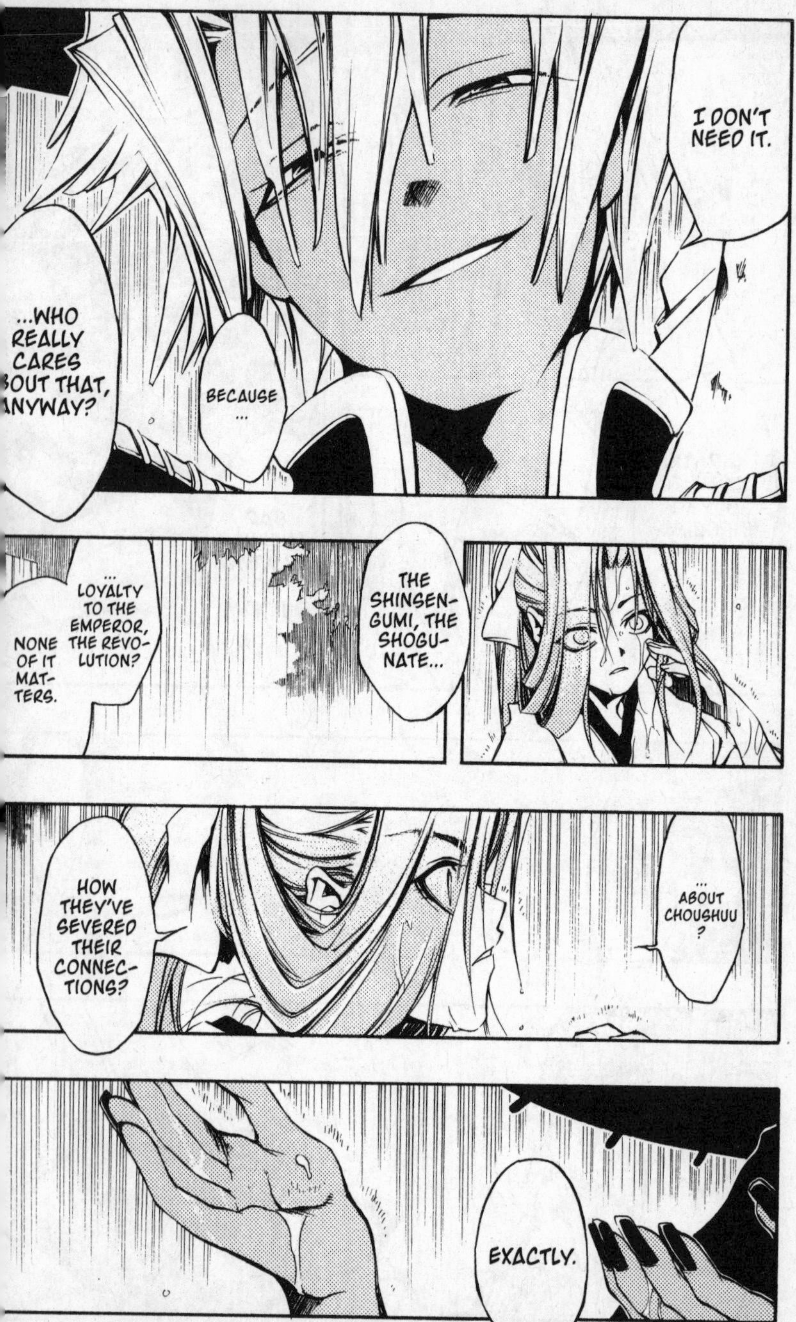
I DON'T NEED IT.
BECAUSE ...
...WHO REALLY CARES BOUT THAT, ANYWAY?
THE SHINSEN-GUMI, THE SHOGU-NATE...
...LOYALTY TO THE EMPEROR, THE REVO-LUTION?
NONE OF IT MAT-TERS.
...ABOUT CHOUSHUU?
HOW THEY'VE SEVERED THEIR CONNEC-TIONS?
EXACTLY.

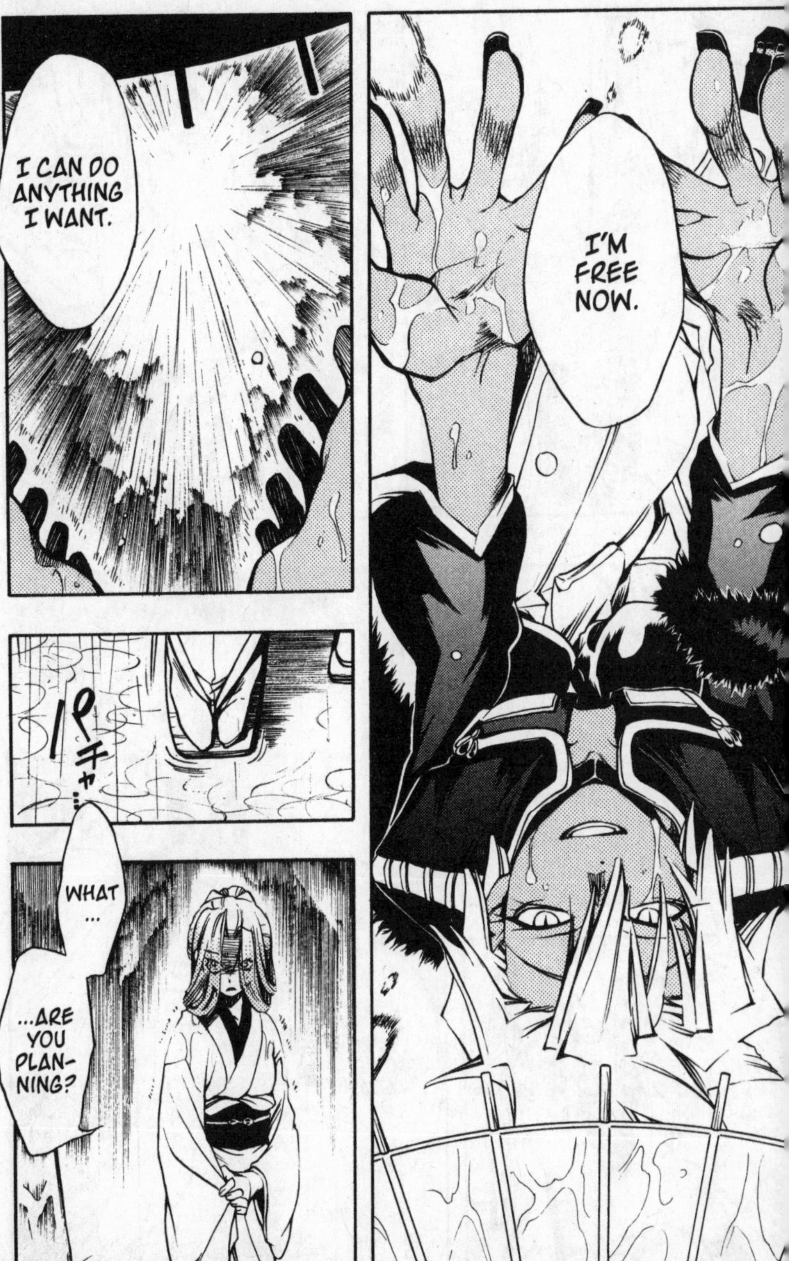
I'M FREE NOW.
I CAN DO ANYTHING I WANT.
パチャ…
WHAT ...
...ARE YOU PLAN-NING?

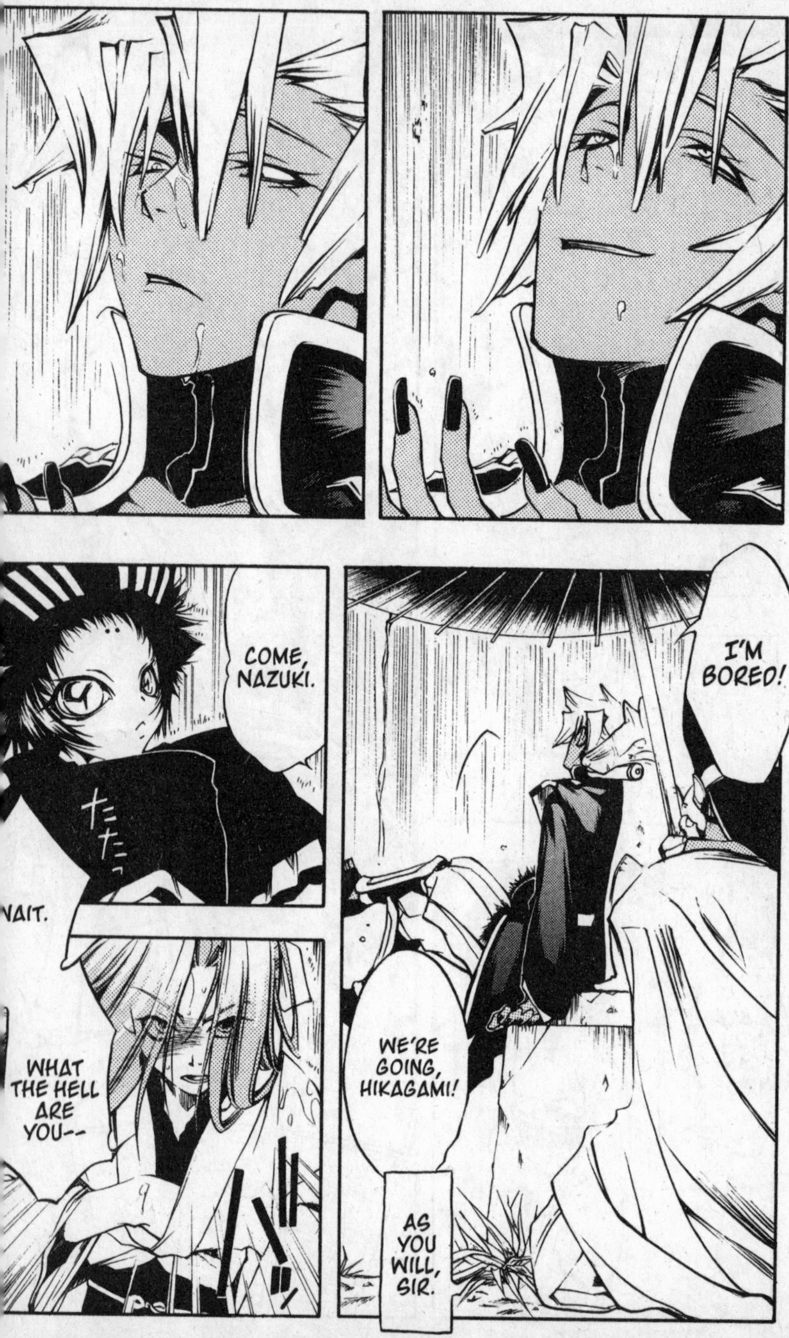
I'M BORED!
WE'RE GOING, HIKAGAMI!
AS YOU WILL, SIR.
COME, NAZUKI.
たたっ
WHAT THE HELL ARE YOU--

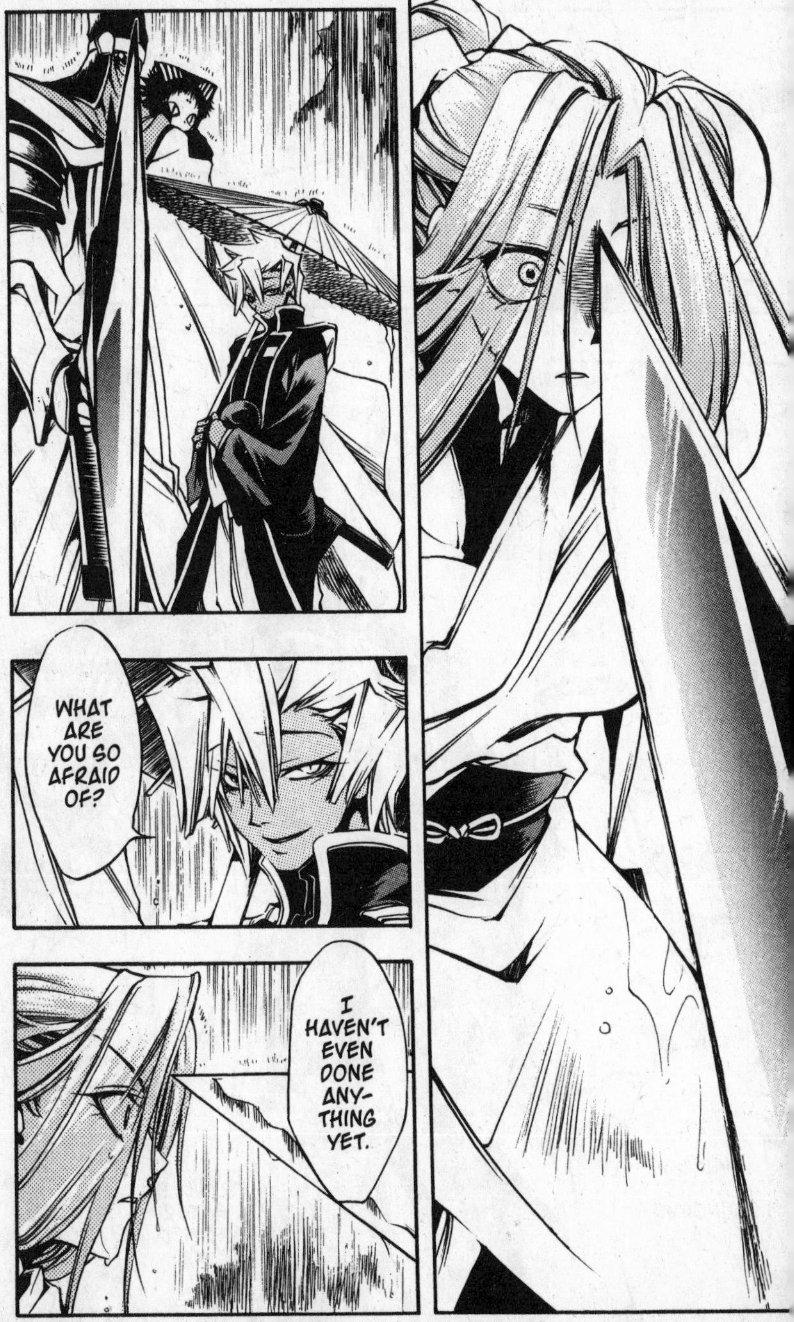
WHAT ARE YOU SO AFRAID OF?
I HAVEN'T EVEN DONE ANYTHING YET.

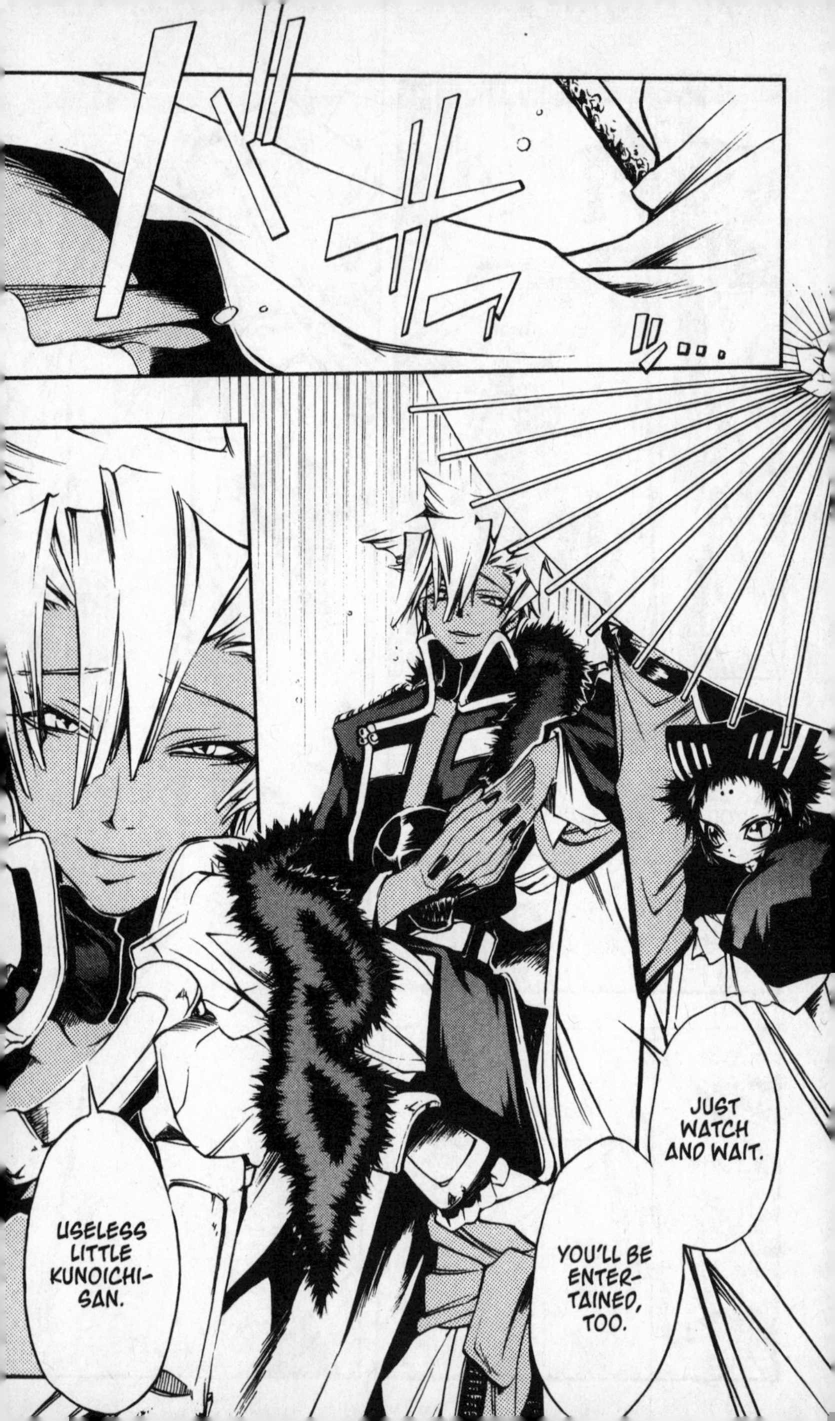
JUST WATCH AND WAIT.
YOU'LL BE ENTER-TAINED, TOO.
USELESS LITTLE KUNOICHI-SAN.

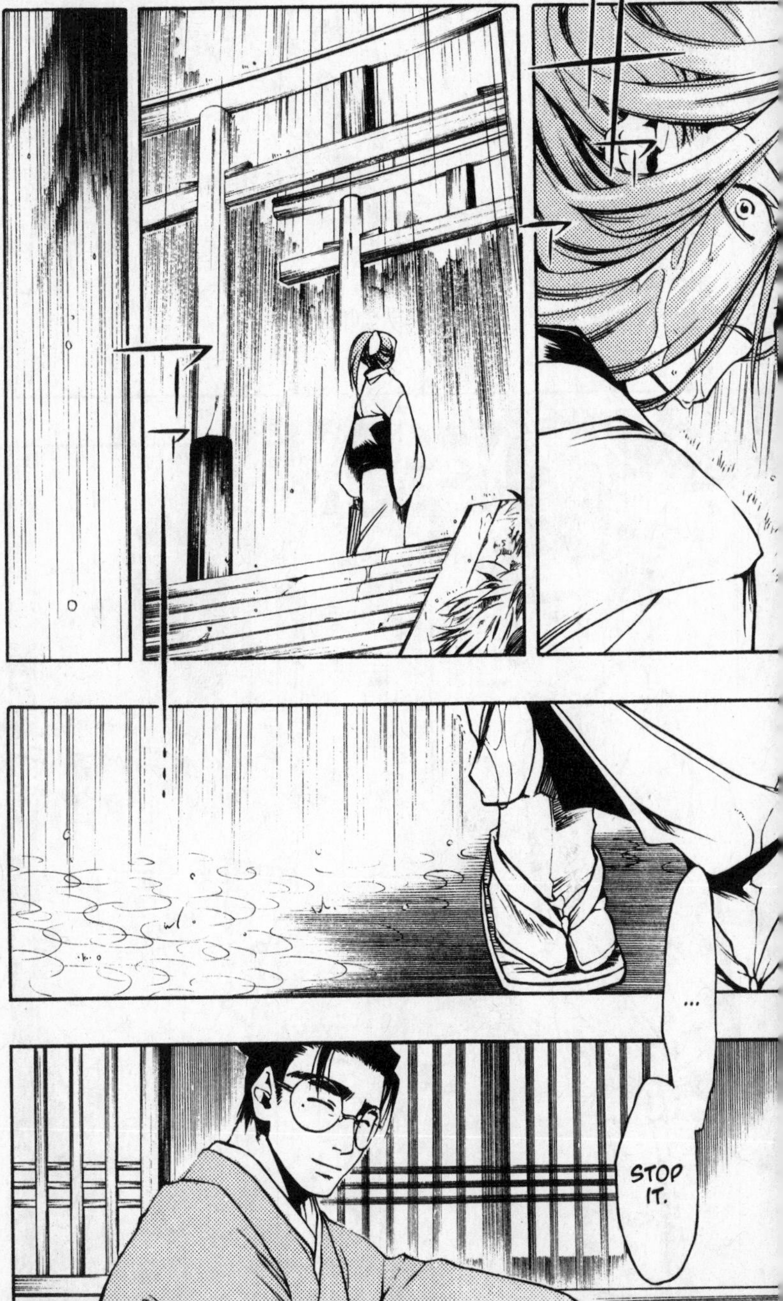
...
STOP IT.

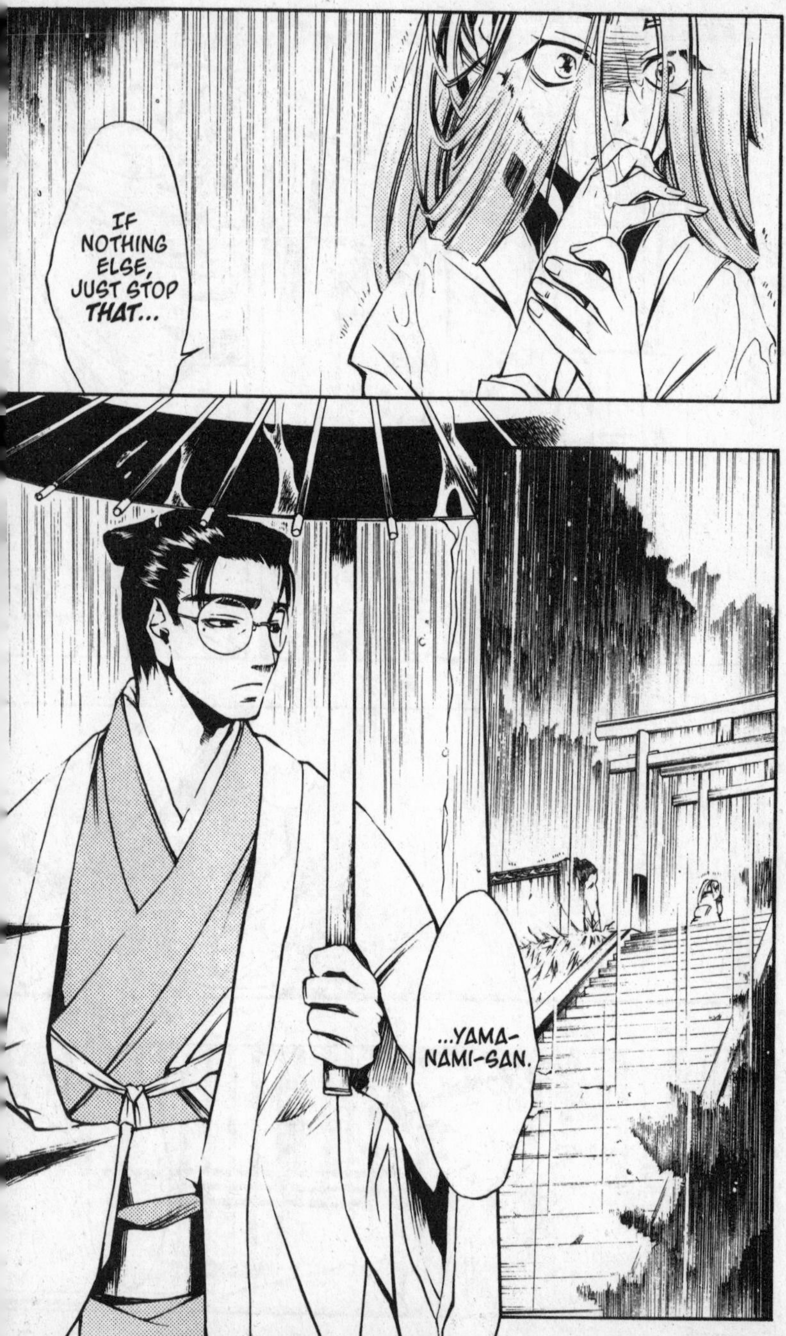
IF NOTHING ELSE, JUST STOP THAT...
...YAMA-NAMI-SAN.

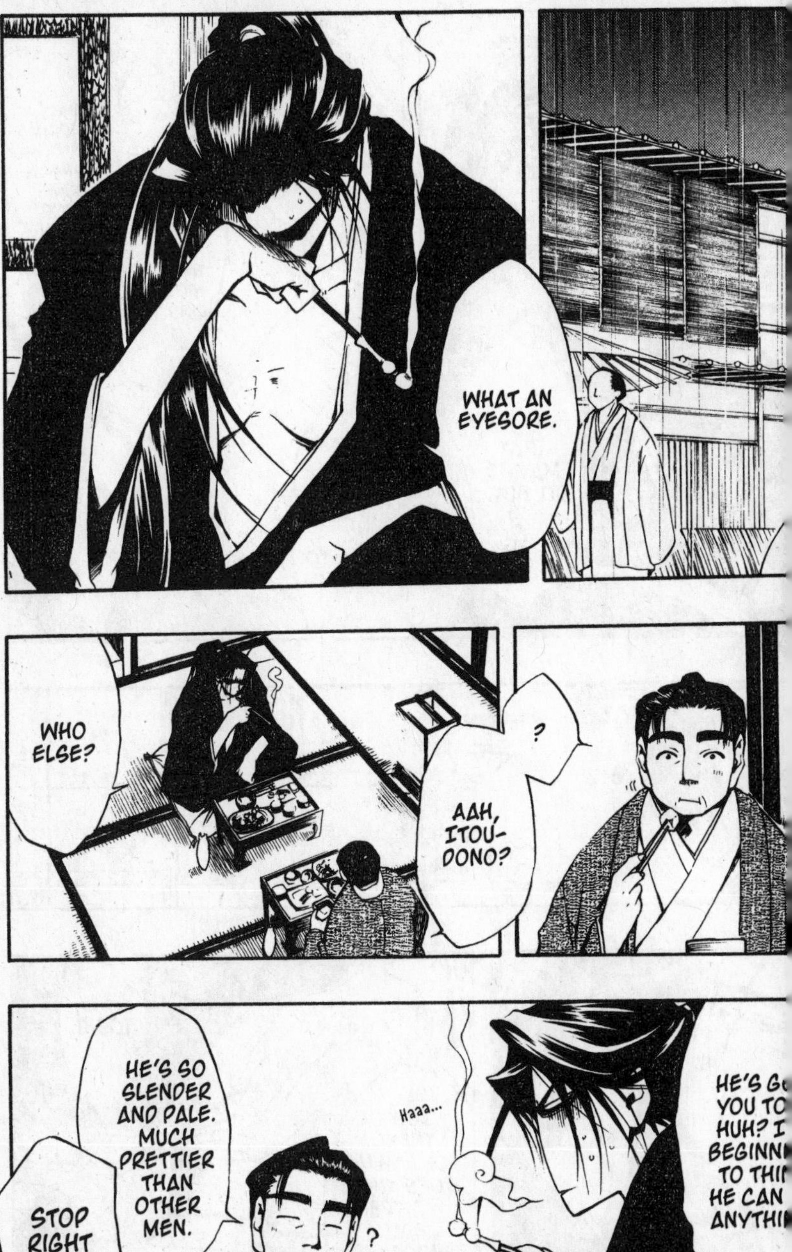
WHAT AN EYESORE.
?
AAH, ITOU-DONO?
WHO ELSE?
HE'S GO YOU TO HUH? I BEGINN TO THI HE CAN ANYTHI
Haaa...
HE'S SO SLENDER AND PALE. MUCH PRETTIER THAN OTHER MEN.
?
STOP RIGHT THERE!

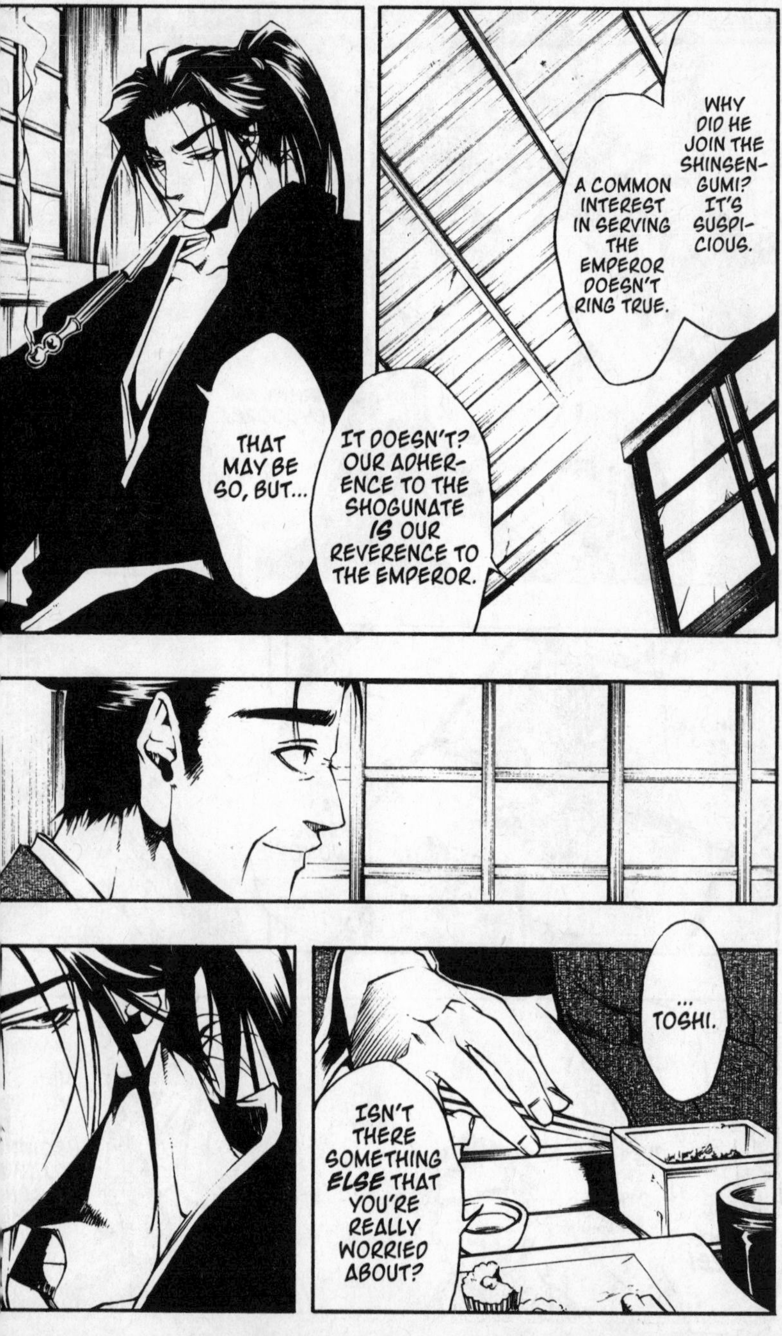
WHY DID HE JOIN THE SHINSEN-GUMI? IT'S SUSPICIOUS.
A COMMON INTEREST IN SERVING THE EMPEROR DOESN'T RING TRUE.
IT DOESN'T? OUR ADHERENCE TO THE SHOGUNATE *IS* OUR REVERENCE TO THE EMPEROR.
THAT MAY BE SO, BUT...
...TOSHI.
ISN'T THERE SOMETHING *ELSE* THAT YOU'RE REALLY WORRIED ABOUT?

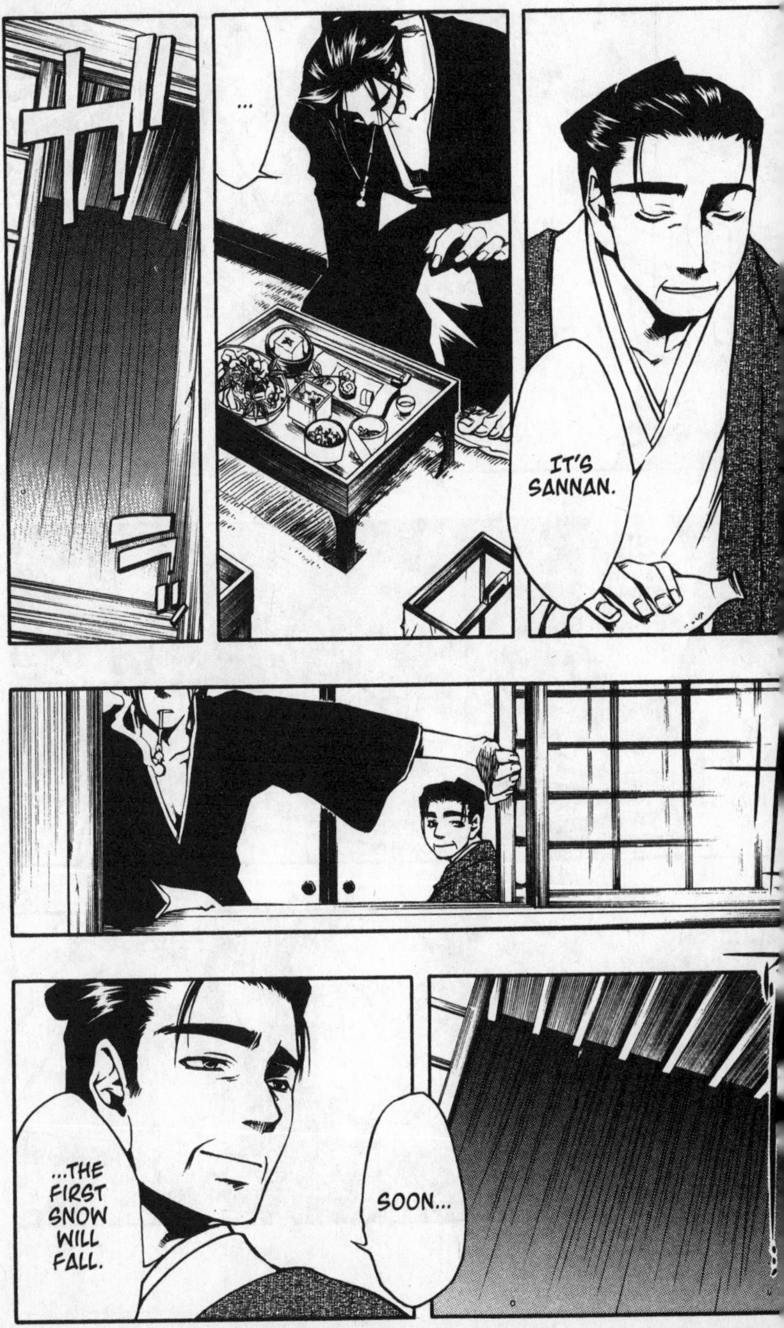
IT'S SANNAN.
...
SOON...
...THE FIRST SNOW WILL FALL.

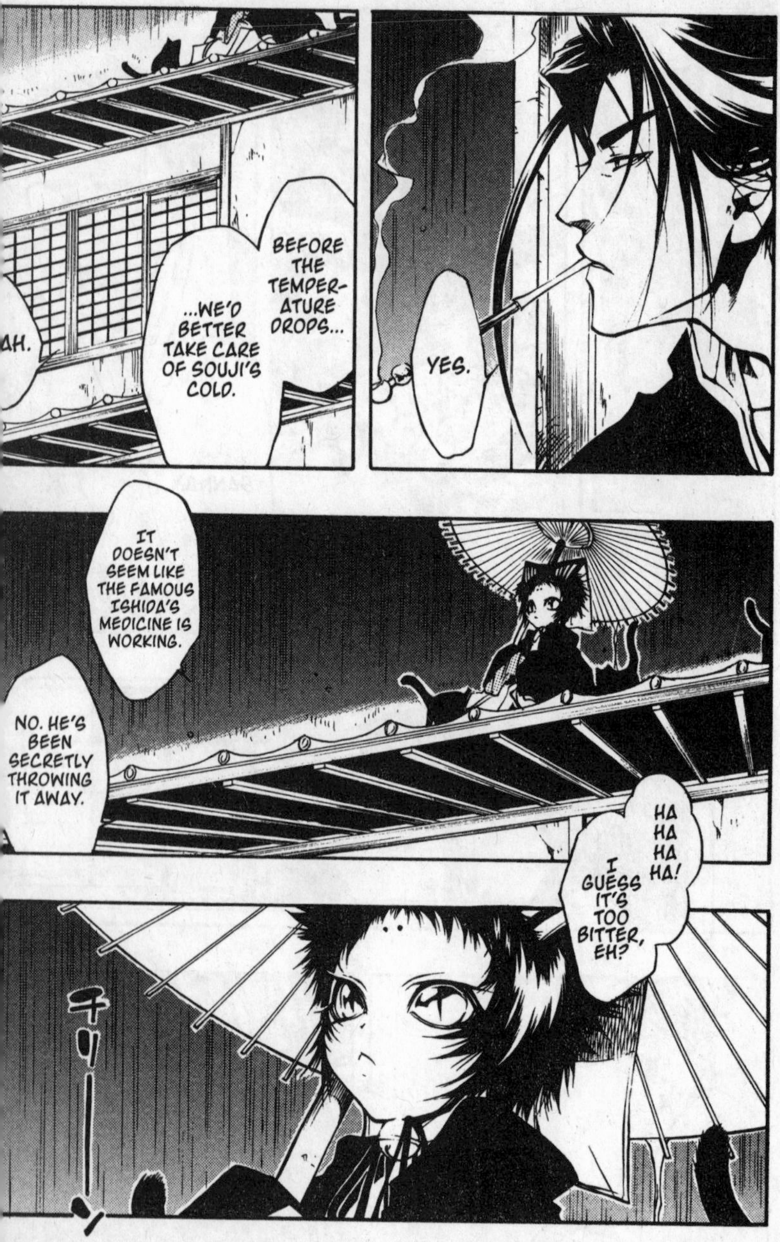

YES.
BEFORE THE TEMPERATURE DROPS...
...WE'D BETTER TAKE CARE OF SOUJI'S COLD.
AH.
IT DOESN'T SEEM LIKE THE FAMOUS ISHIDA'S MEDICINE IS WORKING.
NO. HE'S BEEN SECRETLY THROWING IT AWAY.
HA HA HA HA HA HA HA!
I GUESS IT'S TOO BITTER, EH?
チリーン…

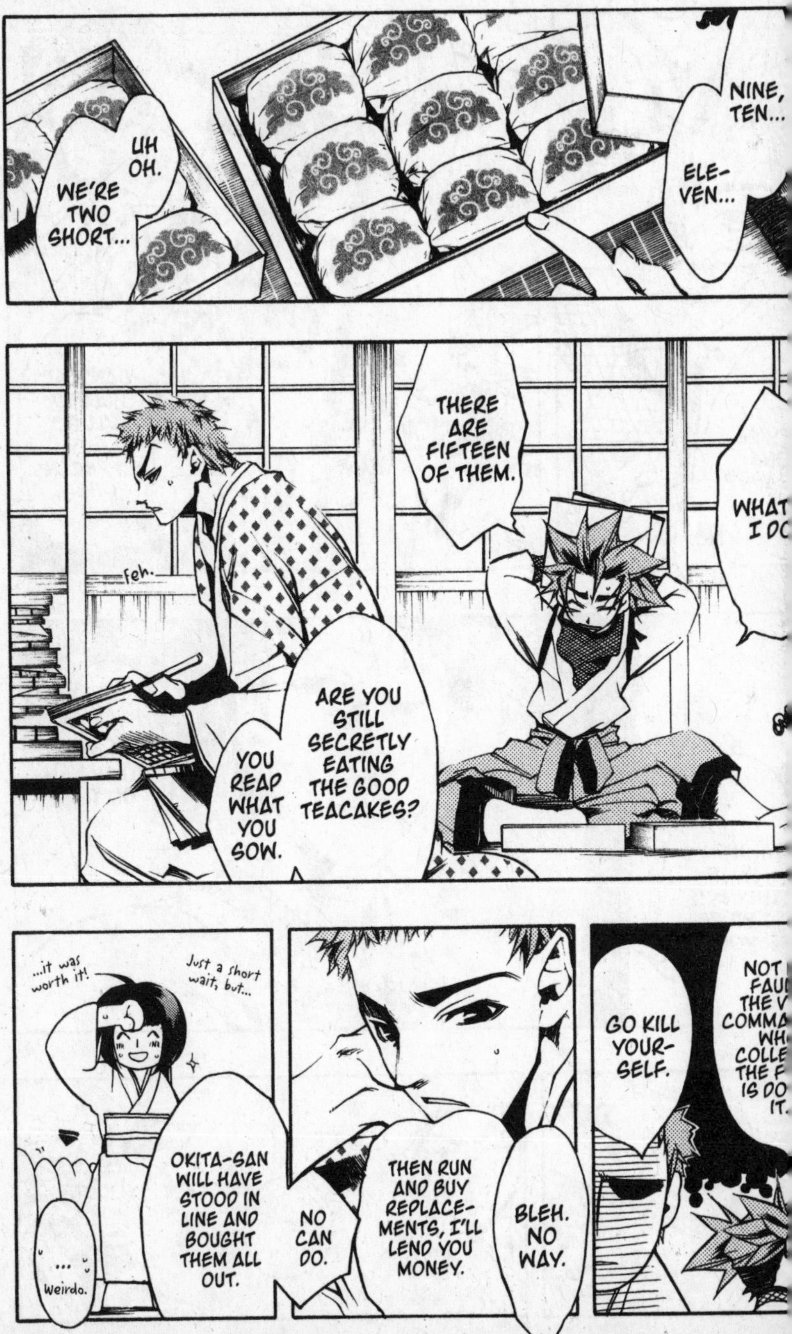

NINE, TEN...
ELE-VEN...
UH OH.
WE'RE TWO SHORT...
WHAT
THERE ARE FIFTEEN OF THEM.
ARE YOU STILL SECRETLY EATING THE GOOD TEACAKES?
YOU REAP WHAT YOU SOW.
feh.
GO KILL YOUR-SELF.
THEN RUN AND BUY REPLACE-MENTS, I'LL LEND YOU MONEY.
BLEH. NO WAY.
NO CAN DO.
Just a short wait, but...
...it was worth it!
OKITA-SAN WILL HAVE STOOD IN LINE AND BOUGHT THEM ALL OUT.
...
Weirdo.

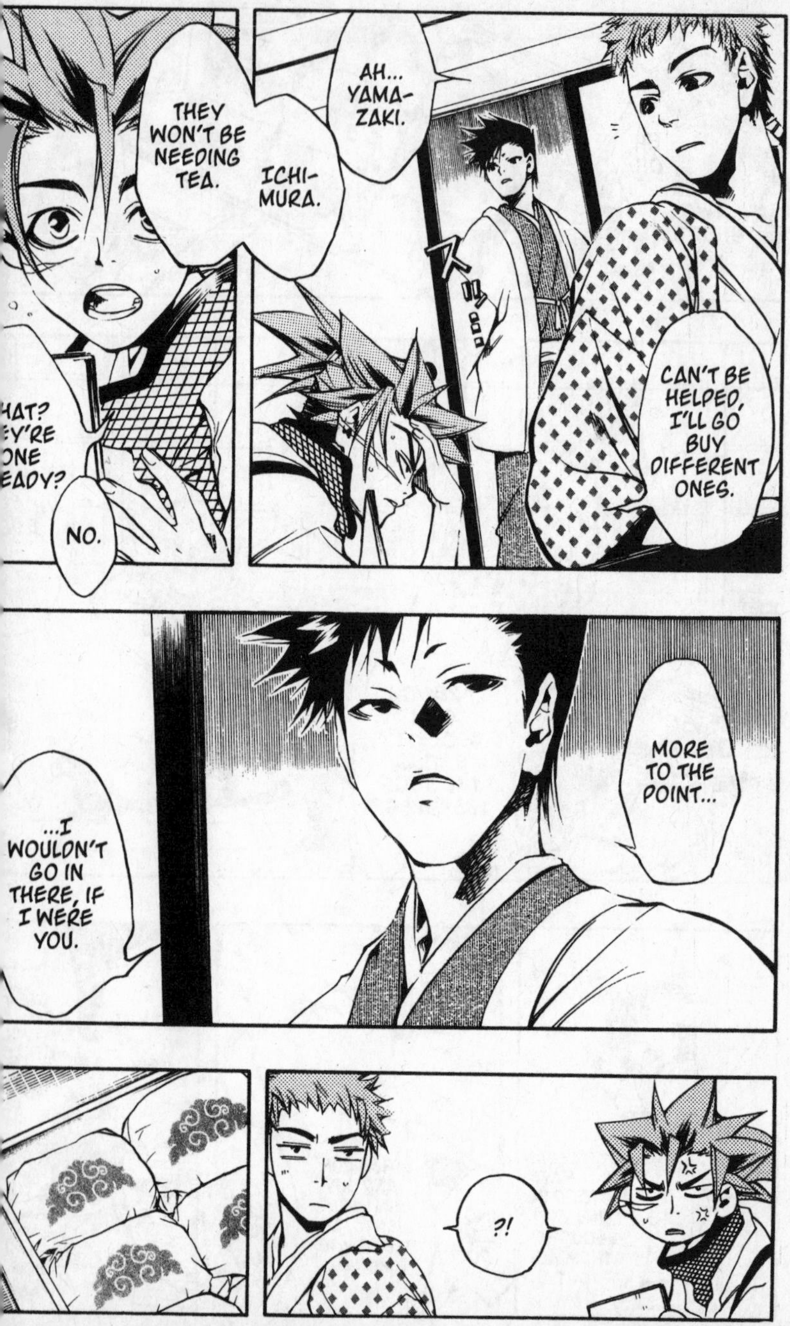
CAN'T BE HELPED, I'LL GO BUY DIFFERENT ONES.
AH... YAMA-ZAKI.
スッ
ICHI-MURA.
THEY WON'T BE NEEDING TEA.
HAT? EY'RE ONE EADY?
NO.
MORE TO THE POINT...
...I WOULDN'T GO IN THERE, IF I WERE YOU.
?!

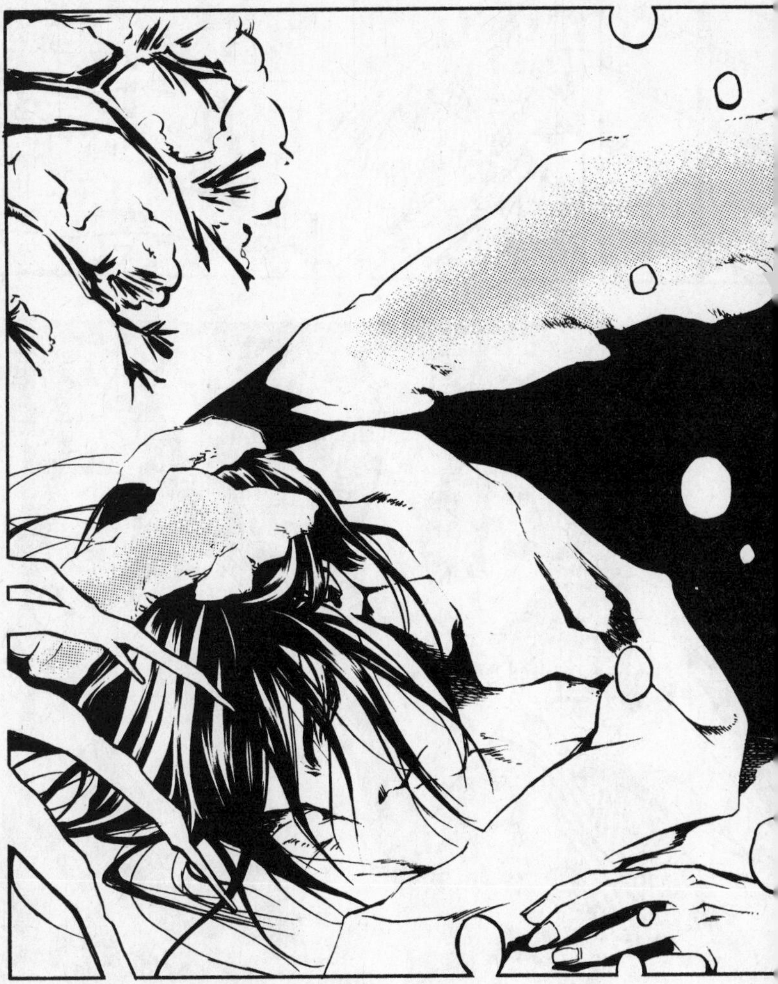

第八話 雪
だいはちわ ゆき

Act 8
Snow

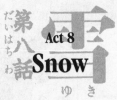

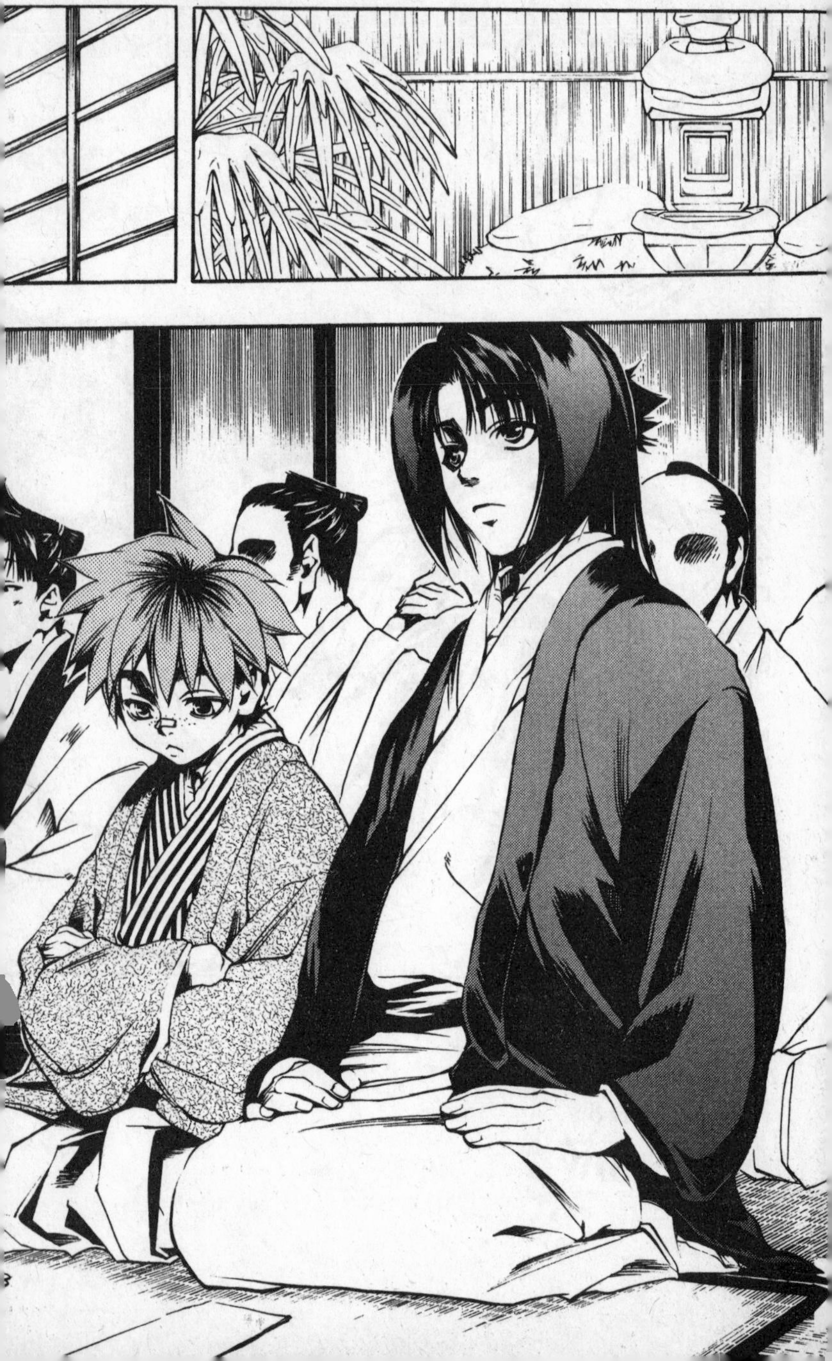

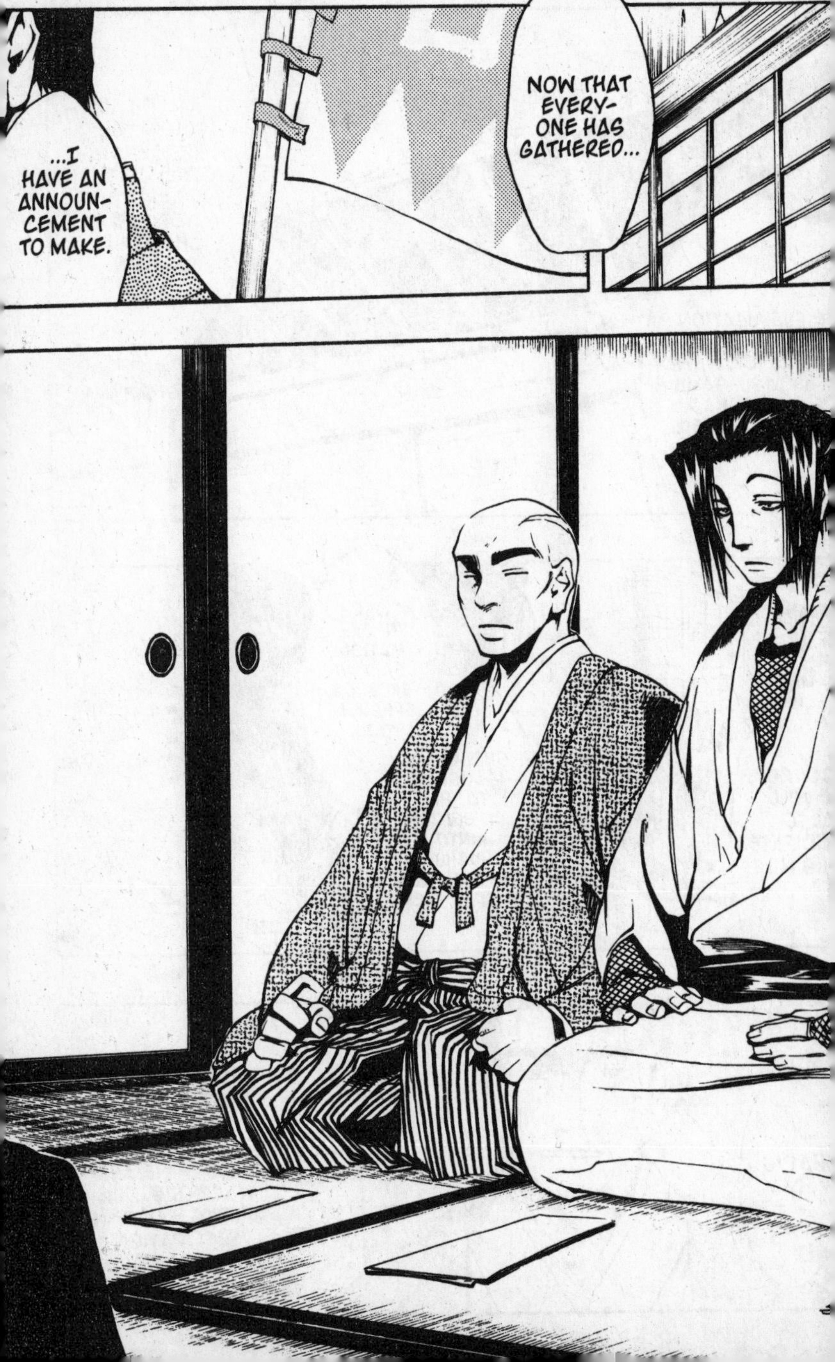
NOW THAT EVERY-ONE HAS GATHERED...
...I HAVE AN ANNOUNCEMENT TO MAKE.

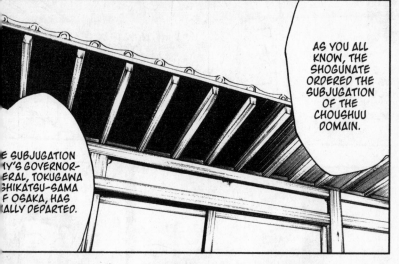

AS YOU ALL KNOW, THE SHOGUNATE ORDERED THE SUBJUGATION OF THE CHOUSHUU DOMAIN.

E SUBJUGATION
MY'S GOVERNOR-
ERAL, TOKUGAWA
SHIKATSU-SAMA
F OSAKA, HAS
ALLY DEPARTED.

OUR INFORMATION BARELY EXCEEDS SPECULATION.

THE SHOGUNATE IS LOOKING TO THIS EXPEDITION INTO CHOUSHUU TO PERMANENTLY SUBDUE THEM.

COURSE,
E WILL
ALSO
TICIPATE
HIS WAR.

BUT WITH OUR LIMITED EXPERIENCE OF POLITICAL STRATEGY, EVEN THOUGH WE ARE WARRIORS, OUR SPIRITS MAY FEEL TREPIDATION AT THIS WAR.

THAT IS
WHY...

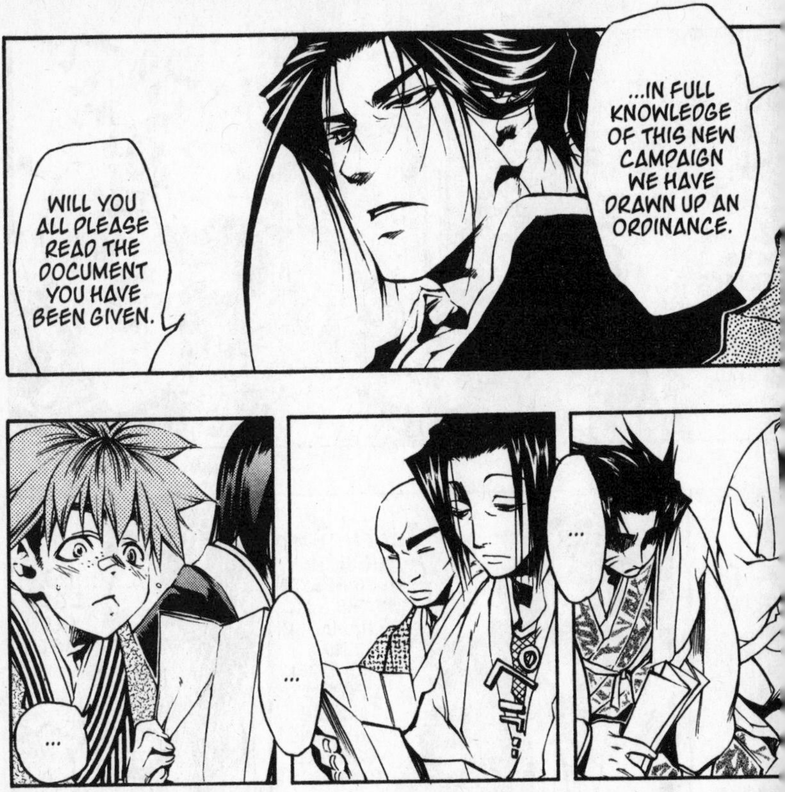
...IN FULL KNOWLEDGE OF THIS NEW CAMPAIGN WE HAVE DRAWN UP AN ORDINANCE.
WILL YOU ALL PLEASE READ THE DOCUMENT YOU HAVE BEEN GIVEN.
...
...
...

- We shall strictly protect the Government and abide by the orders of our leaders.
- We shall stop our enemies' criticisms without hesitation. Furthermore, talk of ghosts, apparitions, and other whimsy will not be tolerated...
- ...and luxurious foods are banned.
- No rebellious conversation will be allowed.
- If one of your comrades engages in a brawl or quarrel, separate yourself from him.
- When eating provisions with your unit, you will keep your weapon sheathed.
- If a group leader dies, the members of that group will commit themselves to fight to the death. If one should flee his group in cowardice, death by decapitation shall be the minimum punishment. We shall strive to be prepared, to be free of lingering attachments, and to do our work.
- After a heated battle, aside from the group leader, no other body is to be removed from the field, even in the case of a high death toll.

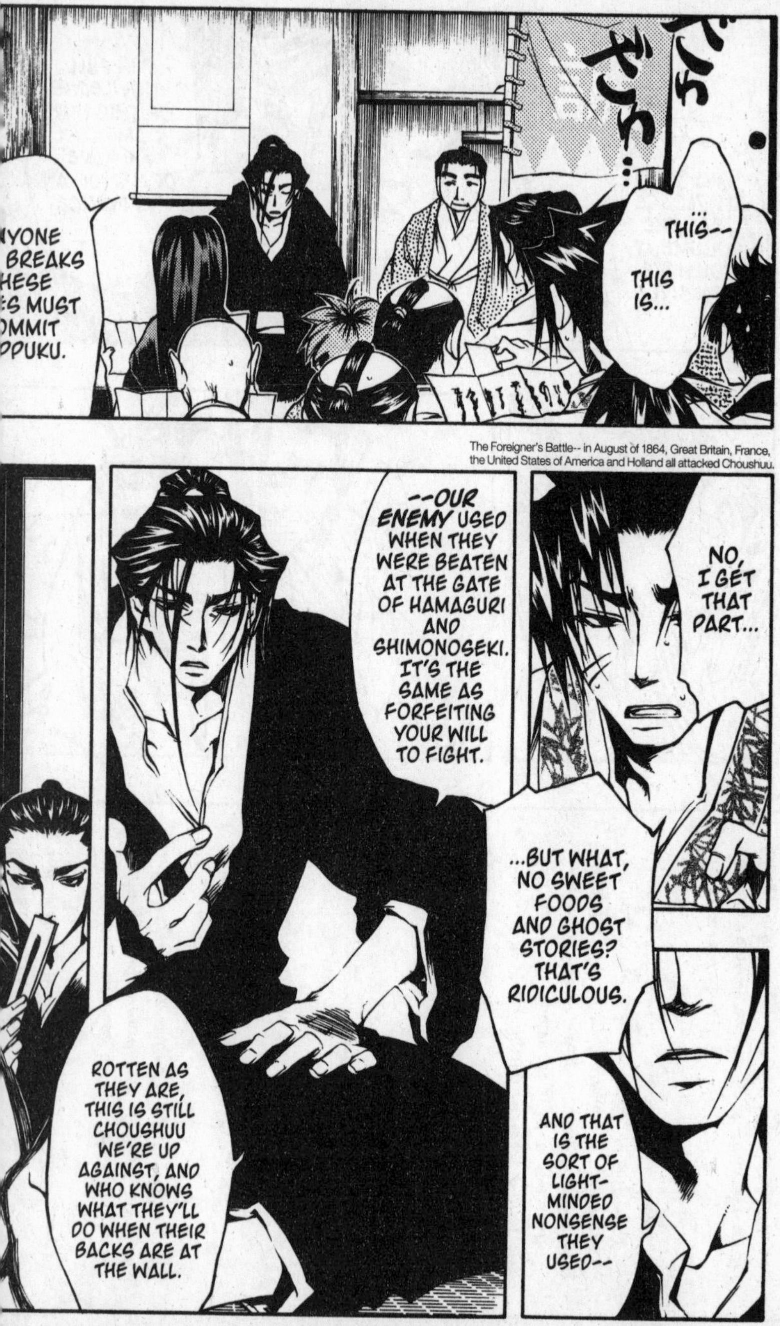

ざわ ざわ...
... THIS--
THIS IS...
NYONE BREAKS HESE ES MUST OMMIT PPUKU.
NO, I GET THAT PART...
...BUT WHAT, NO SWEET FOODS AND GHOST STORIES? THAT'S RIDICULOUS.
AND THAT IS THE SORT OF LIGHT-MINDED NONSENSE THEY USED--
--OUR ENEMY USED WHEN THEY WERE BEATEN AT THE GATE OF HAMAGURI AND SHIMONOSEKI. IT'S THE SAME AS FORFEITING YOUR WILL TO FIGHT.
ROTTEN AS THEY ARE, THIS IS STILL CHOUSHUU WE'RE UP AGAINST, AND WHO KNOWS WHAT THEY'LL DO WHEN THEIR BACKS ARE AT THE WALL.

The Foreigner's Battle-- in August of 1864, Great Britain, France, the United States of America and Holland all attacked Choushuu.

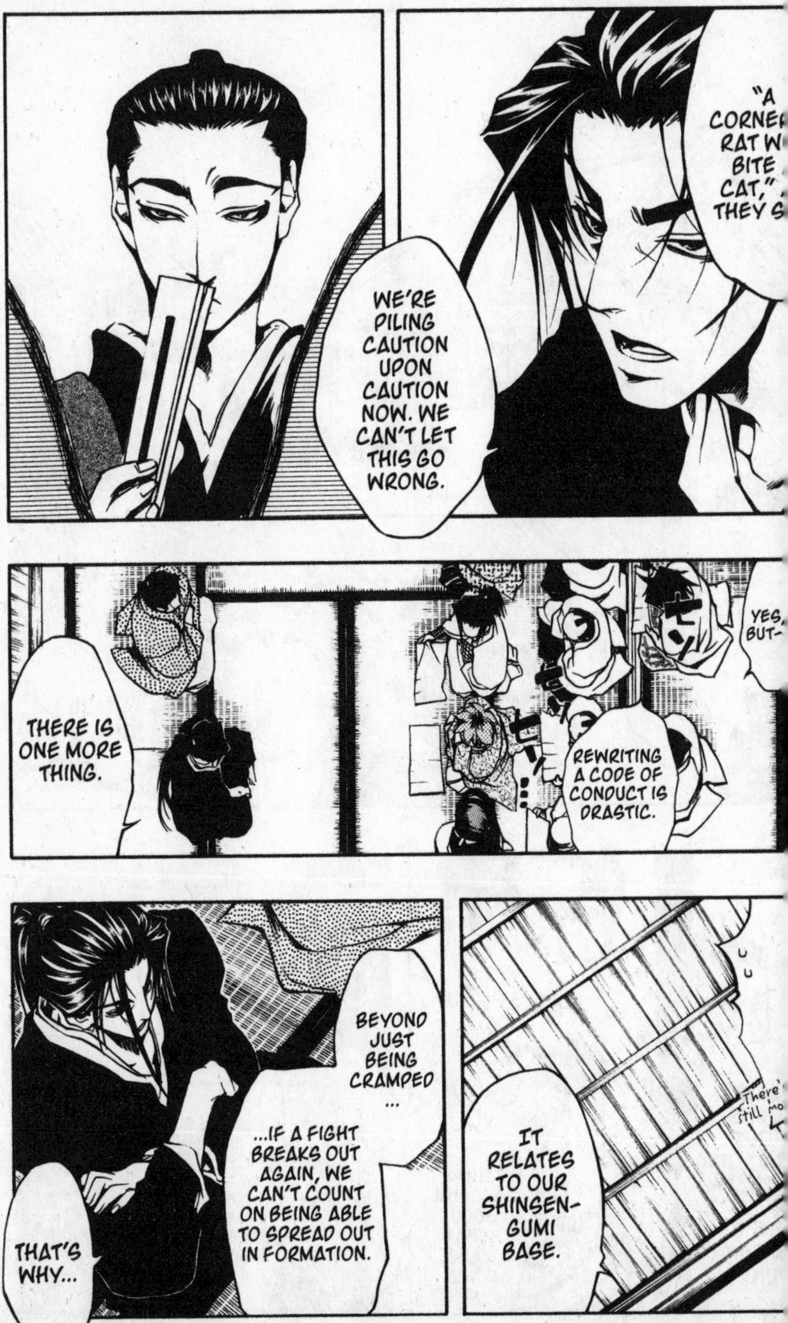
"A CORNEF RAT W BITE CAT," THEY S
WE'RE PILING CAUTION UPON CAUTION NOW. WE CAN'T LET THIS GO WRONG.
YES, BUT-
REWRITING A CODE OF CONDUCT IS DRASTIC.
THERE IS ONE MORE THING.
There's still mo
IT RELATES TO OUR SHINSEN-GUMI BASE.
BEYOND JUST BEING CRAMPED...
...IF A FIGHT BREAKS OUT AGAIN, WE CAN'T COUNT ON BEING ABLE TO SPREAD OUT IN FORMATION.
THAT'S WHY...

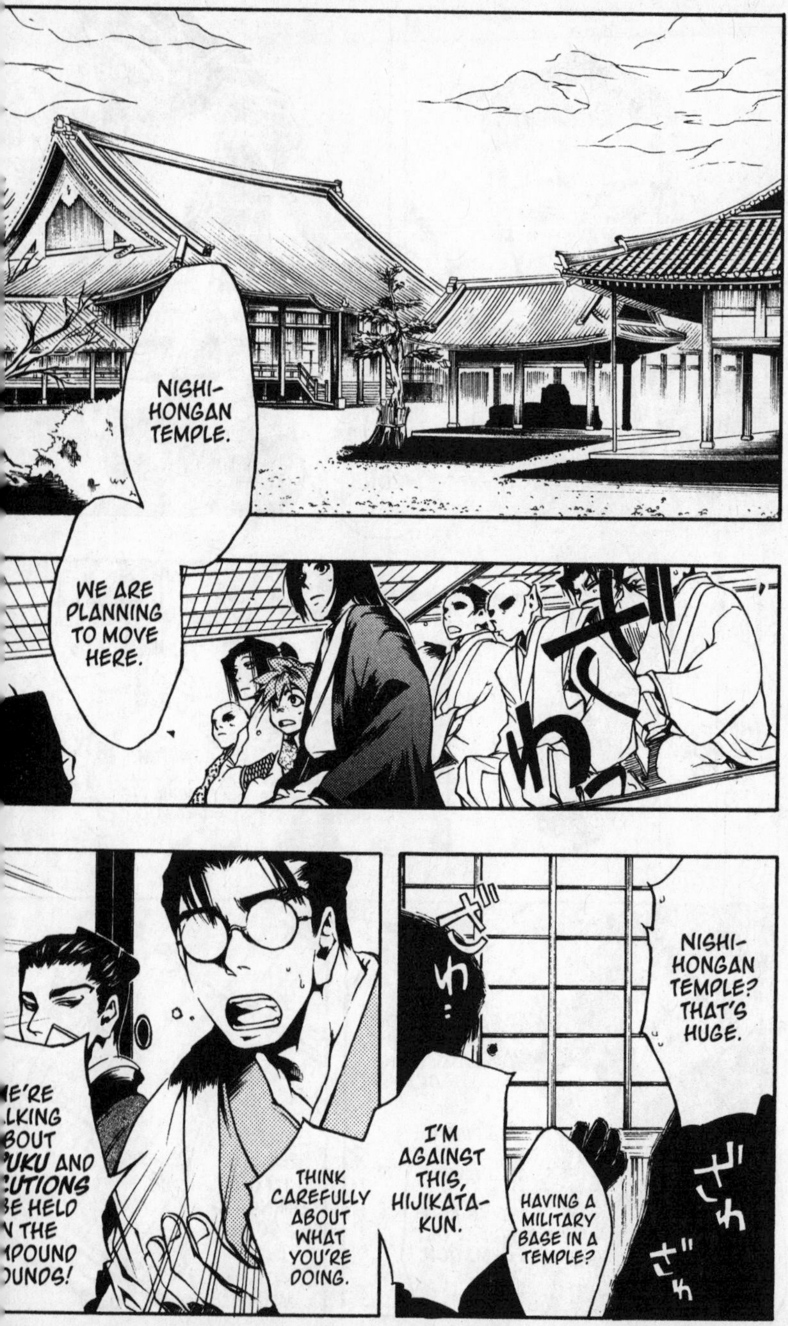
NISHI-HONGAN TEMPLE.
WE ARE PLANNING TO MOVE HERE.
NISHI-HONGAN TEMPLE? THAT'S HUGE.
HAVING A MILITARY BASE IN A TEMPLE?
I'M AGAINST THIS, HIJIKATA-KUN.
THINK CAREFULLY ABOUT WHAT YOU'RE DOING.
E'RE LKING BOUT PUKU AND CUTIONS BE HELD N THE MPOUND OUNDS!

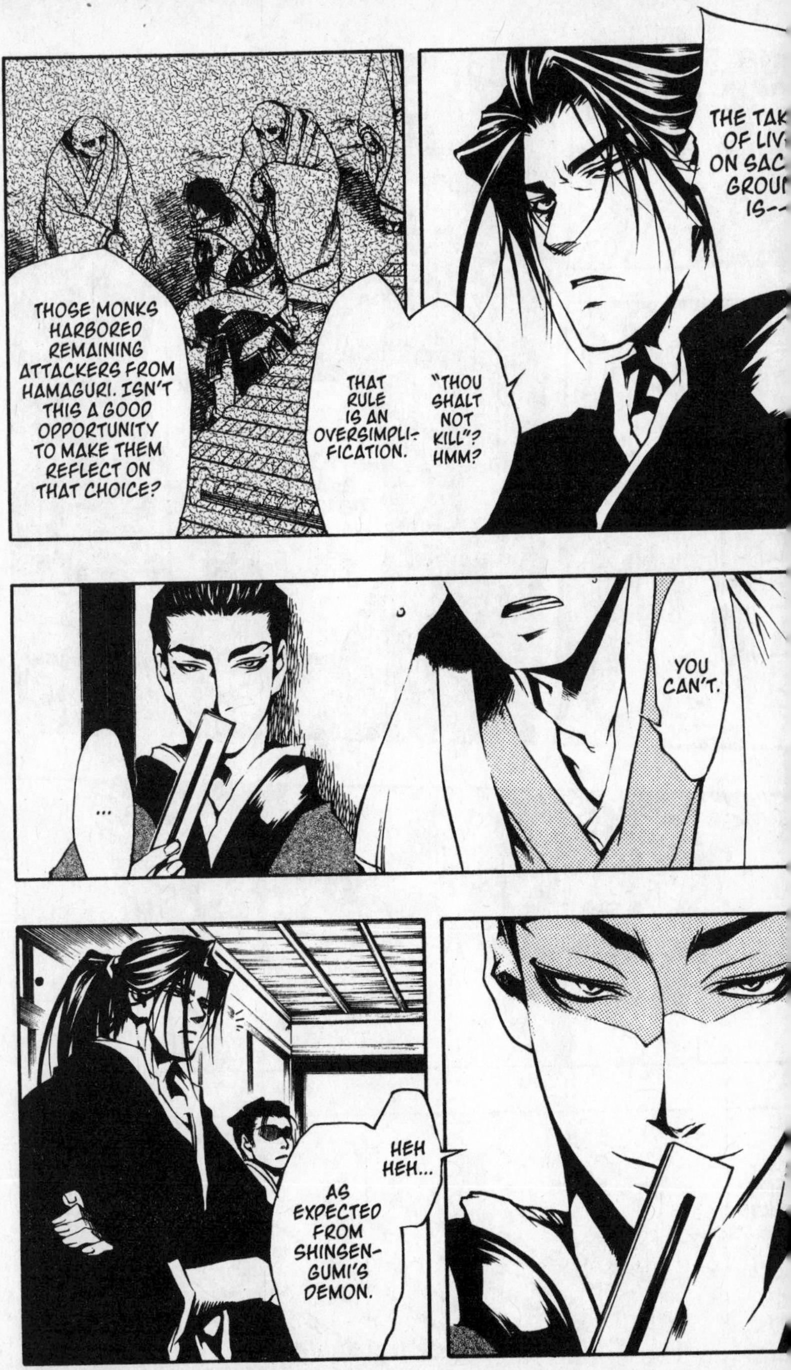
THE TAK OF LIV ON SAC GROUN IS--
"THOU SHALT NOT KILL"? HMM?
THAT RULE IS AN OVERSIMPLI-FICATION.
THOSE MONKS HARBORED REMAINING ATTACKERS FROM HAMAGURI. ISN'T THIS A GOOD OPPORTUNITY TO MAKE THEM REFLECT ON THAT CHOICE?
YOU CAN'T.
...
HEH HEH...
AS EXPECTED FROM SHINSEN-GUMI'S DEMON.

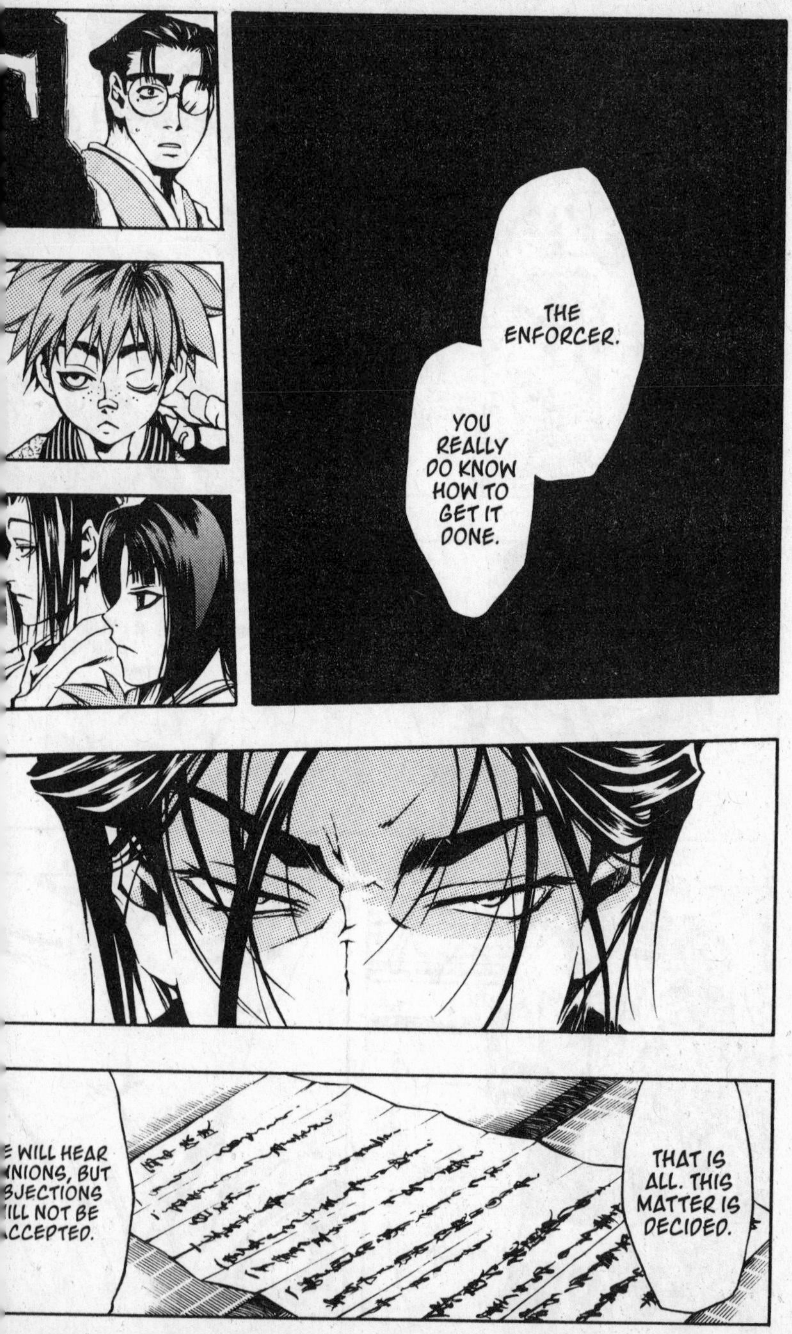
THE ENFORCER.
YOU REALLY DO KNOW HOW TO GET IT DONE.
THAT IS ALL. THIS MATTER IS DECIDED.
E WILL HEAR NIONS, BUT BJECTIONS ILL NOT BE CCEPTED.

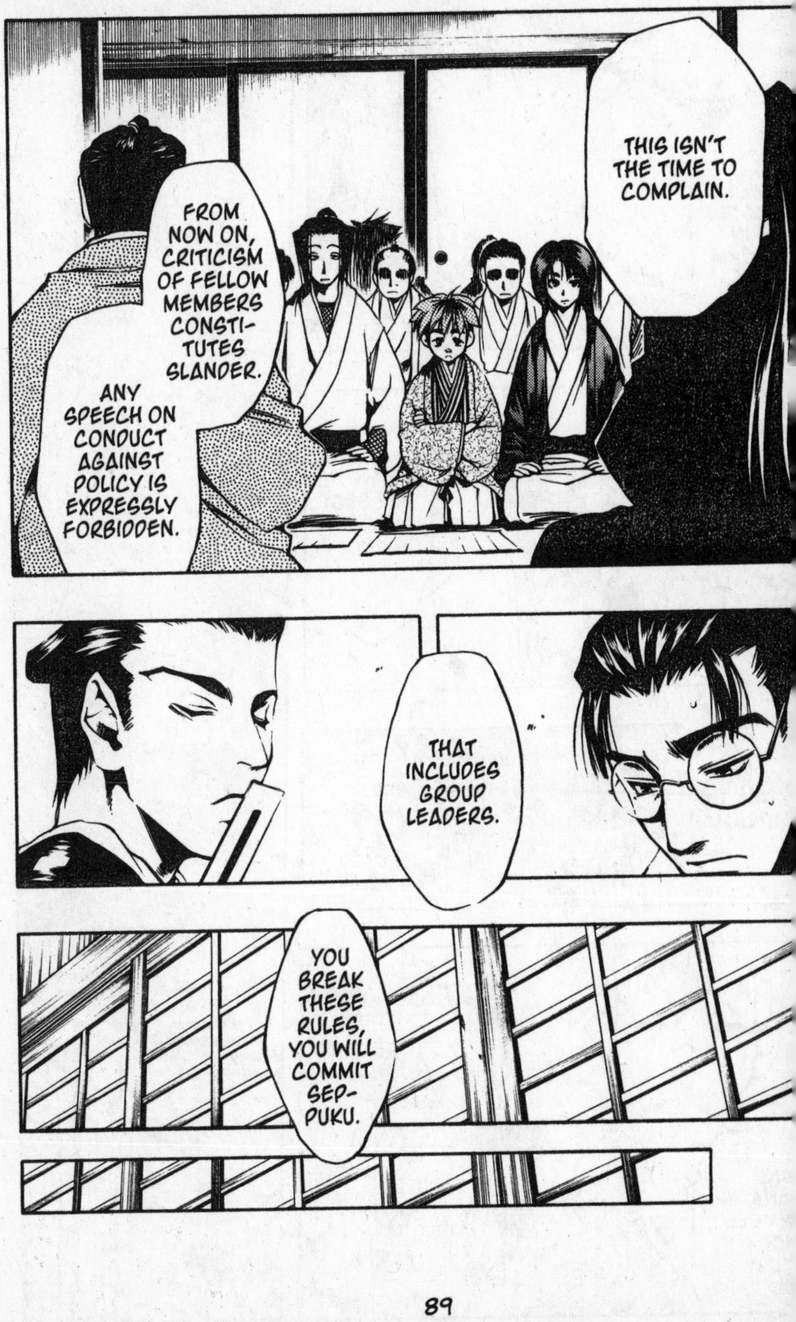
THIS ISN'T THE TIME TO COMPLAIN.
FROM NOW ON, CRITICISM OF FELLOW MEMBERS CONSTITUTES SLANDER.
ANY SPEECH ON CONDUCT AGAINST POLICY IS EXPRESSLY FORBIDDEN.
THAT INCLUDES GROUP LEADERS.
YOU BREAK THESE RULES, YOU WILL COMMIT SEP-PUKU.

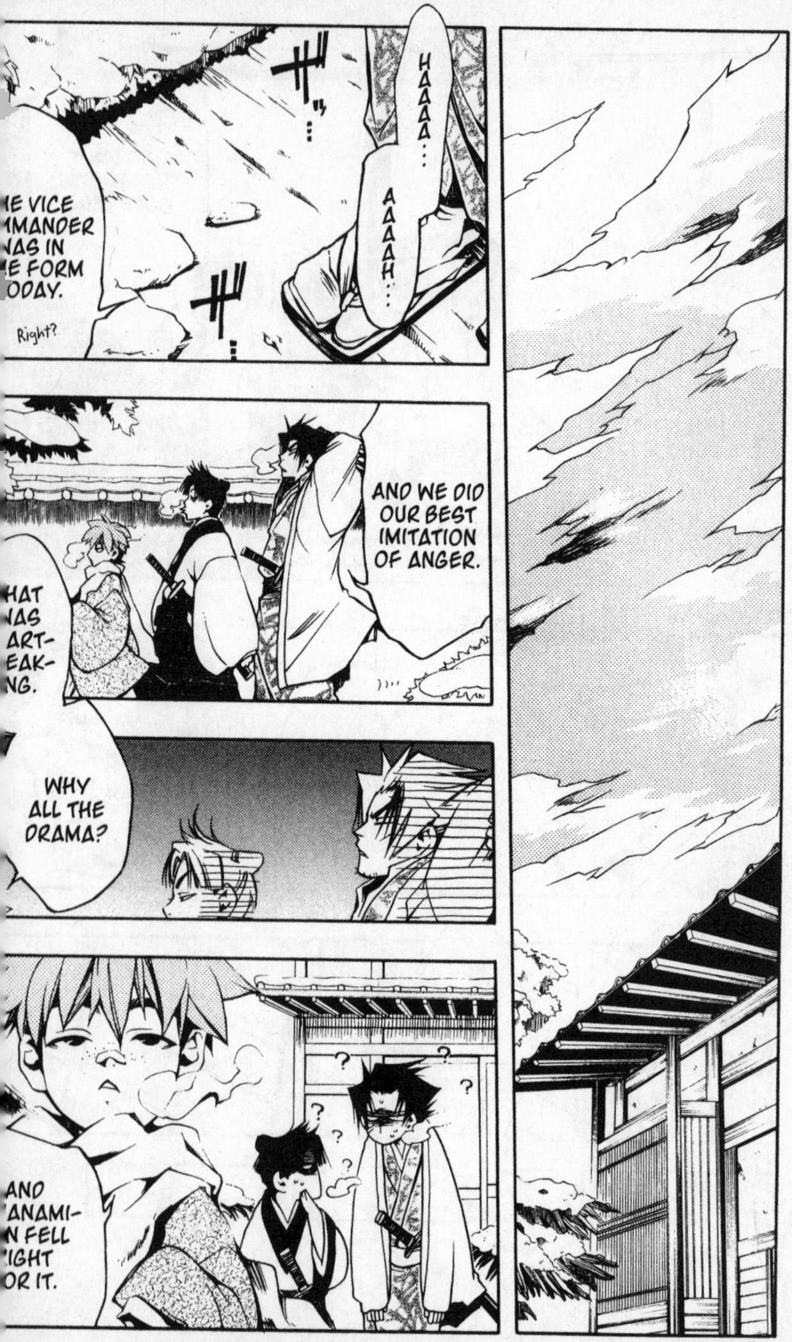
HAAAA... AAAAH...
E VICE MMANDER WAS IN E FORM ODAY.
Right?
AND WE DID OUR BEST IMITATION OF ANGER.
HAT WAS ART- EAK- NG.
WHY ALL THE DRAMA?
AND ANAMI- N FELL IGHT OR IT.

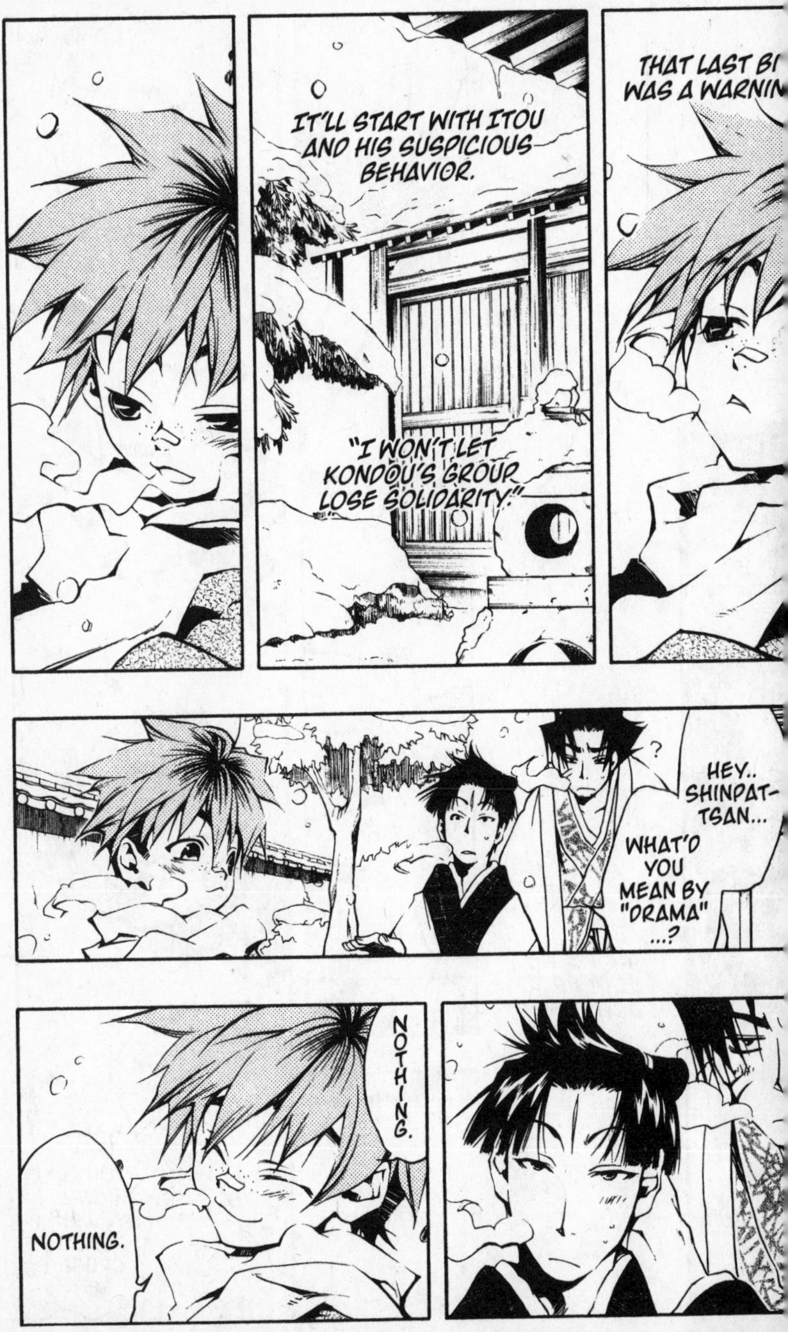
THAT LAST BI
WAS A WARNIN
IT'LL START WITH ITOU AND HIS SUSPICIOUS BEHAVIOR.
"I WON'T LET KONDOU'S GROUP LOSE SOLIDARITY."
HEY.. SHINPAT-TSAN...
WHAT'D YOU MEAN BY "DRAMA" ...?
NOTHING.
NOTHING.

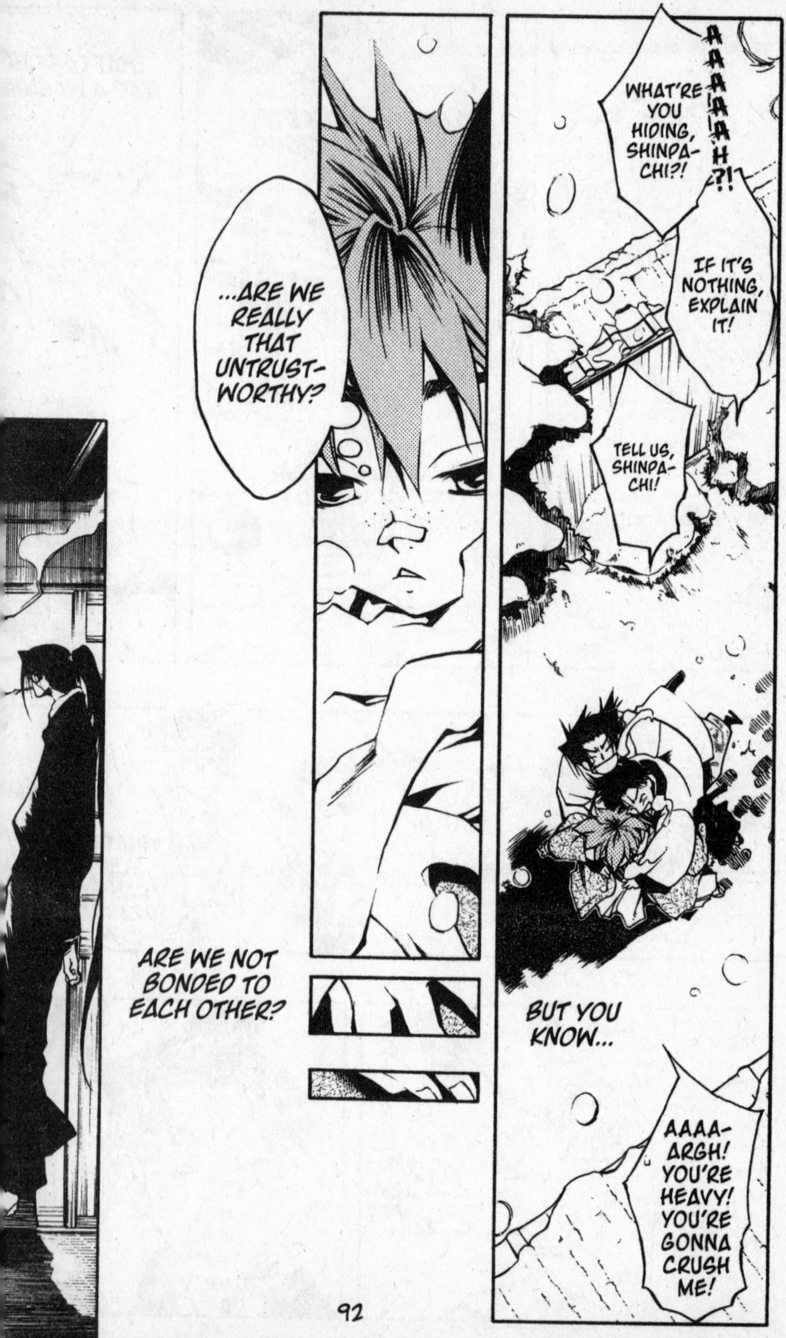
AAAAAH?!
WHAT'RE YOU HIDING, SHINPA-CHI?!
IF IT'S NOTHING, EXPLAIN IT!
TELL US, SHINPA-CHI!
BUT YOU KNOW...
AAAA-ARGH! YOU'RE HEAVY! YOU'RE GONNA CRUSH ME!
...ARE WE REALLY THAT UNTRUST-WORTHY?
ARE WE NOT BONDED TO EACH OTHER?

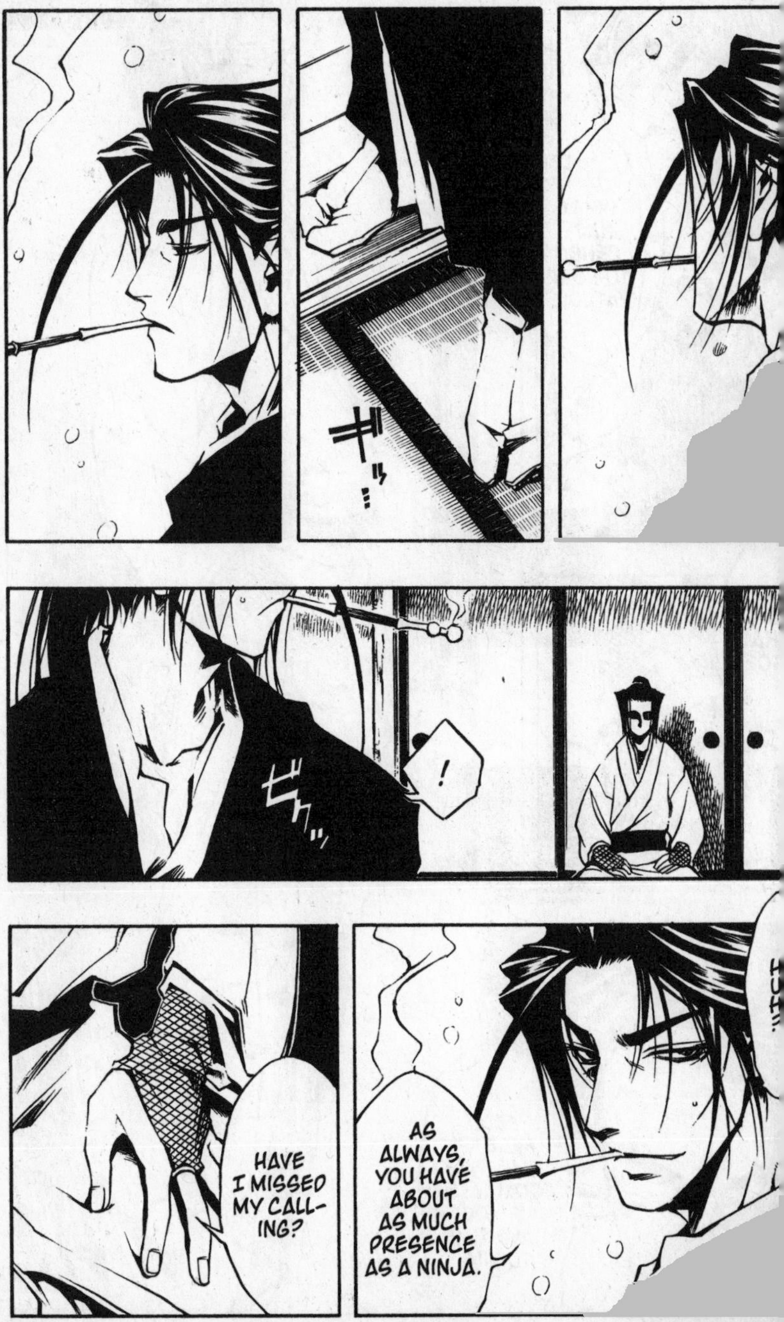
!
AS ALWAYS, YOU HAVE ABOUT AS MUCH PRESENCE AS A NINJA.
HAVE I MISSED MY CALLING?

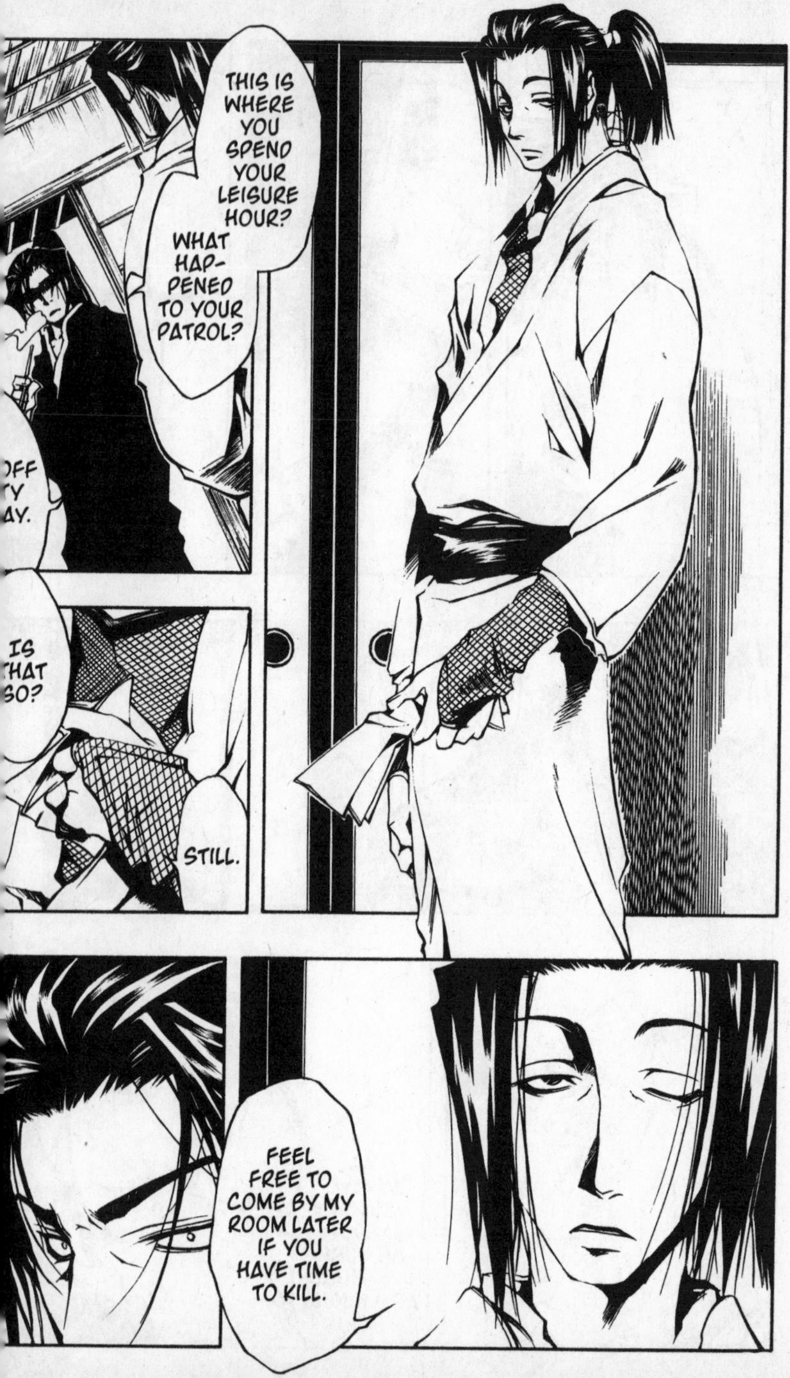
THIS IS WHERE YOU SPEND YOUR LEISURE HOUR? WHAT HAP-PENED TO YOUR PATROL?
STILL.
FEEL FREE TO COME BY MY ROOM LATER IF YOU HAVE TIME TO KILL.

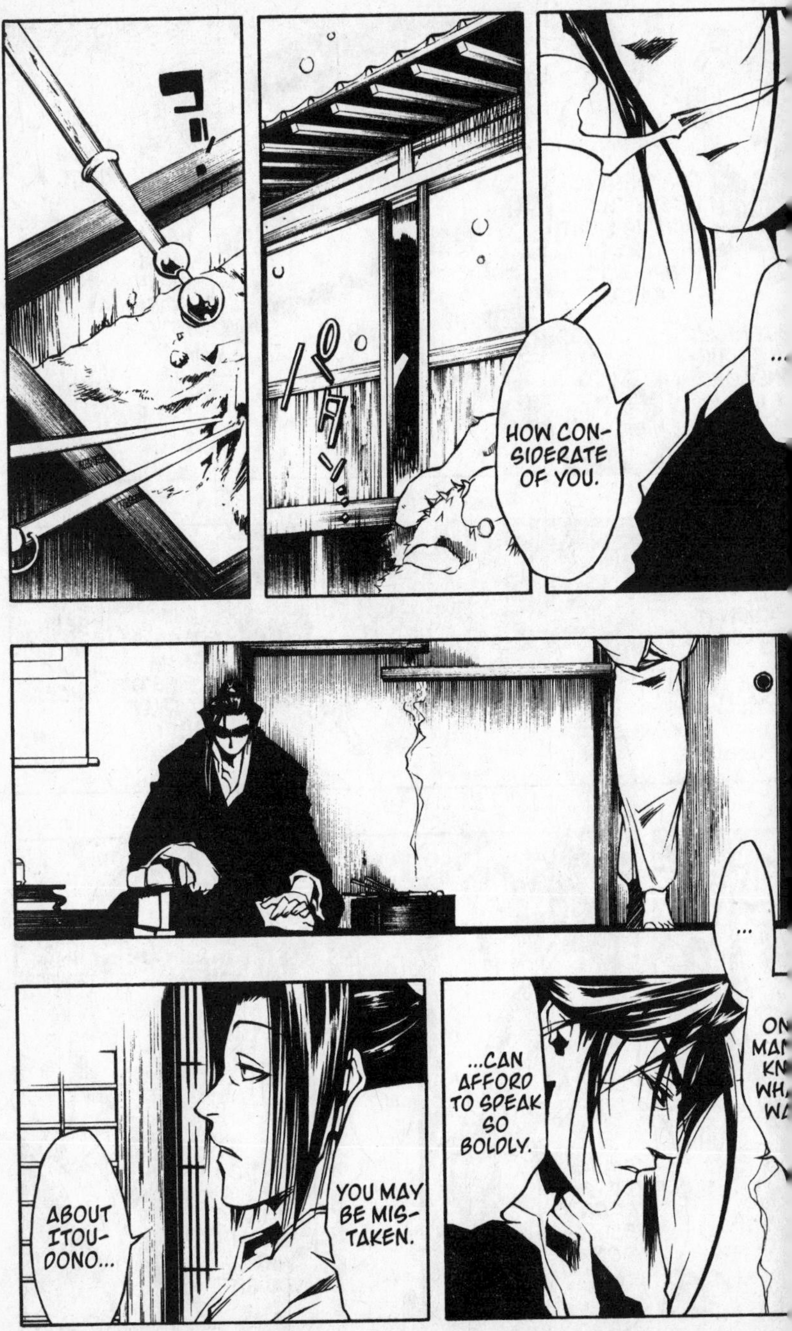
...
HOW CON-SIDERATE OF YOU.
...
...CAN AFFORD TO SPEAK SO BOLDLY.
YOU MAY BE MIS-TAKEN.
ABOUT ITOU-DONO...

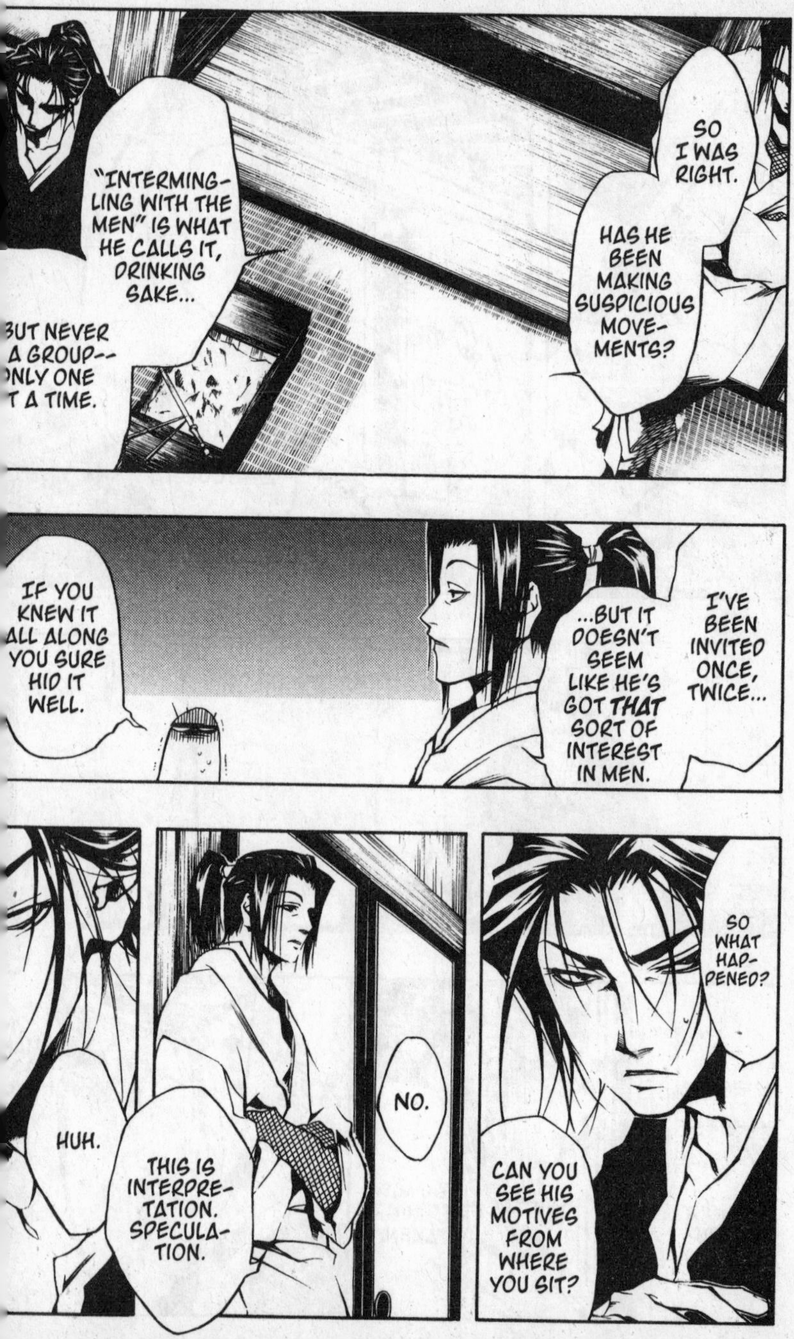
SO I WAS RIGHT.
HAS HE BEEN MAKING SUSPICIOUS MOVE-MENTS?
"INTERMING-LING WITH THE MEN" IS WHAT HE CALLS IT, DRINKING SAKE...
UT NEVER A GROUP-- NLY ONE T A TIME.
I'VE BEEN INVITED ONCE, TWICE...
...BUT IT DOESN'T SEEM LIKE HE'S GOT **THAT** SORT OF INTEREST IN MEN.
IF YOU KNEW IT ALL ALONG YOU SURE HID IT WELL.
SO WHAT HAP-PENED?
CAN YOU SEE HIS MOTIVES FROM WHERE YOU SIT?
NO.
THIS IS INTERPRE-TATION. SPECULA-TION.
HUH.

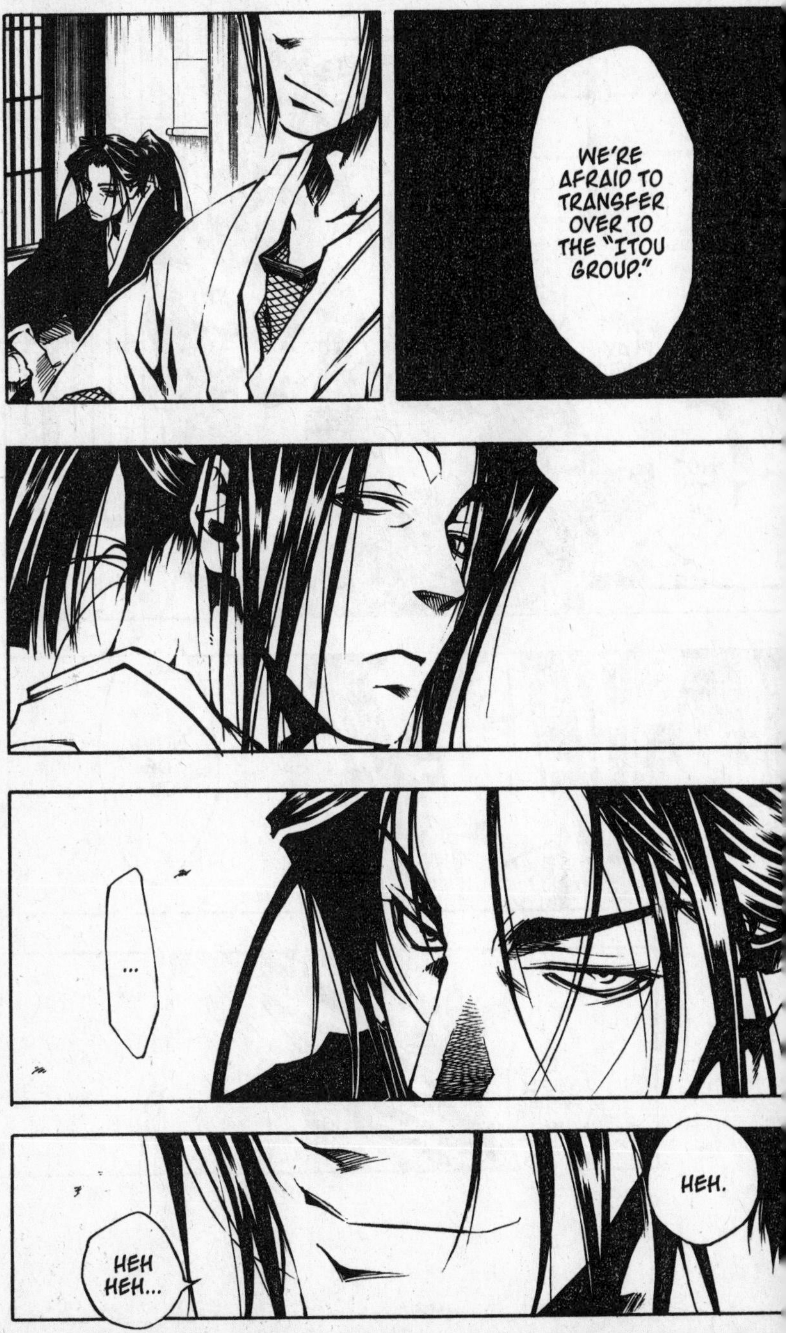
WE'RE AFRAID TO TRANSFER OVER TO THE "ITOU GROUP."
...
HEH.
HEH HEH...

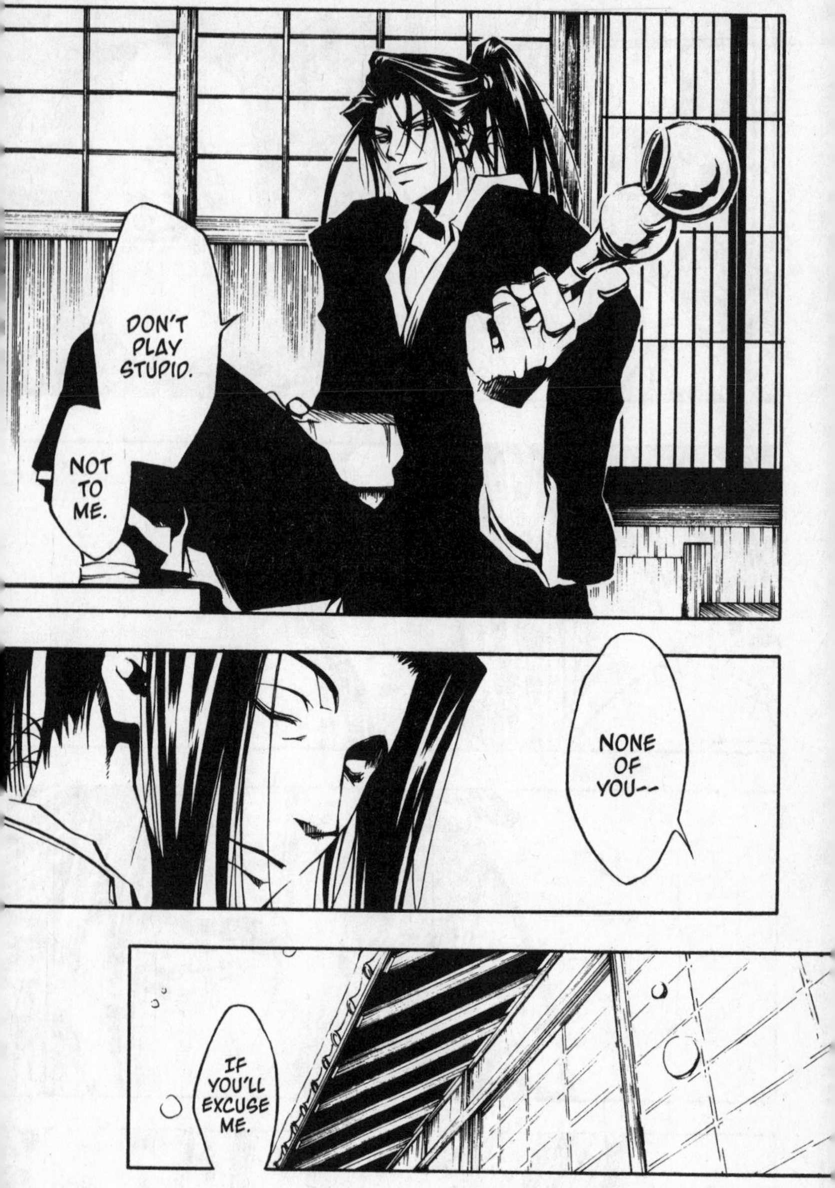
DON'T PLAY STUPID.
NOT TO ME.
NONE OF YOU--
IF YOU'LL EXCUSE ME.

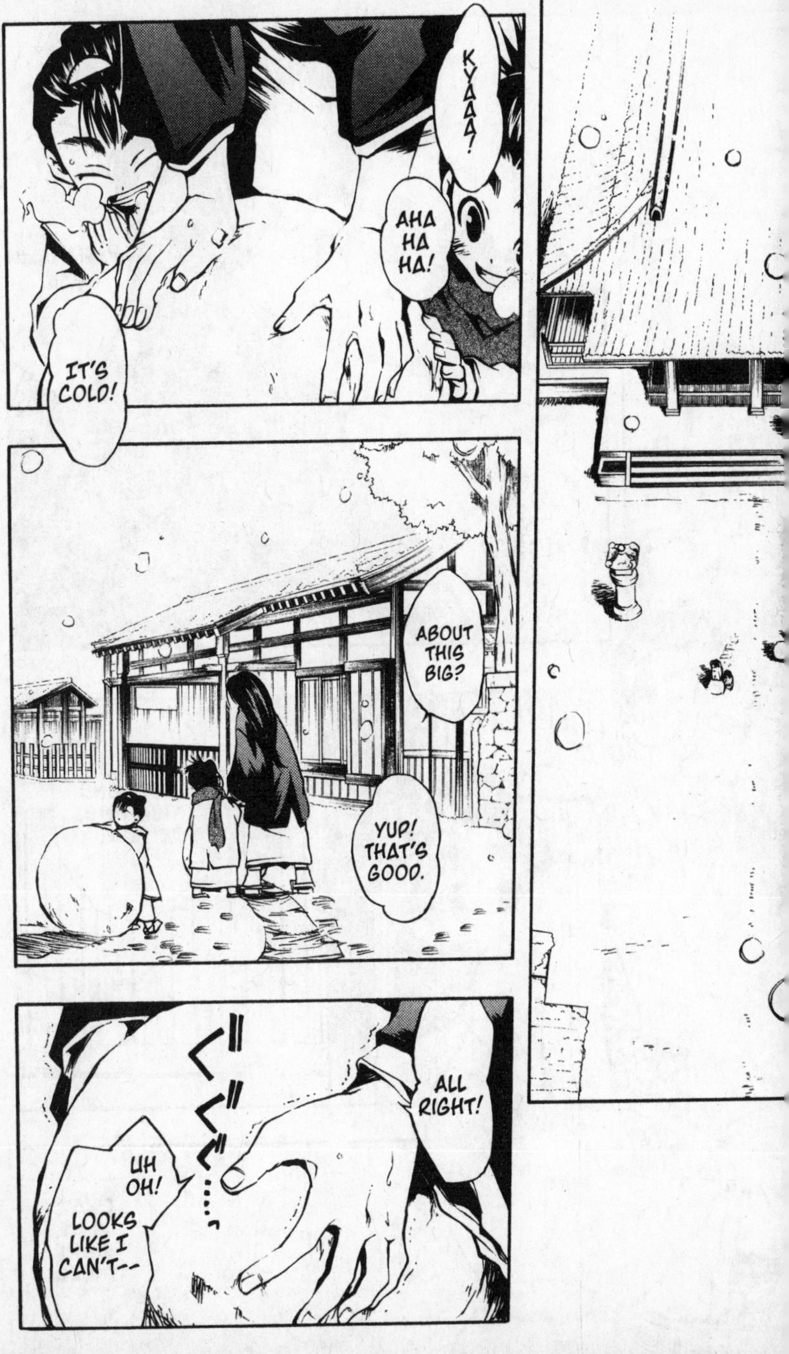
KYAAA!
AHA HA HA!
IT'S COLD!
ABOUT THIS BIG?
YUP! THAT'S GOOD.
ALL RIGHT!
ぐぐぐ……
UH OH!
LOOKS LIKE I CAN'T--

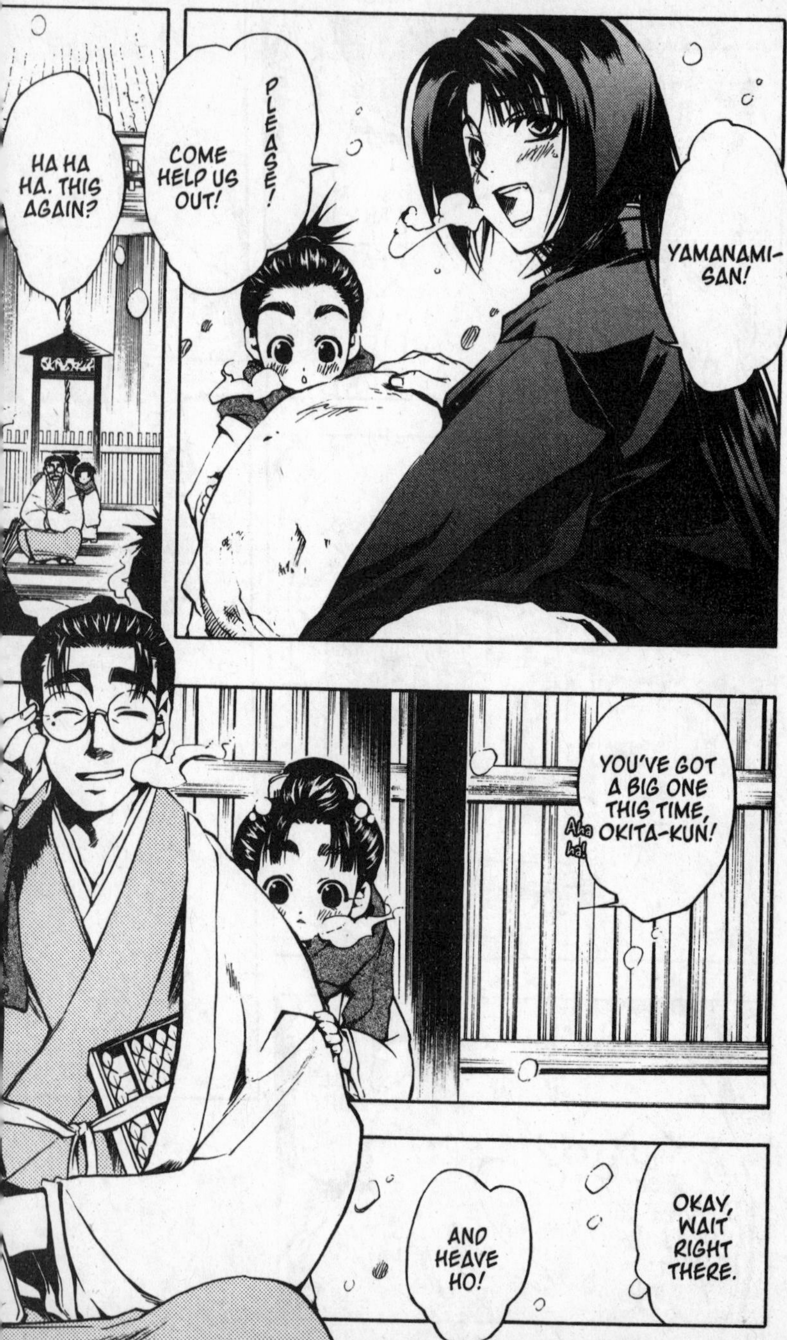
YAMANAMI-SAN!
PLEASE!
COME HELP US OUT!
HA HA HA. THIS AGAIN?
YOU'VE GOT A BIG ONE THIS TIME, OKITA-KUN!
Aha ha!
OKAY, WAIT RIGHT THERE.
AND HEAVE HO!

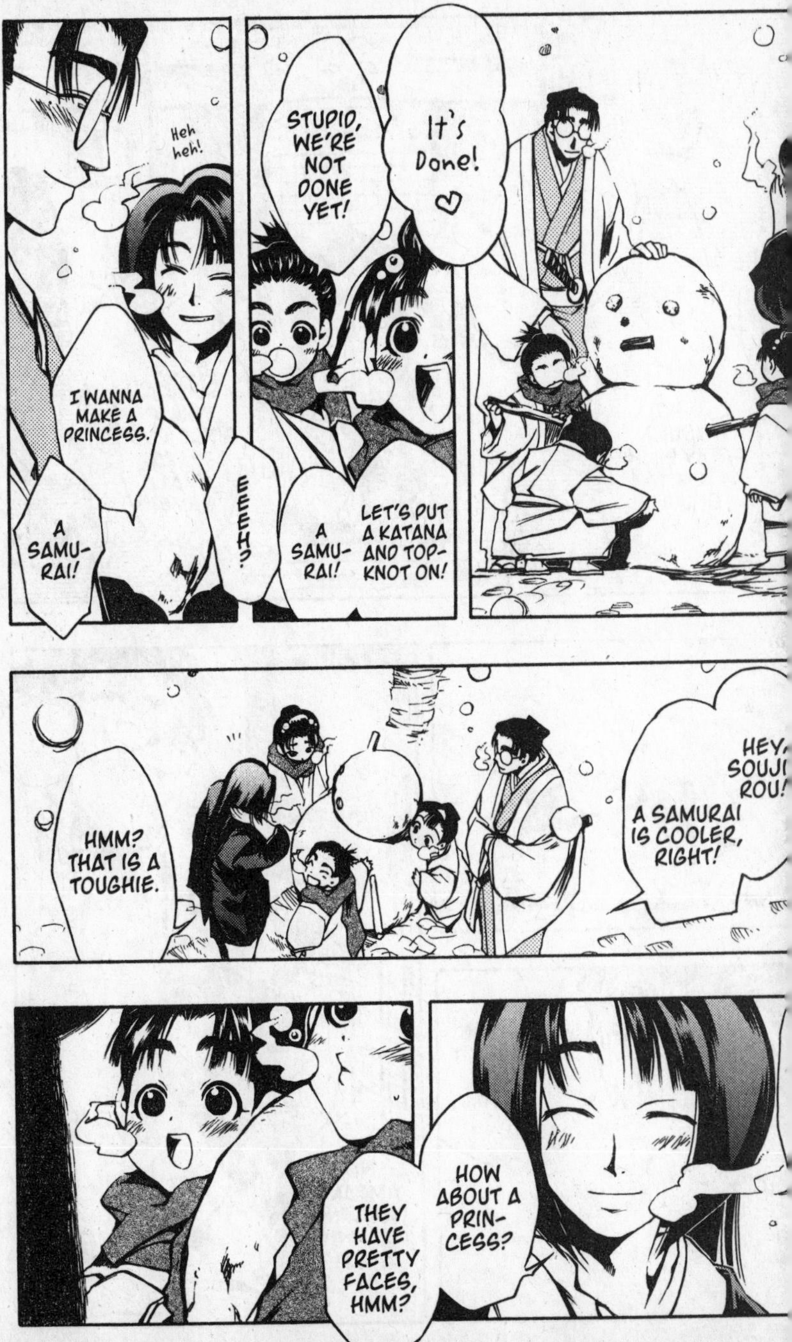
It's Done! ♡
STUPID, WE'RE NOT DONE YET!
LET'S PUT A KATANA AND TOP-KNOT ON!
A SAMU-RAI!
EEEH?
Heh heh!
I WANNA MAKE A PRINCESS.
A SAMU-RAI!
HEY, SOUJI ROU!
A SAMURAI IS COOLER, RIGHT!
HMM? THAT IS A TOUGHIE.
HOW ABOUT A PRIN-CESS?
THEY HAVE PRETTY FACES, HMM?

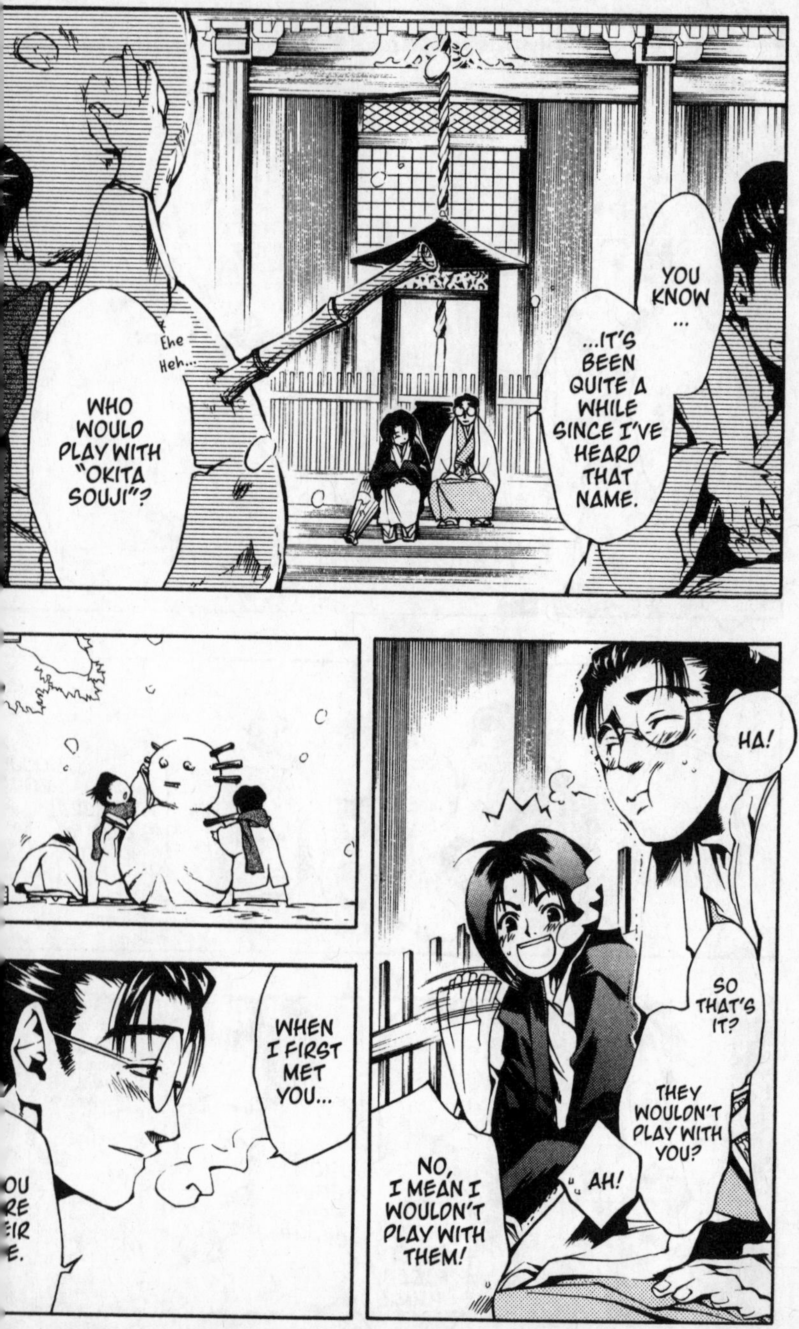
YOU KNOW ...
...IT'S BEEN QUITE A WHILE SINCE I'VE HEARD THAT NAME.
Ehe Heh...
WHO WOULD PLAY WITH "OKITA SOUJI"?
HA!
SO THAT'S IT?
THEY WOULDN'T PLAY WITH YOU?
AH!
NO, I MEAN I WOULDN'T PLAY WITH THEM!
WHEN I FIRST MET YOU...

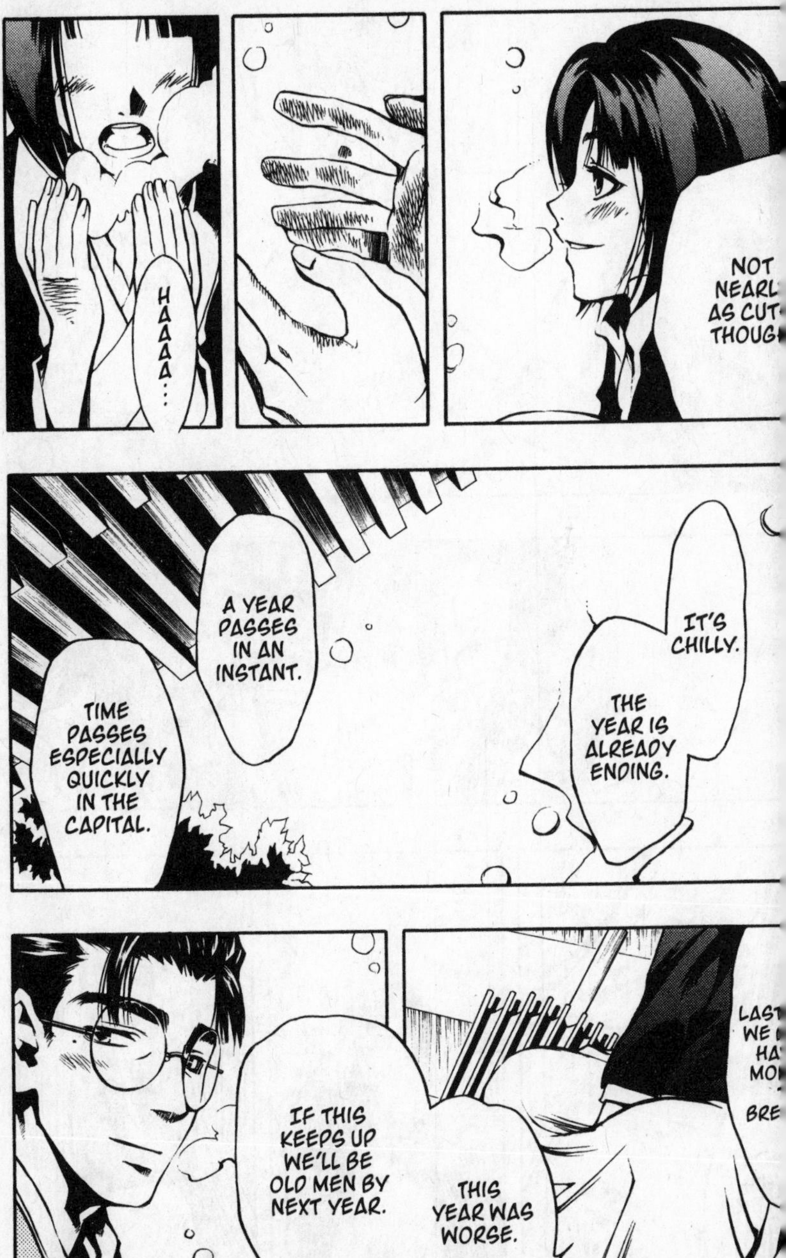
NOT NEARL AS CUT THOUG
HAAAA...
IT'S CHILLY.
THE YEAR IS ALREADY ENDING.
A YEAR PASSES IN AN INSTANT.
TIME PASSES ESPECIALLY QUICKLY IN THE CAPITAL.
LAST WE HA MO
BRE
THIS YEAR WAS WORSE.
IF THIS KEEPS UP WE'LL BE OLD MEN BY NEXT YEAR.

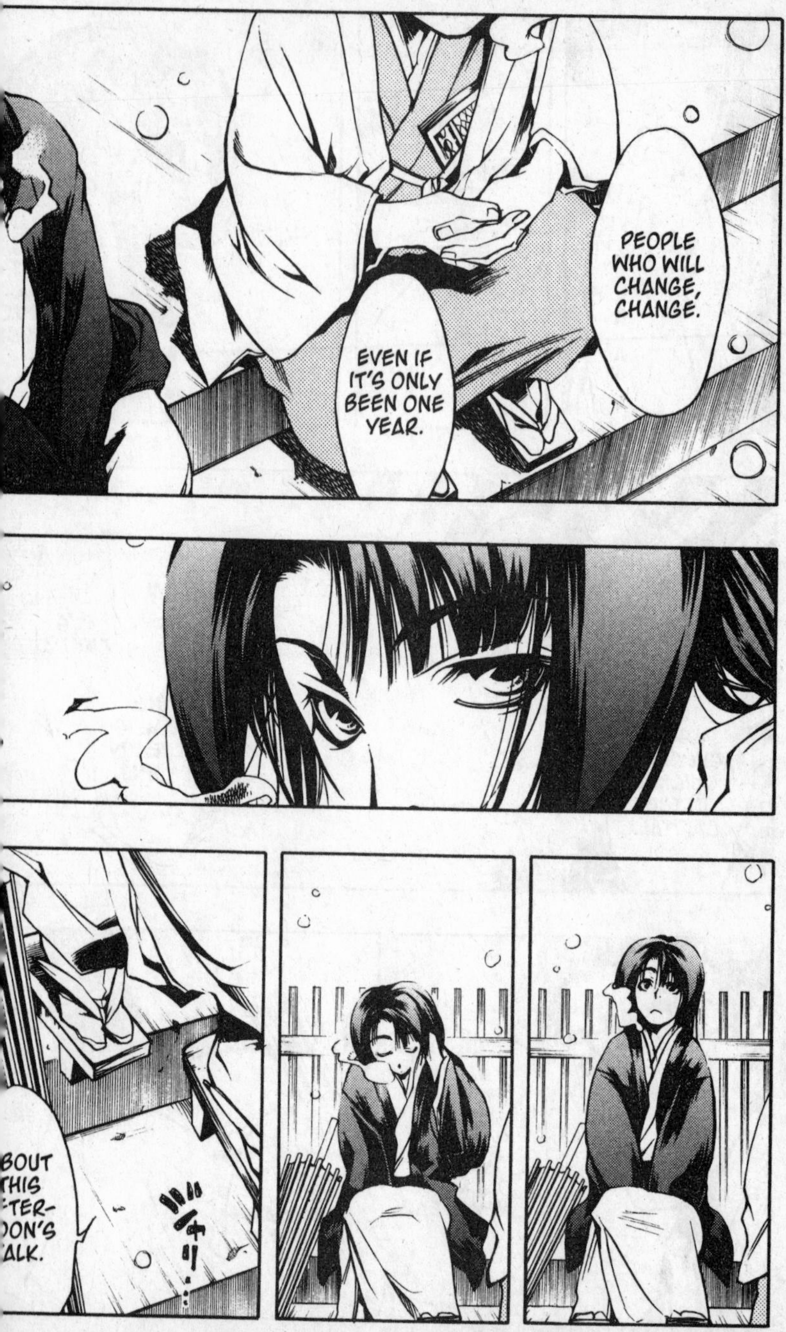
PEOPLE WHO WILL CHANGE, CHANGE.
EVEN IF IT'S ONLY BEEN ONE YEAR.
BOUT THIS TER- OON'S ALK.
ニヤリ…

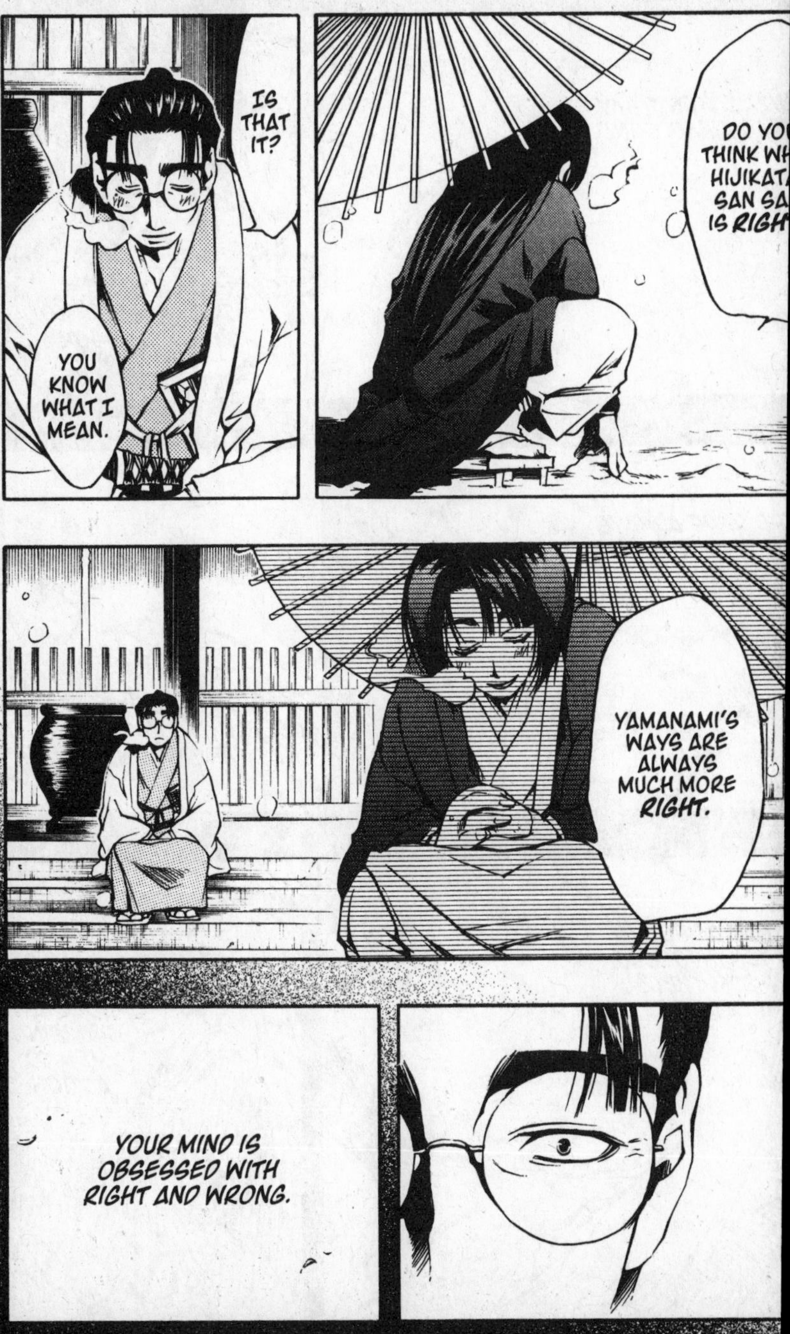
DO YO THINK WH HIJIKATA SAN SA IS RIGHT
IS THAT IT?
YOU KNOW WHAT I MEAN.
YAMANAMI'S WAYS ARE ALWAYS MUCH MORE RIGHT.
YOUR MIND IS OBSESSED WITH RIGHT AND WRONG.

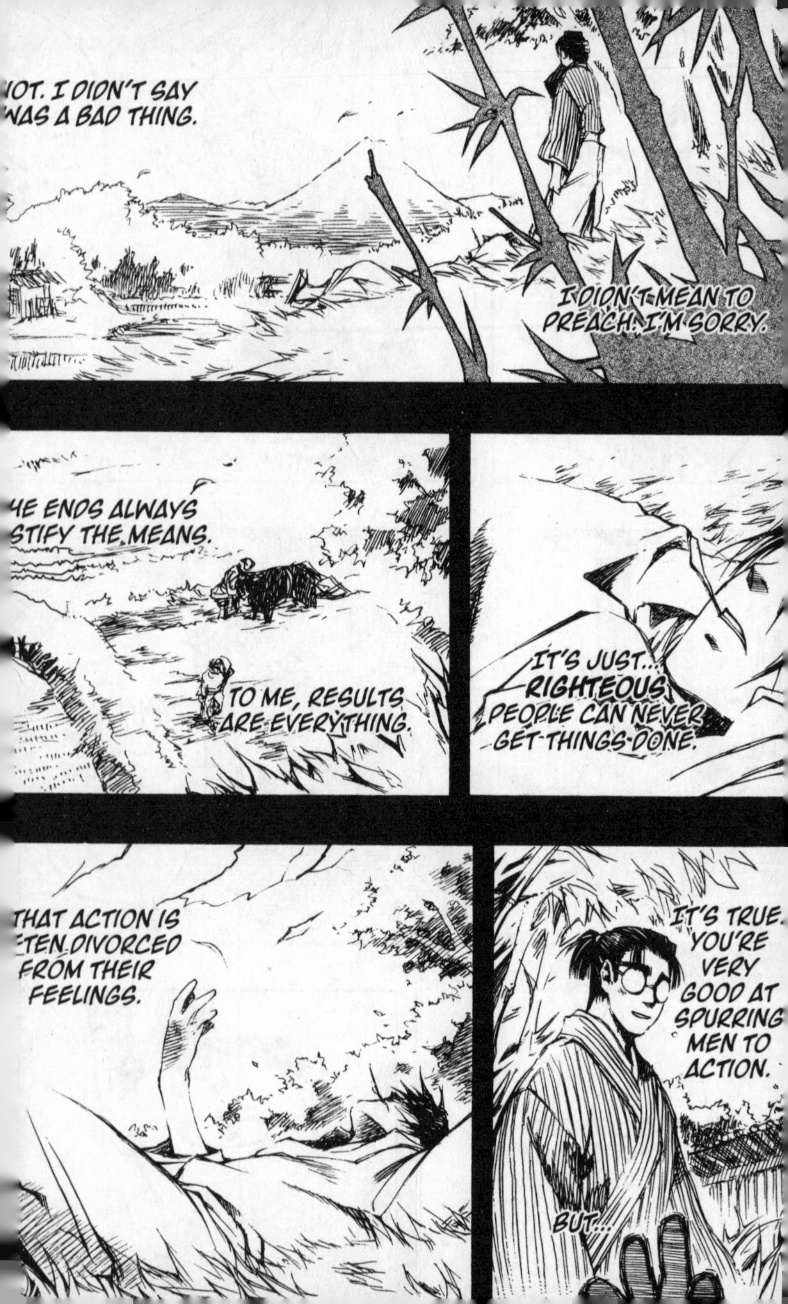
I DIDN'T MEAN TO PREACH. I'M SORRY.
OT. I DIDN'T SAY
AS A BAD THING.
IT'S JUST... RIGHTEOUS PEOPLE CAN NEVER GET THINGS DONE.
TO ME, RESULTS ARE EVERYTHING.
HE ENDS ALWAYS
STIFY THE MEANS.
IT'S TRUE. YOU'RE VERY GOOD AT SPURRING MEN TO ACTION.
BUT...
THAT ACTION IS
TEN DIVORCED FROM THEIR FEELINGS.

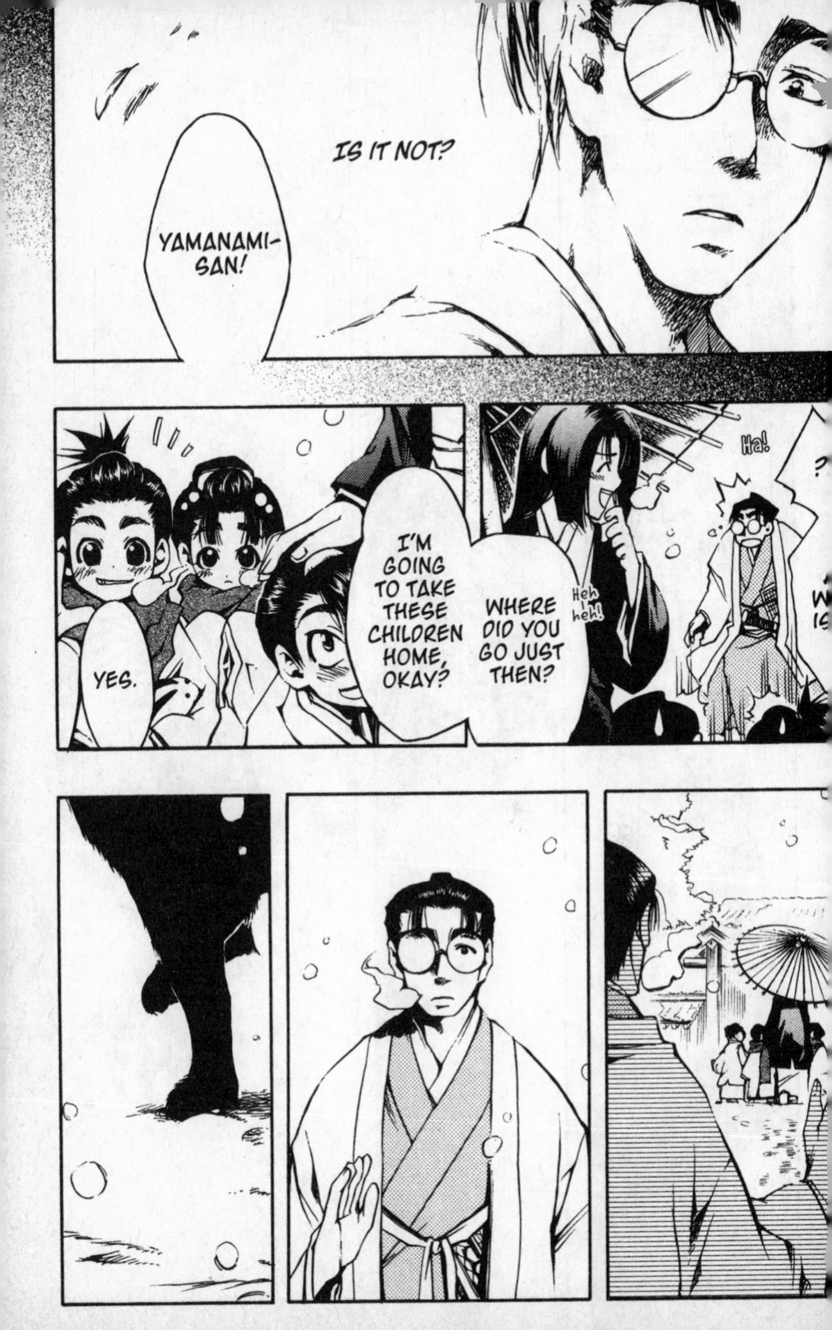
IS IT NOT?
YAMANAMI-SAN!
Ha!
?
Heh heh!
WHERE DID YOU GO JUST THEN?
I'M GOING TO TAKE THESE CHILDREN HOME, OKAY?
YES.

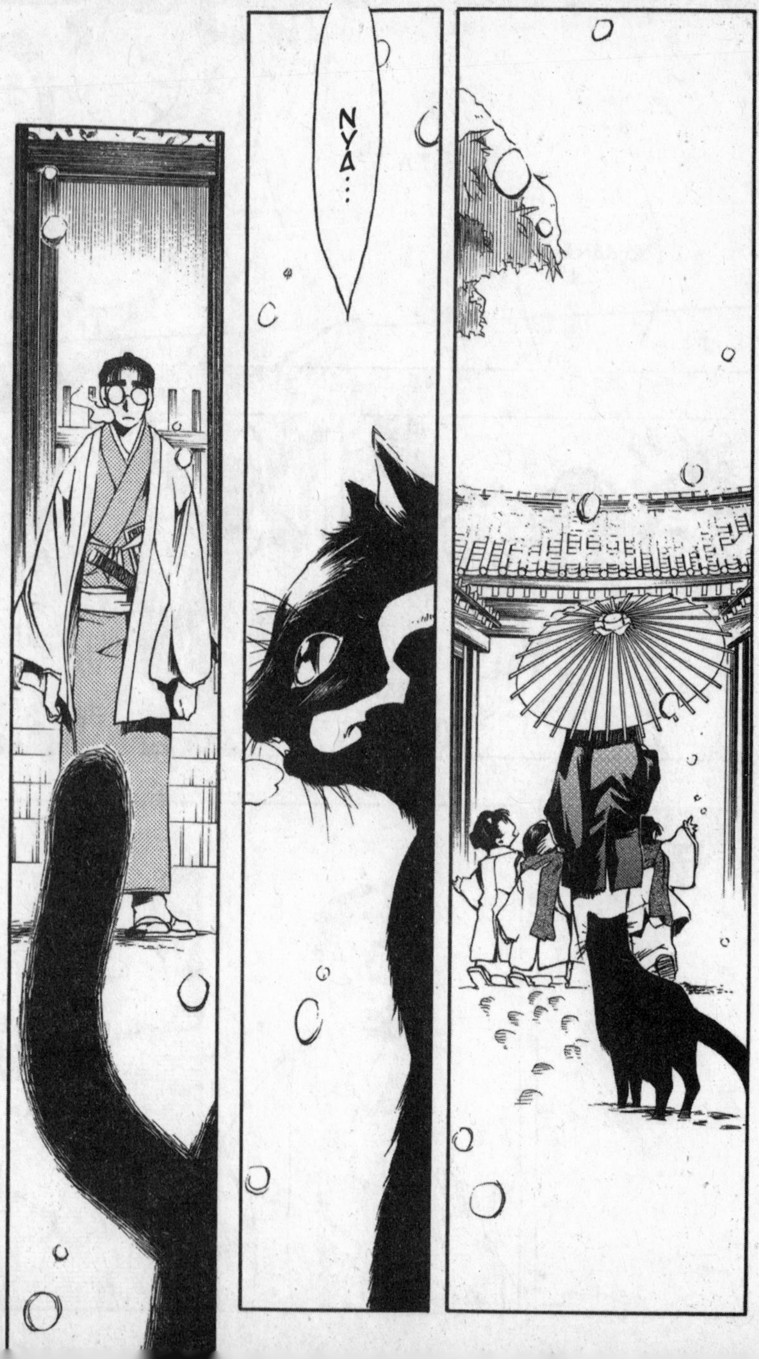
NYA...

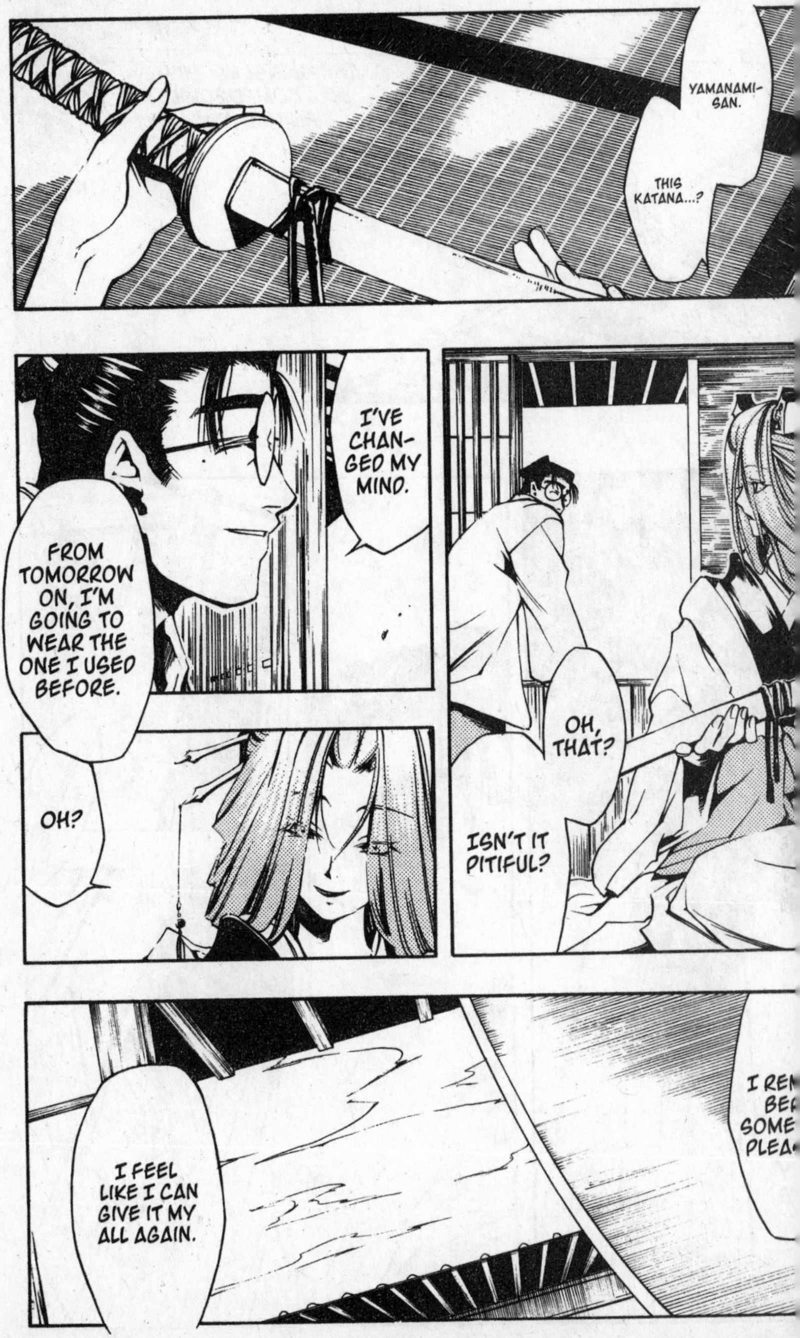
YAMANAMI-SAN.
THIS KATANA...?
OH, THAT?
ISN'T IT PITIFUL?
I'VE CHANGED MY MIND.
FROM TOMORROW ON, I'M GOING TO WEAR THE ONE I USED BEFORE.
OH?
I FEEL LIKE I CAN GIVE IT MY ALL AGAIN.

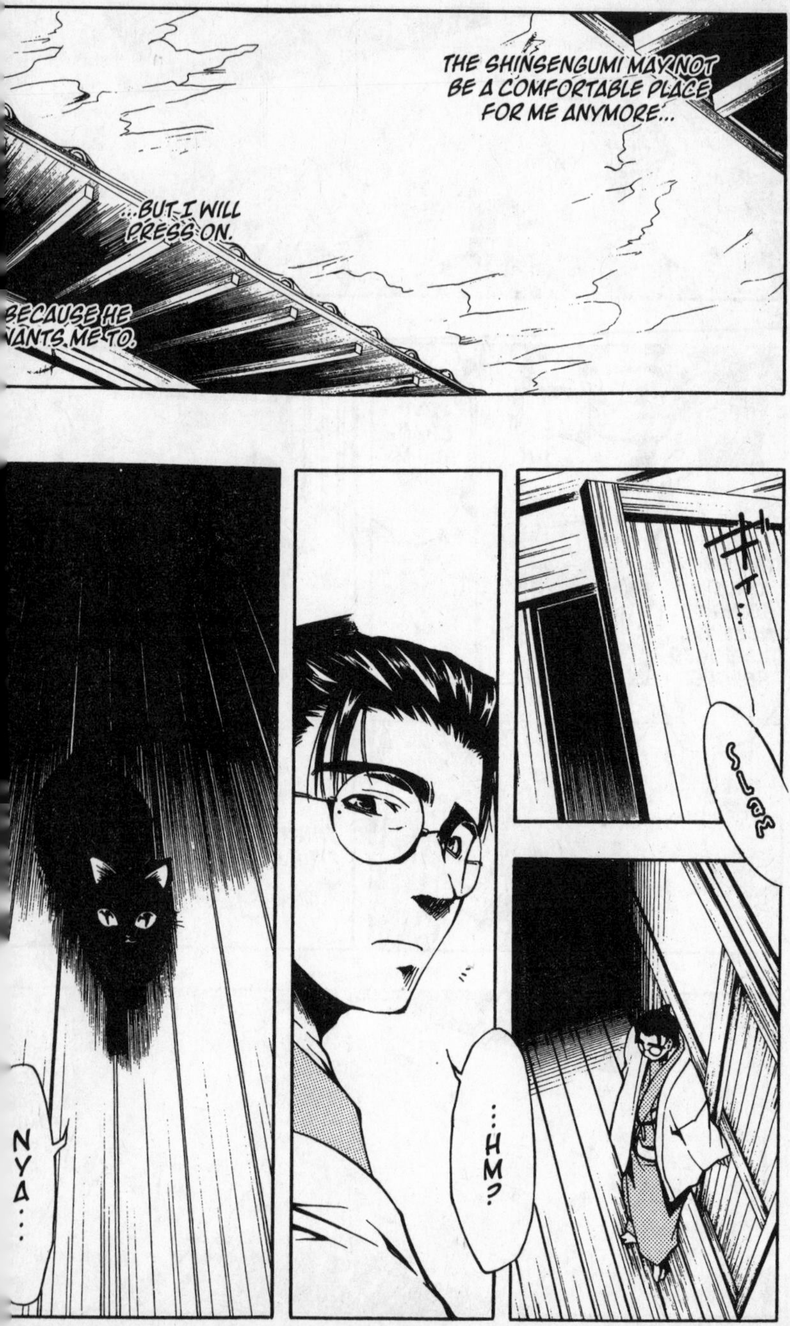
THE SHINSENGUMI MAY NOT BE A COMFORTABLE PLACE FOR ME ANYMORE...
...BUT I WILL PRESS ON.
BECAUSE HE WANTS ME TO.
SLAM
...HM?
NYA...

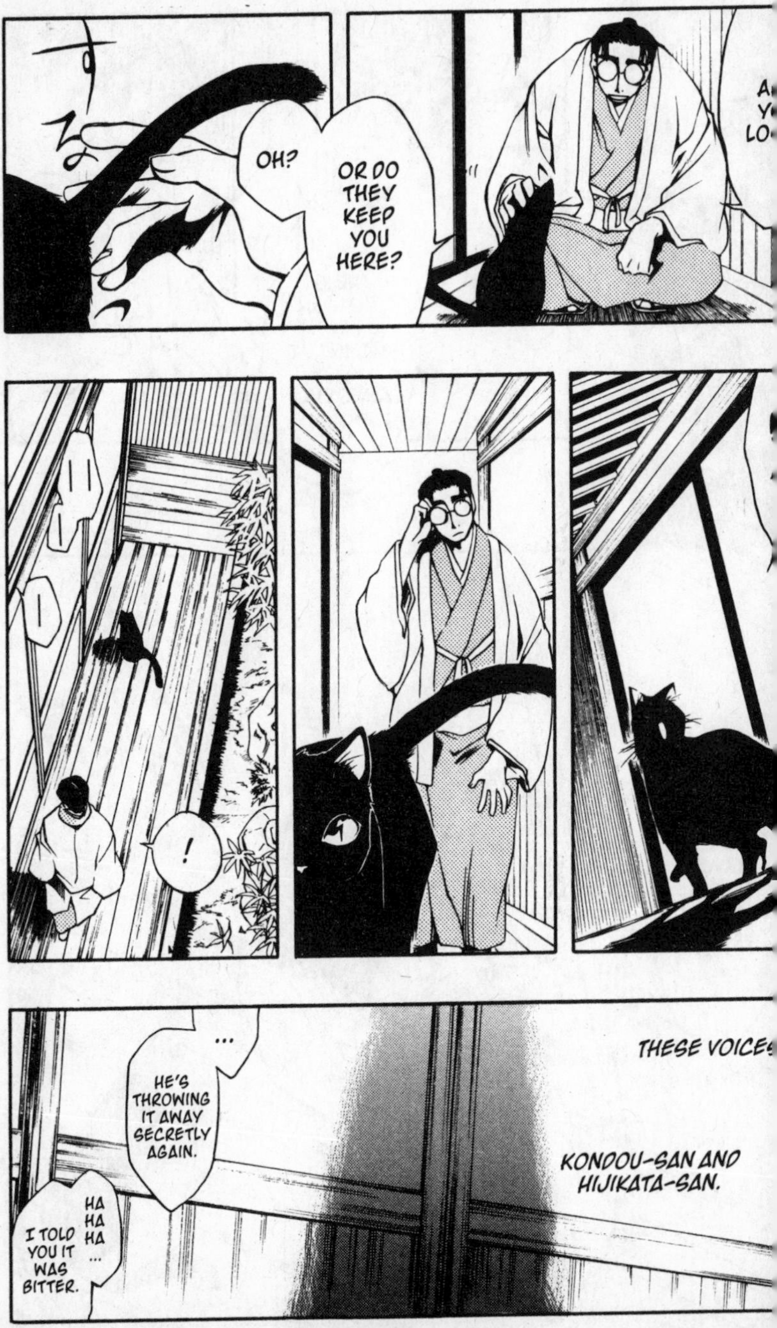

OH?
OR DO THEY KEEP YOU HERE?
!
THESE VOICES
KONDOU-SAN AND HIJIKATA-SAN.
...
HE'S THROWING IT AWAY SECRETLY AGAIN.
HA HA HA ...
I TOLD YOU IT WAS BITTER.

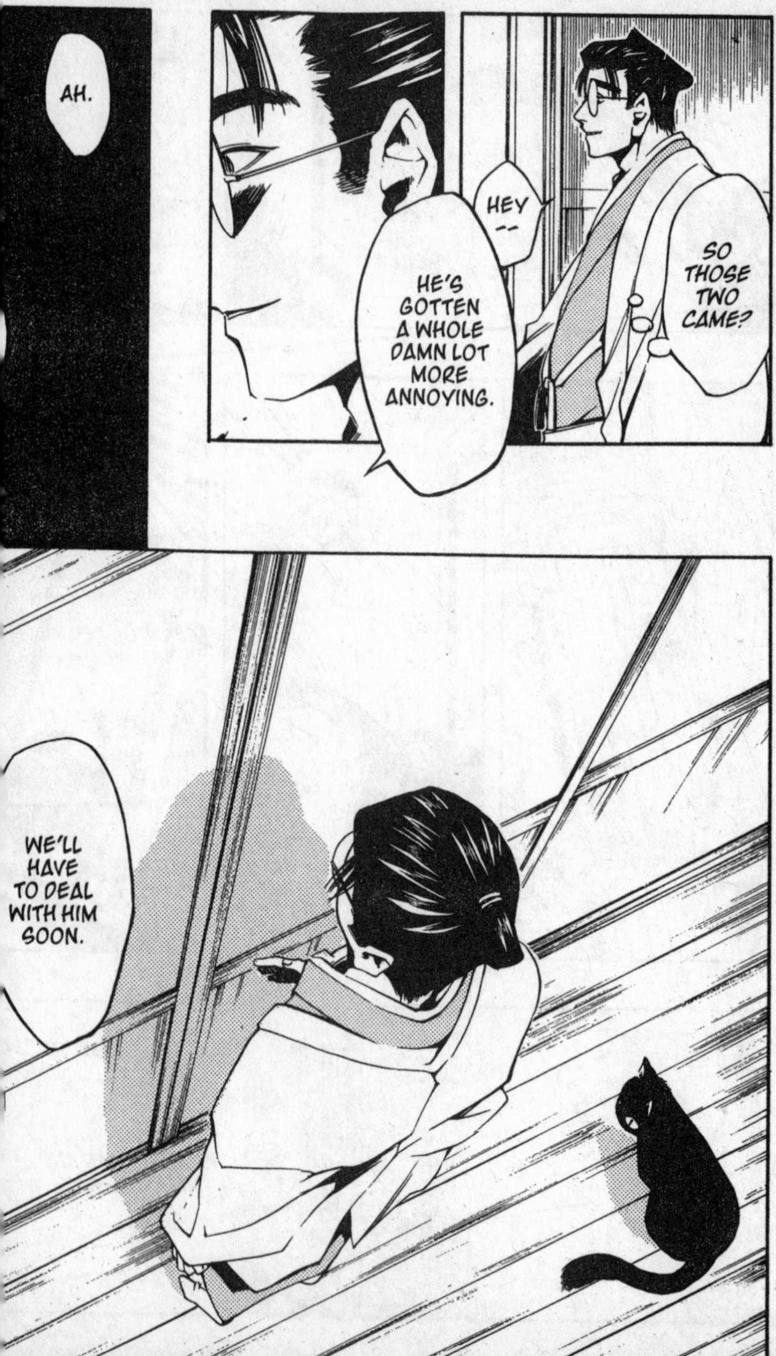
SO THOSE TWO CAME?
HEY --
HE'S GOTTEN A WHOLE DAMN LOT MORE ANNOYING.
AH.
WE'LL HAVE TO DEAL WITH HIM SOON.

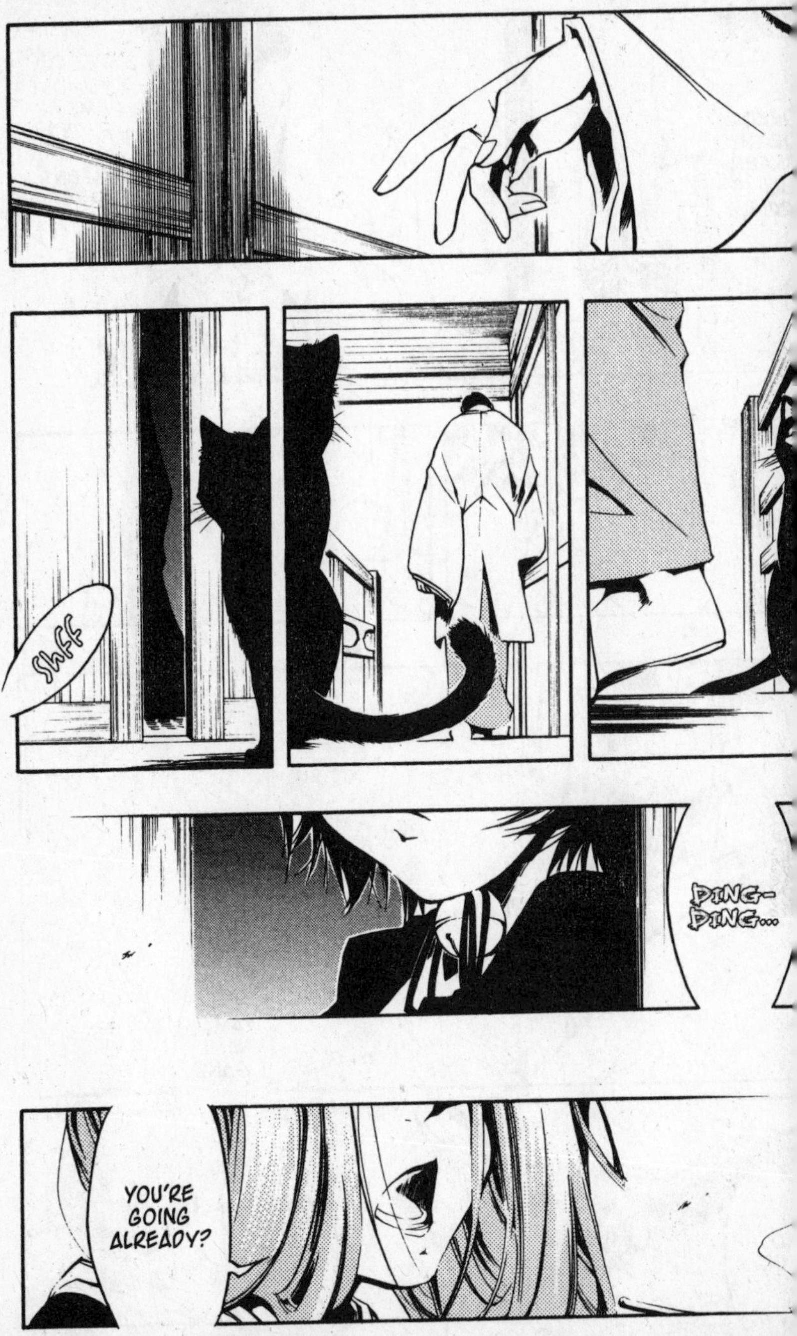
Shff
DING-DING...
YOU'RE GOING ALREADY?

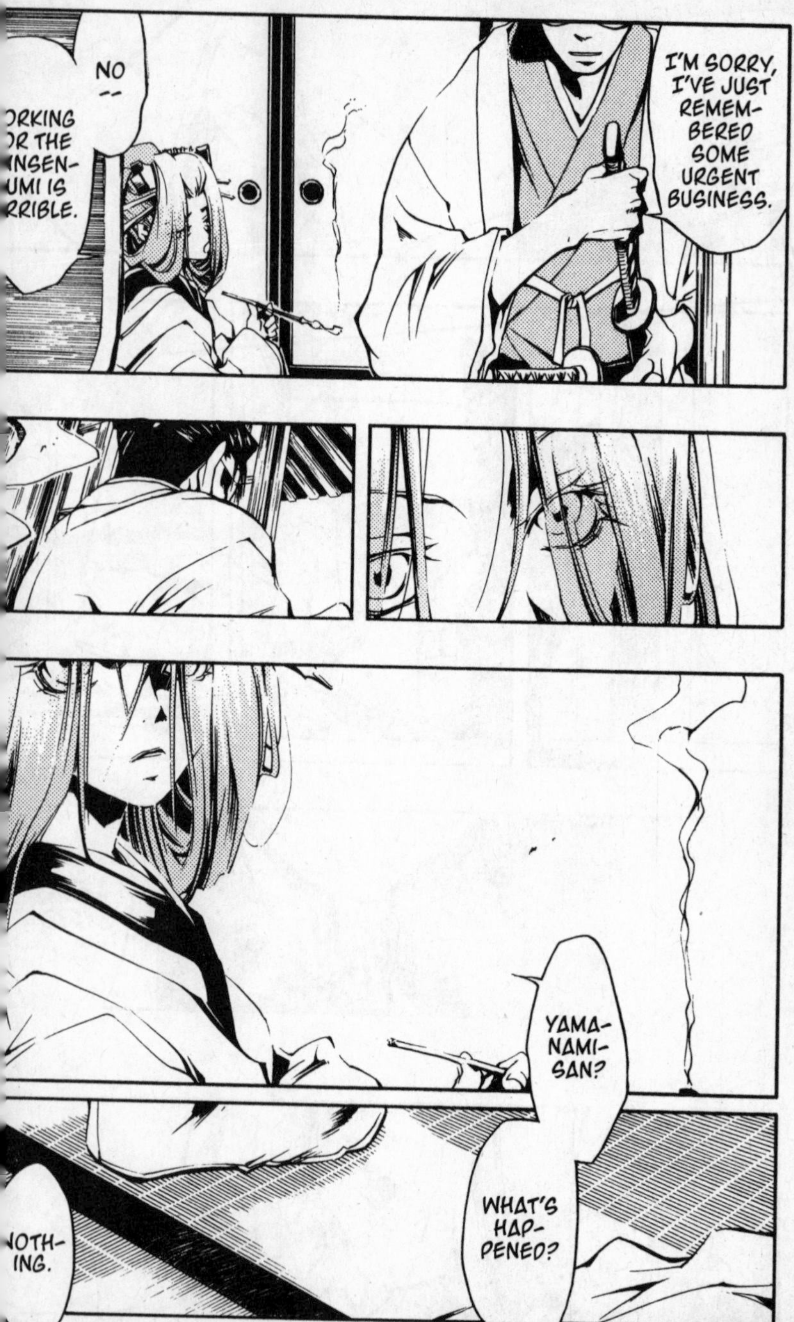
I'M SORRY, I'VE JUST REMEM-BERED SOME URGENT BUSINESS.
NO --
ORKING OR THE INSEN-UMI IS RRIBLE.
YAMA-NAMI-SAN?
WHAT'S HAP-PENED?
NOTH-ING.

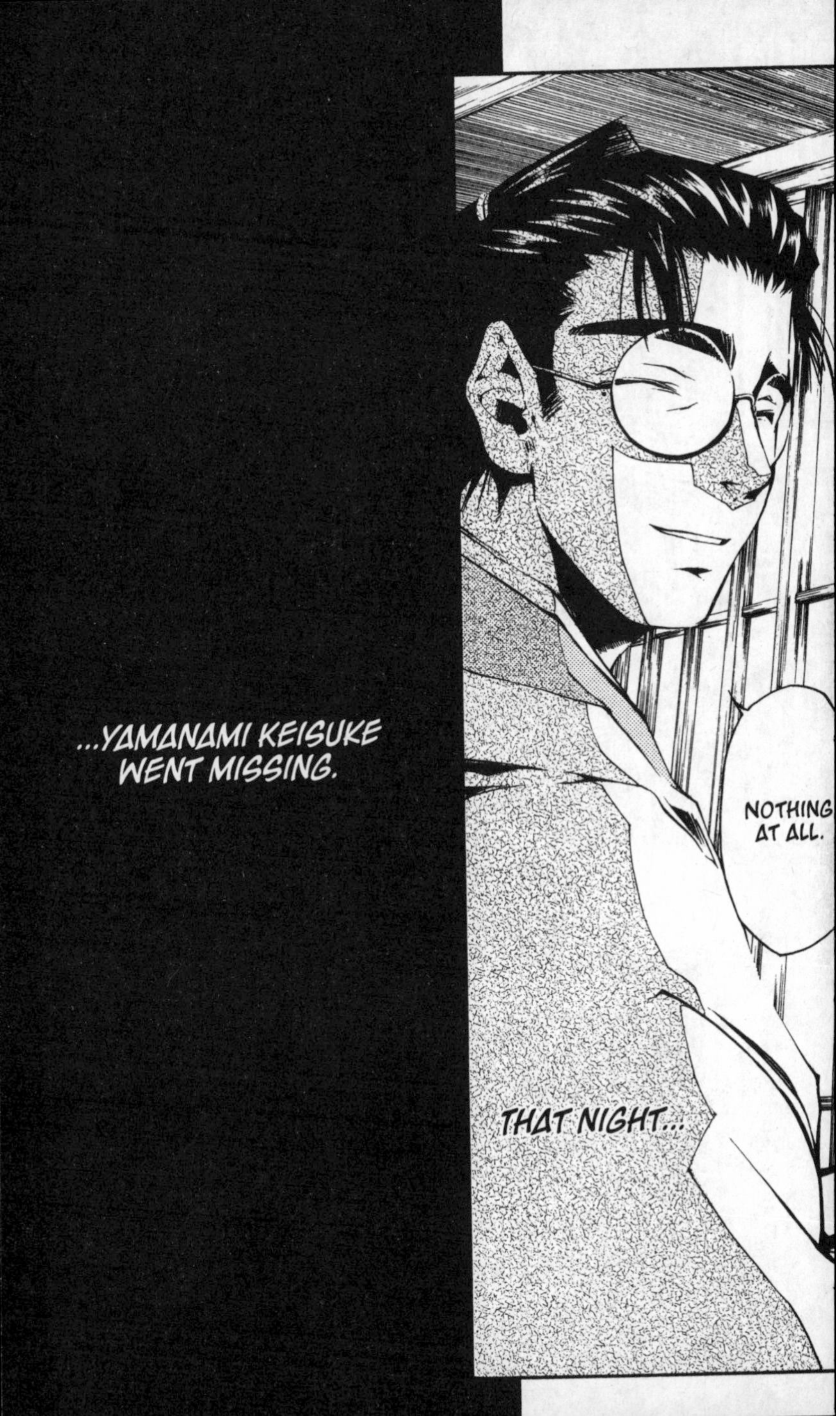
NOTHING AT ALL.
THAT NIGHT...
...YAMANAMI KEISUKE WENT MISSING.

第九話
Act.9
Voices
だいきゅうわ
こえ

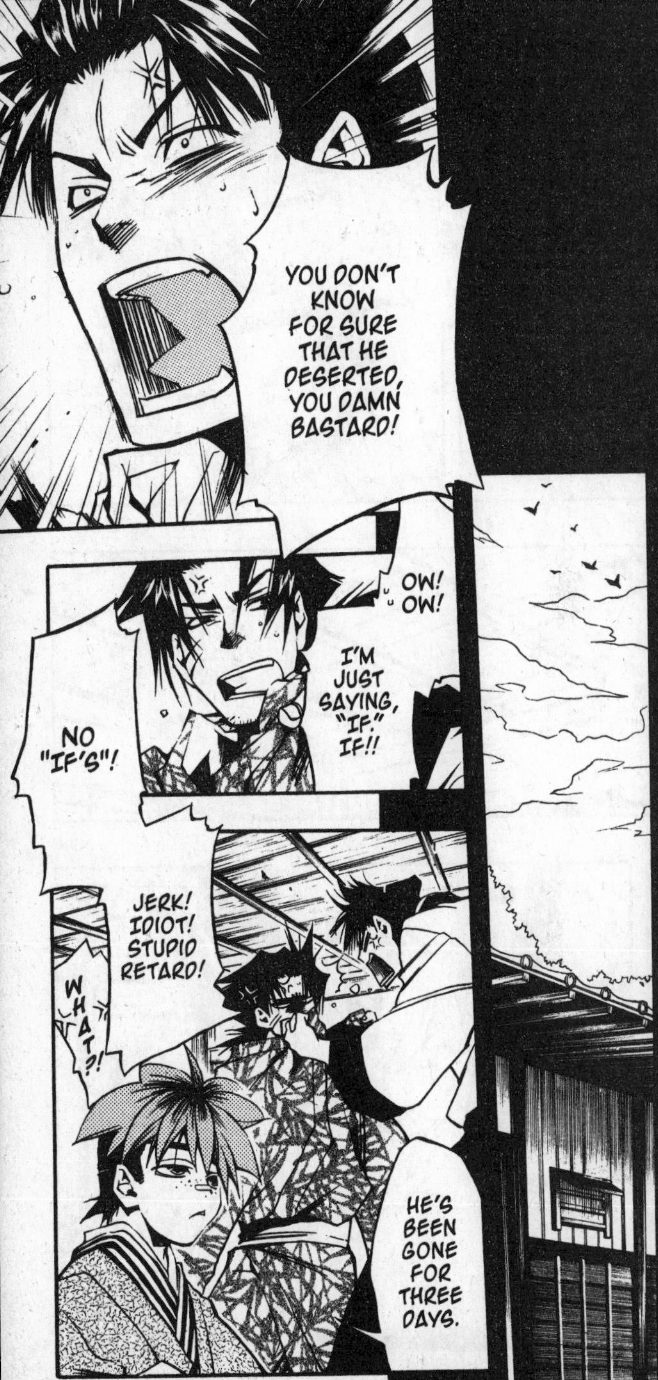
YOU DON'T KNOW FOR SURE THAT HE DESERTED, YOU DAMN BASTARD!
OW! OW!
I'M JUST SAYING, "IF." IF!!
NO "IF'S"!
JERK! IDIOT! STUPID RETARD!
WHAT?!
HE'S BEEN GONE FOR THREE DAYS.

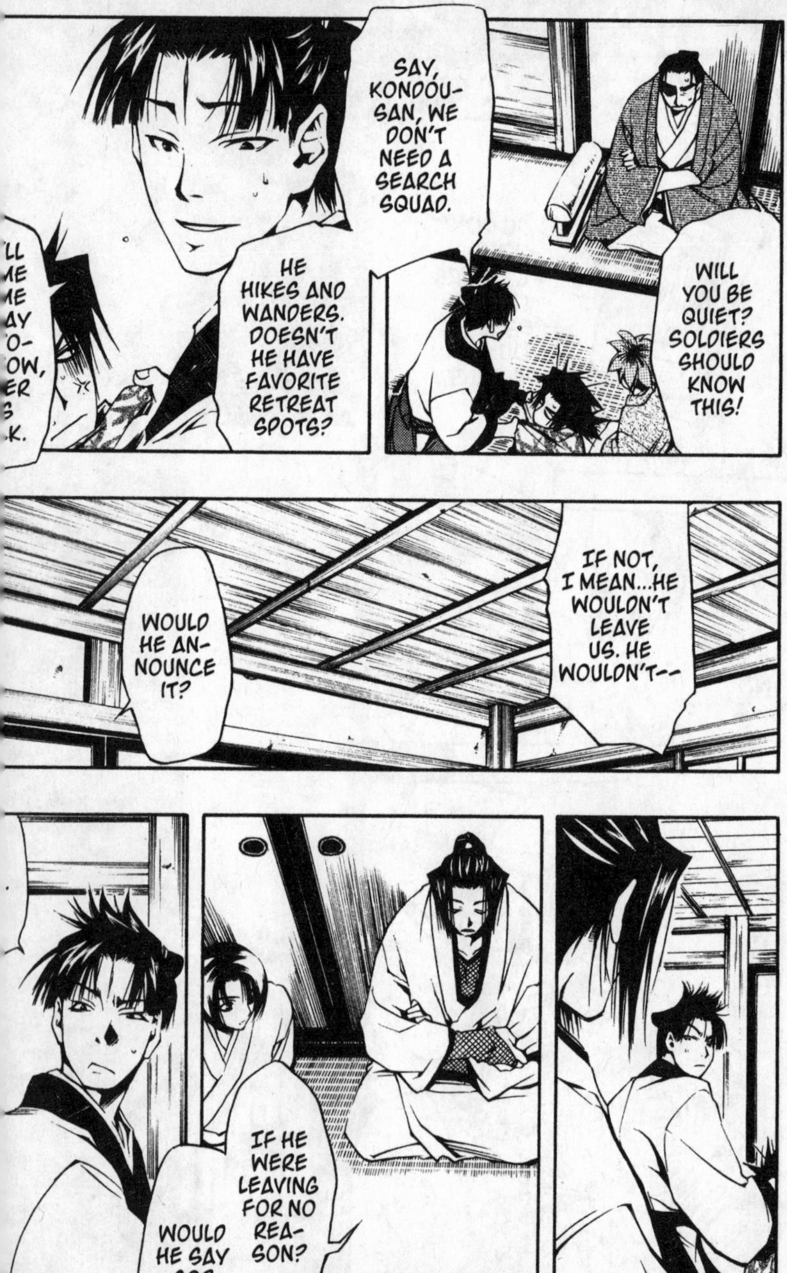
SAY, KONDOU-SAN, WE DON'T NEED A SEARCH SQUAD.
HE HIKES AND WANDERS. DOESN'T HE HAVE FAVORITE RETREAT SPOTS?
WILL YOU BE QUIET? SOLDIERS SHOULD KNOW THIS!
IF NOT, I MEAN...HE WOULDN'T LEAVE US. HE WOULDN'T--
WOULD HE ANNOUNCE IT?
IF HE WERE LEAVING FOR NO REASON?
WOULD HE SAY SO?

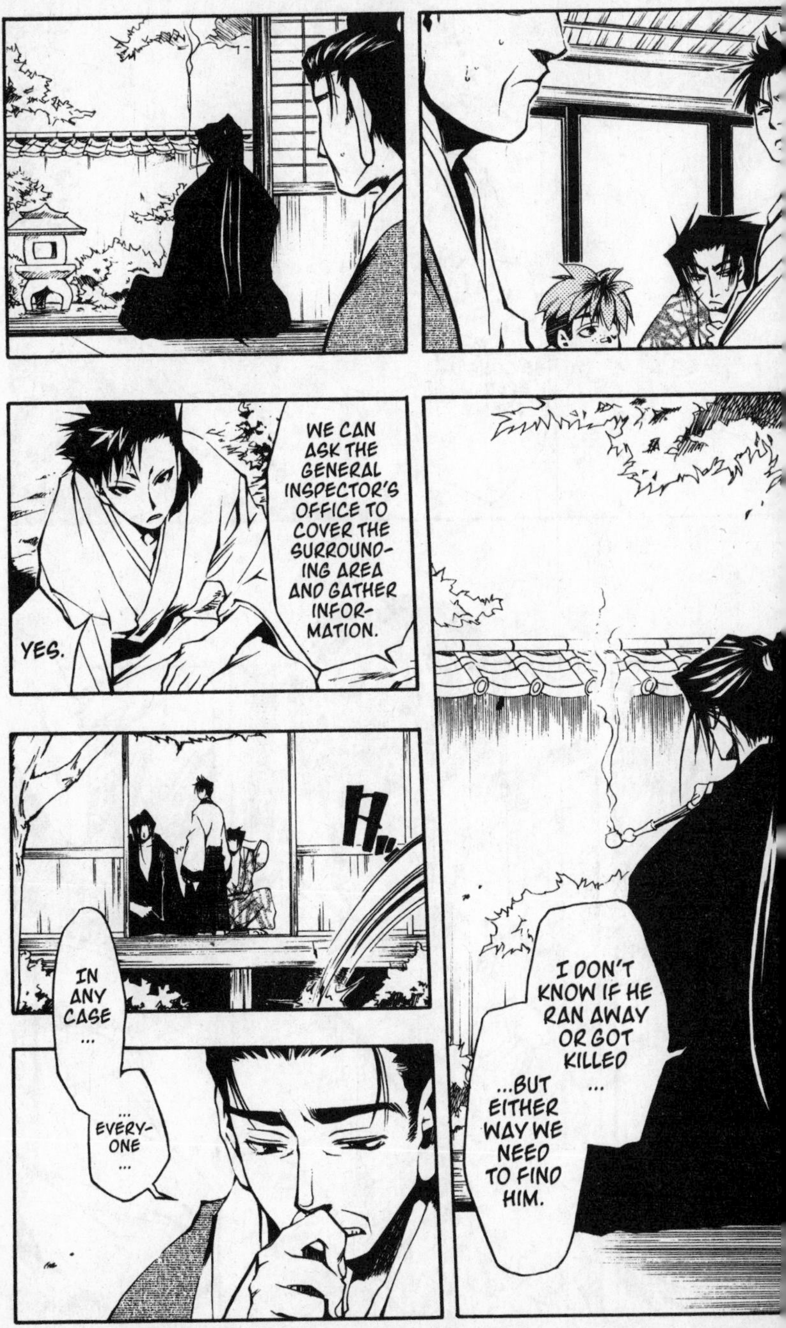
I DON'T KNOW IF HE RAN AWAY OR GOT KILLED ...
...BUT EITHER WAY WE NEED TO FIND HIM.
WE CAN ASK THE GENERAL INSPECTOR'S OFFICE TO COVER THE SURROUNDING AREA AND GATHER INFORMATION.
YES.
IN ANY CASE ...
... EVERYONE ...

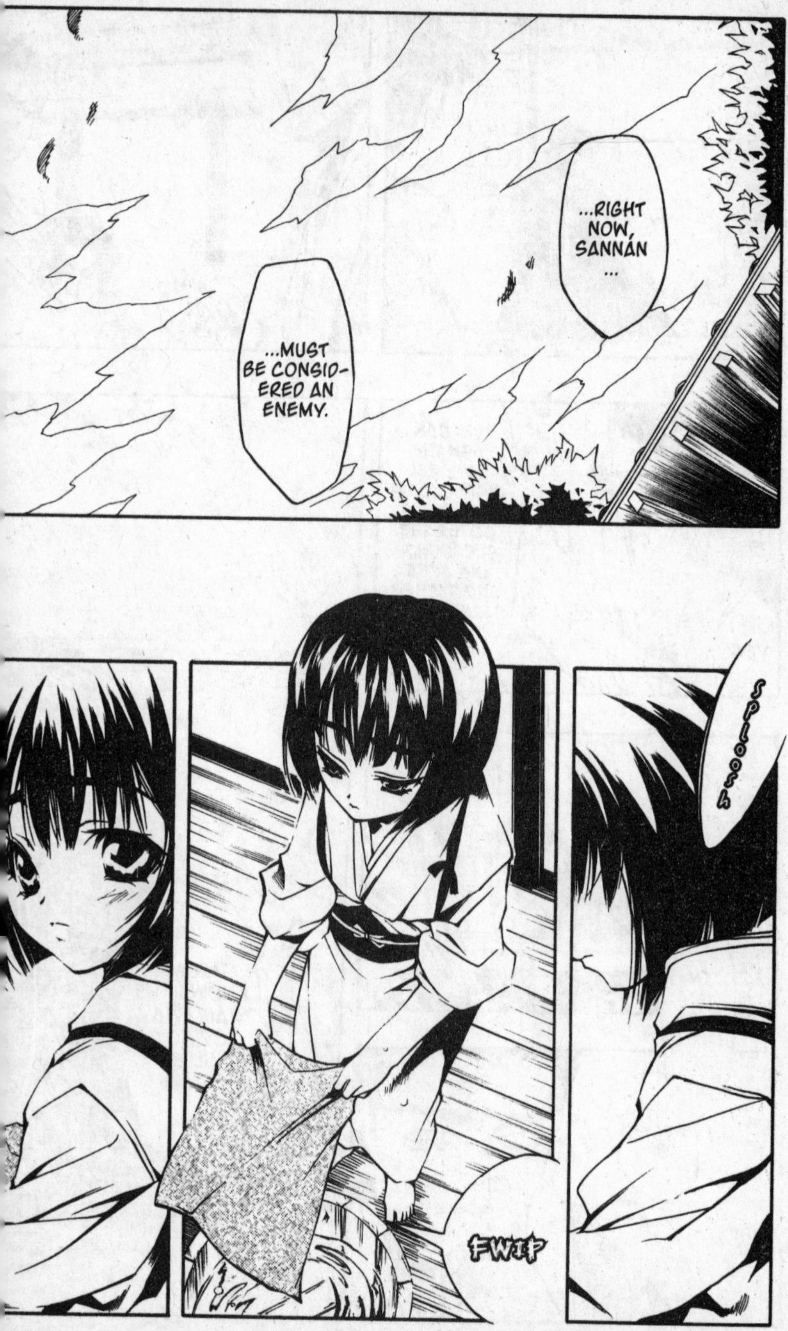
...RIGHT NOW, SANNAN ...
...MUST BE CONSIDERED AN ENEMY.
SPLOOSH
FWIP

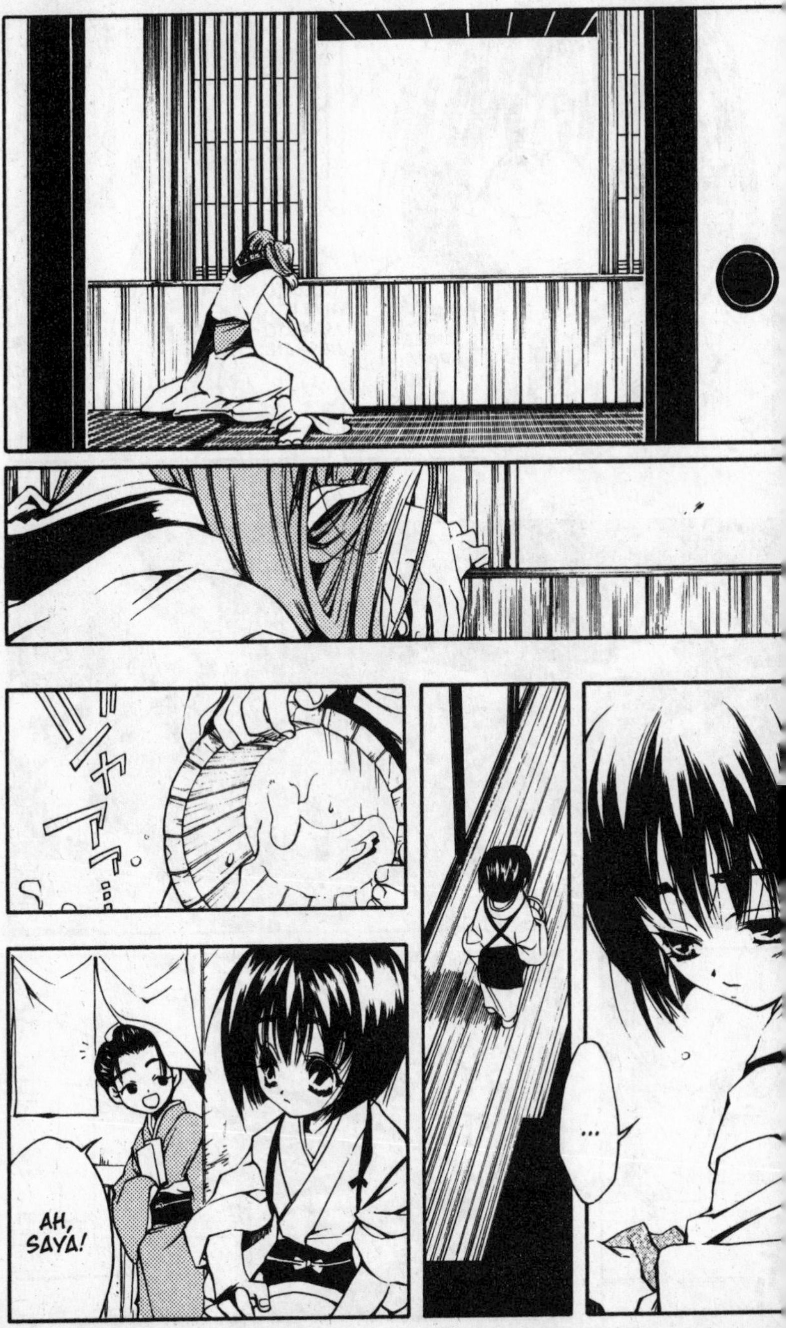
...
ジャアア…
AH, SAYA!

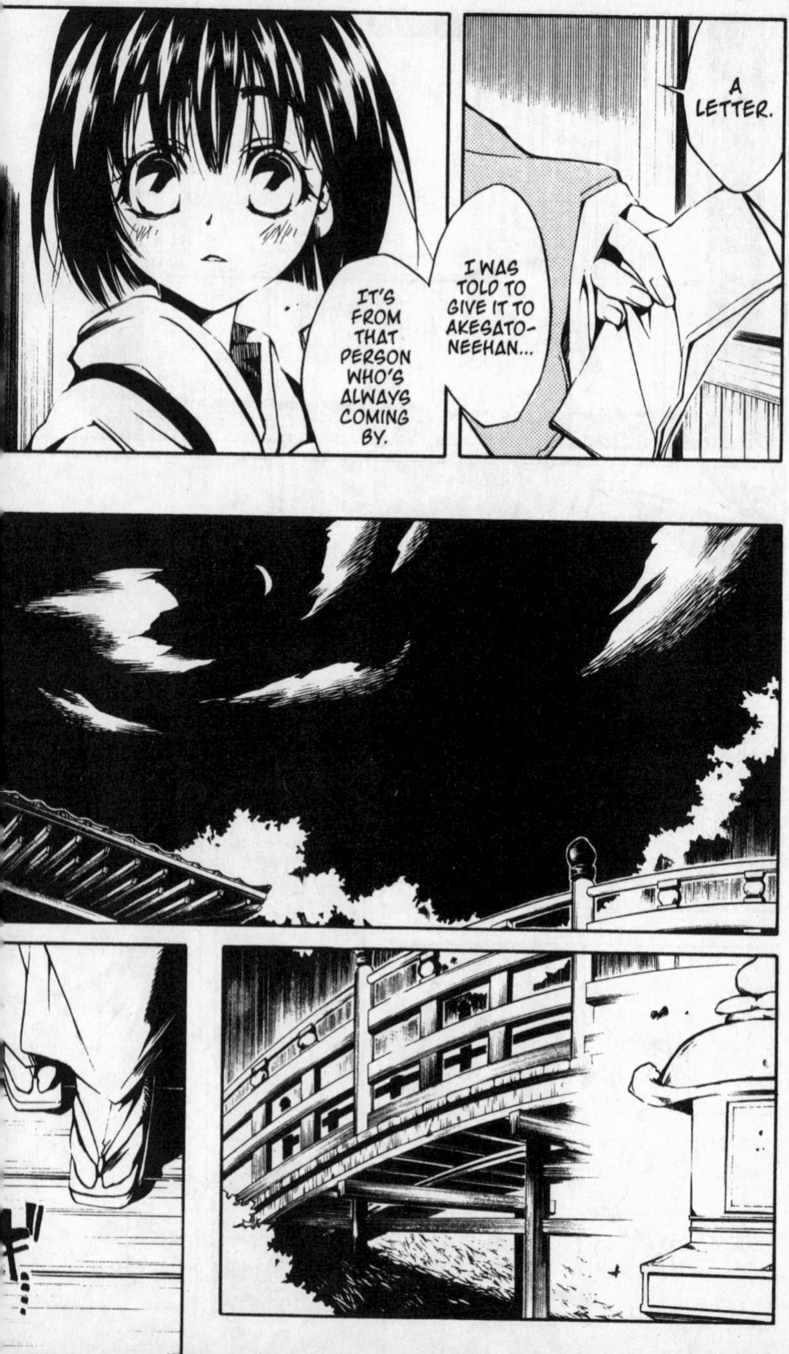
A LETTER.
I WAS TOLD TO GIVE IT TO AKESATO-NEEHAN...
IT'S FROM THAT PERSON WHO'S ALWAYS COMING BY.

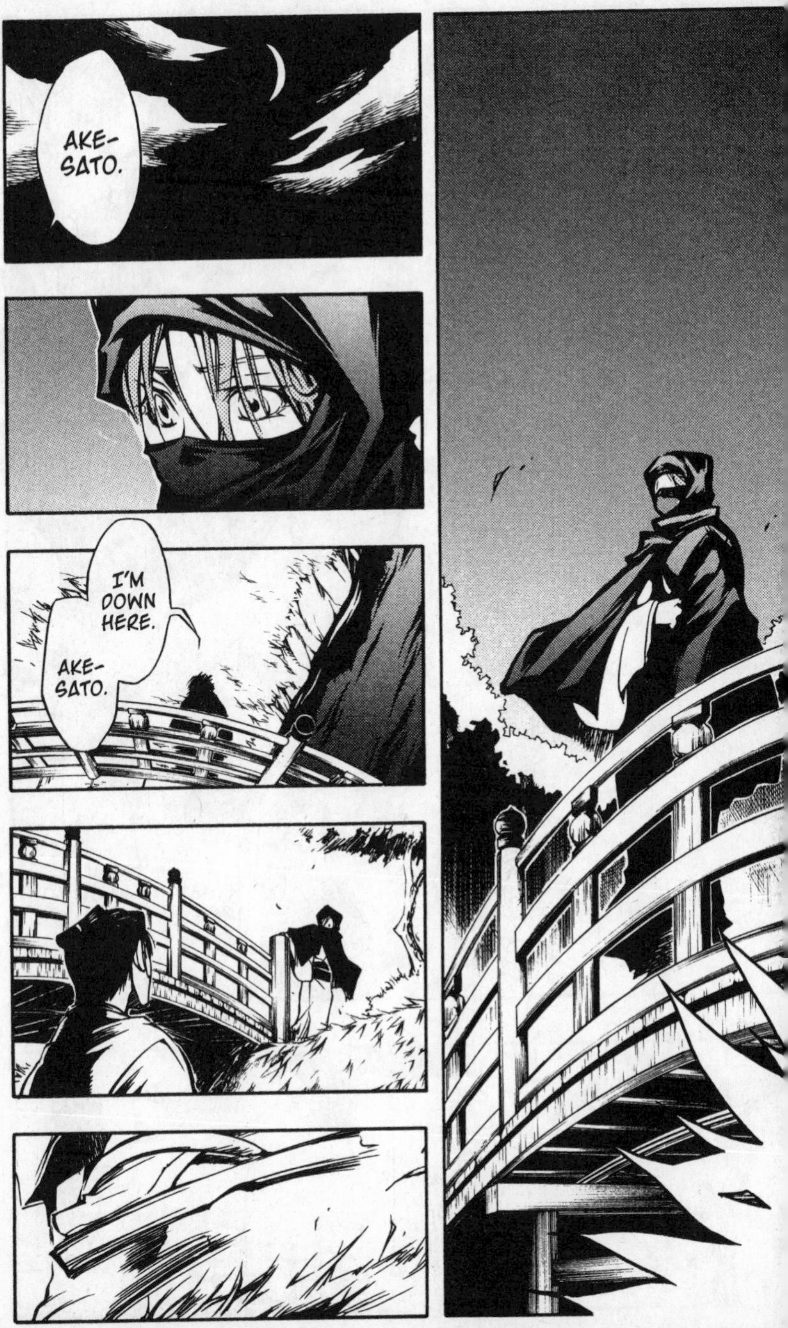
AKE-SATO.
I'M DOWN HERE. AKE-SATO.

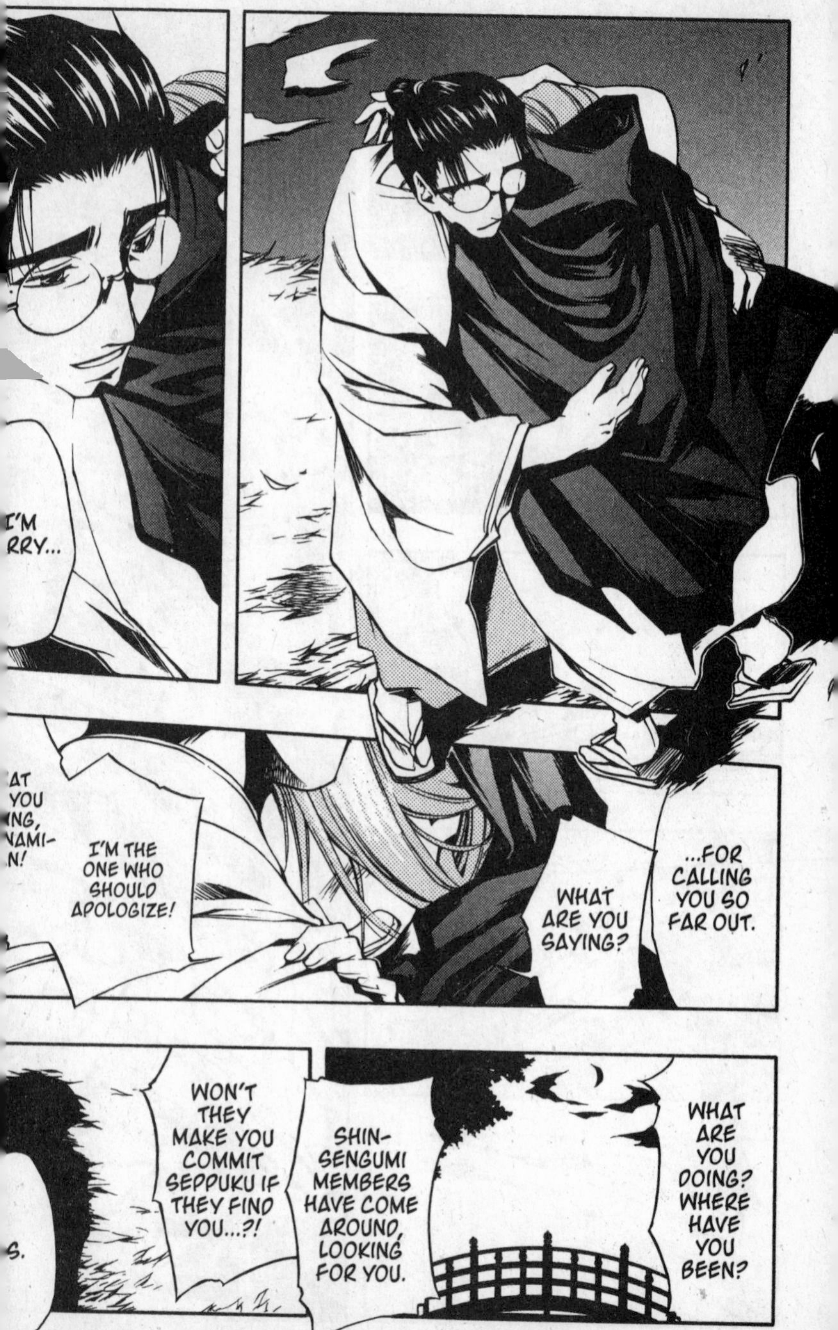
...FOR CALLING YOU SO FAR OUT.
WHAT ARE YOU SAYING?
I'M THE ONE WHO SHOULD APOLOGIZE!
WHAT ARE YOU DOING? WHERE HAVE YOU BEEN?
SHIN-SENGUMI MEMBERS HAVE COME AROUND, LOOKING FOR YOU.
WON'T THEY MAKE YOU COMMIT SEPPUKU IF THEY FIND YOU...?!

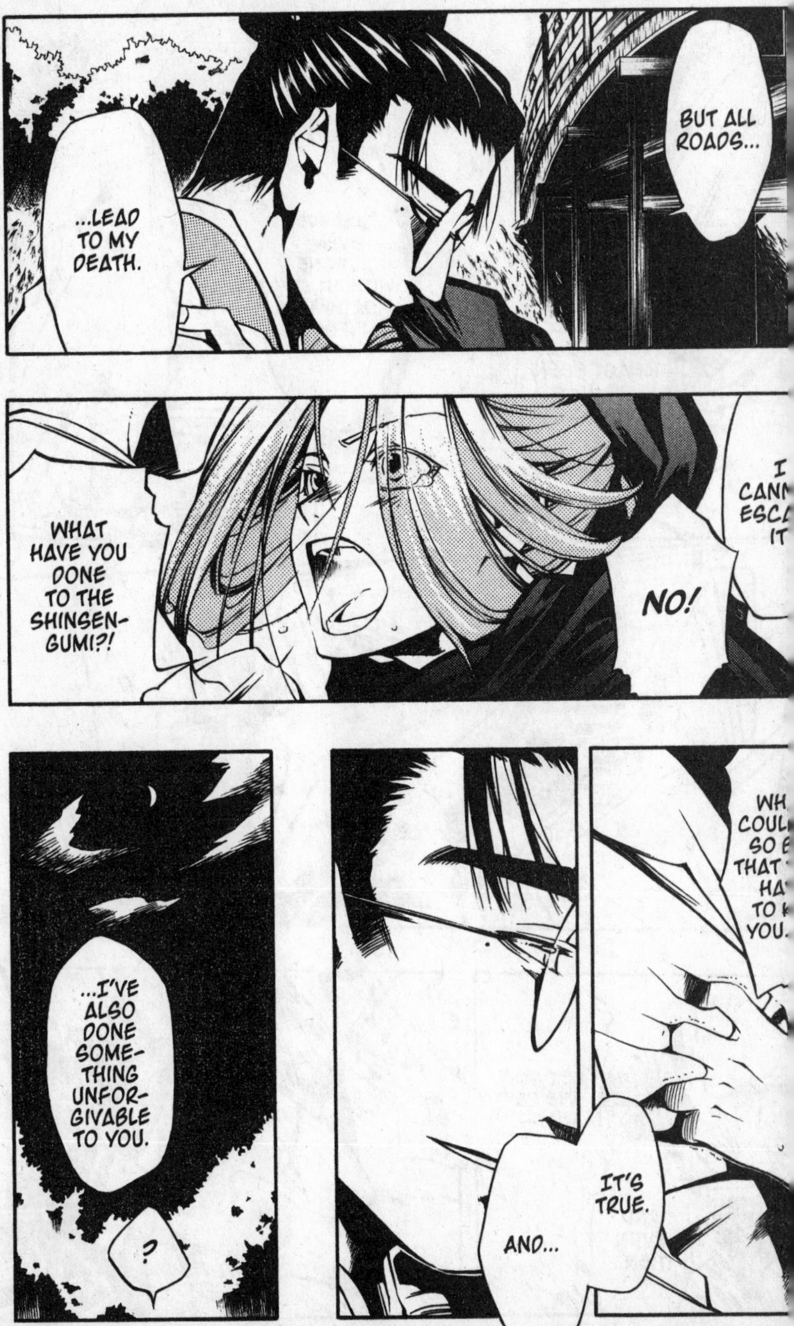
BUT ALL ROADS...
...LEAD TO MY DEATH.
I CANN ESCA IT
NO!
WHAT HAVE YOU DONE TO THE SHINSEN-GUMI?!
WH COUL SO E THAT HA TO K YOU.
IT'S TRUE.
AND...
...I'VE ALSO DONE SOME-THING UNFOR-GIVABLE TO YOU.
?

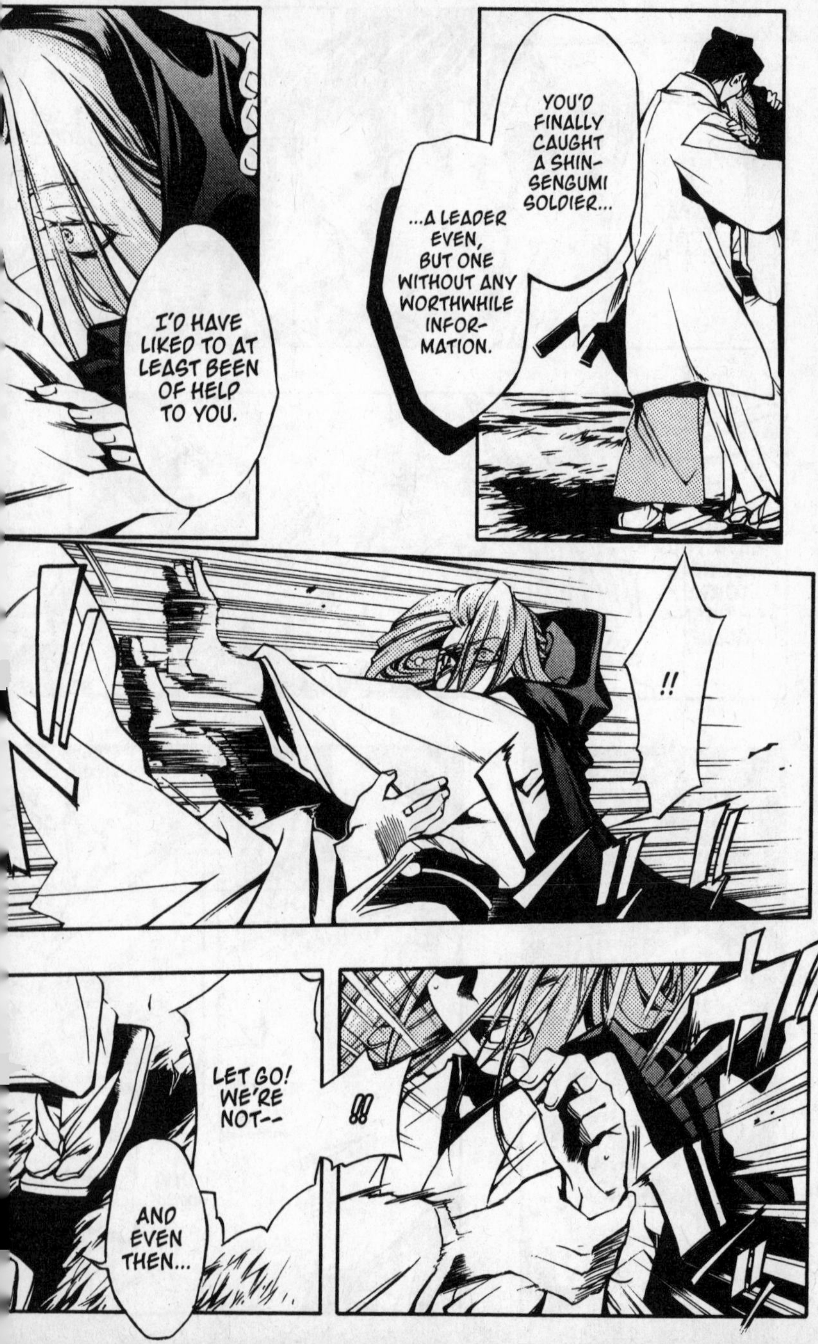
YOU'D FINALLY CAUGHT A SHIN-SENGUMI SOLDIER...
...A LEADER EVEN, BUT ONE WITHOUT ANY WORTHWHILE INFORMATION.
I'D HAVE LIKED TO AT LEAST BEEN OF HELP TO YOU.
!!
!!
LET GO! WE'RE NOT--
AND EVEN THEN...

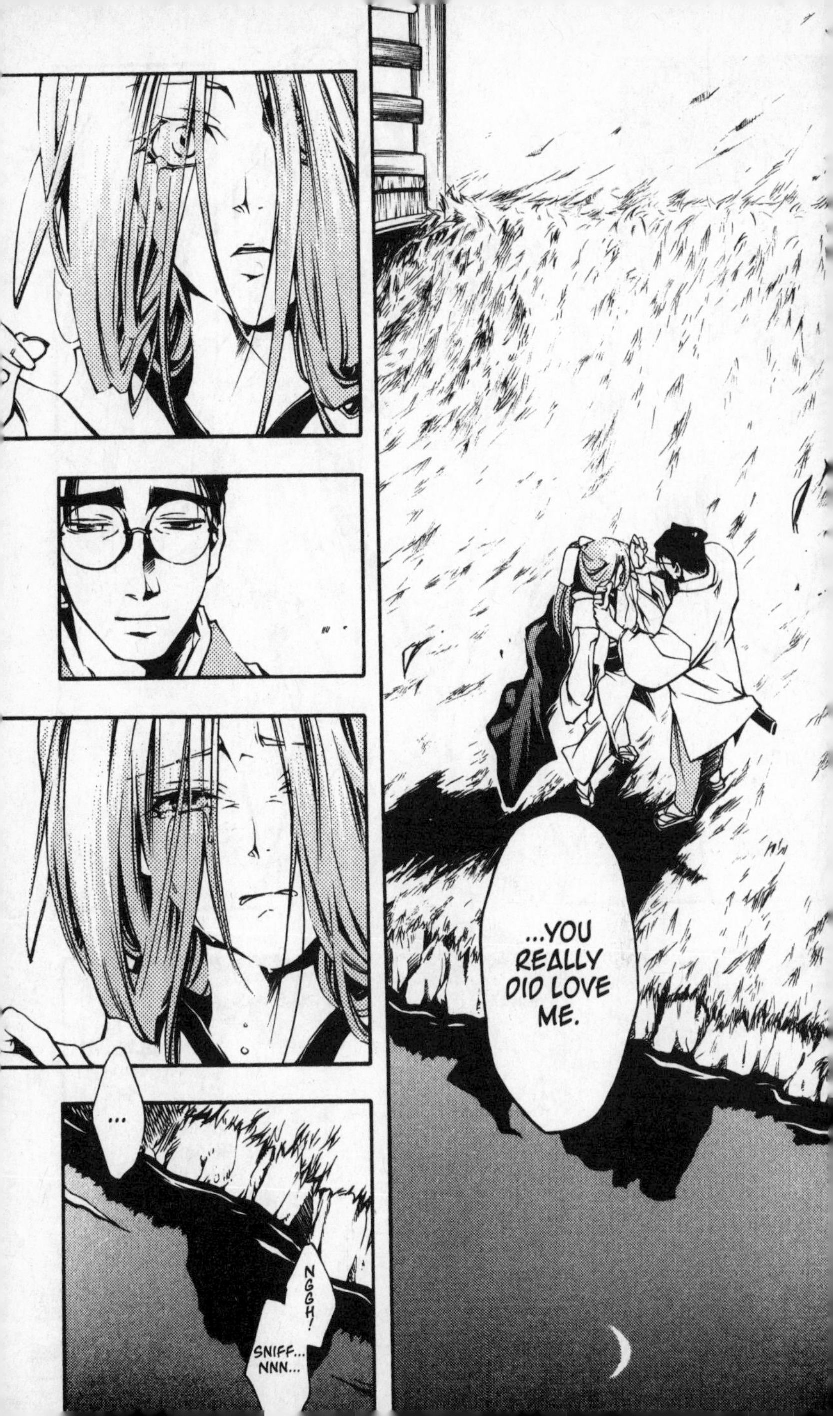
...YOU REALLY DID LOVE ME.
...
NGGH!
SNIFF... NNN...

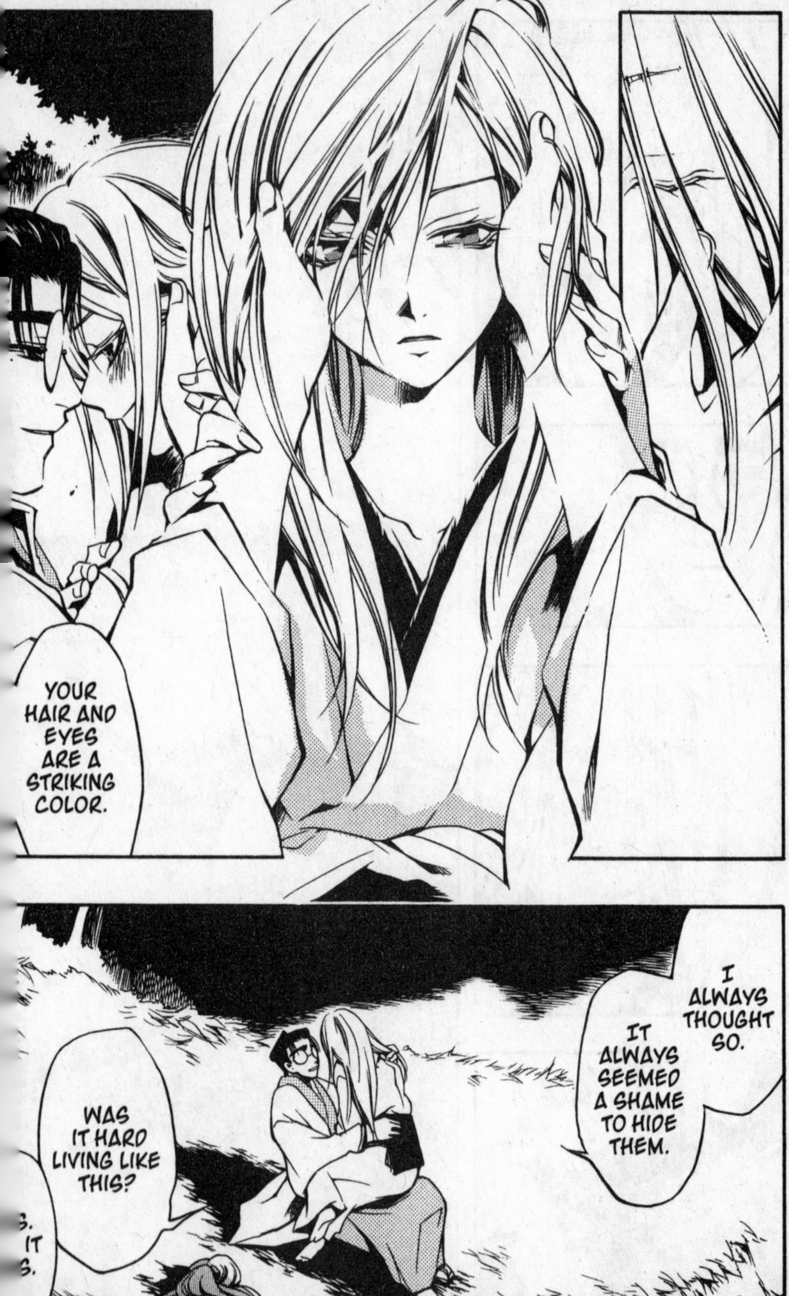
YOUR HAIR AND EYES ARE A STRIKING COLOR.
I ALWAYS THOUGHT SO.
IT ALWAYS SEEMED A SHAME TO HIDE THEM.
WAS IT HARD LIVING LIKE THIS?

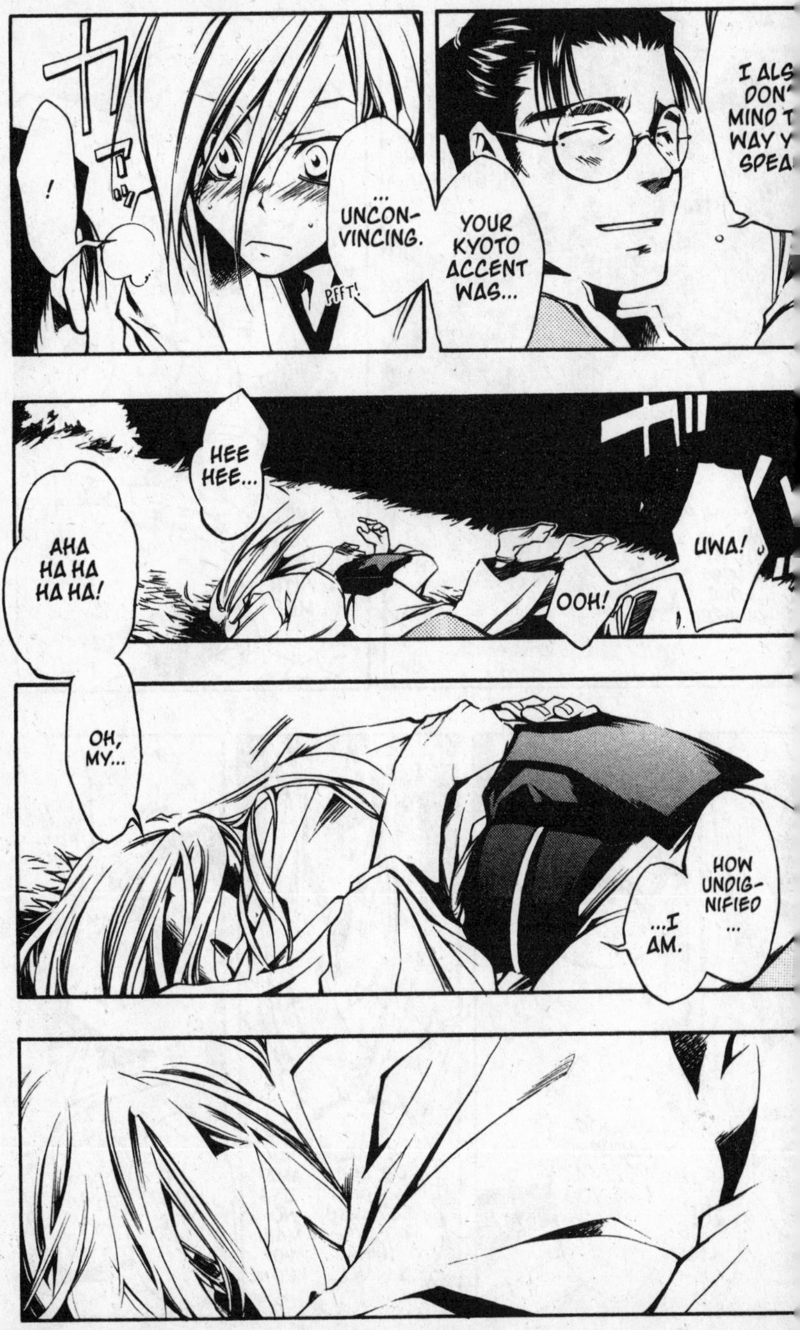
I ALS DON' MIND T WAY Y SPEA
YOUR KYOTO ACCENT WAS...
...UNCONVINCING.
PFFT!
!
UWA!
OOH!
HEE HEE...
AHA HA HA HA HA!
HOW UNDIGNIFIED...
...I AM.
OH, MY...

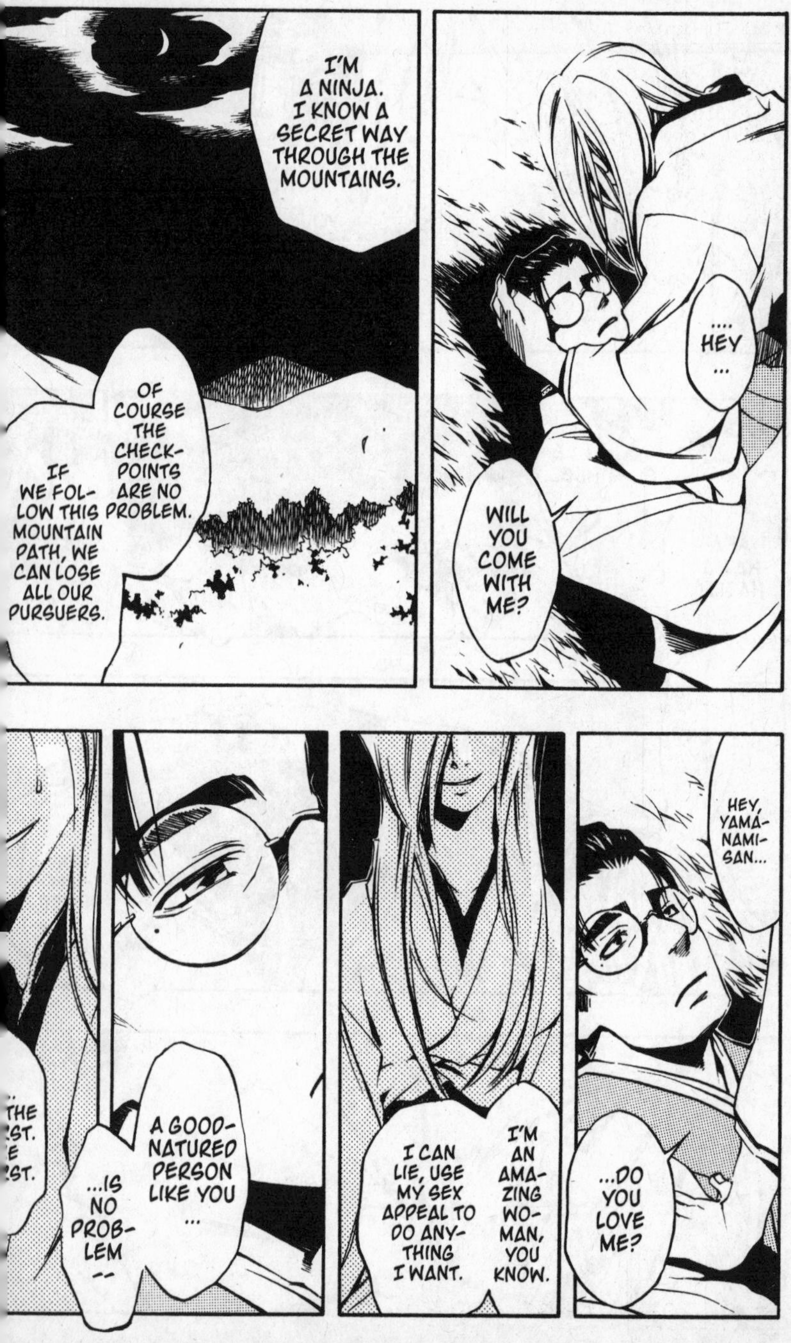
....HEY...
WILL YOU COME WITH ME?
I'M A NINJA. I KNOW A SECRET WAY THROUGH THE MOUNTAINS.
OF COURSE THE CHECKPOINTS ARE NO PROBLEM.
IF WE FOLLOW THIS MOUNTAIN PATH, WE CAN LOSE ALL OUR PURSUERS.
HEY, YAMANAMI-SAN...
...DO YOU LOVE ME?
I'M AN AMAZING WOMAN, YOU KNOW.
I CAN LIE, USE MY SEX APPEAL TO DO ANYTHING I WANT.
A GOOD-NATURED PERSON LIKE YOU ...
...IS NO PROBLEM --

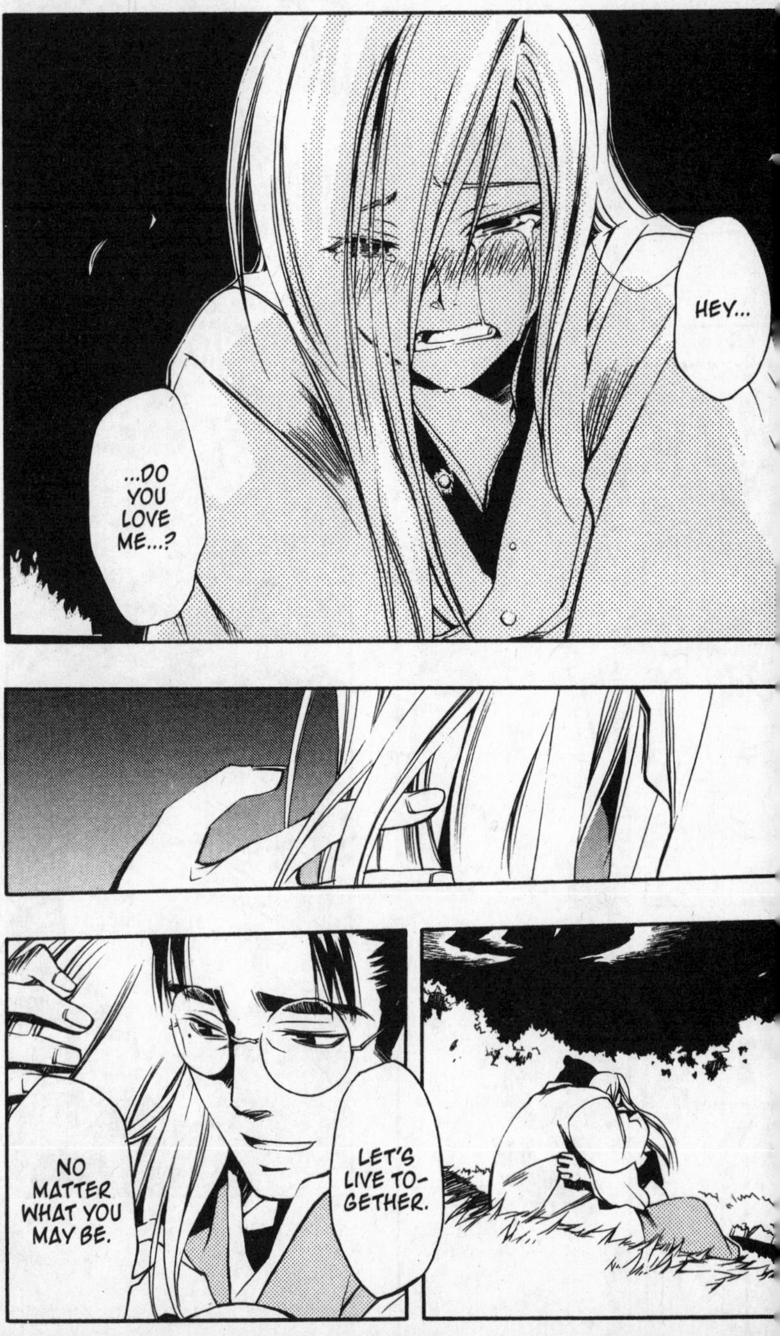
HEY...
...DO YOU LOVE ME...?
LET'S LIVE TO-GETHER.
NO MATTER WHAT YOU MAY BE.

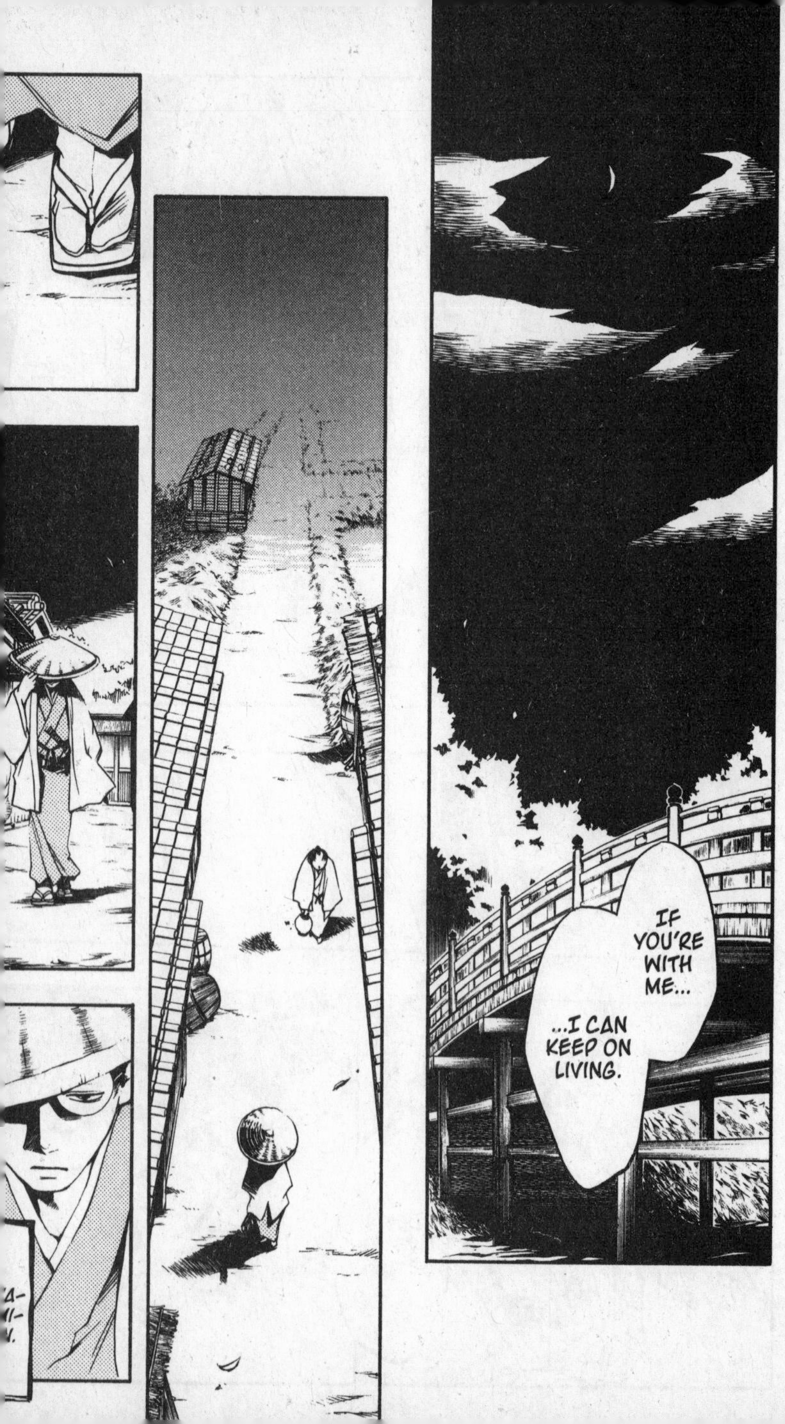
IF YOU'RE WITH ME...
...I CAN KEEP ON LIVING.

HIDE YOUR SELF UNTIL THREE IN THE MORNING.

I WILL PREPARE OUR JOURNEY, AND WAIT FOR YOU AT THE PLACE MARKED FOR THE HOUR OF THE TIGER.

I WILL THE

BELIEVE IN ME.

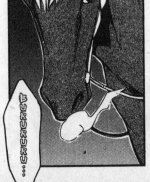

BURURURU...

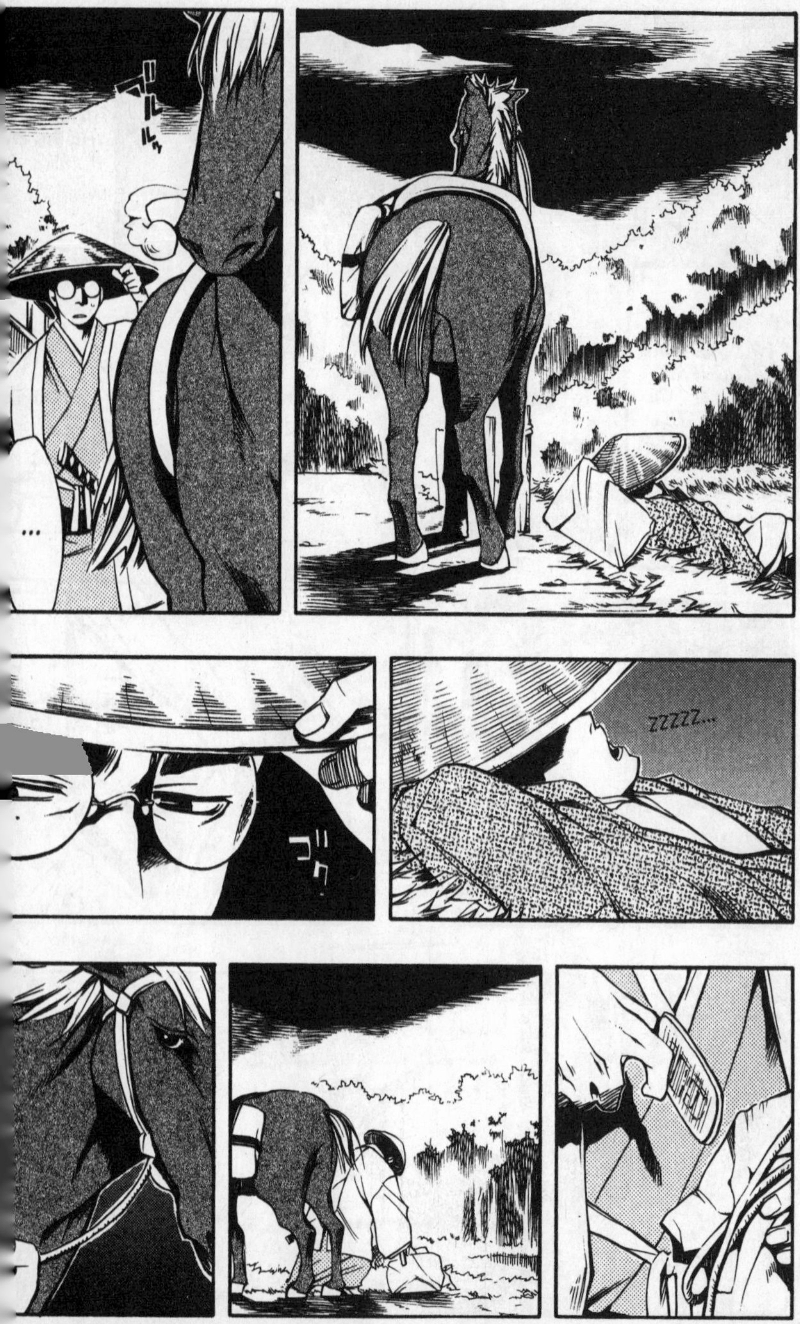
ブルルッ
...
ZZZZZ...
ニコッ!

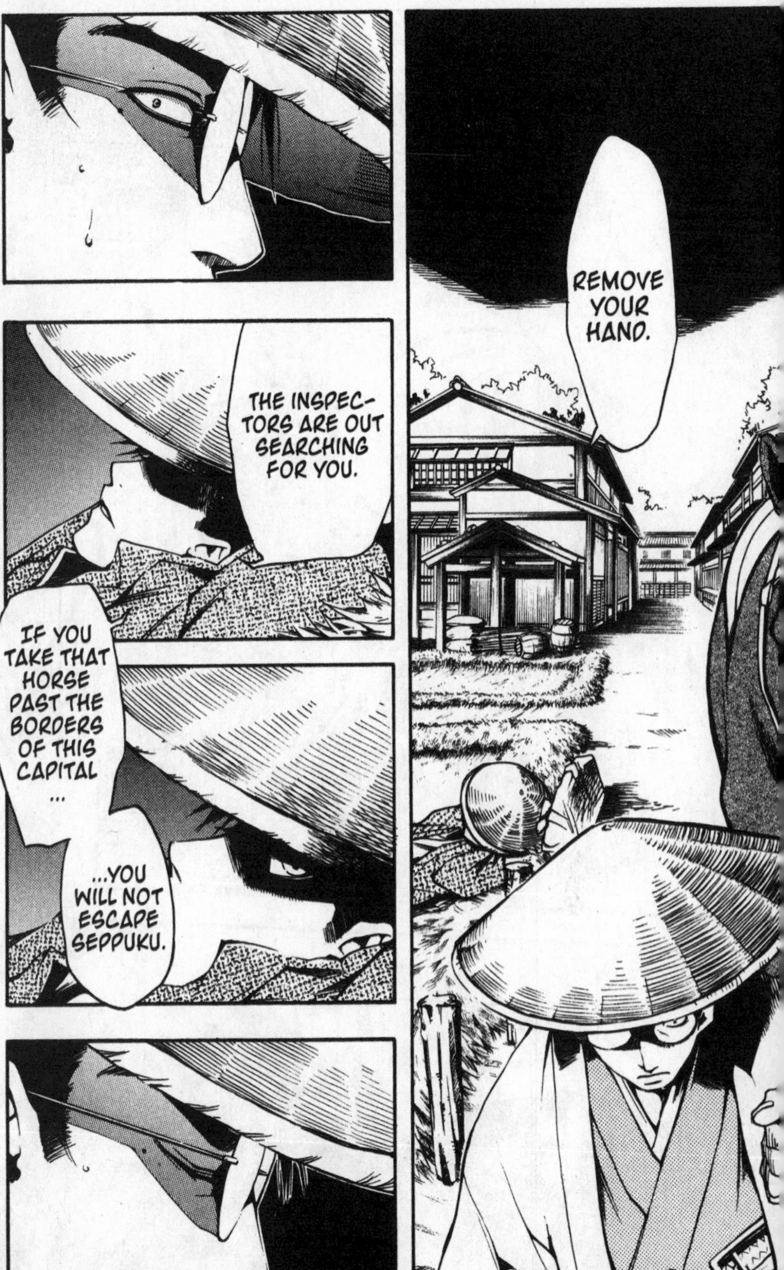
REMOVE YOUR HAND.
THE INSPECTORS ARE OUT SEARCHING FOR YOU.
IF YOU TAKE THAT HORSE PAST THE BORDERS OF THIS CAPITAL ...
...YOU WILL NOT ESCAPE SEPPUKU.

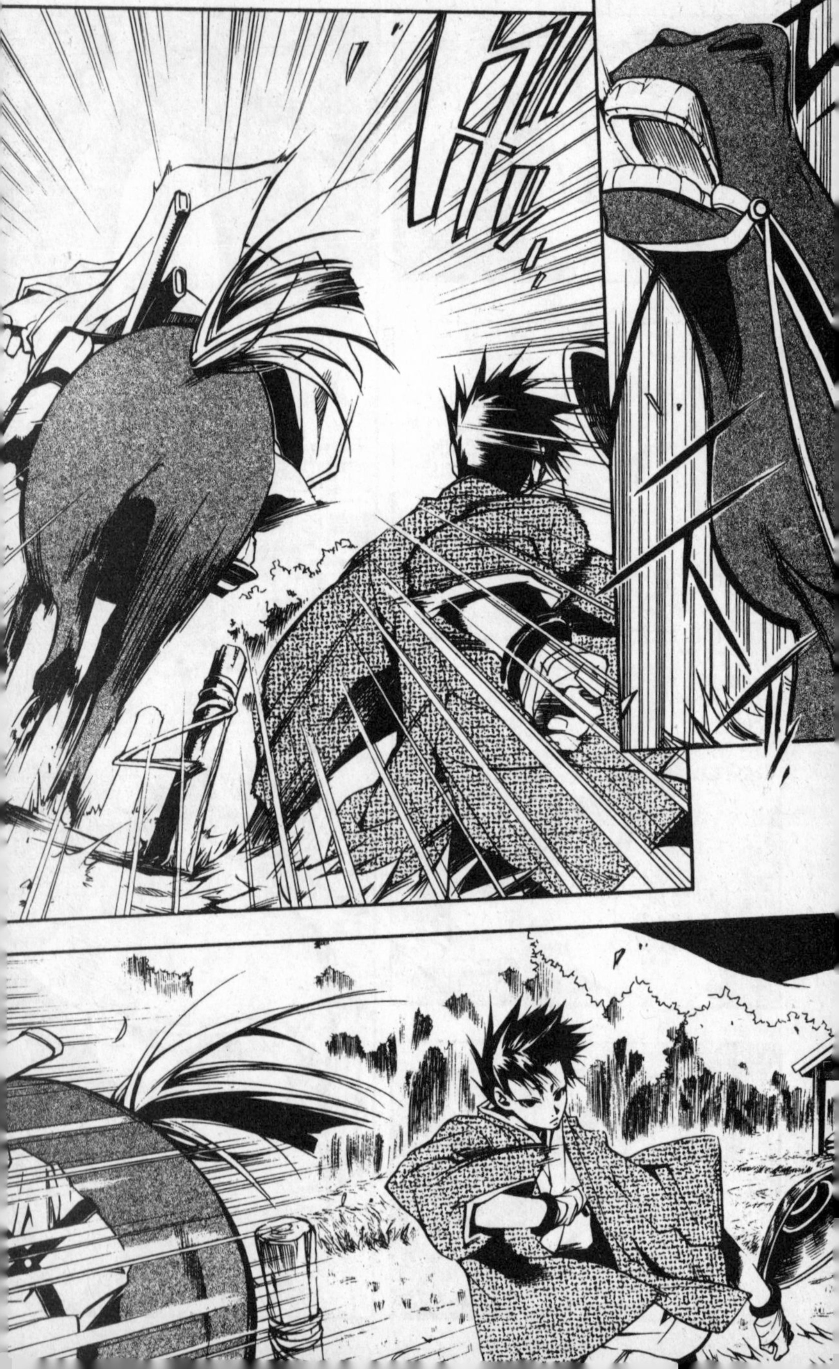

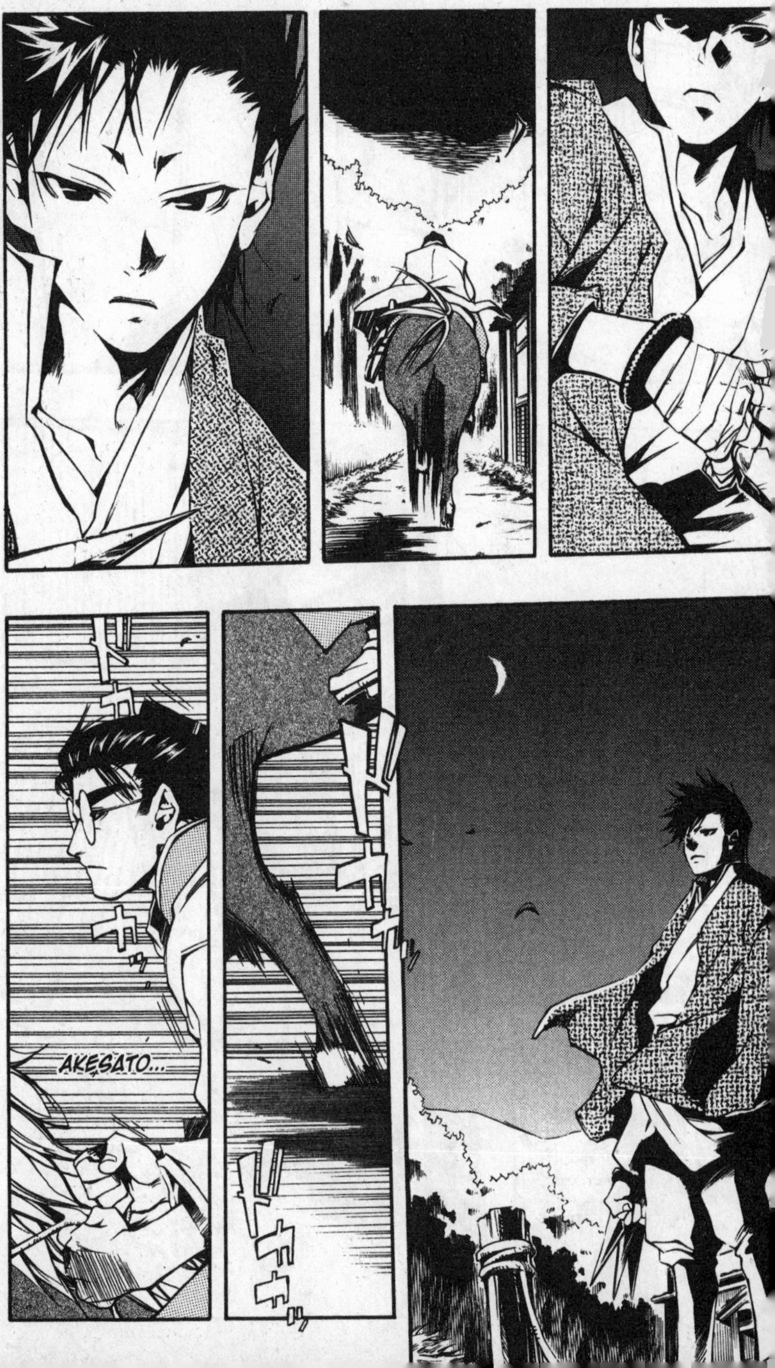
AKESATO...

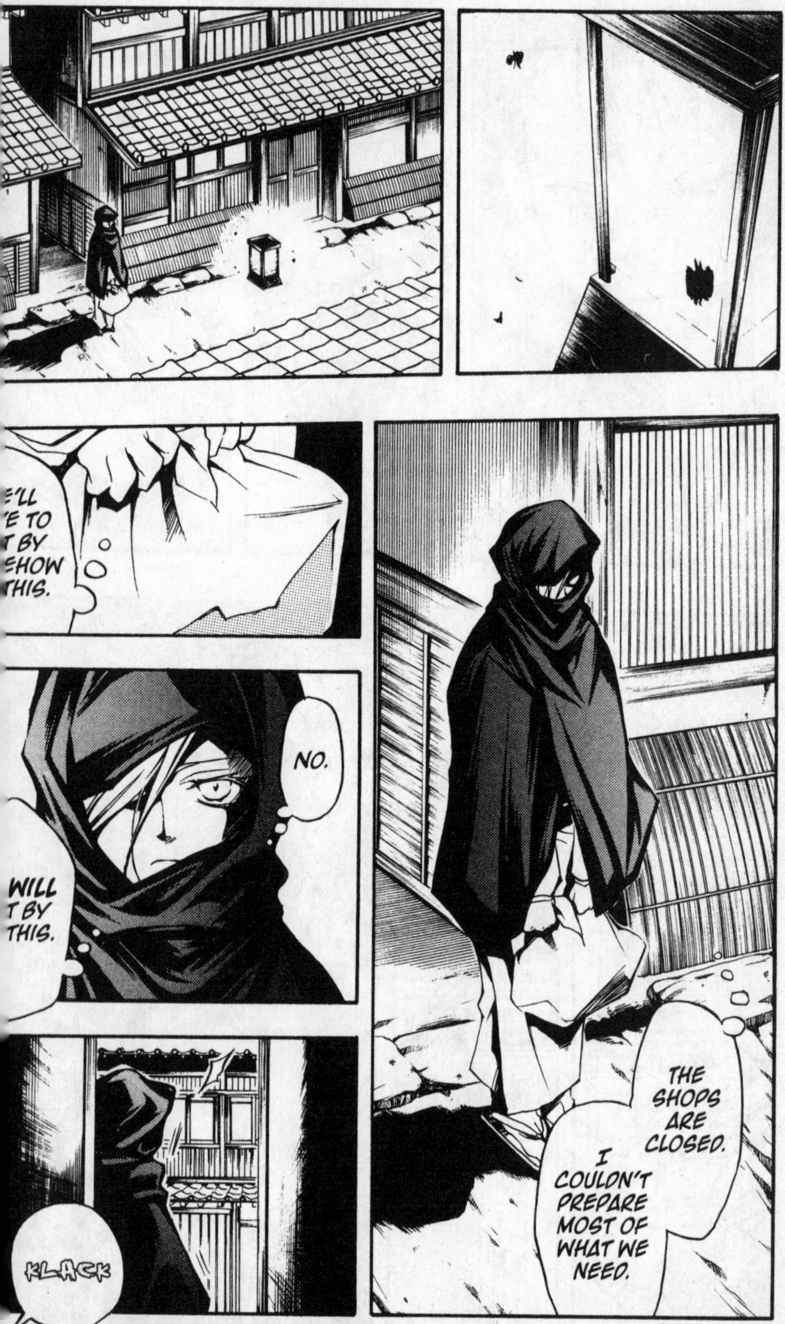
THE SHOPS ARE CLOSED.
I COULDN'T PREPARE MOST OF WHAT WE NEED.
E'LL E TO T BY EHOW THIS.
NO.
WILL T BY THIS.
KLACK

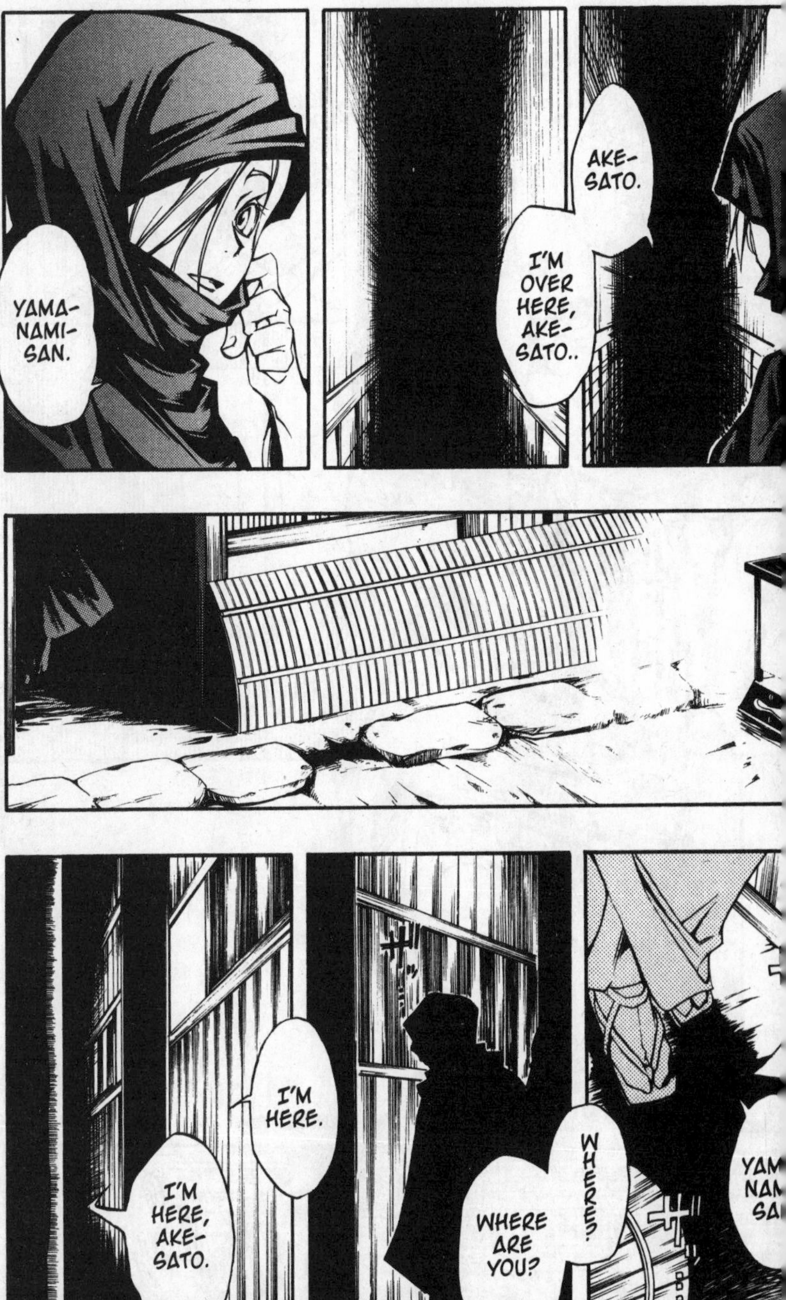
AKE-SATO.
I'M OVER HERE, AKE-SATO..
YAMA-NAMI-SAN.
YAM NAM SA
WHERE?
WHERE ARE YOU?
I'M HERE.
I'M HERE, AKE-SATO.

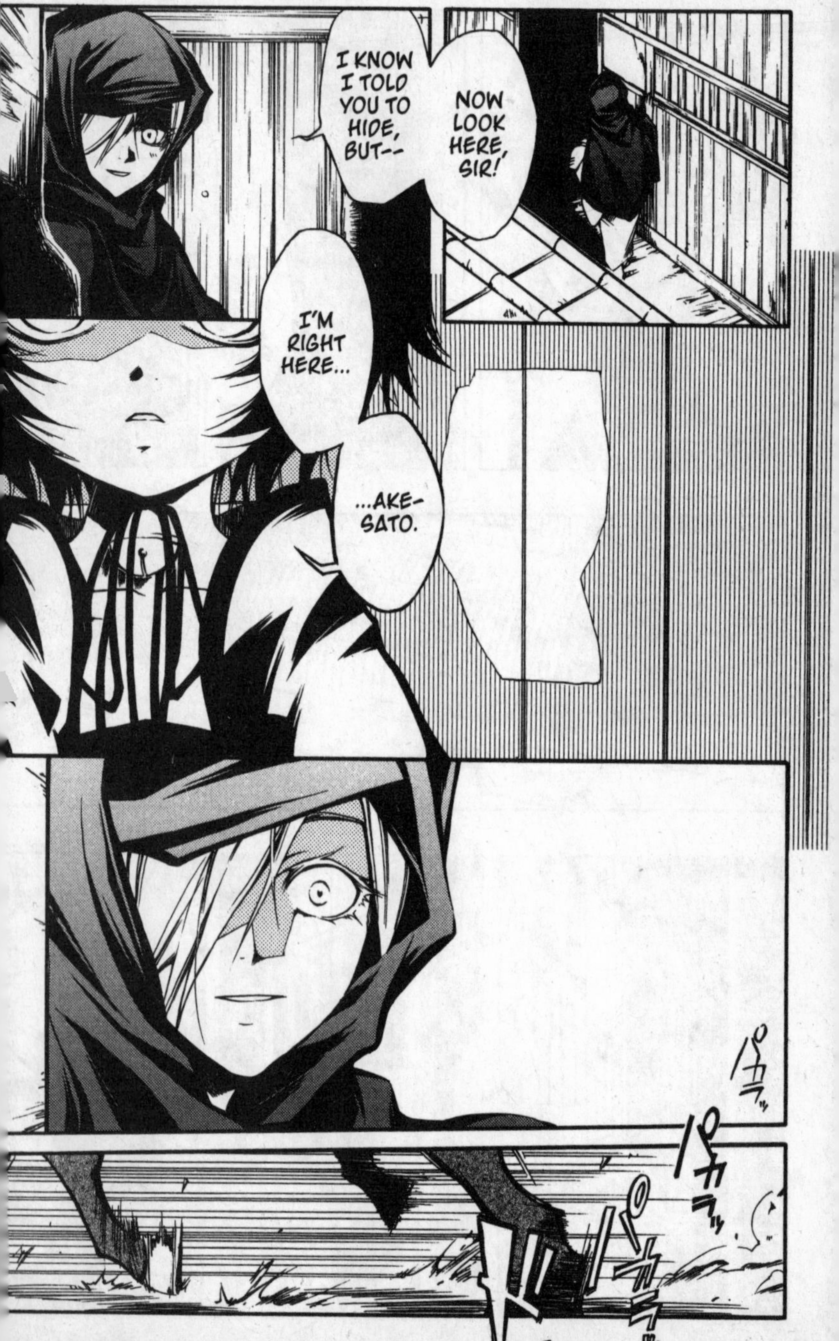
NOW LOOK HERE, SIR!
I KNOW I TOLD YOU TO HIDE, BUT--
I'M RIGHT HERE...
...AKE-SATO.

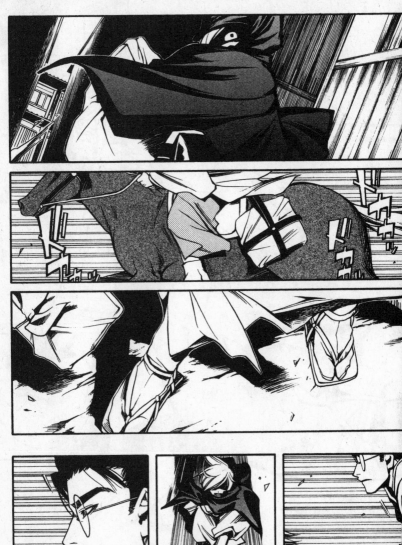

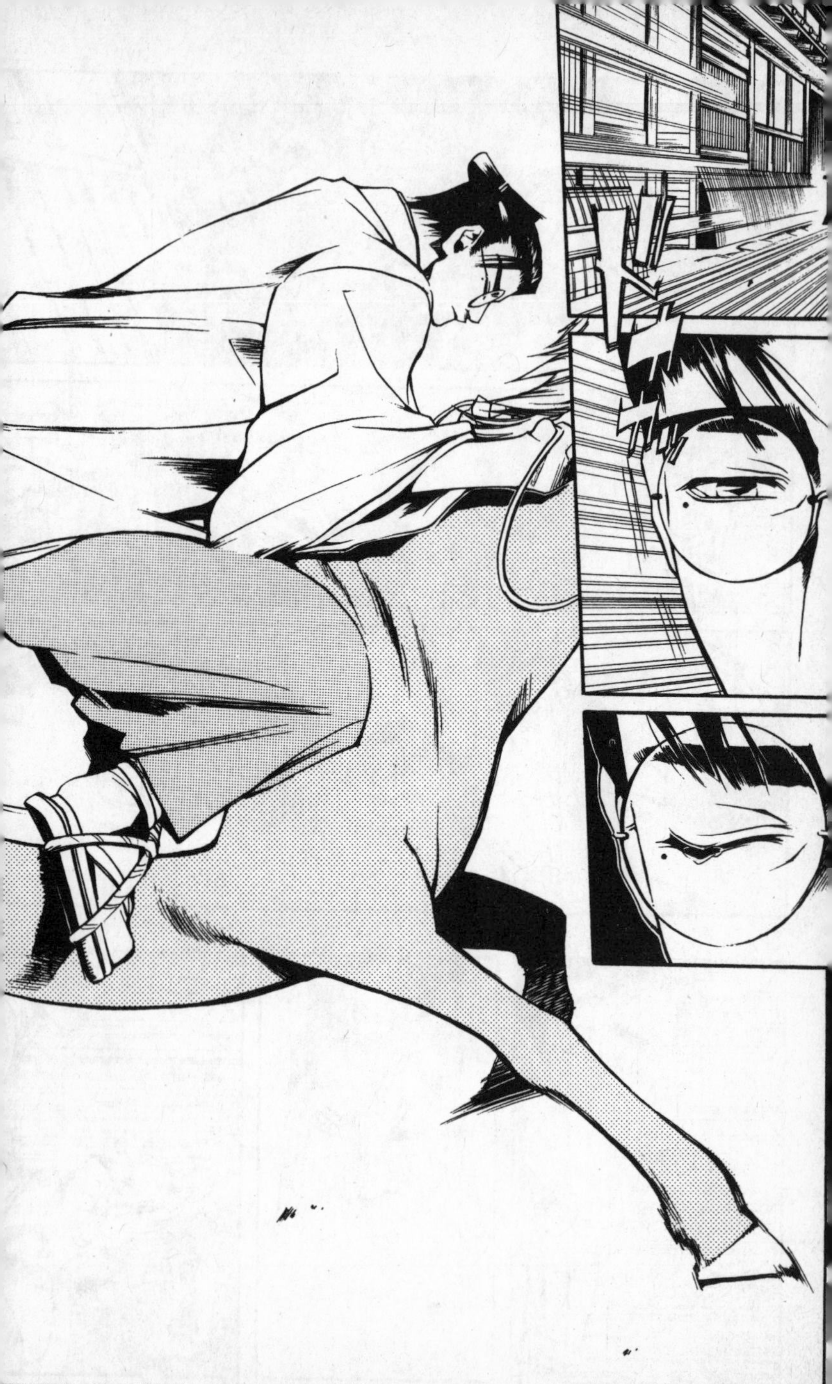

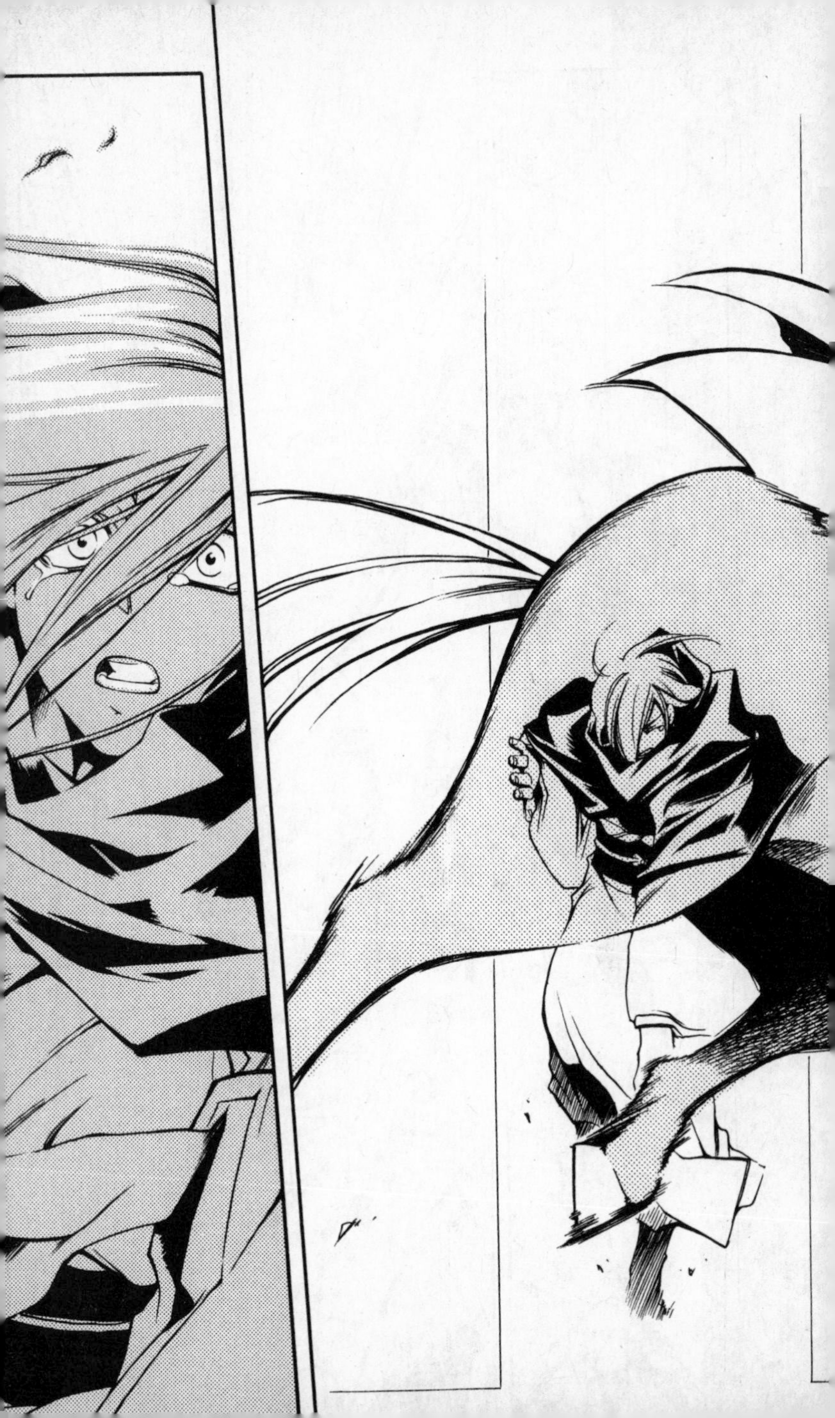

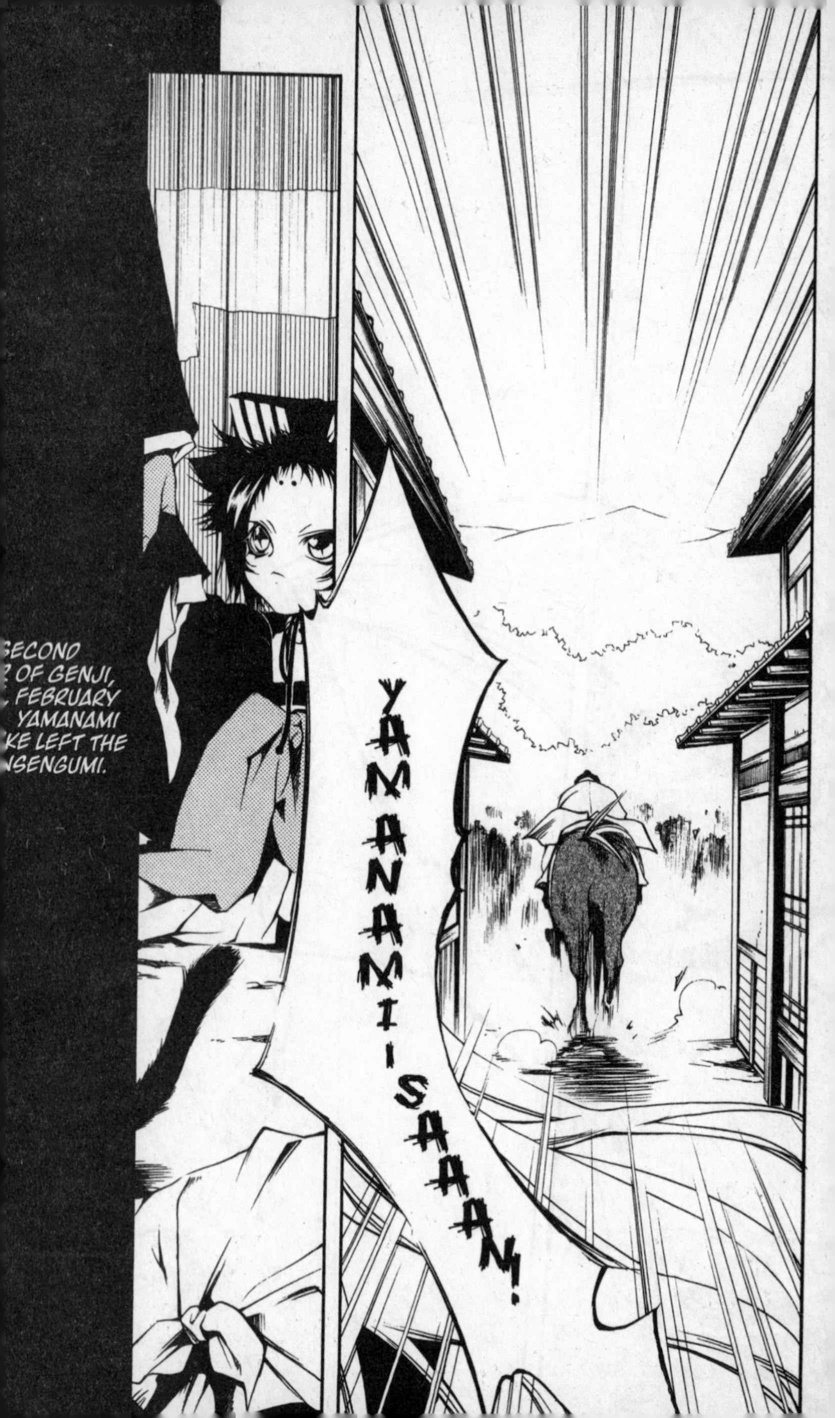
YAMANAMI-SAAAN!
SECOND
OF GENJI,
FEBRUARY
YAMANAMI
KE LEFT THE
NSENGUMI.

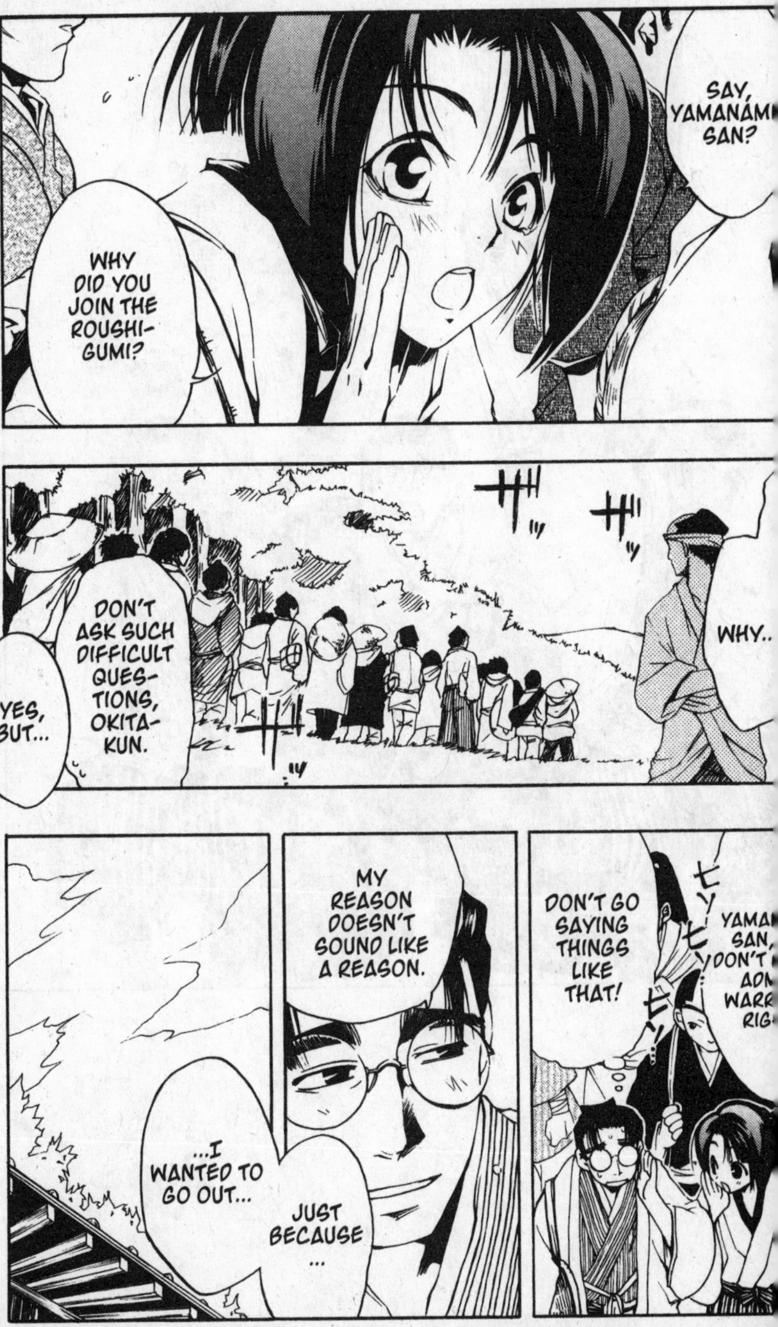
SAY, YAMANAM SAN?
WHY DID YOU JOIN THE ROUSHI-GUMI?
WHY..
DON'T ASK SUCH DIFFICULT QUES-TIONS, OKITA-KUN.
YES, BUT...
YAMA SAN, DON'T ADM WARR RIG
DON'T GO SAYING THINGS LIKE THAT!
MY REASON DOESN'T SOUND LIKE A REASON.
...I WANTED TO GO OUT...
JUST BECAUSE ...

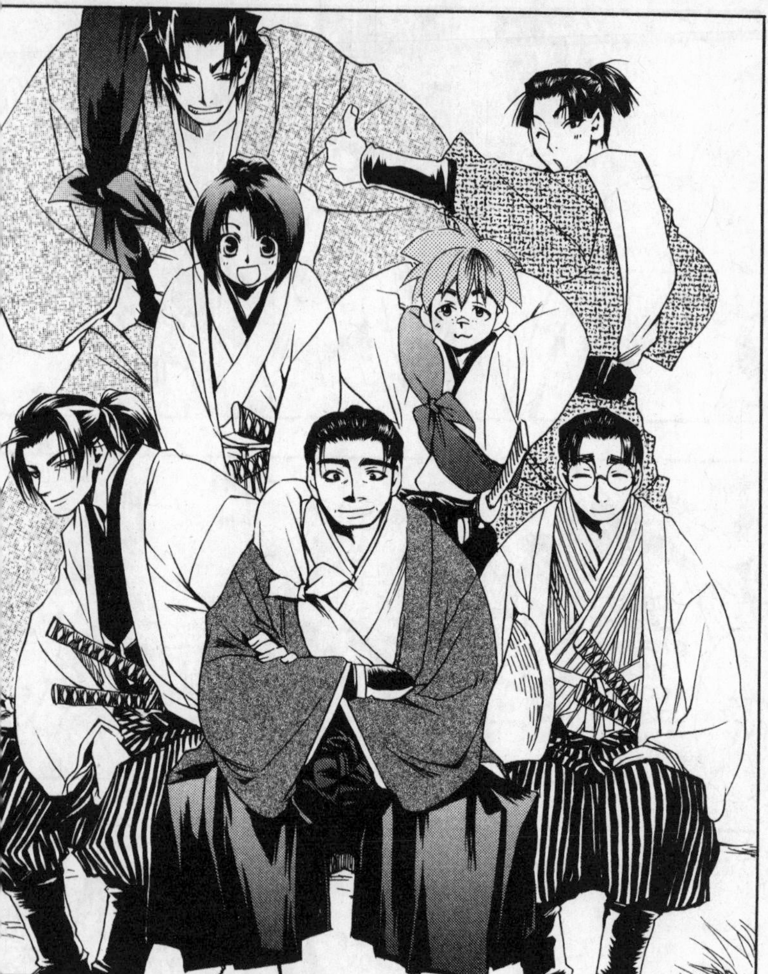

第拾話（だいじゅうわ） 縄（なわ）

Act 10 Rope

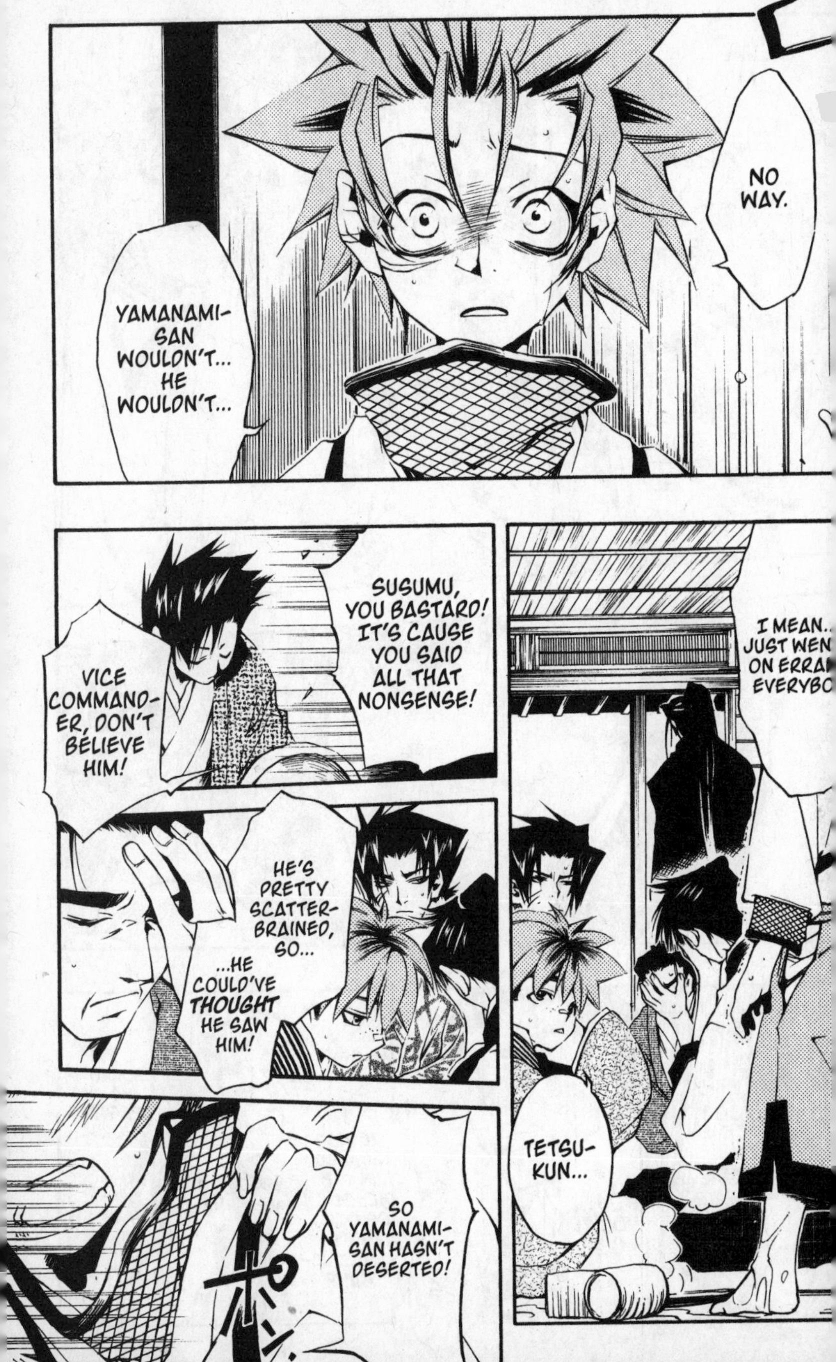
NO WAY.
YAMANAMI-SAN WOULDN'T... HE WOULDN'T...
I MEAN.. JUST WEN ON ERRA EVERYBO
TETSU-KUN...
SUSUMU, YOU BASTARD! IT'S CAUSE YOU SAID ALL THAT NONSENSE!
VICE COMMANDER, DON'T BELIEVE HIM!
HE'S PRETTY SCATTER-BRAINED, SO...
...HE COULD'VE **THOUGHT** HE SAW HIM!
SO YAMANAMI-SAN HASN'T DESERTED!
ポン

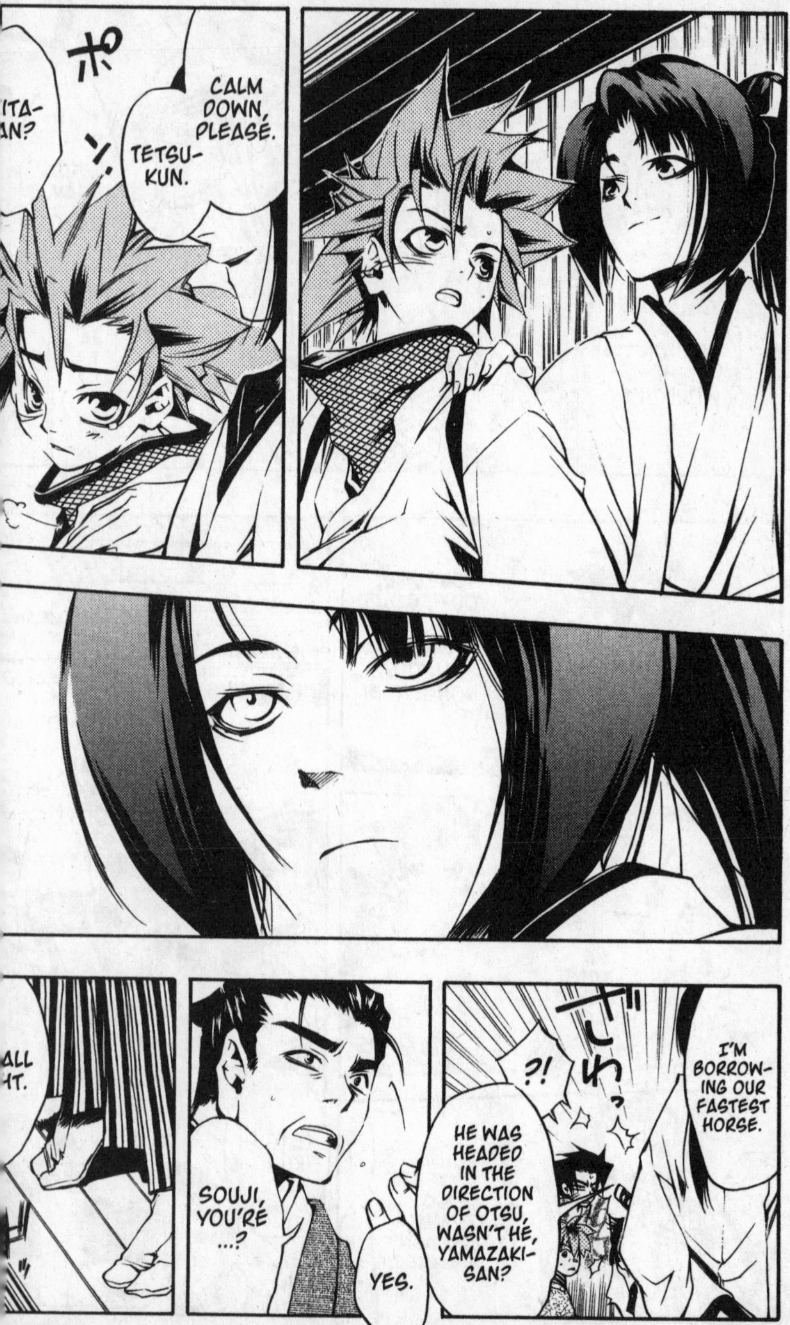
ポン
CALM DOWN, PLEASE.
TETSU-KUN.
I'M BORROWING OUR FASTEST HORSE.
ざわ
?!
HE WAS HEADED IN THE DIRECTION OF OTSU, WASN'T HE, YAMAZAKI-SAN?
YES.
SOUJI, YOU'RE ...?

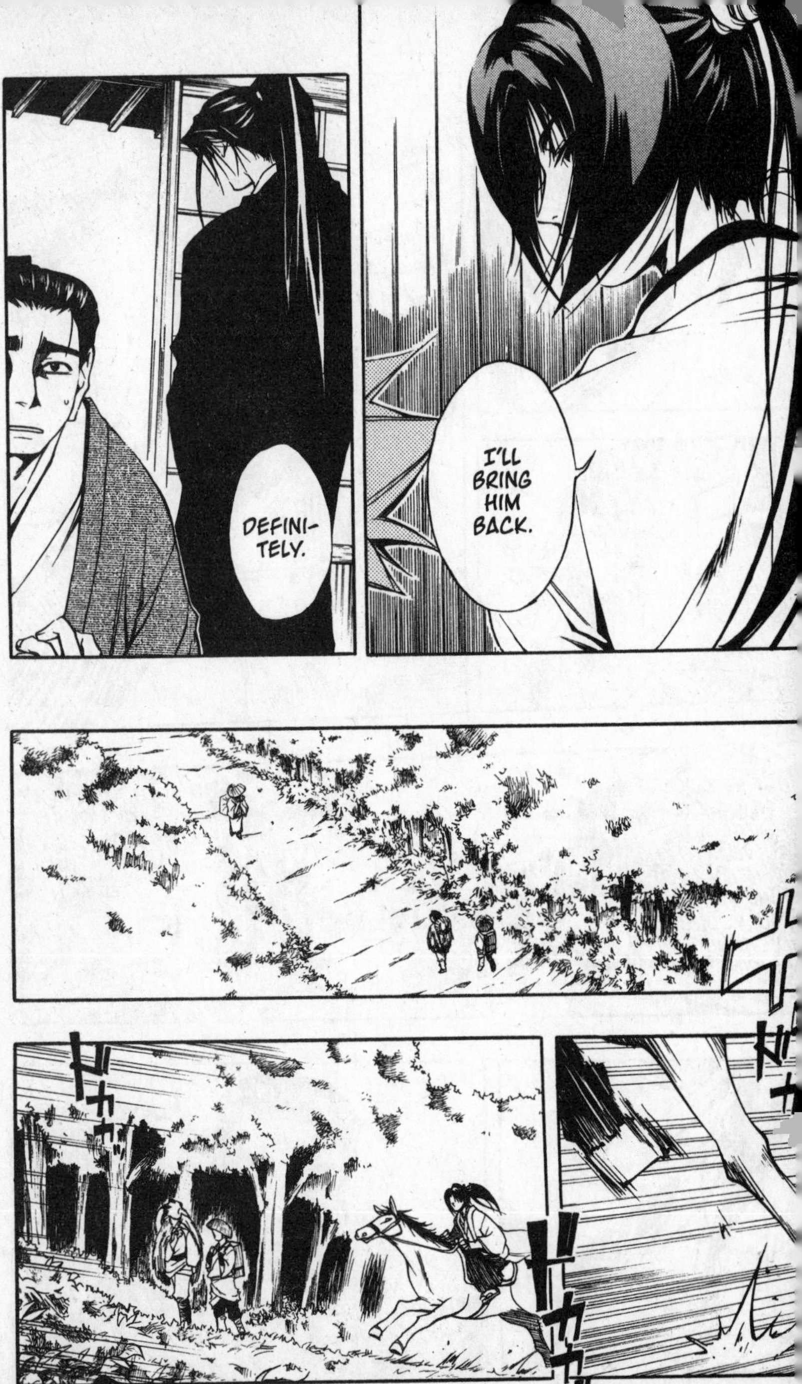
I'LL BRING HIM BACK.
DEFINI-TELY.

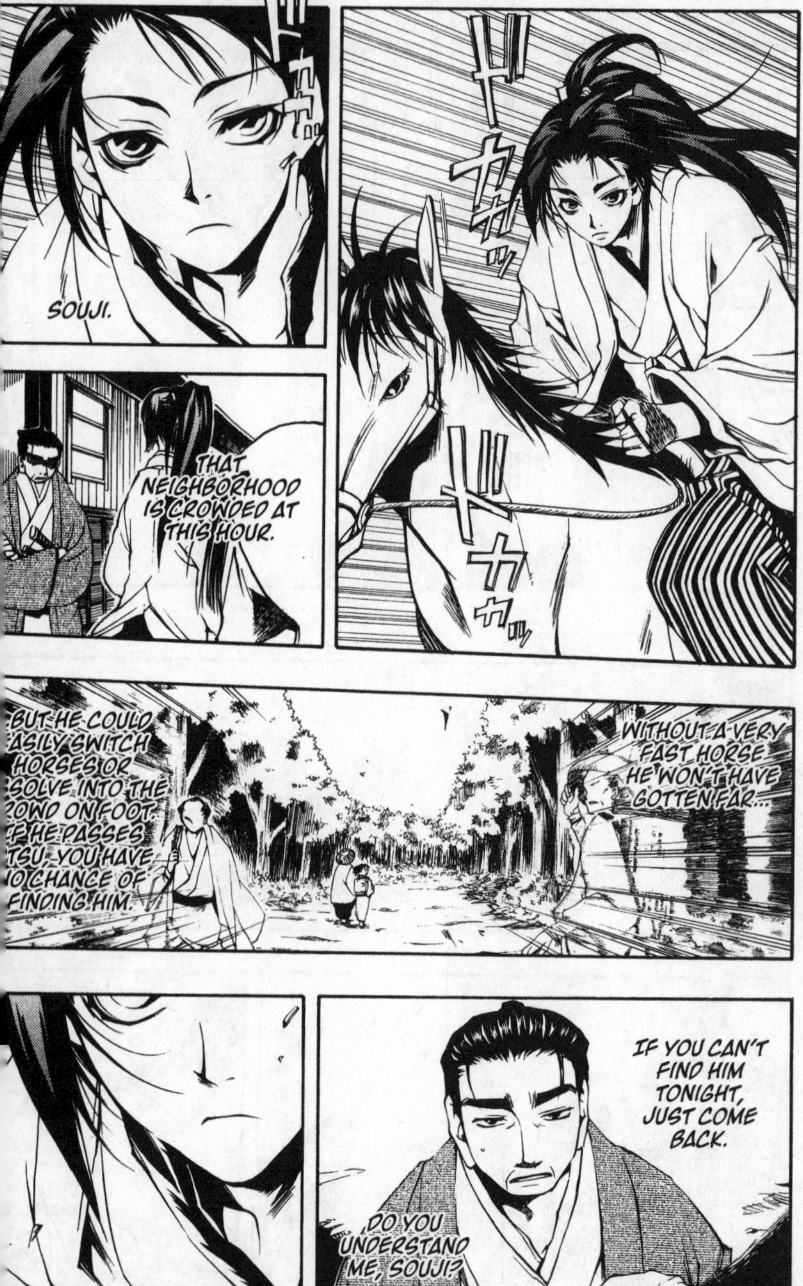
SOUJI.
THAT NEIGHBORHOOD IS CROWDED AT THIS HOUR.
WITHOUT A VERY FAST HORSE HE WON'T HAVE GOTTEN FAR...
BUT HE COULD ASILY SWITCH HORSES OR SOLVE INTO THE OWD ON FOOT. F HE PASSES TSU, YOU HAVE O CHANCE OF FINDING HIM.
IF YOU CAN'T FIND HIM TONIGHT, JUST COME BACK.
DO YOU UNDERSTAND ME, SOUJI?

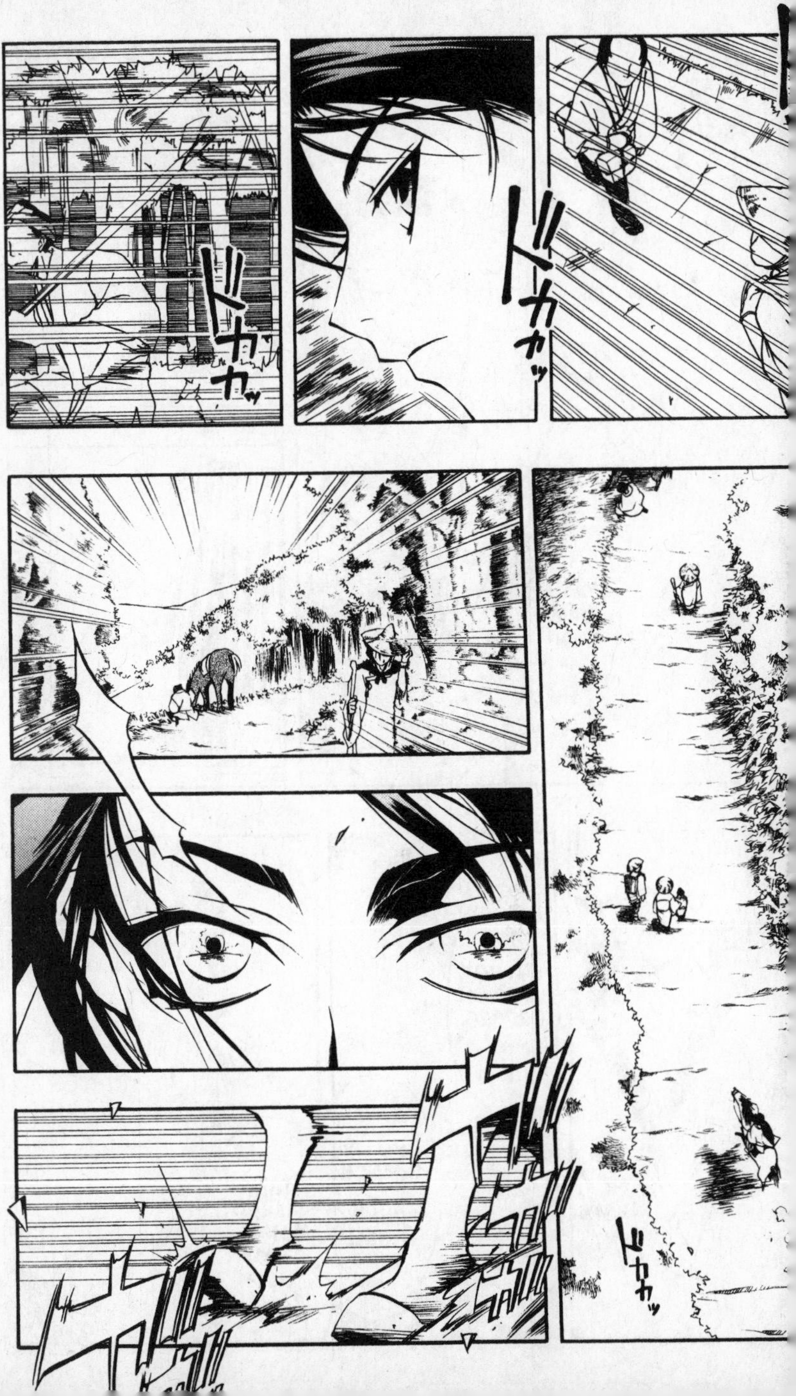
ドカカッ
ドカカッ
ドカカッ

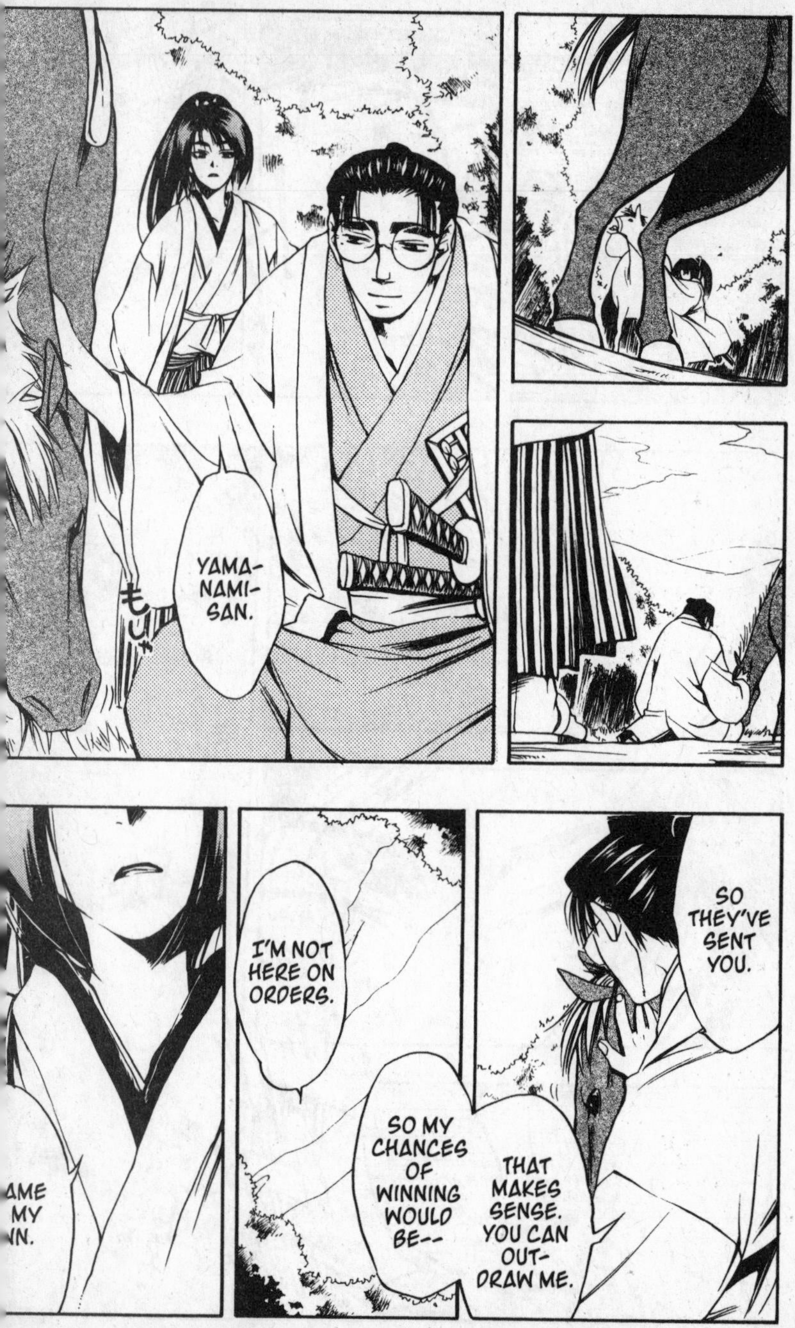
YAMA-NAMI-SAN.
もしゃ
SO THEY'VE SENT YOU.
THAT MAKES SENSE. YOU CAN OUT-DRAW ME.
I'M NOT HERE ON ORDERS.
SO MY CHANCES OF WINNING WOULD BE--
AME MY NN.

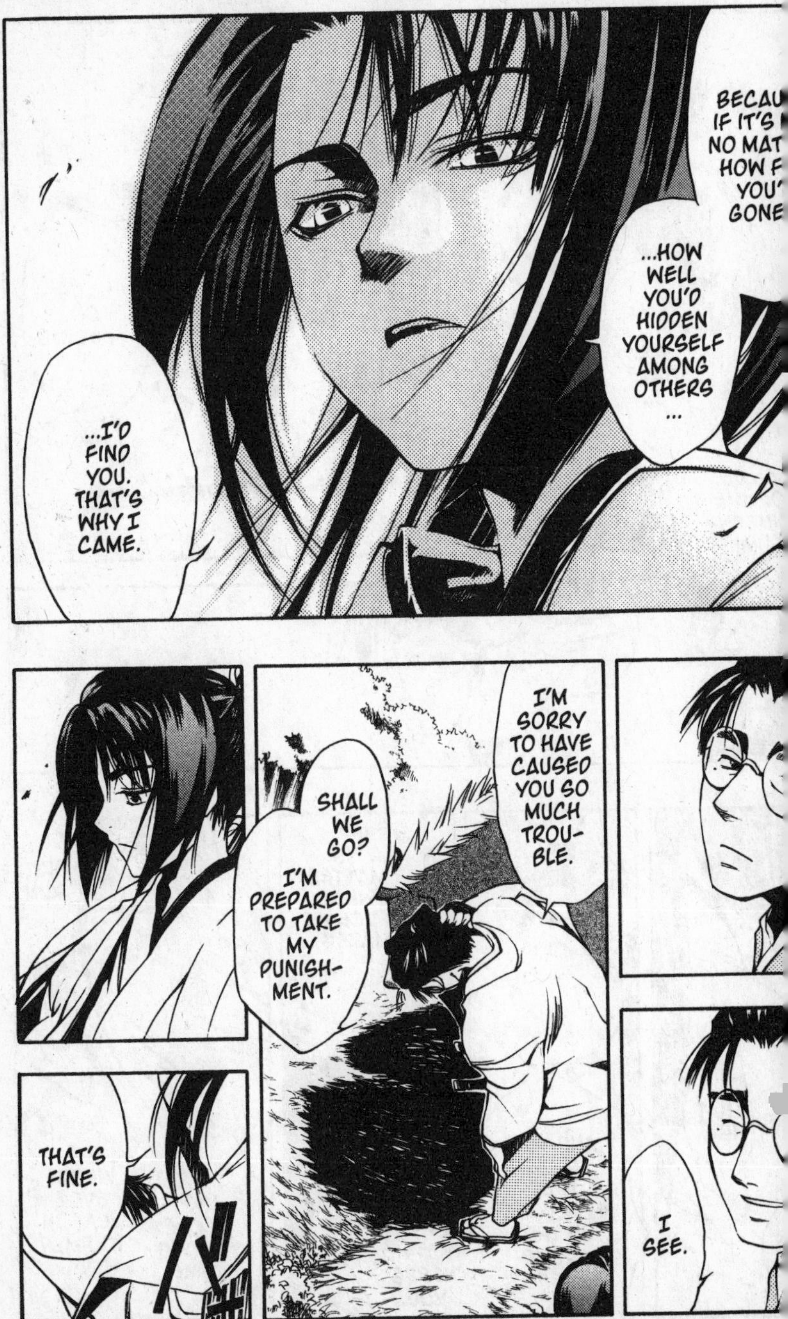
BECAU IF IT'S NO MAT HOW F YOU' GONE
...HOW WELL YOU'D HIDDEN YOURSELF AMONG OTHERS ...
...I'D FIND YOU. THAT'S WHY I CAME.
I SEE.
I'M SORRY TO HAVE CAUSED YOU SO MUCH TROU-BLE.
SHALL WE GO?
I'M PREPARED TO TAKE MY PUNISHMENT.
THAT'S FINE.

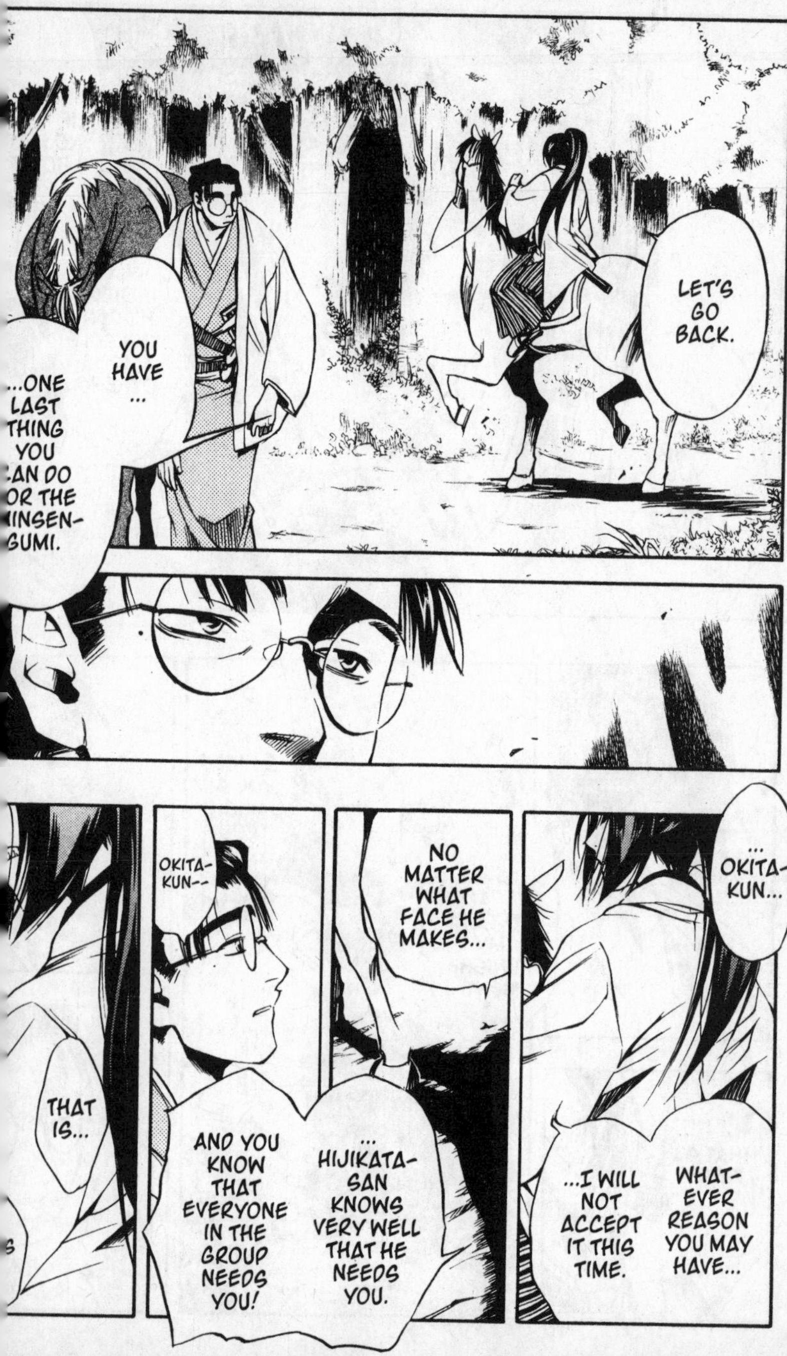
LET'S GO BACK.
YOU HAVE ...
...ONE LAST THING YOU AN DO OR THE INSEN-GUMI.
... OKITA-KUN...
WHAT-EVER REASON YOU MAY HAVE...
...I WILL NOT ACCEPT IT THIS TIME.
NO MATTER WHAT FACE HE MAKES...
... HIJIKATA-SAN KNOWS VERY WELL THAT HE NEEDS YOU.
OKITA-KUN--
AND YOU KNOW THAT EVERYONE IN THE GROUP NEEDS YOU!
THAT IS...

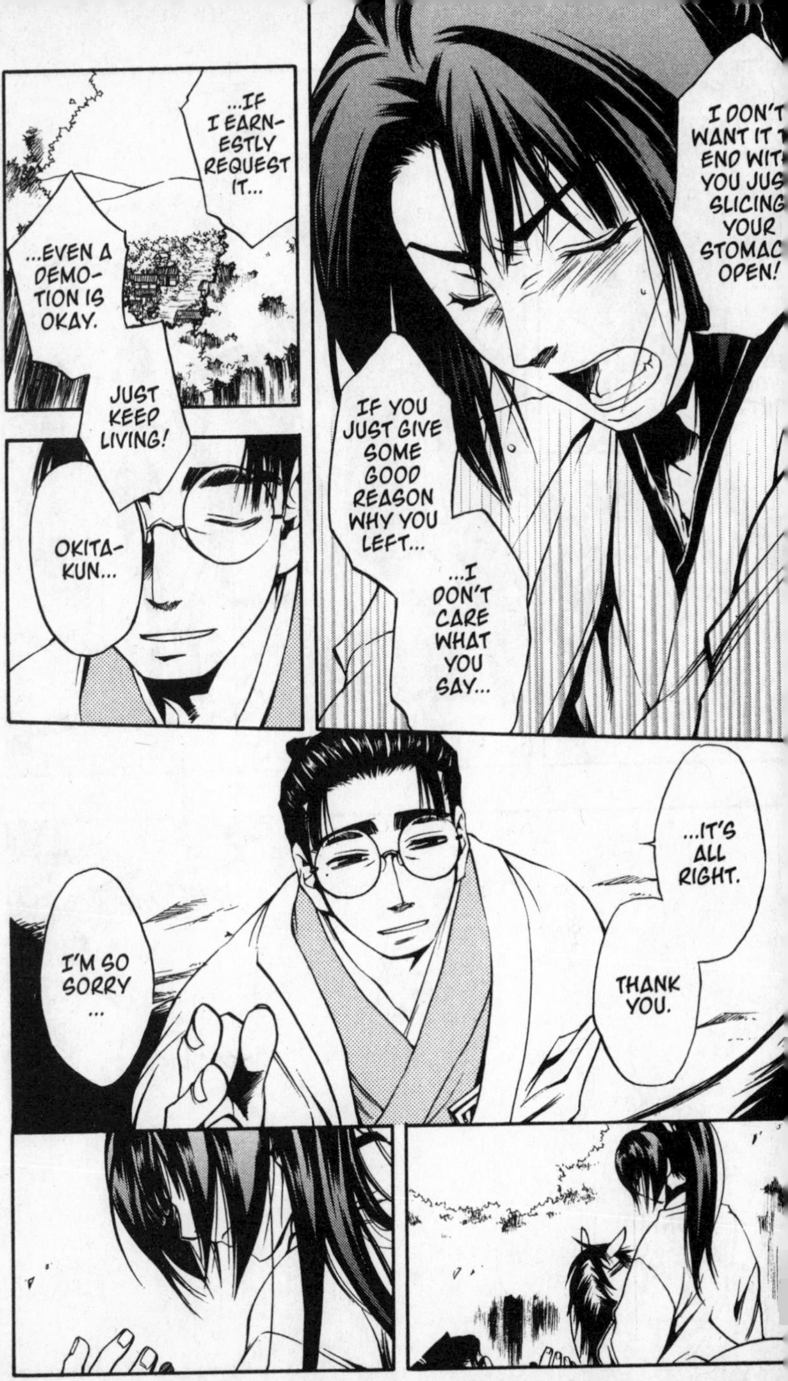
I DON'T WANT IT T END WIT YOU JUS SLICING YOUR STOMAC OPEN!
IF YOU JUST GIVE SOME GOOD REASON WHY YOU LEFT...
...I DON'T CARE WHAT YOU SAY...
...IF I EARNESTLY REQUEST IT...
...EVEN A DEMOTION IS OKAY.
JUST KEEP LIVING!
OKITA-KUN...
...IT'S ALL RIGHT.
THANK YOU.
I'M SO SORRY ...

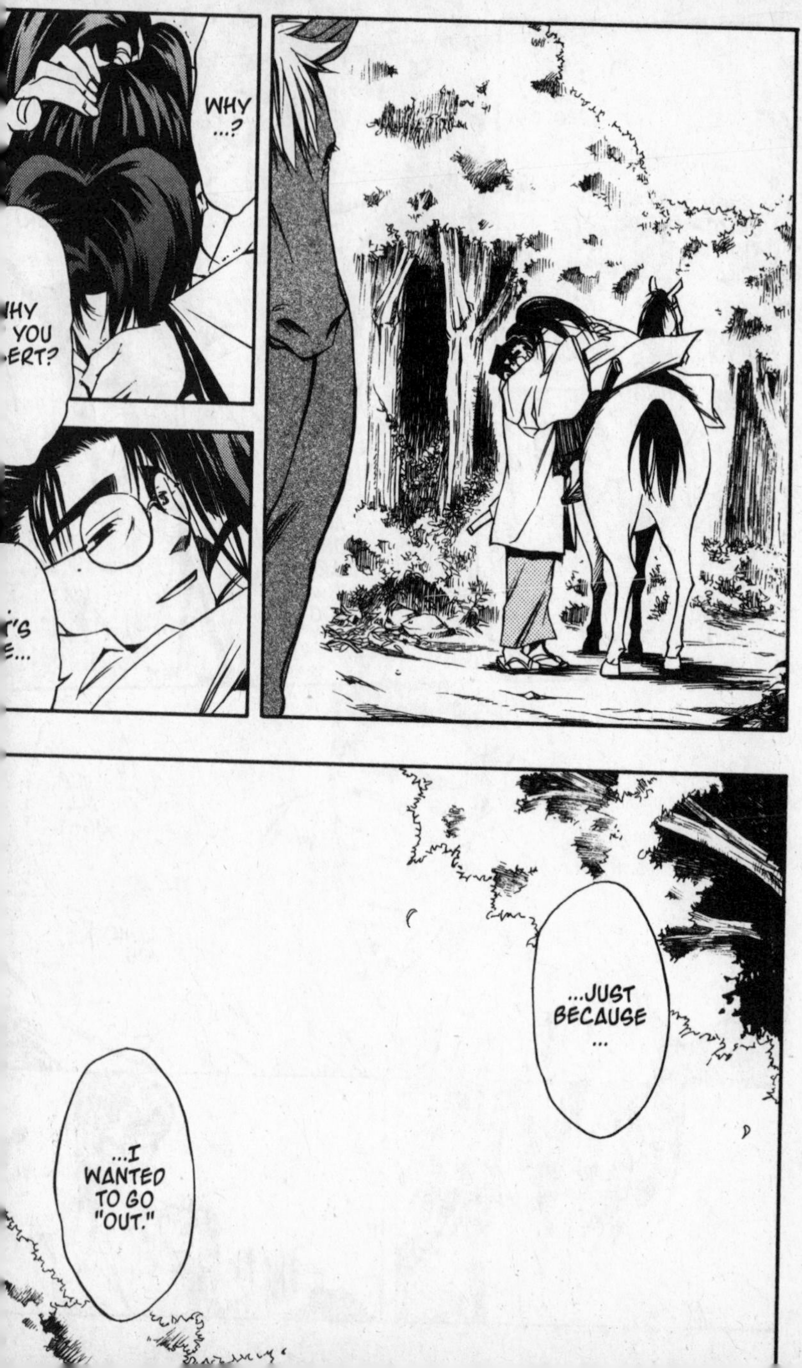

WHY ...?
HY YOU ERT?
T'S E...
...JUST BECAUSE ...
...I WANTED TO GO "OUT."

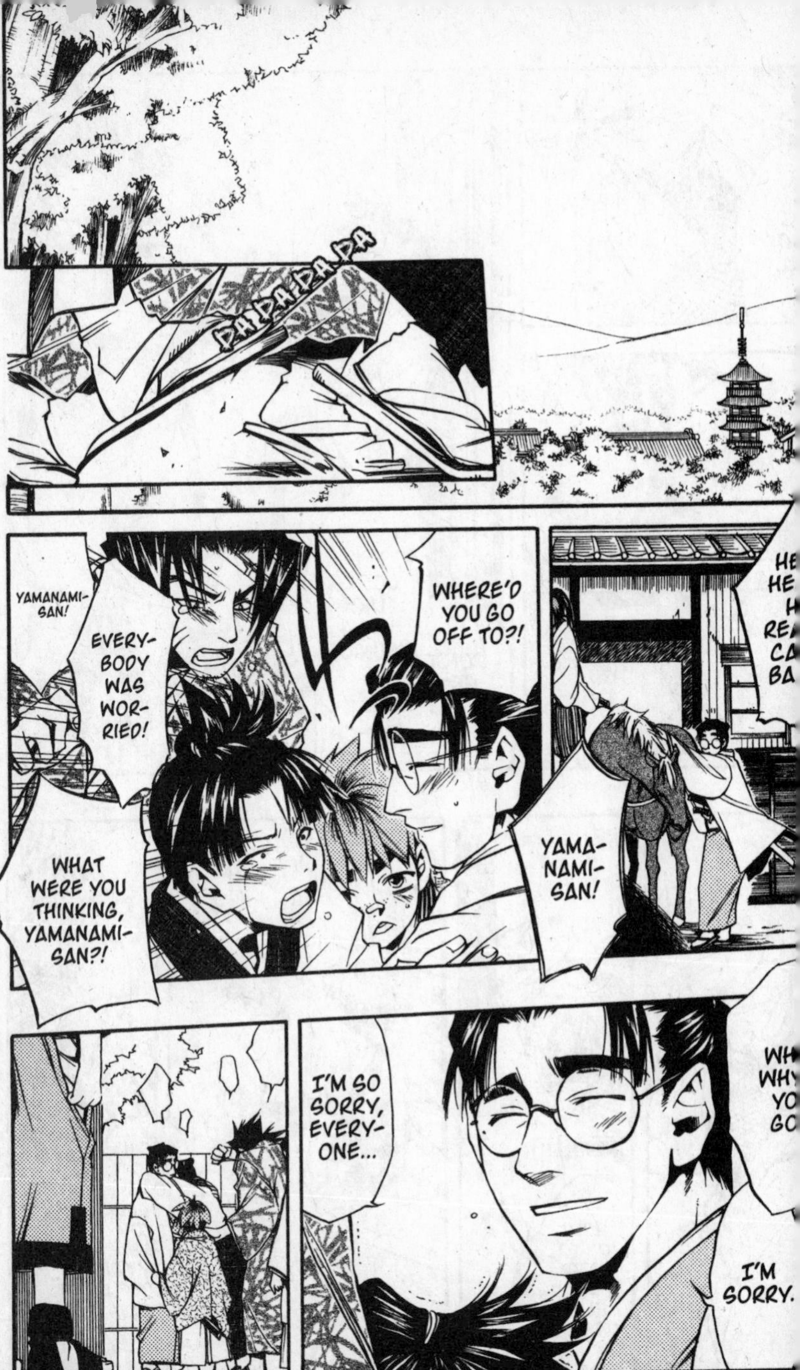
DA PA PA PA PA
YAMA-NAMI-SAN!
WHERE'D YOU GO OFF TO?!
YAMANAMI-SAN!
EVERY-BODY WAS WOR-RIED!
WHAT WERE YOU THINKING, YAMANAMI-SAN?!
I'M SORRY.
I'M SO SORRY, EVERY-ONE...

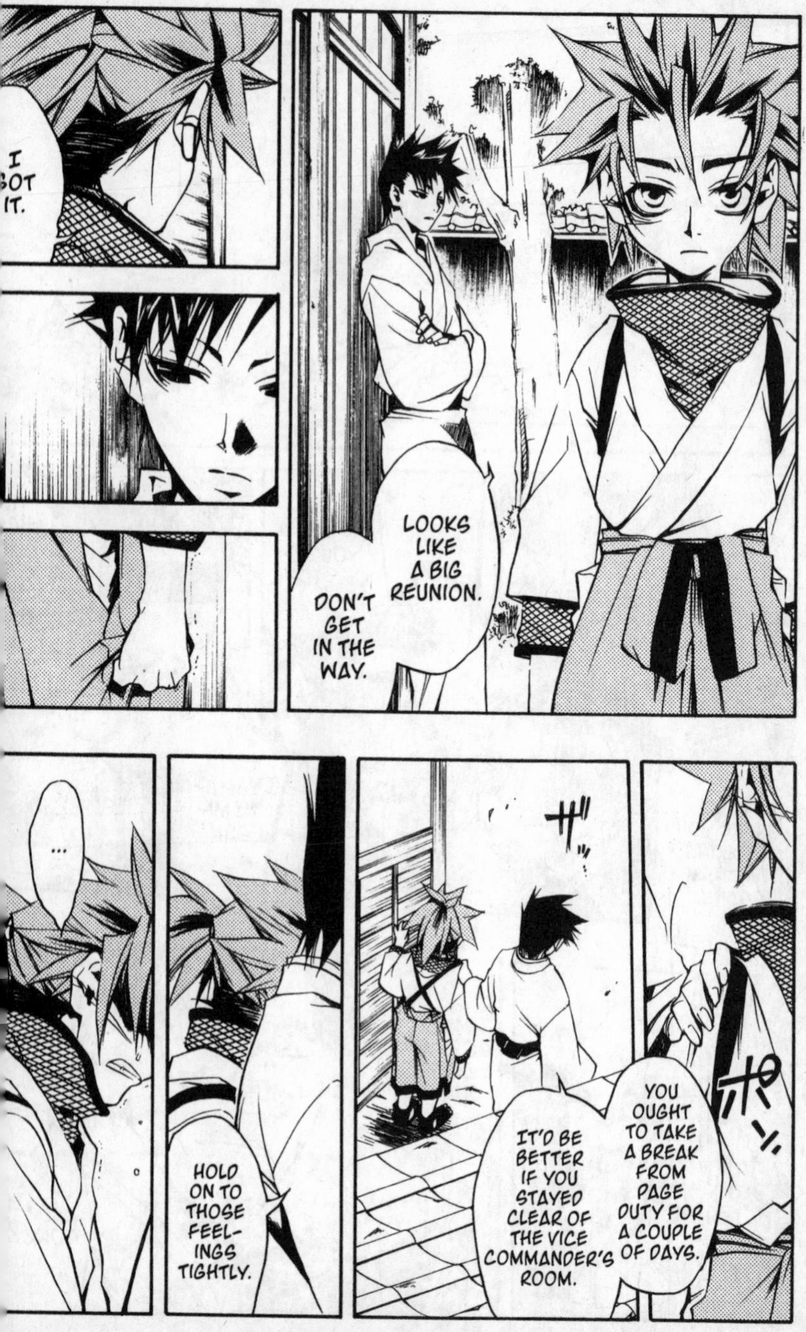
LOOKS LIKE A BIG REUNION.
DON'T GET IN THE WAY.
I GOT IT.
YOU OUGHT TO TAKE A BREAK FROM PAGE DUTY FOR A COUPLE OF DAYS.
IT'D BE BETTER IF YOU STAYED CLEAR OF THE VICE COMMANDER'S ROOM.
HOLD ON TO THOSE FEEL-INGS TIGHTLY.
...

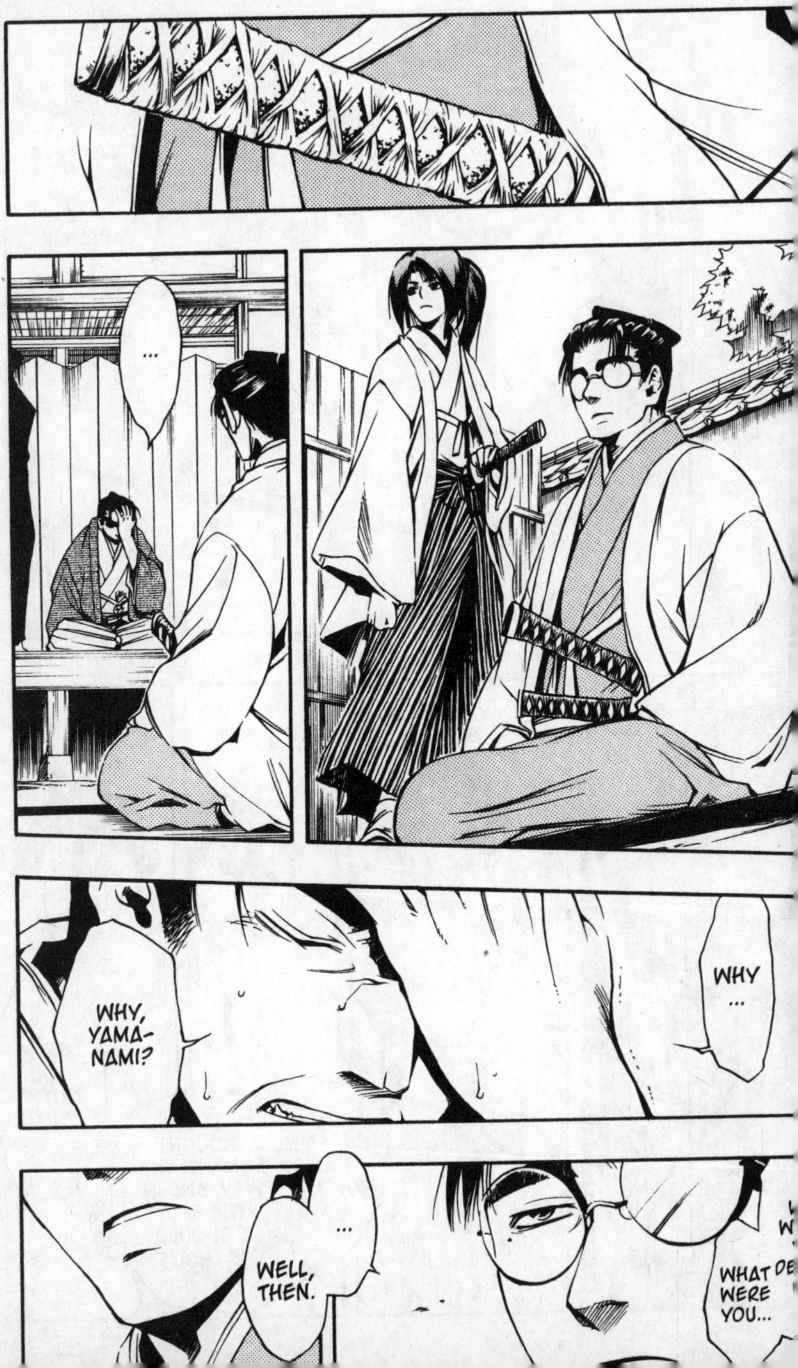
...
WHY ...
WHY, YAMANAMI?
WHAT DE
WERE YOU...
...
WELL, THEN.

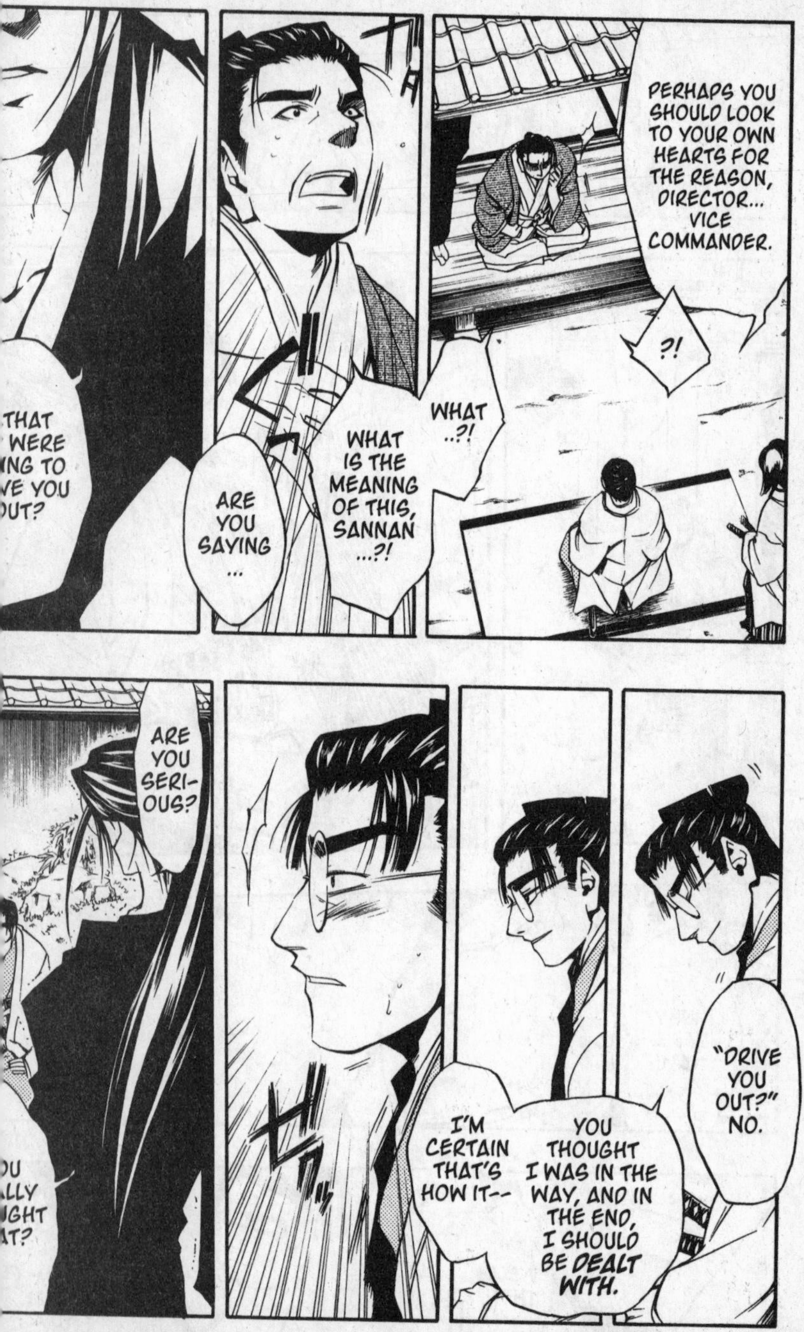

PERHAPS YOU SHOULD LOOK TO YOUR OWN HEARTS FOR THE REASON, DIRECTOR... VICE COMMANDER.
?!
WHAT ...?!
WHAT IS THE MEANING OF THIS, SANNAN ...?!
ARE YOU SAYING ...
THAT WERE NG TO VE YOU OUT?
"DRIVE YOU OUT?" NO.
YOU THOUGHT I WAS IN THE WAY, AND IN THE END, I SHOULD BE *DEALT WITH.*
I'M CERTAIN THAT'S HOW IT--
ARE YOU SERI-OUS?
OU LLY UGHT AT?

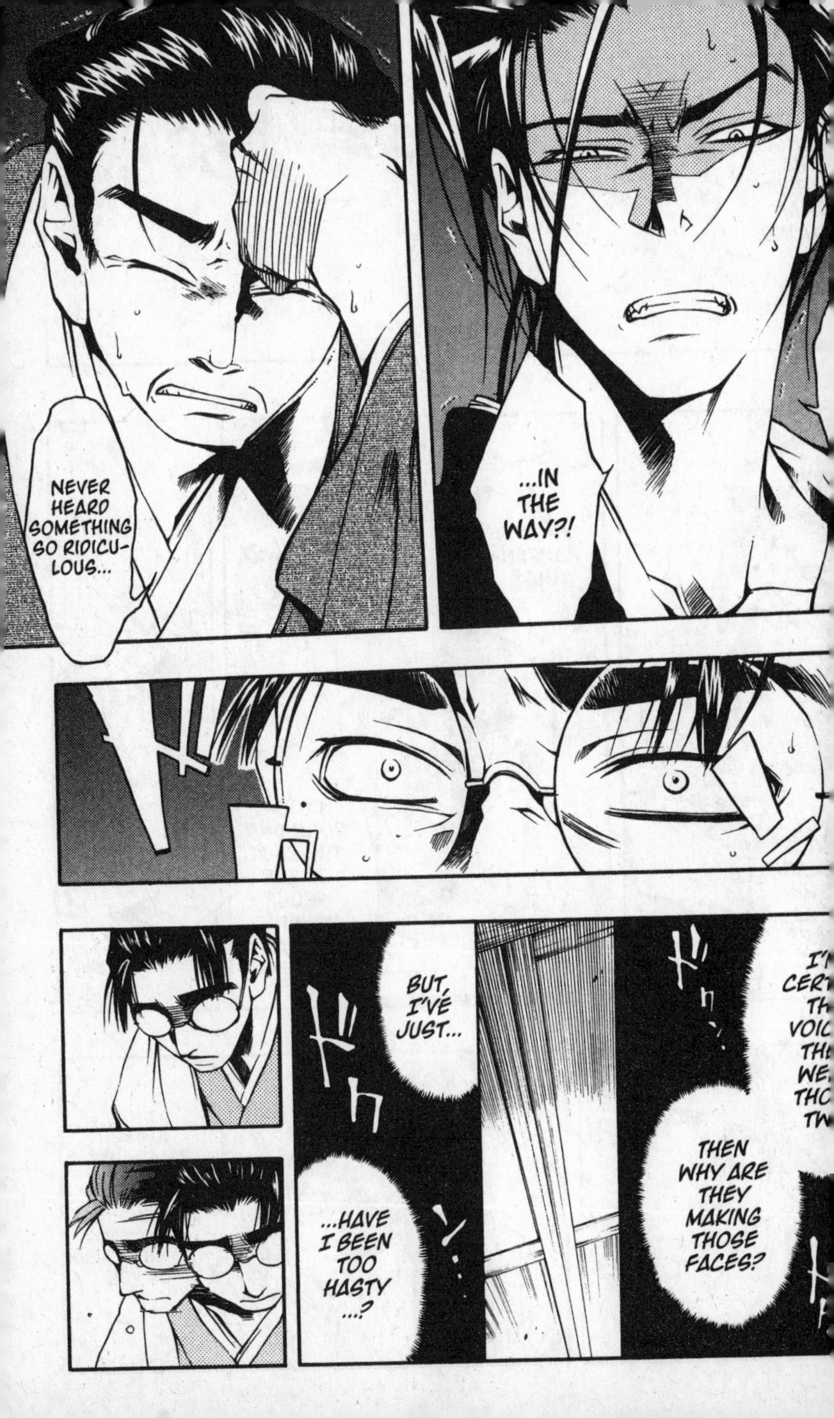
...IN THE WAY?!
NEVER HEARD SOMETHING SO RIDICULOUS...
THEN WHY ARE THEY MAKING THOSE FACES?
BUT, I'VE JUST...
...HAVE I BEEN TOO HASTY ...?

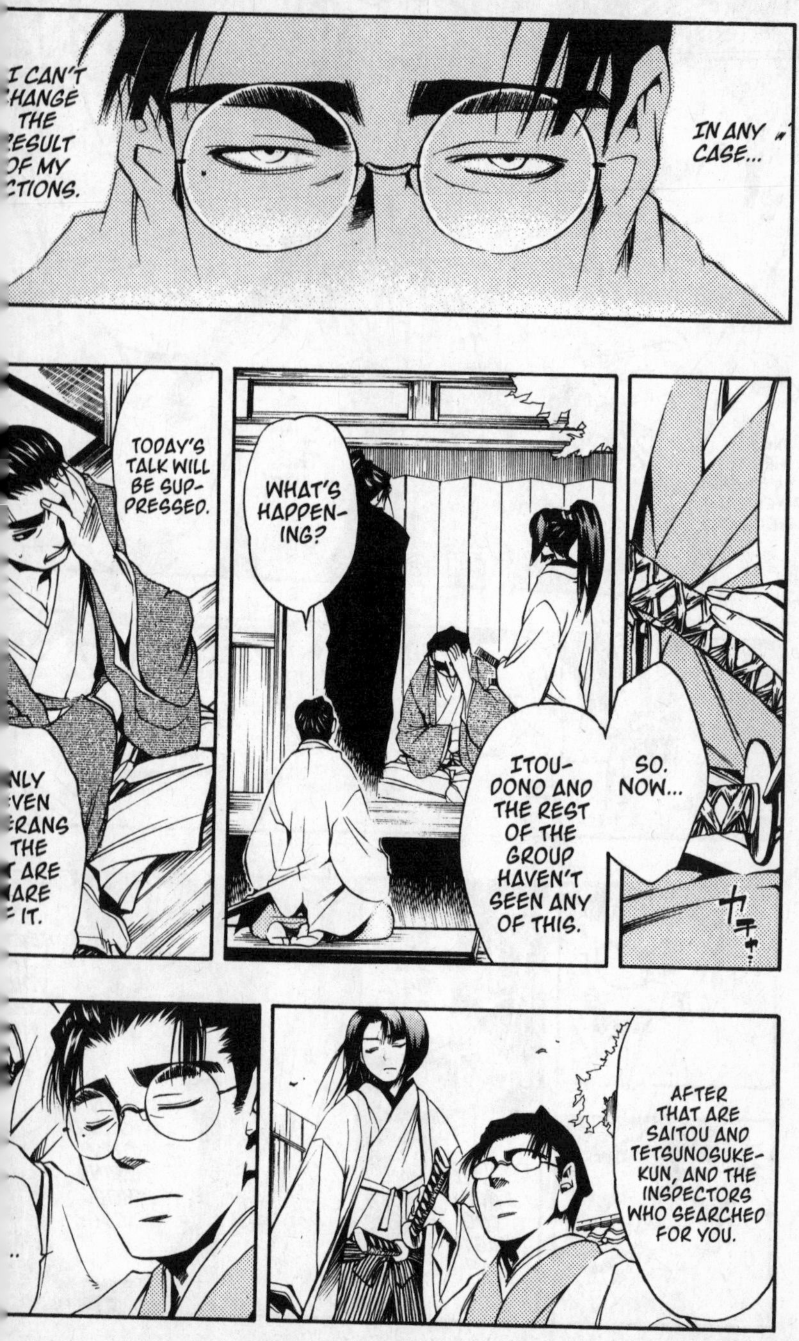
IN ANY CASE...
I CAN'T HANGE THE ESULT OF MY CTIONS.
SO. NOW...
ITOU-DONO AND THE REST OF THE GROUP HAVEN'T SEEN ANY OF THIS.
カチャ...
WHAT'S HAPPEN-ING?
TODAY'S TALK WILL BE SUP-PRESSED.
NLY VEN ERANS THE T ARE ARE IT.
AFTER THAT ARE SAITOU AND TETSUNOSUKE-KUN, AND THE INSPECTORS WHO SEARCHED FOR YOU.
..

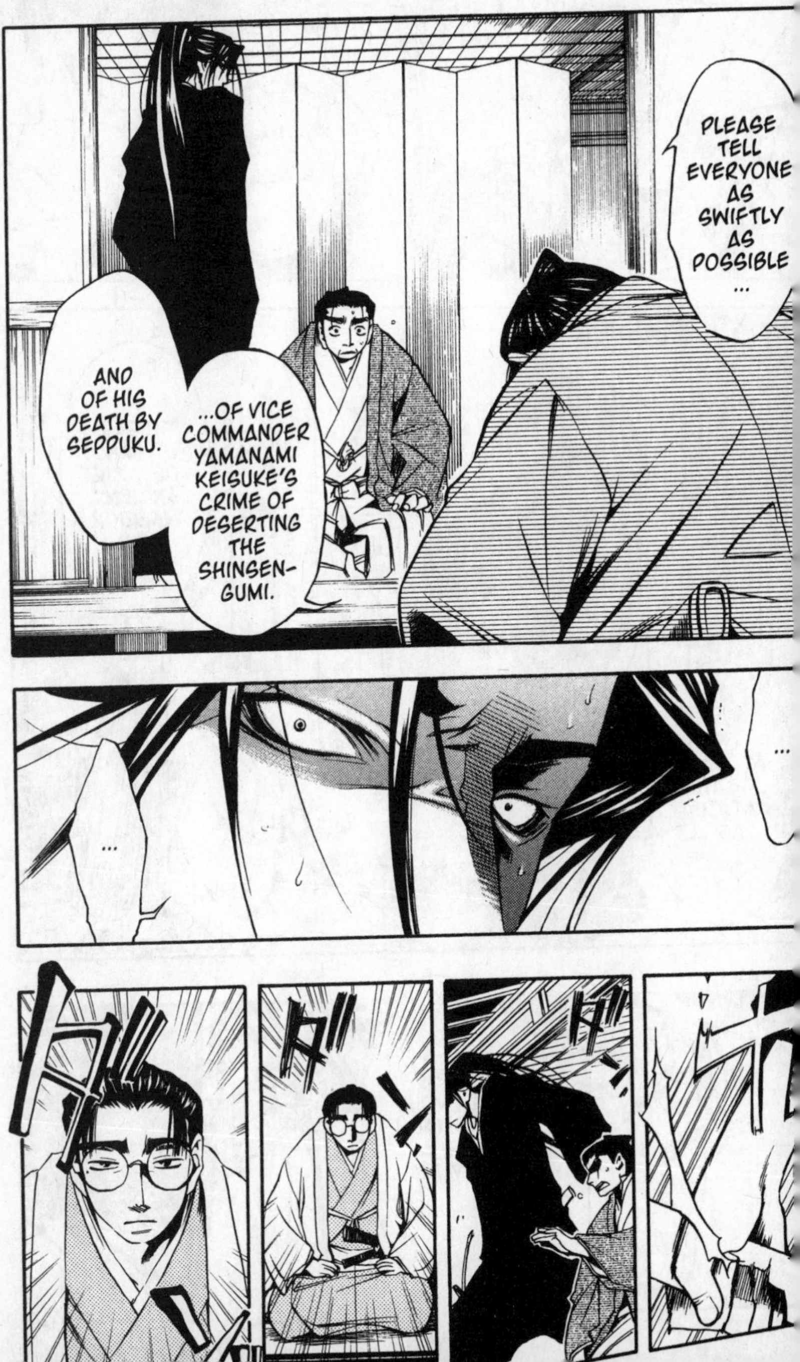
PLEASE TELL EVERYONE AS SWIFTLY AS POSSIBLE ...
...OF VICE COMMANDER YAMANAMI KEISUKE'S CRIME OF DESERTING THE SHINSEN-GUMI.
AND OF HIS DEATH BY SEPPUKU.
...
...

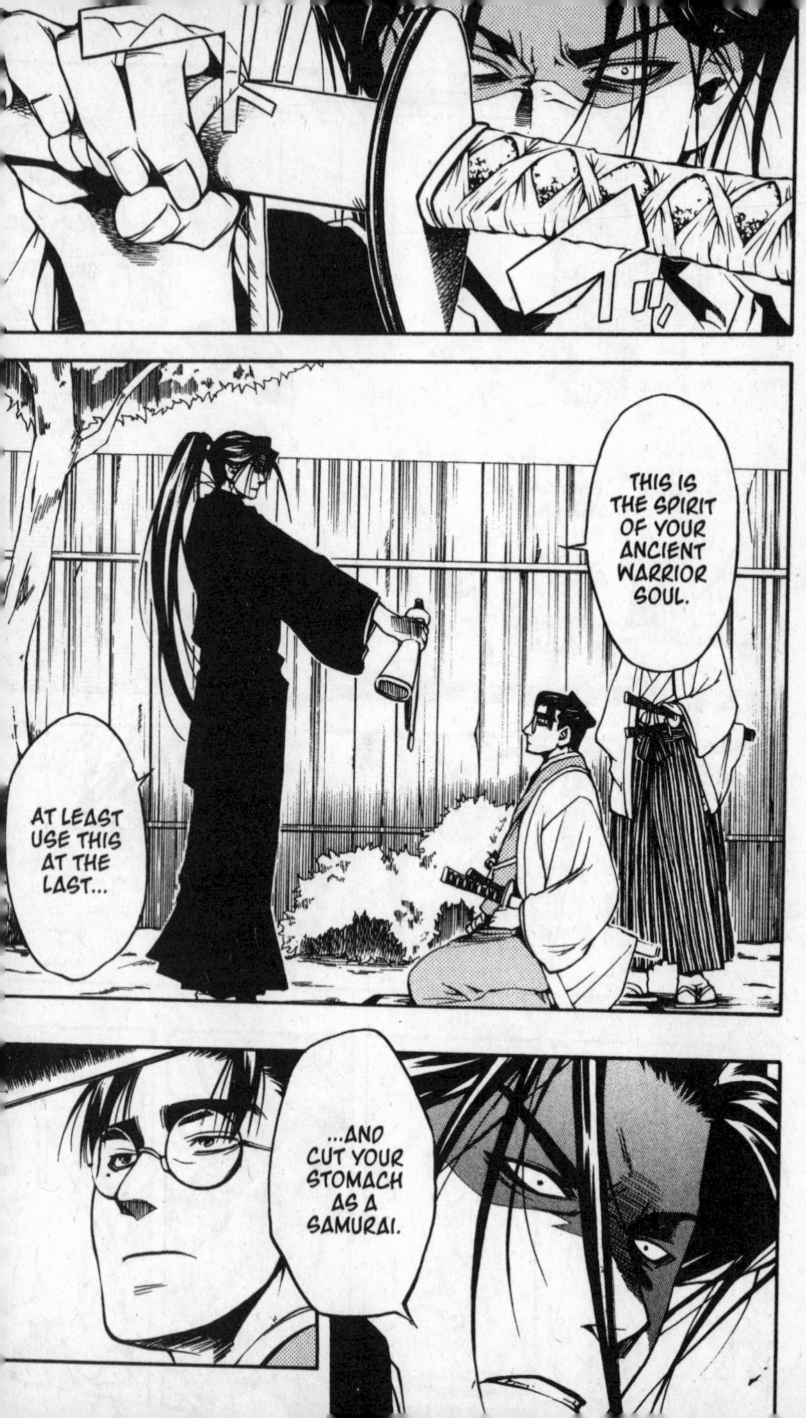
THIS IS THE SPIRIT OF YOUR ANCIENT WARRIOR SOUL.
AT LEAST USE THIS AT THE LAST...
...AND CUT YOUR STOMACH AS A SAMURAI.

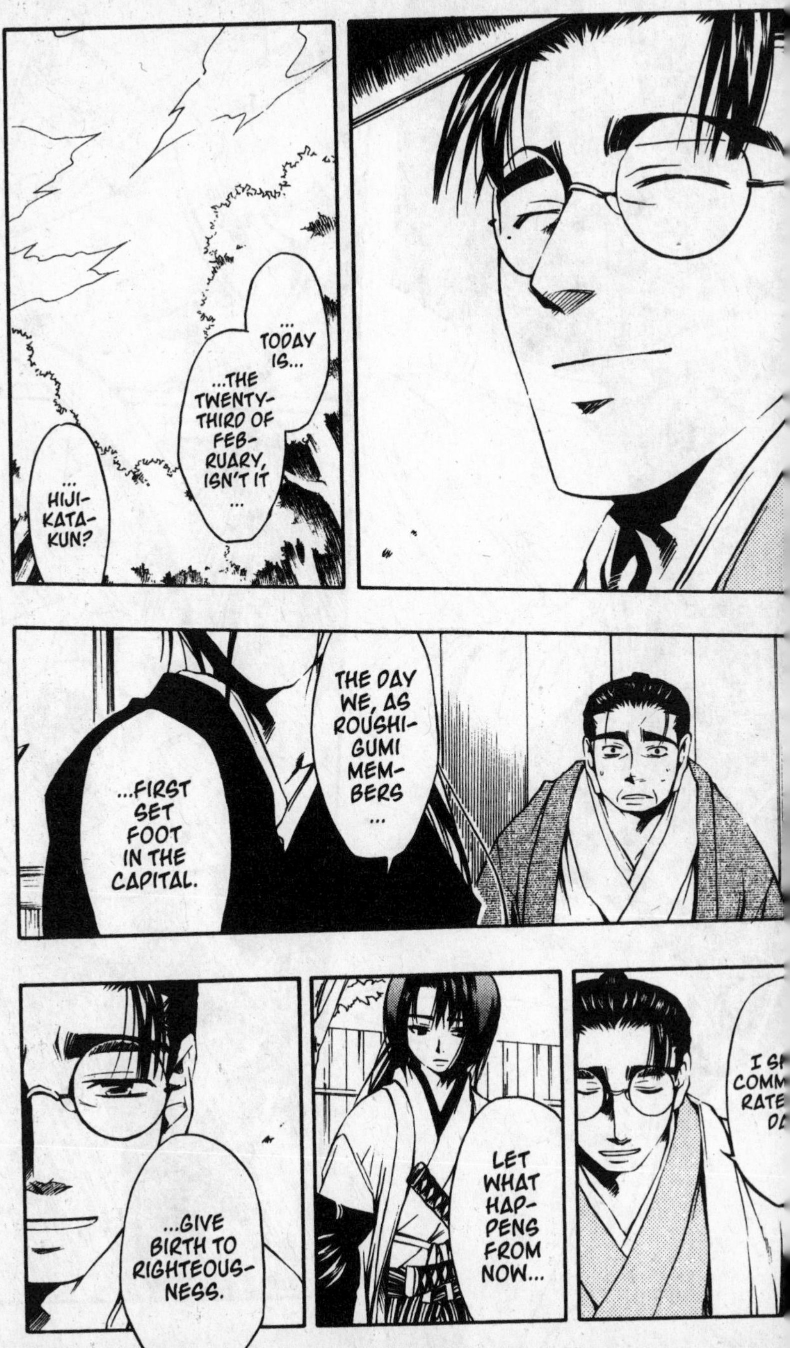
... TODAY IS... ...THE TWENTY-THIRD OF FEB-RUARY, ISN'T IT ...
... HIJI-KATA-KUN?
THE DAY WE, AS ROUSHI-GUMI MEM-BERS ...
...FIRST SET FOOT IN THE CAPITAL.
LET WHAT HAP-PENS FROM NOW...
...GIVE BIRTH TO RIGHTEOUS-NESS.

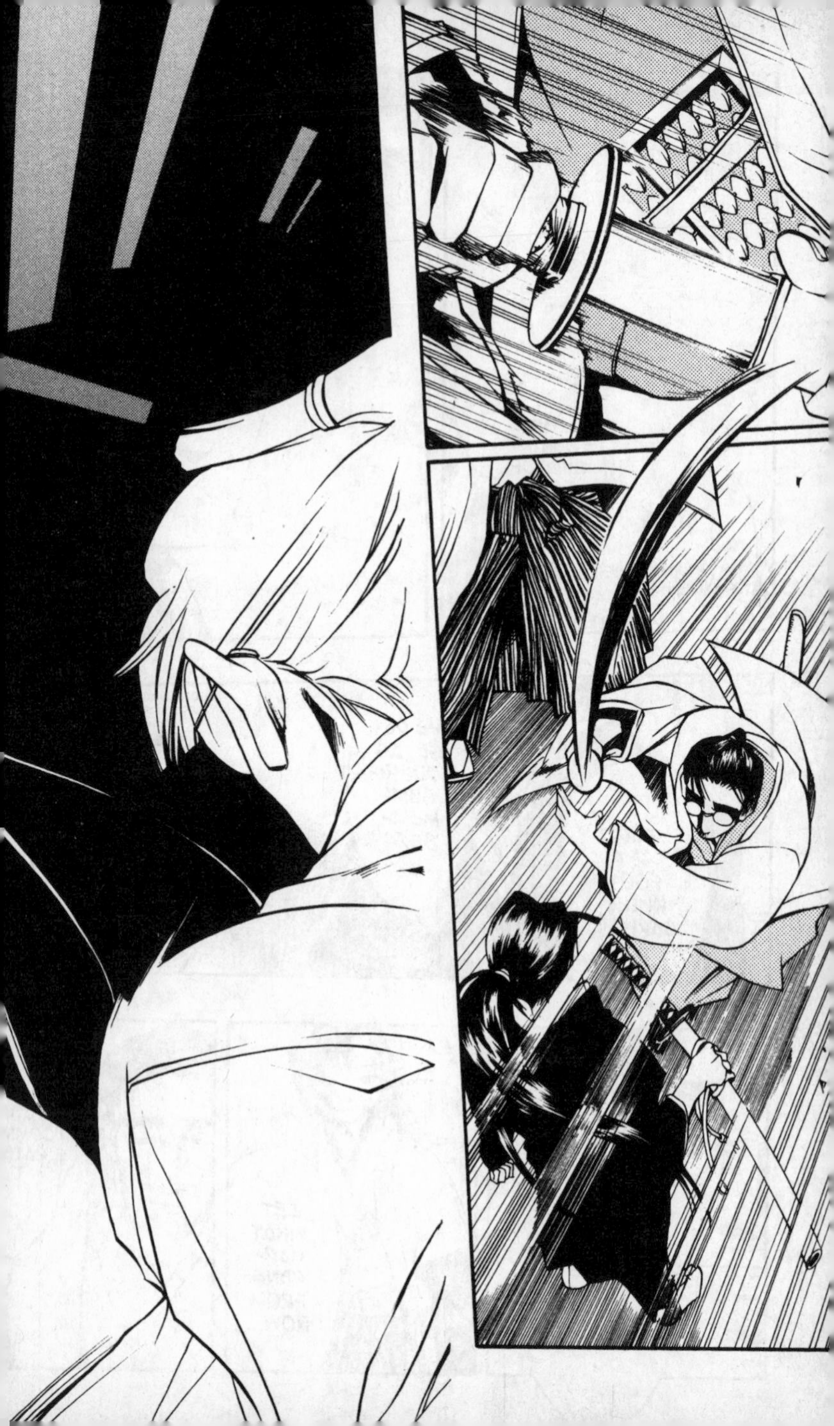

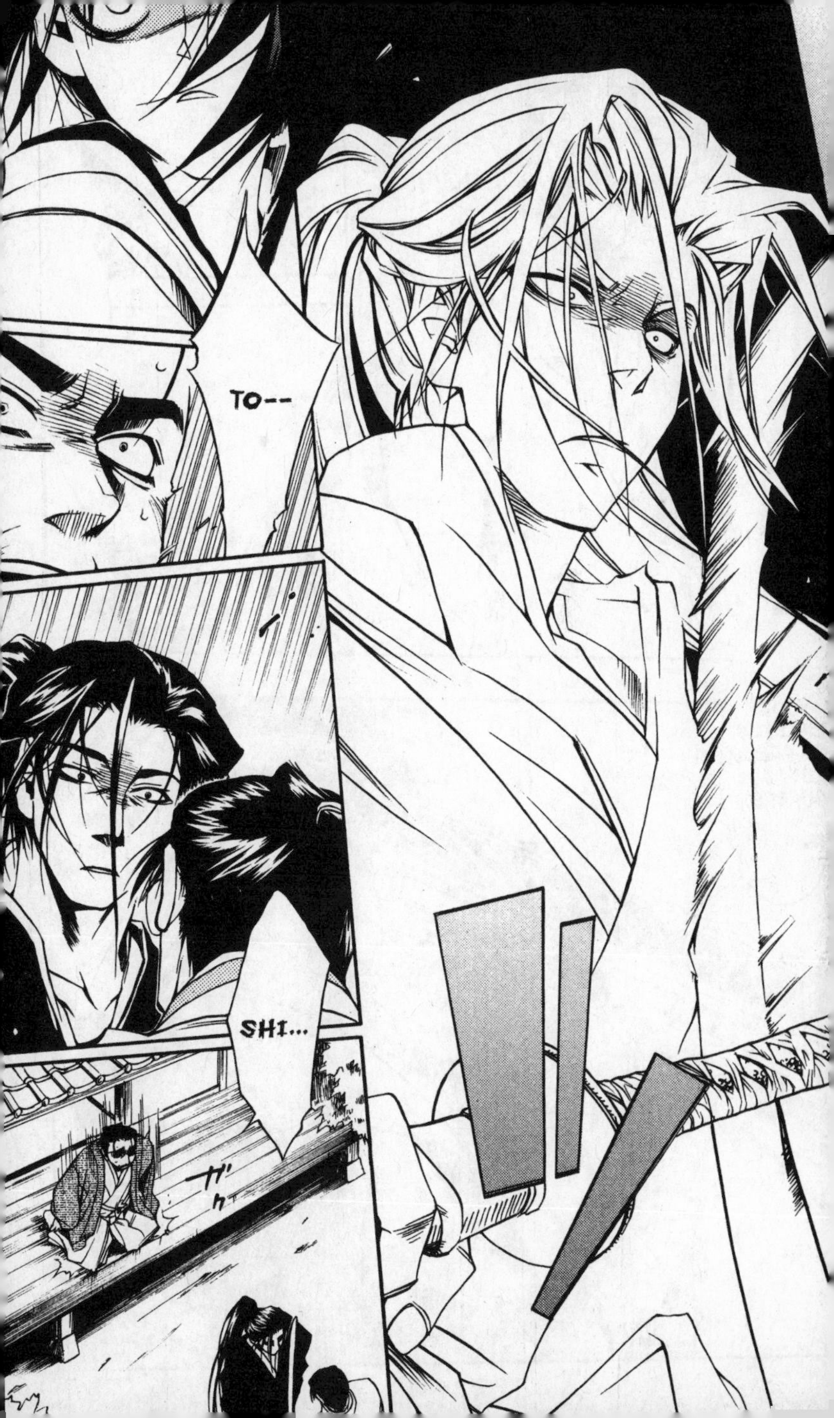
TO--
SHI...
ガク

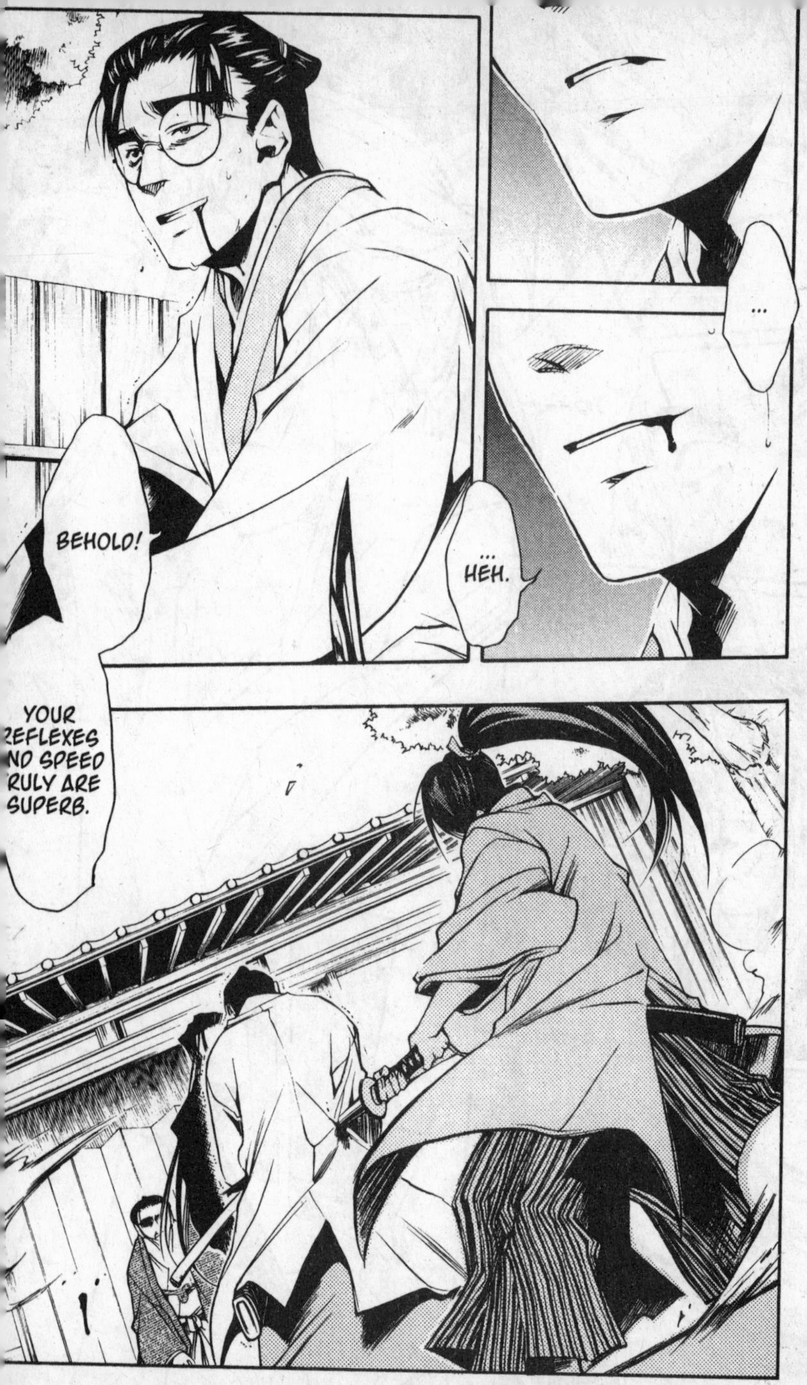
...
...HEH.
BEHOLD!
YOUR REFLEXES ND SPEED RULY ARE SUPERB.

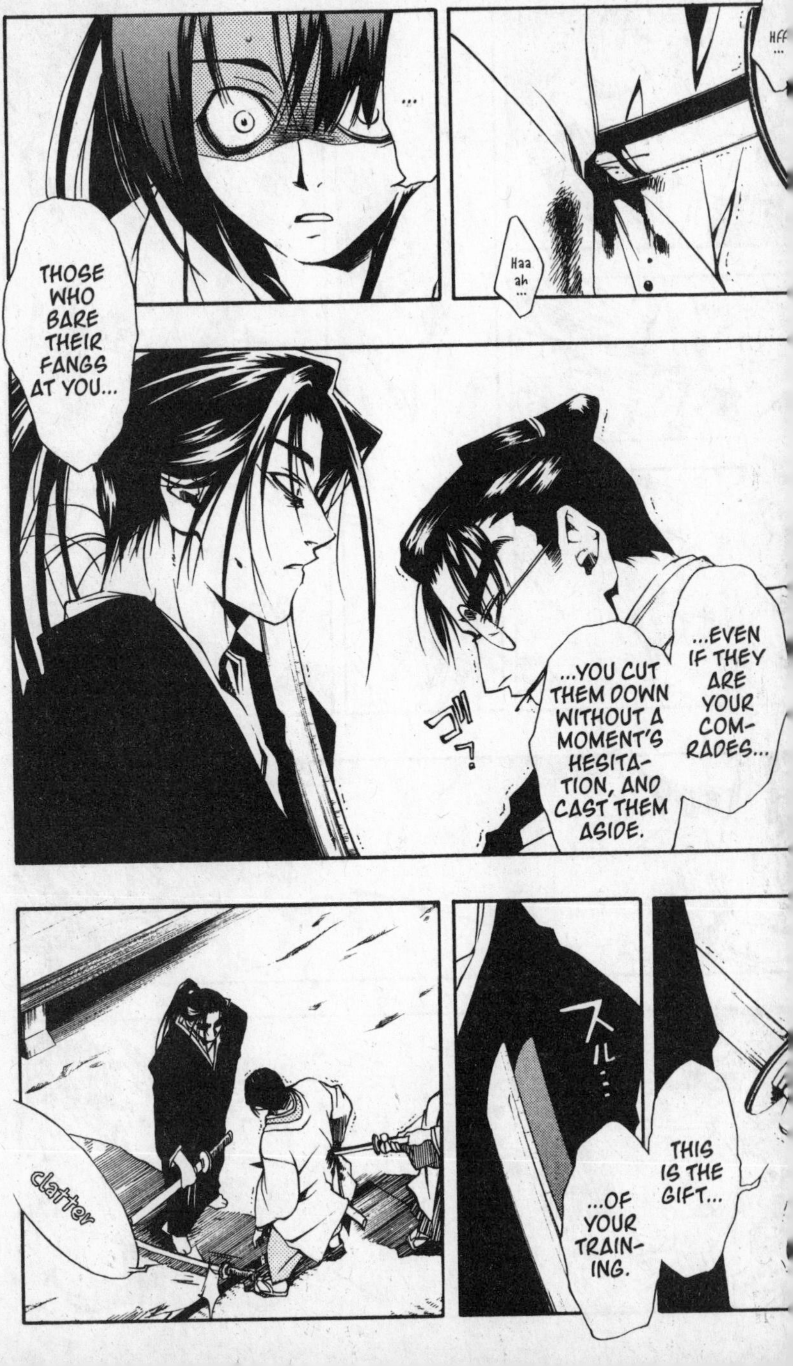
Hff...
Haa ah...
...
THOSE WHO BARE THEIR FANGS AT YOU...
...EVEN IF THEY ARE YOUR COMRADES...
...YOU CUT THEM DOWN WITHOUT A MOMENT'S HESITATION, AND CAST THEM ASIDE.
スル…
THIS IS THE GIFT...
...OF YOUR TRAINING.
clatter

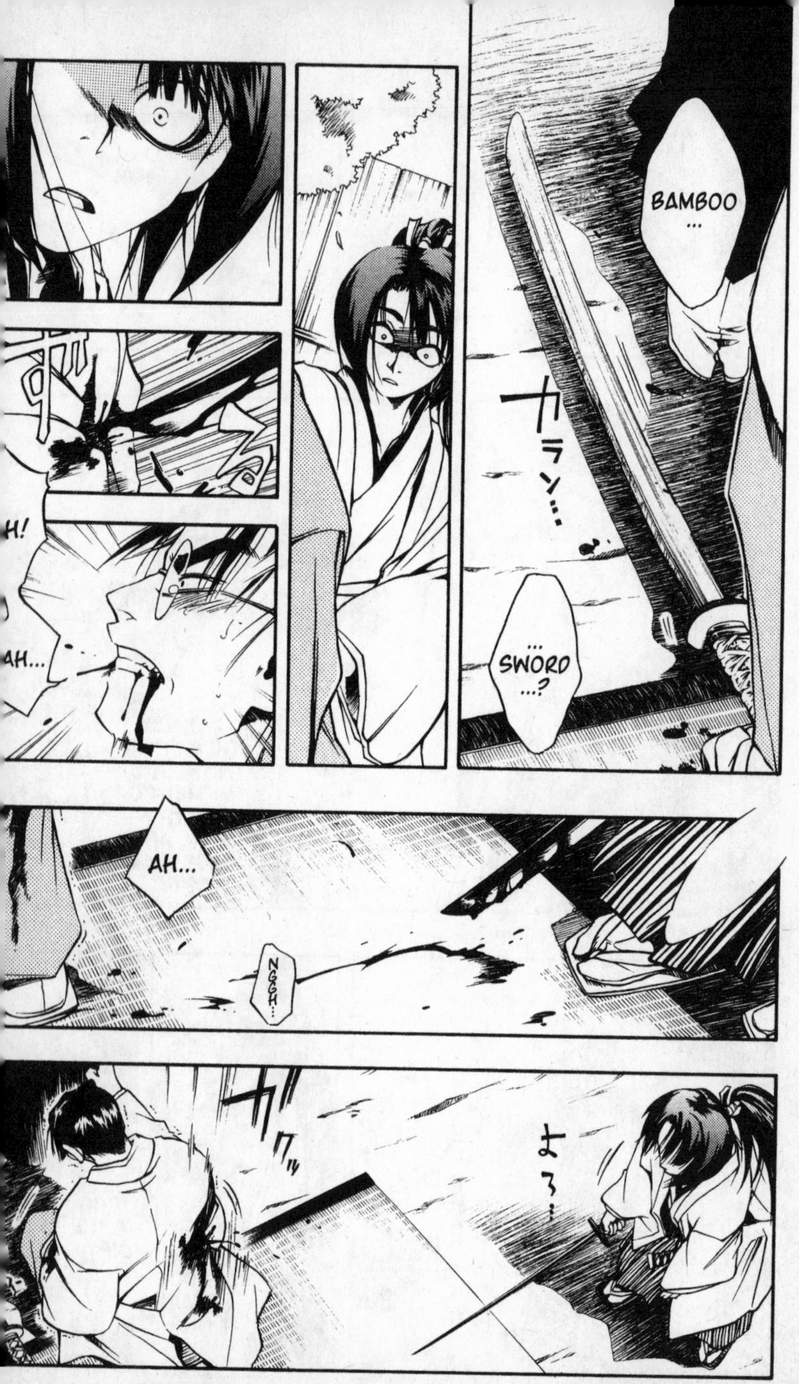
BAMBOO ...
カラン…
... SWORD ...?
H!
AH...
AH...
NGGH...
ガクッ
よろ…

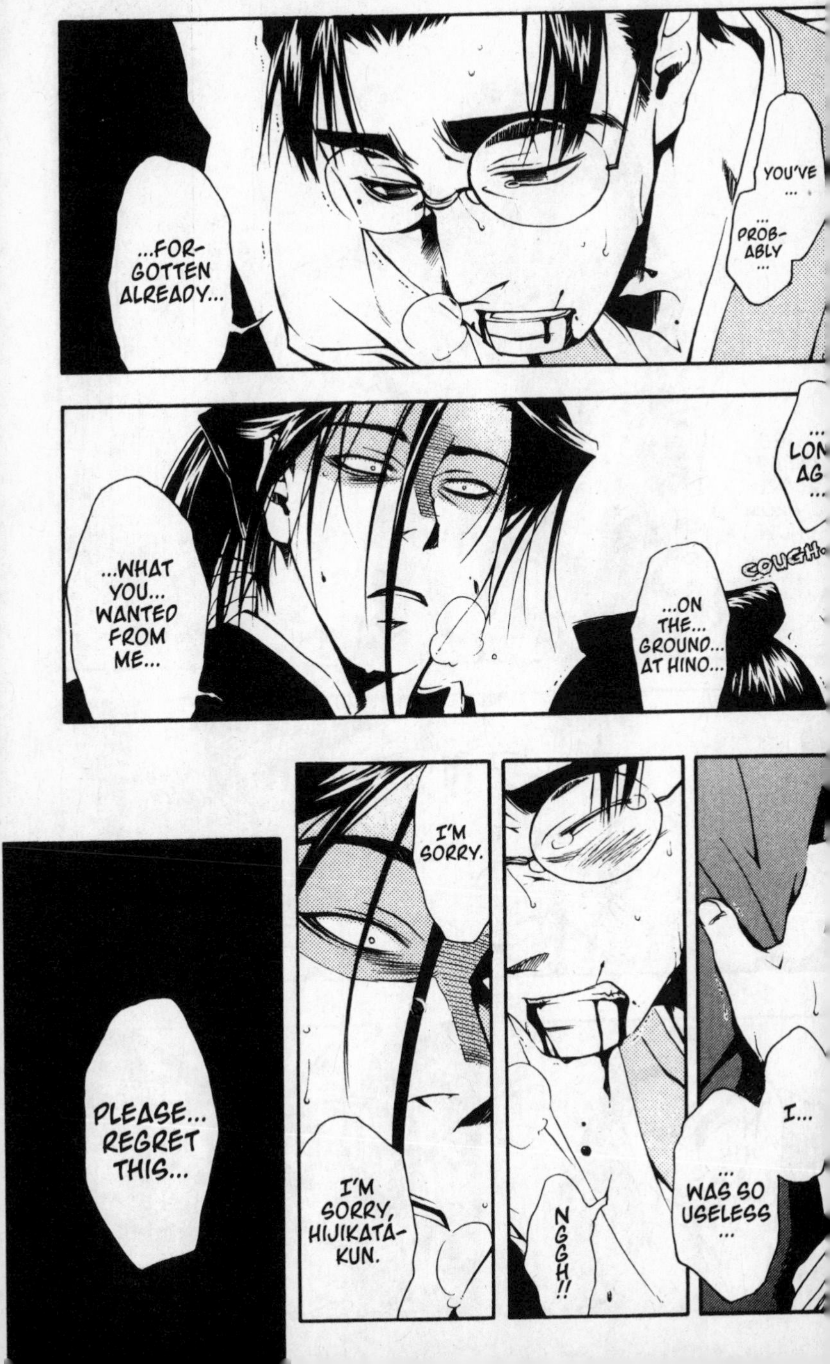
YOU'VE... ...PROBABLY...
...FORGOTTEN ALREADY...
... LON AG ...
COUGH.
...ON THE... GROUND... AT HINO...
...WHAT YOU... WANTED FROM ME...
I...
...WAS SO USELESS...
NGGH!!
I'M SORRY.
I'M SORRY, HIJIKATA-KUN.
PLEASE... REGRET THIS...

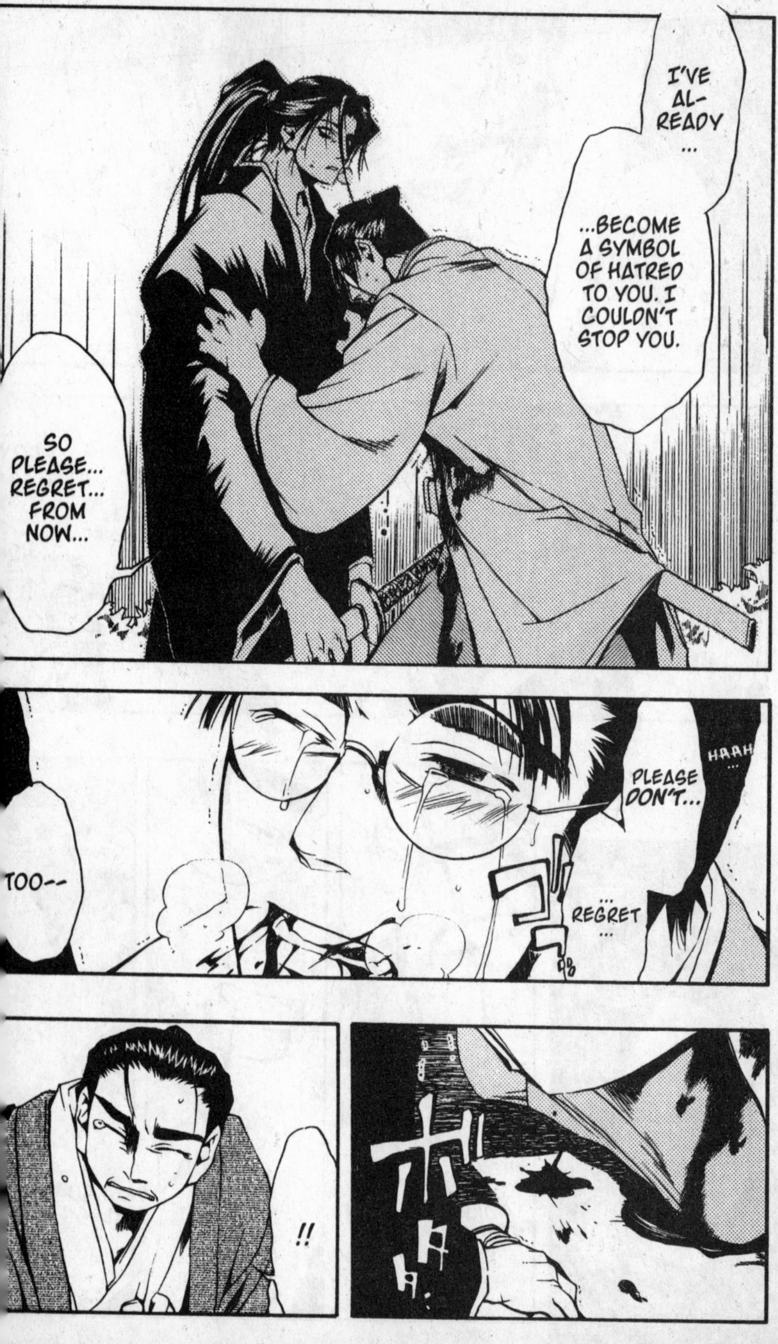
I'VE AL-READY...
...BECOME A SYMBOL OF HATRED TO YOU. I COULDN'T STOP YOU.
SO PLEASE... REGRET... FROM NOW...
HAAH...
PLEASE DON'T...
...REGRET...
TOO--
!!

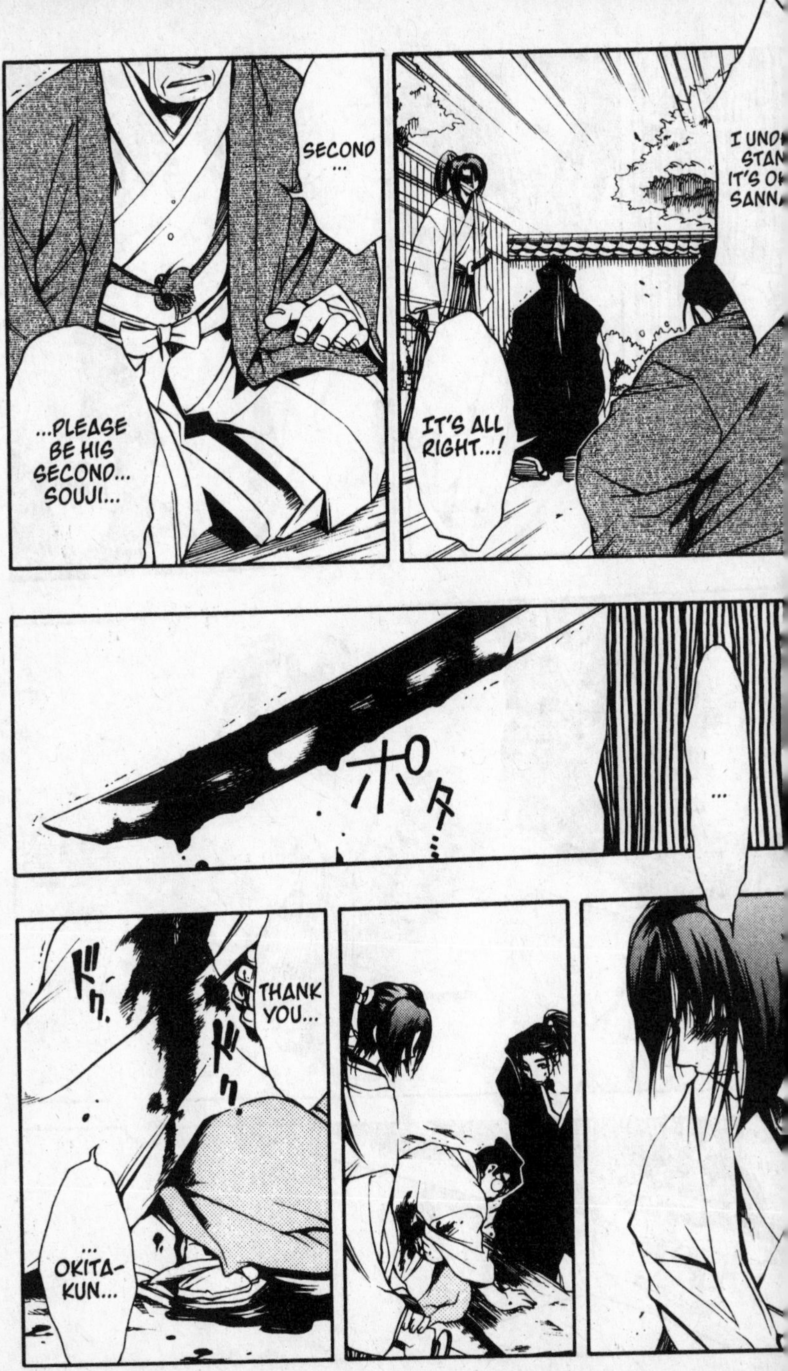
I UND STAN IT'S OK SANN
IT'S ALL RIGHT...!
SECOND ...
...PLEASE BE HIS SECOND... SOUJI...
...
ポタ...
THANK YOU...
ドク.
ドク
... OKITA-KUN...

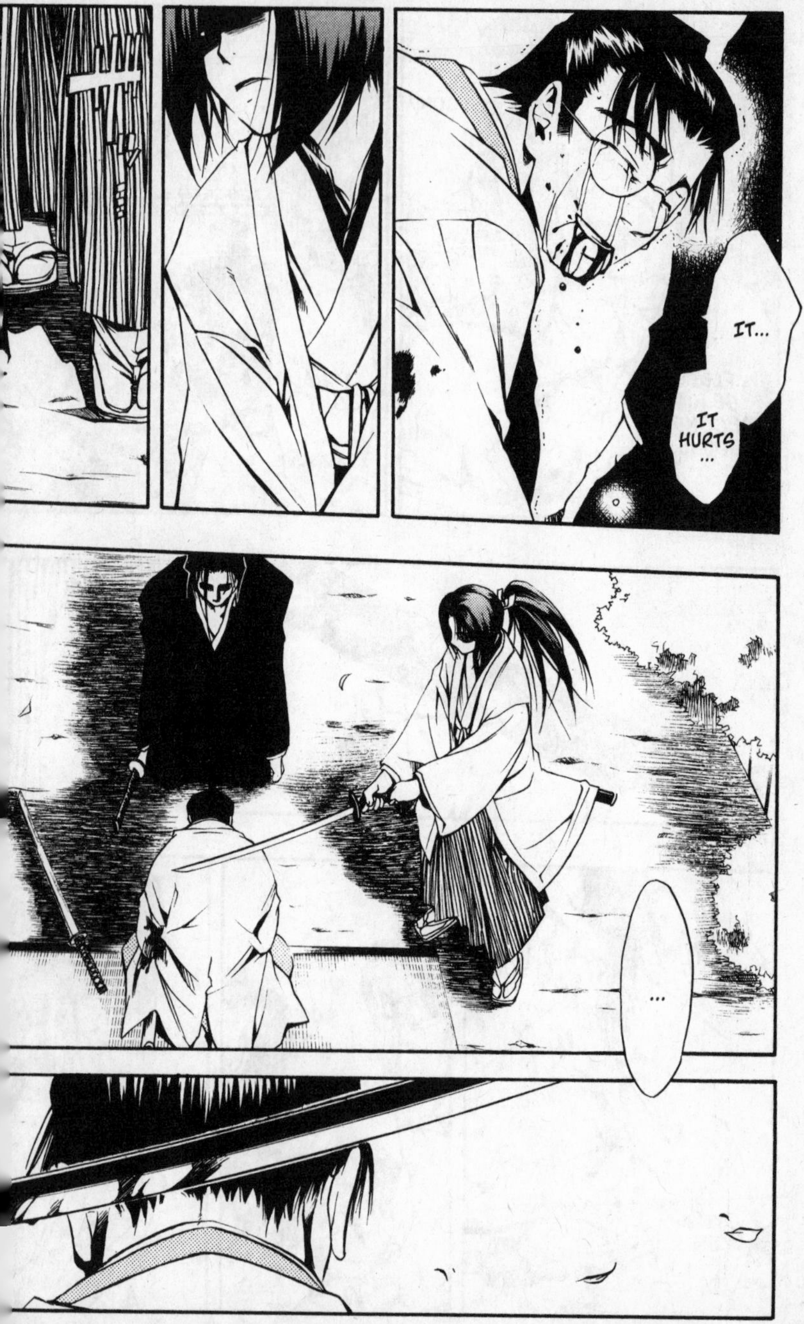
IT...
IT HURTS ...
...

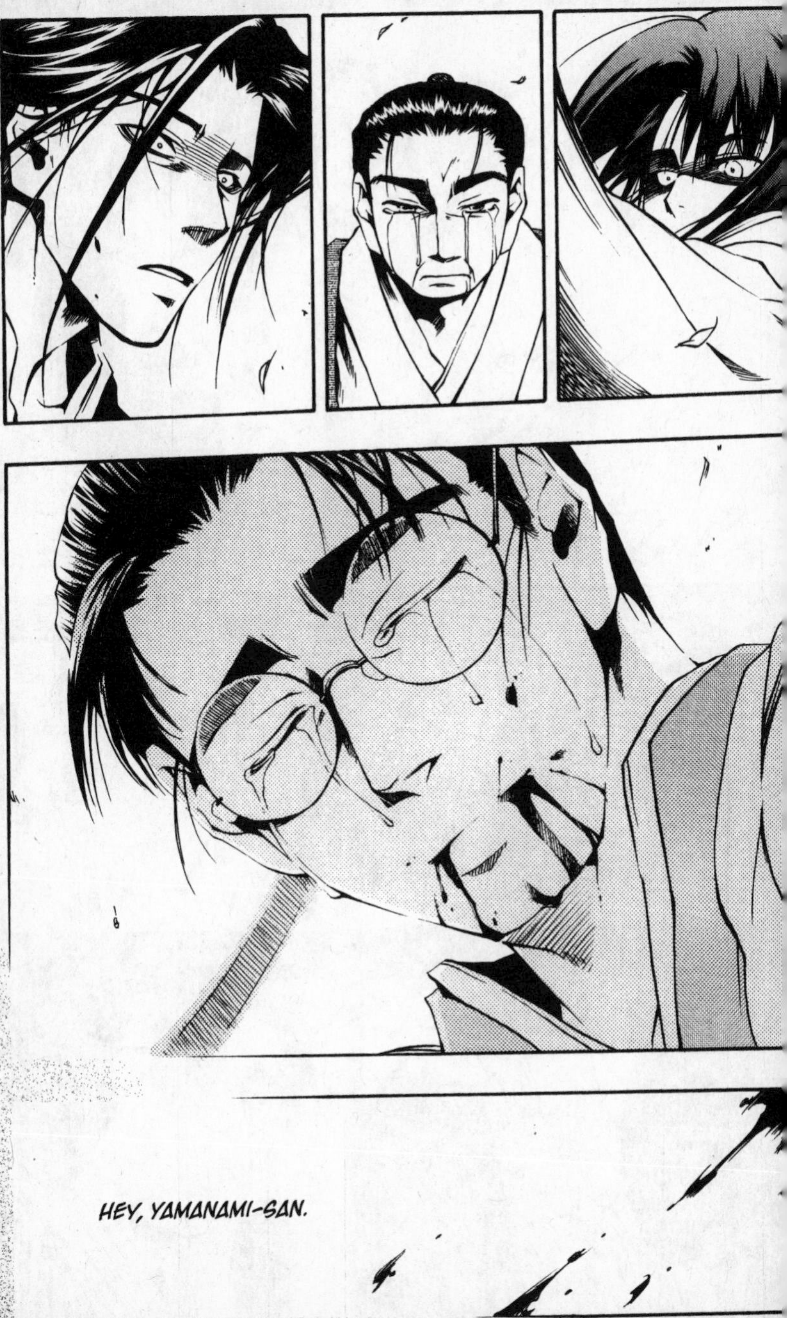
HEY, YAMANAMI-SAN.

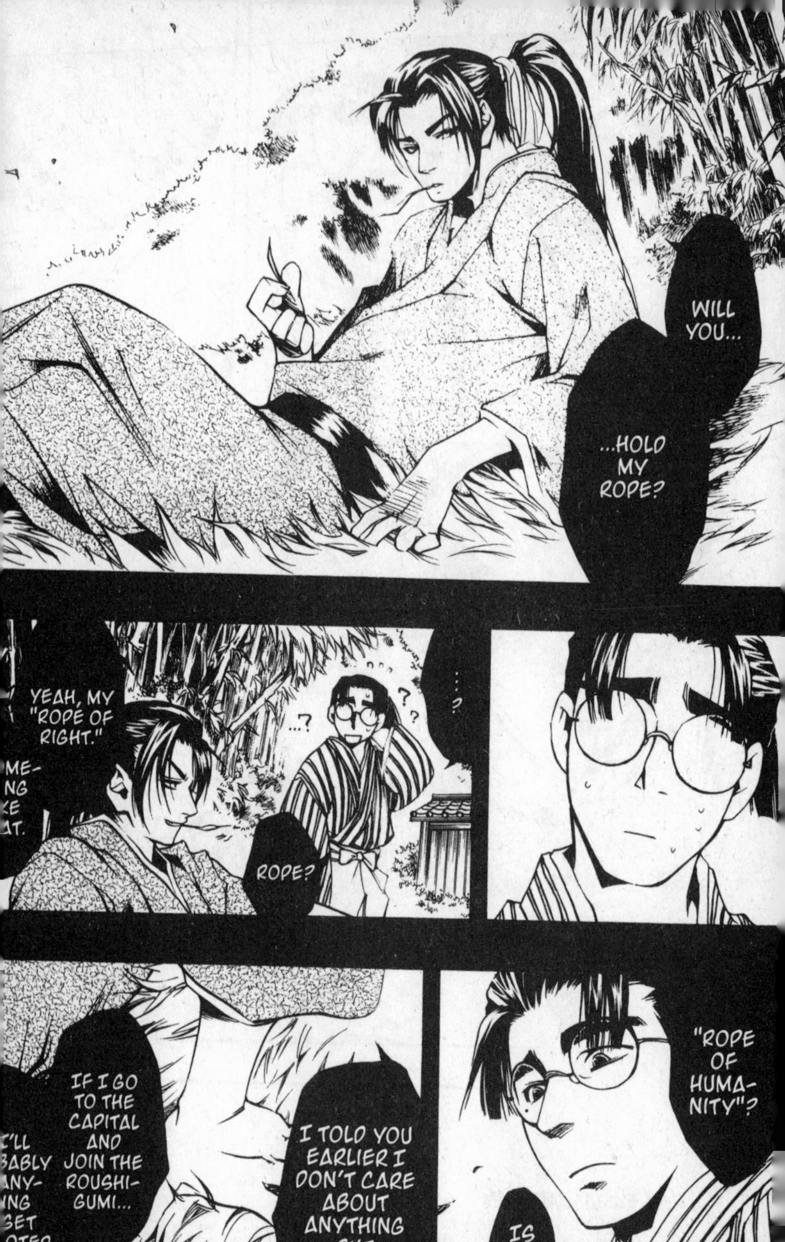
WILL YOU...
...HOLD MY ROPE?
...?
...?
ROPE?
YEAH, MY "ROPE OF RIGHT."
"ROPE OF HUMANITY"?
IS THAT IT?
I TOLD YOU EARLIER I DON'T CARE ABOUT ANYTHING BUT RESULTS.
IF I GO TO THE CAPITAL AND JOIN THE ROUSHIGUMI...

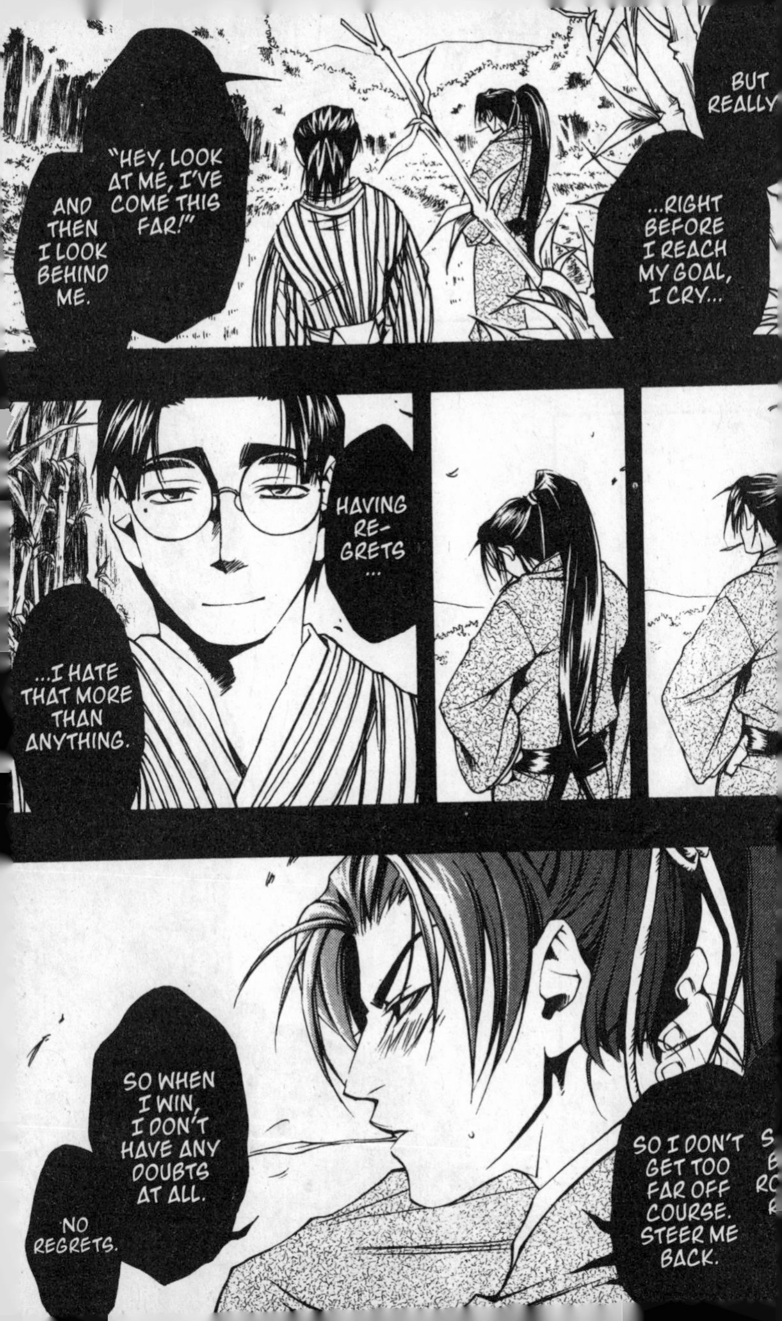
BUT REALLY
...RIGHT BEFORE I REACH MY GOAL, I CRY...
"HEY, LOOK AT ME, I'VE COME THIS FAR!"
AND THEN I LOOK BEHIND ME.
HAVING REGRETS...
...I HATE THAT MORE THAN ANYTHING.
SO I DON'T GET TOO FAR OFF COURSE. STEER ME BACK.
SO WHEN I WIN, I DON'T HAVE ANY DOUBTS AT ALL.
NO REGRETS.

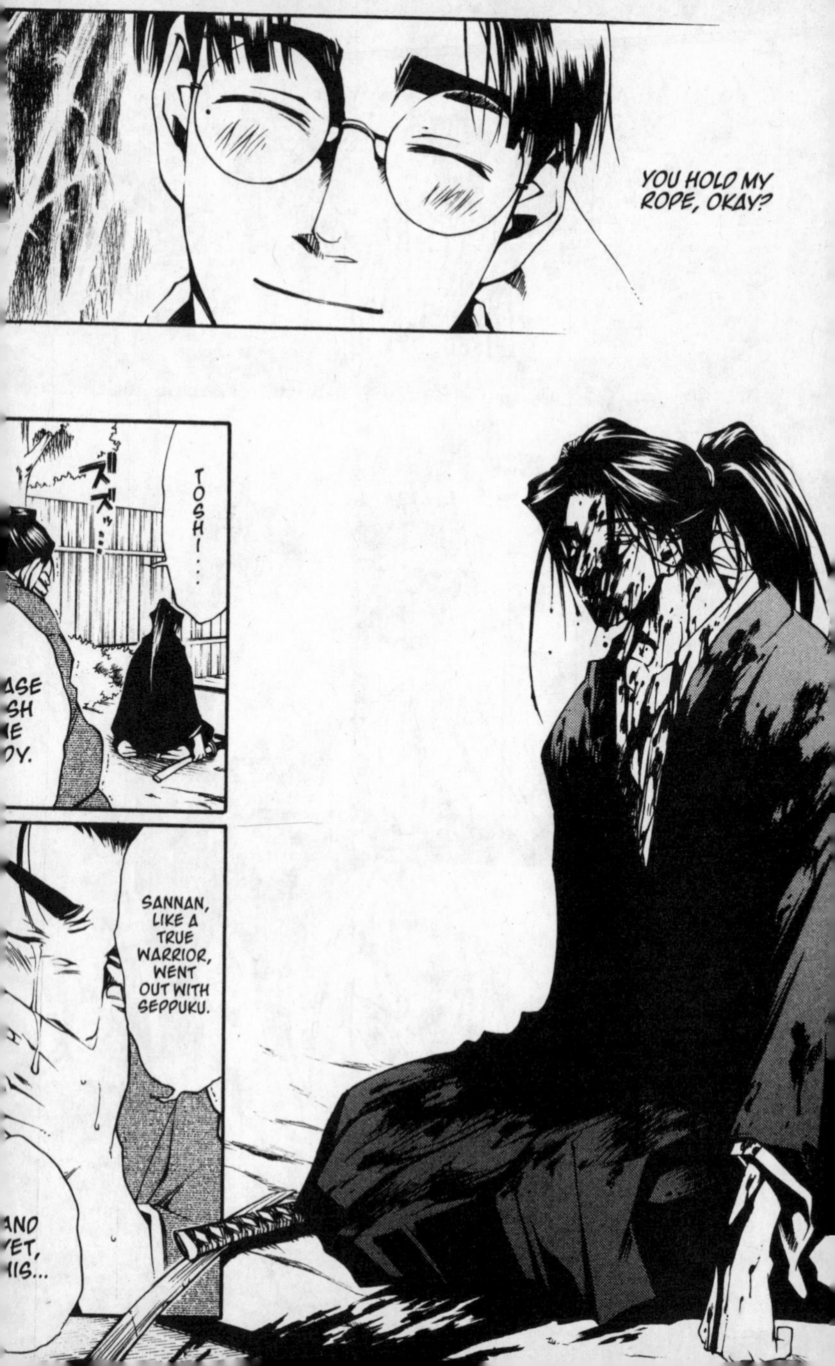
YOU HOLD MY ROPE, OKAY?
TOSHI...
ズズッ...
ASE SH E DY.
SANNAN, LIKE A TRUE WARRIOR, WENT OUT WITH SEPPUKU.
AND ET, IS...

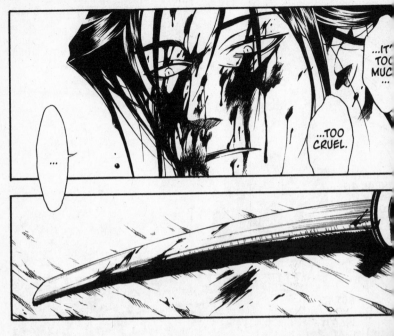

...IT'...
TOO
MUC...

...TOO
CRUEL.

...

THIS
THING
OF
YOURS?

WAS IT
THAT
HEAVY?

WAS IT
HEAVY
...?

A
WOOD...
SWO...

...

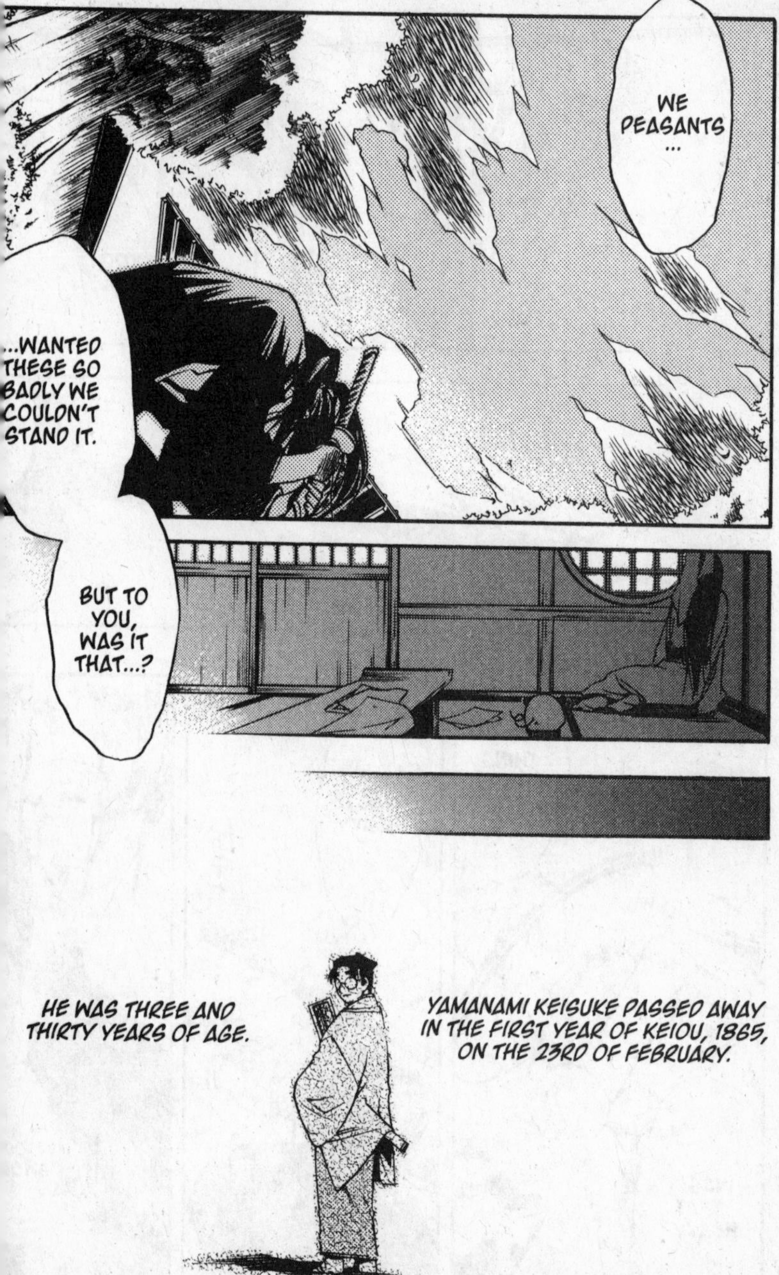
WE PEASANTS ...
...WANTED THESE SO BADLY WE COULDN'T STAND IT.
BUT TO YOU, WAS IT THAT...?
YAMANAMI KEISUKE PASSED AWAY IN THE FIRST YEAR OF KEIOU, 1865, ON THE 23RD OF FEBRUARY.
HE WAS THREE AND THIRTY YEARS OF AGE.

Peace Maker Kurogane 2 End

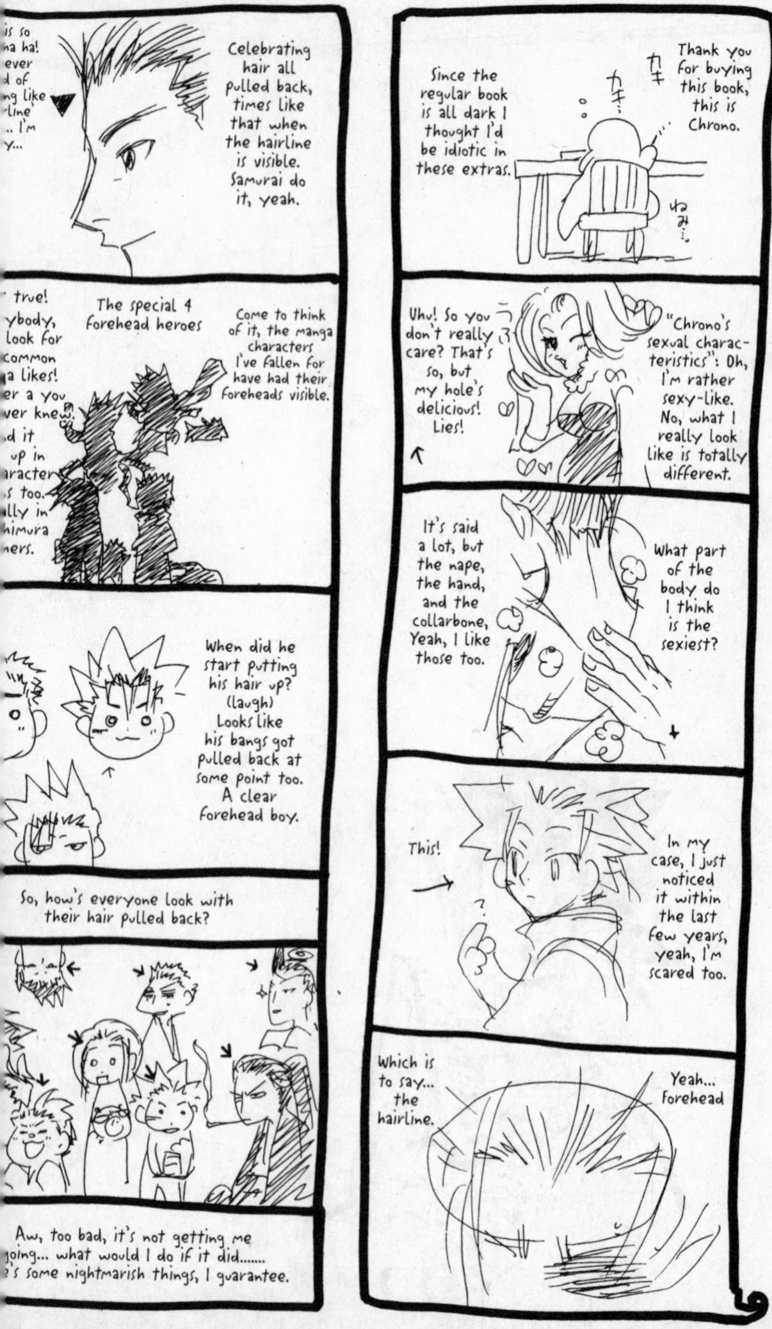
Thank you for buying this book, this is Chrono.
カキ…
Since the regular book is all dark I thought I'd be idiotic in these extras.
ねみ…
"Chrono's sexual characteristics": Oh, I'm rather sexy-like. No, what I really look like is totally different.
Uhu! So you don't really care? That's so, but my hole's delicious! Lies!
What part of the body do I think is the sexiest?
It's said a lot, but the nape, the hand, and the collarbone, Yeah, I like those too.
In my case, I just noticed it within the last few years, yeah, I'm scared too.
This!
?
Yeah... Forehead
Which is to say... the hairline.
Celebrating hair all pulled back, times like that when the hairline is visible. Samurai do it, yeah.
is so ha ha! ever d of ng like rline' .. I'm y...
Come to think of it, the manga characters I've fallen for have had their foreheads visible.
The special 4 forehead heroes
true! ybody, look for common a likes! er a you ver knew! d it up in aracter s too. lly in himura ners.
When did he start putting his hair up? (laugh) Looks like his bangs got pulled back at some point too. A clear forehead boy.
So, how's everyone look with their hair pulled back?
Aw, too bad, it's not getting me oing... what would I do if it did....... e's some nightmarish things, I guarantee.

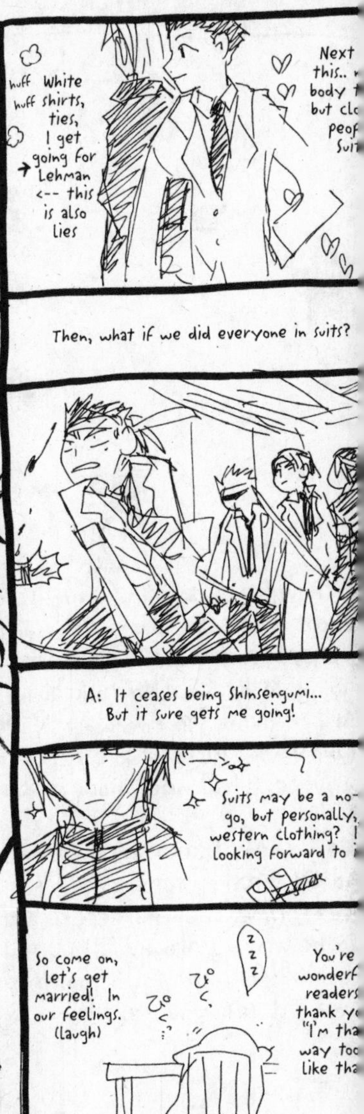
Next this..
huff huff White shirts, ties, I get going for Lehman <-- this is also lies
Then, what if we did everyone in suits?
A: It ceases being Shinsengumi... But it sure gets me going!
Suits may be a no- go, but personally, western clothing?
looking forward to
You're
So come on, let's get married! In our feelings. (laugh)
z z z
★ Bye! Write and run!
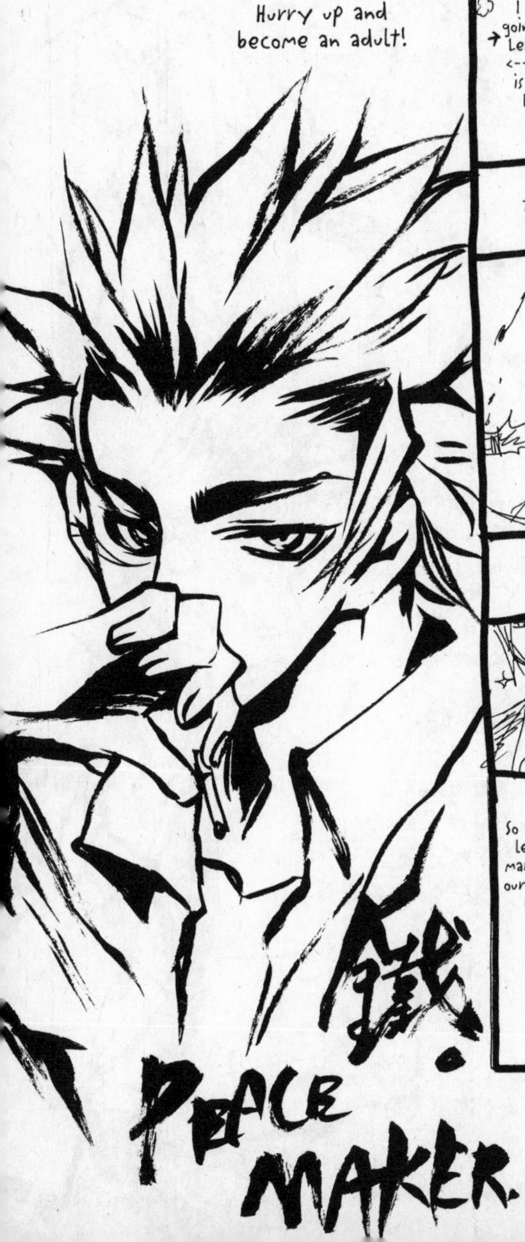
Hurry up and become an adult!
鐵
PEACE MAKER.

I thought of a lot of things to say about the way Yamanami-san died here, but it doesn't look like I'm going to be able to talk about it, so I'm giving up. Anyway, if people who know history are shocked, I'm a success. I wonder how it was...

Well then, I keep writing on, I have no excuse. I'm very sorry for this! Next time the characters are going to be moving around a lot, so I'm looking forward to it too. If you like, I'll see you next time. Bye!

NANAE CHRONO.

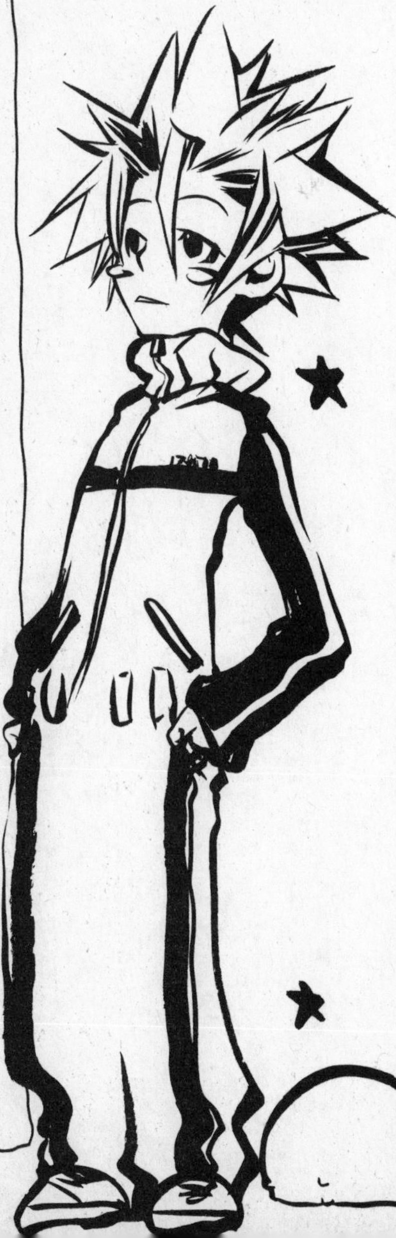

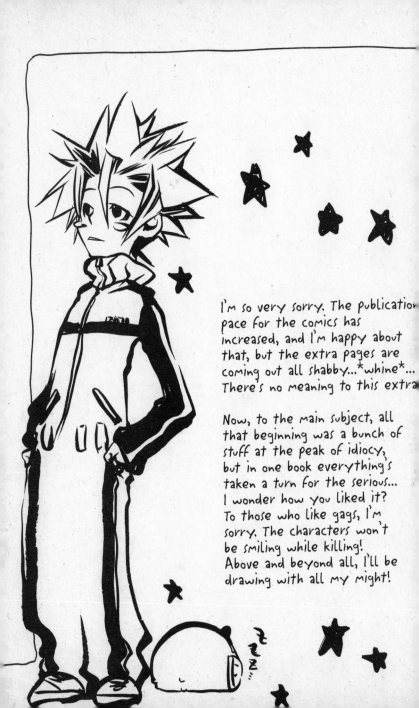

I'm so very sorry. The publication pace for the comics has increased, and I'm happy about that, but the extra pages are coming out all shabby...*whine*... There's no meaning to this extra

Now, to the main subject, all that beginning was a bunch of stuff at the peak of idiocy, but in one book everything's taken a turn for the serious... I wonder how you liked it? To those who like gags, I'm sorry. The characters won't be smiling while killing! Above and beyond all, I'll be drawing with all my might!

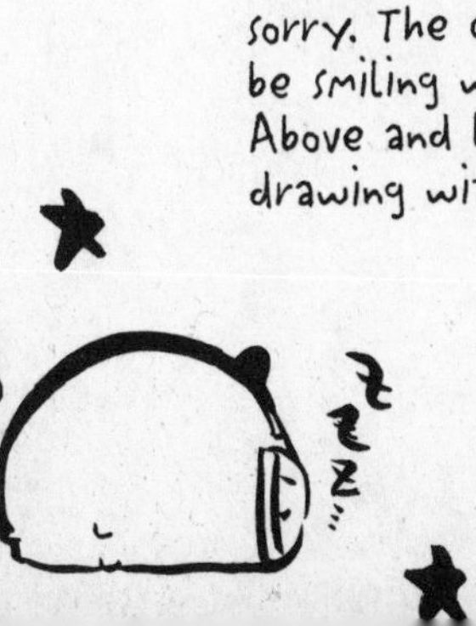

鐵

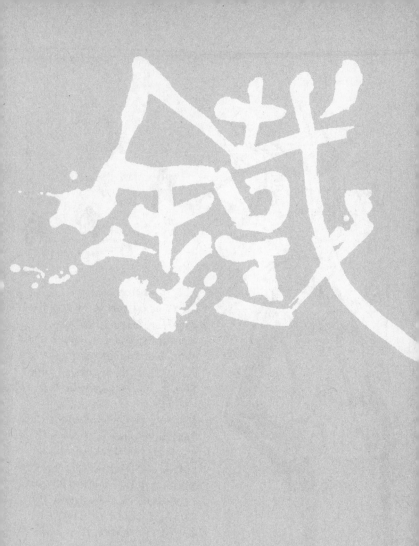

In the next

PEACE MAKER 鐵
KUROGANE

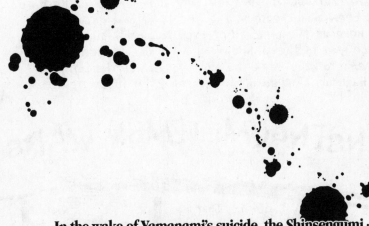

In the wake of Yamanami's suicide, the Shinsengumi are left tense and brooding, but no one is more distraught than Akesato. New arrivals at the new base of operations (and the return of Sakamoto Ryouma) do little to lighten the mood, and Tetsunosuke has a terrifying run-in with his former friend...

der-Cover series:

Original one-shot?! SPECIAL!!

Moronic.

ɔo-san's assistant staff "Hasshi," "Mura-chan", and Yuu-
are continuing to do their best (summer 2002). Recently
e's been an increase in the amount of odd discussions &
es here at the office (Get back to work!). SO, I'll just
duce you to the "Shinsengumi Super Occult Action!!" story
seems to have been the most popular of the lot. Even
r Hagimori chipped in on the story. I'm SO excited!!

★

INSENGUMI DEMON WARS

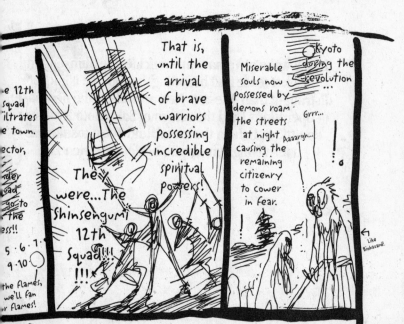

Kyoto during the revolution...
Miserable souls now possessed by demons roam the streets at night causing the remaining citizenry to cower in fear.
Grrr...
Aaaargh...
Like Biohazard!
That is, until the arrival of brave warriors possessing incredible spiritual powers!
They were...The Shinsengumi 12th Squad!!!
!!!
e 12th Squad iltrates e town.
ector,
der
uad
go to
the
ess!!
5 · 6 · 7 ·
9 · 10
the flames, we'll fan r flames!
Huh?

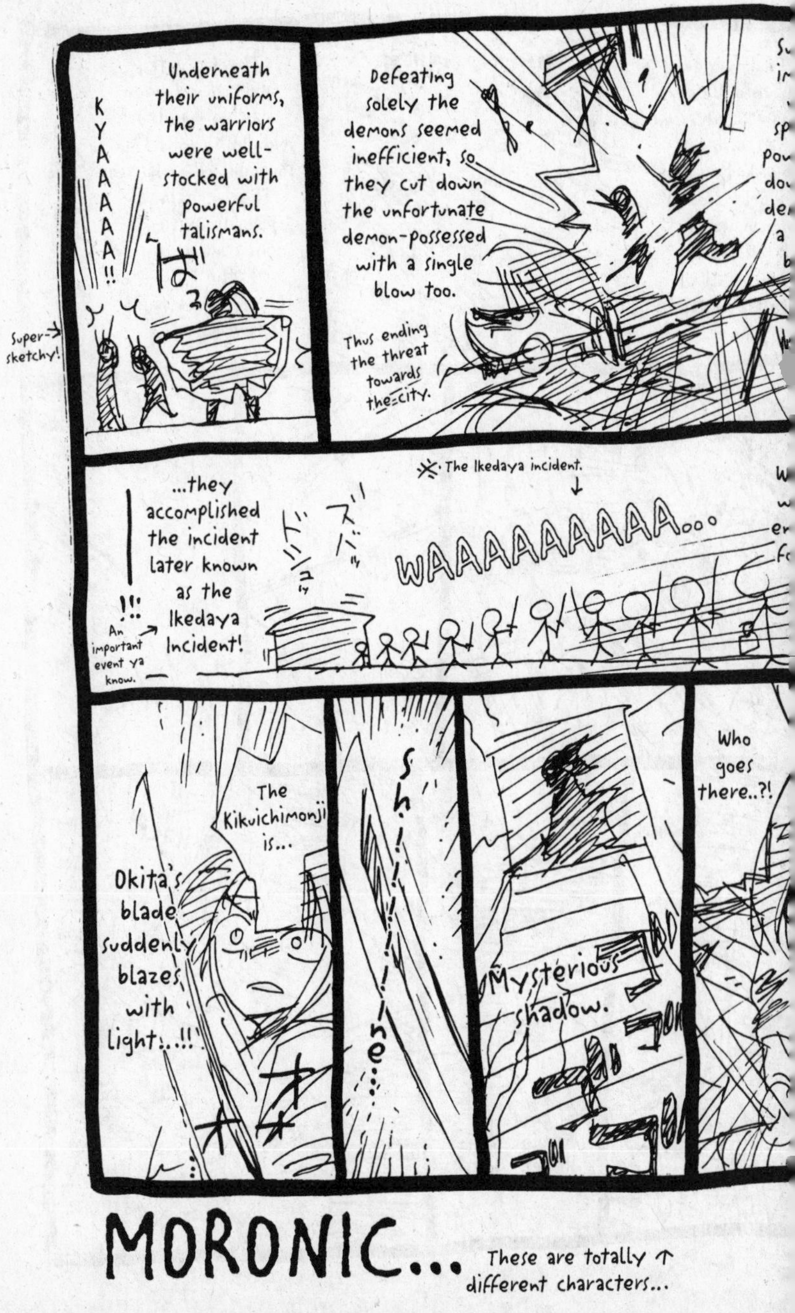

Defeating solely the demons seemed inefficient, so they cut down the unfortunate demon-possessed with a single blow too.
Thus ending the threat towards the city.
Underneath their uniforms, the warriors were well-stocked with powerful talismans.
KYAAAAA!!
はっ
Super-sketchy!
※ The Ikedaya incident.
WAAAAAAAAA...
ズバッ
ドシュッ
...they accomplished the incident later known as the Ikedaya Incident!
!!
An important event ya know.
Who goes there..?!
Mysterious shadow.
Shi...ne...
The Kikuichimonji is...
Okita's blade suddenly blazes with light...!!
MORONIC...
These are totally different characters...

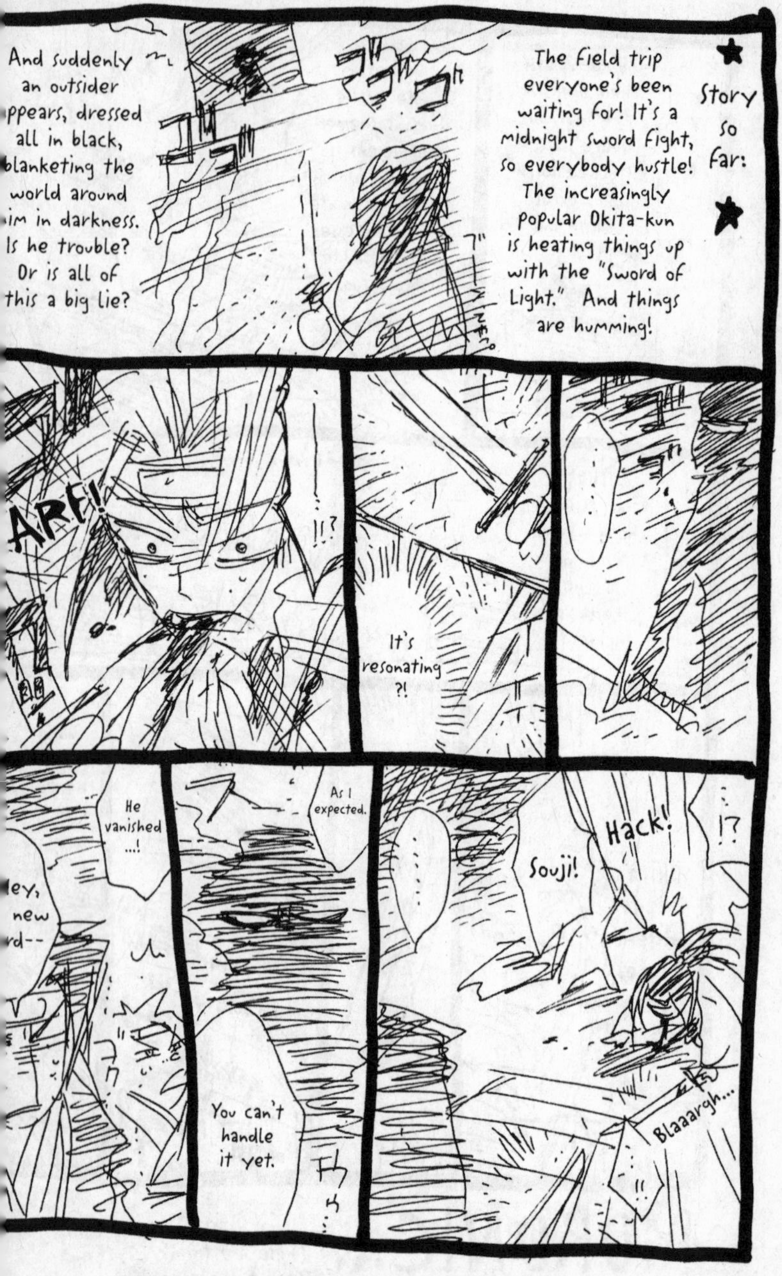

Story so far:
The field trip everyone's been waiting for! It's a midnight sword fight, so everybody hustle! The increasingly popular Okita-kun is heating things up with the "Sword of Light." And things are humming!
And suddenly an outsider ppears, dressed all in black, blanketing the world around im in darkness. Is he trouble? Or is all of this a big lie?
It's resonating ?!
!!?
ARF!
!?
Hack!
Souji!
Blaaargh...
!!
As I expected.
You can't handle it yet.
He vanished ...!
ley, new rd--

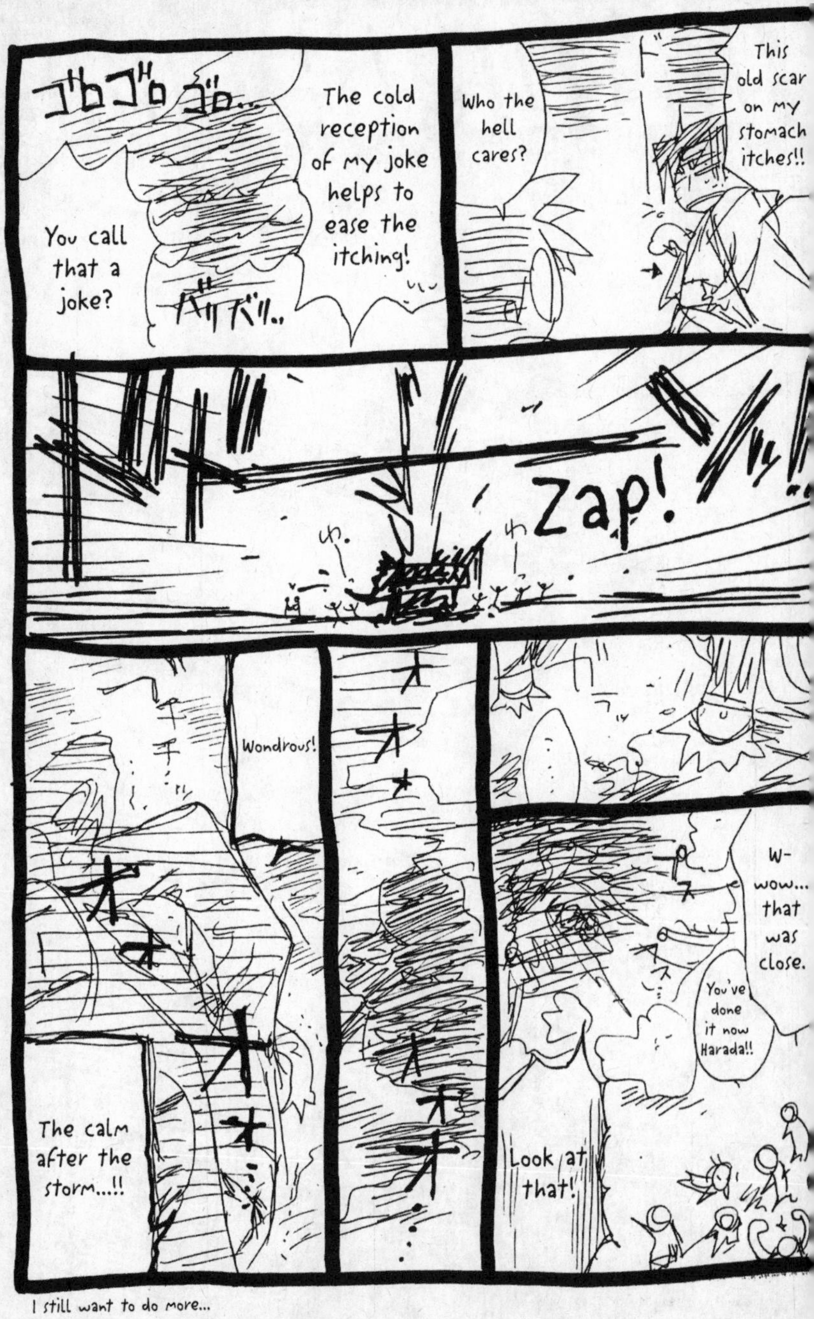
This old scar on my stomach itches!!
Who the hell cares?
The cold reception of my joke helps to ease the itching!
ゴロゴロゴロ...
You call that a joke?
バリバリ..
Zap!
W- wow... that was close.
You've done it now Harada!!
Look at that!
Wondrous!
The calm after the storm...!!

I still want to do more...

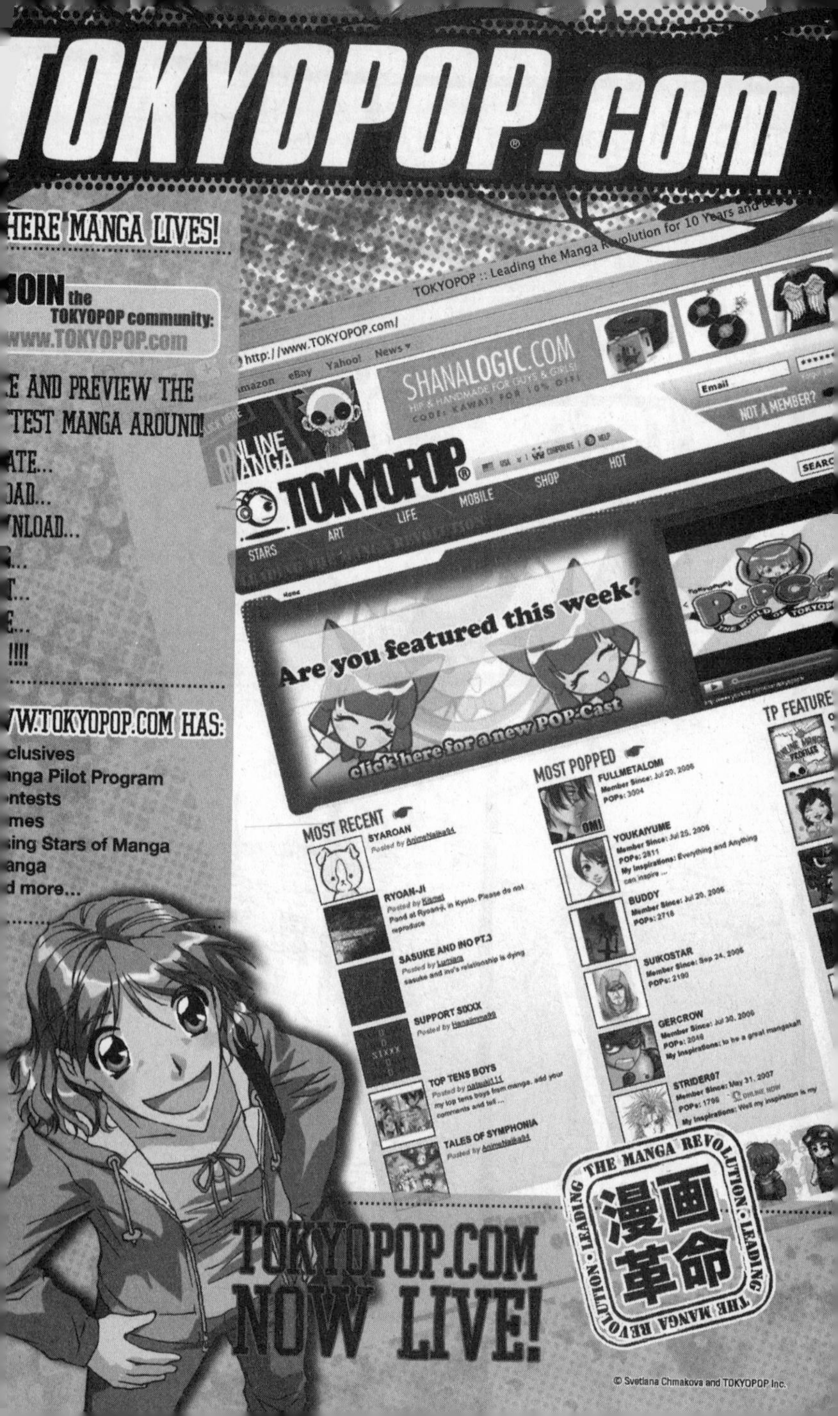
TOKYOPOP.com
HERE MANGA LIVES!
JOIN the TOKYOPOP community:
www.TOKYOPOP.com
E AND PREVIEW THE
TEST MANGA AROUND!
ATE...
OAD...
NLOAD...
WWW.TOKYOPOP.COM HAS:
clusives
anga Pilot Program
ntests
mes
ing Stars of Manga
anga
d more...
TOKYOPOP :: Leading the Manga Revolution for 10 Years and
http://www.TOKYOPOP.com/
SHANALOGIC.COM
NOT A MEMBER?
TOKYOPOP
STARS
ART
LIFE
MOBILE
SHOP
HOT
Are you featured this week?
click here for a new POP-Cast
MOST RECENT
SYAROAN
RYOAN-JI
SASUKE AND INO PT.3
SUPPORT SIXXX
TOP TENS BOYS
TALES OF SYMPHONIA
MOST POPPED
FULLMETALOMI
YOUKAIYUME
BUDDY
SUIKOSTAR
GERCROW
STRIDER07
TP FEATURE
TOKYOPOP.COM NOW LIVE!
LEADING THE MANGA REVOLUTION
漫画革命
© Svetlana Chmakova and TOKYOPOP Inc.

STOP!

This is the back of the book.
You wouldn't want to spoil a great ending!

This book is printed "manga-style," in the authentic Japanese right-to-left format. Since none of the artwork has been flipped or altered, readers get to experience the story just as the creator intended. You've been asking for it, so TOKYOPOP® delivered: authentic, hot-off-the-press, and far more fun!

DIRECTIONS

If this is your first time reading manga-style, here's a quick guide to help you understand how it works.

It's easy... just start in the top right panel and follow the numbers. Have fun, and look for more 100% authentic manga from TOKYOPOP®!

漫画革命

THE MANGA REVOLUTION · LEADING · THE MANGA REVOLUTION · LEADING